Citizen Soldiers

The popular image of the British soldier in the First World War is of a passive, obedient victim, caught up in events beyond his control, and isolated from civilian society. This book offers a different vision of the soldier's experience of war. Using letters, diaries and official sources relating to Liverpool units, Helen B. McCartney shows how ordinary men were able to retain their civilian outlook through four years of war and use it to influence their experience in the trenches. These citizen soldiers came to rely on local, civilian loyalties and strong links with home to bolster their morale, whilst their civilian backgrounds and beliefs gave them the ability to challenge those in command if they felt they were being treated unfairly. *Citizen Soldiers* examines the British soldier not only in his military context but in terms of his local, social and cultural life. It will appeal to anyone wishing to understand how the British soldier thought and behaved during the First World War.

HELEN B. McCARTNEY is a Senior Lecturer in the Defence Studies Department, King's College London, based at the Joint Services Command and Staff College.

Studies in the Social and Cultural History of Modern Warfare

General Editor
Jay Winter *Yale University*

Advisory Editors
Omer Bartov *Brown University*
Carol Gluck *Columbia University*
David M. Kennedy *Stanford University*
Paul Kennedy *Yale University*
Antoine Prost *Université de Paris-Sorbonne*
Emmanuel Sivan *Hebrew University of Jerusalem*
Robert Wohl *University of California, Los Angeles*

In recent years the field of modern history has been enriched by the exploration of two parallel histories. These are the social and cultural history of armed conflict, and the impact of military events on social and cultural history.

Studies in the Social and Cultural History of Modern Warfare presents the fruits of this growing area of research, reflecting both the colonization of military history by cultural historians and the reciprocal interest of military historians in social and cultural history, to the benefit of both. The series offers the latest scholarship in European and non-European events from the 1850s to the present day.

For a list of titles in the series, please see end of book.

Citizen Soldiers
The Liverpool Territorials in the First World War

Helen B. McCartney

CAMBRIDGE UNIVERSITY PRESS
Cambridge, New York, Melbourne, Madrid, Cape Town, Singapore,
São Paulo, Delhi, Dubai, Tokyo, Mexico City

Cambridge University Press
The Edinburgh Building, Cambridge CB2 8RU, UK

Published in the United States of America by Cambridge University Press, New York

www.cambridge.org
Information on this title: www.cambridge.org/9780521187770

© Helen B. McCartney 2005

This publication is in copyright. Subject to statutory exception
and to the provisions of relevant collective licensing agreements,
no reproduction of any part may take place without the written
permission of the copyright holder.

First published 2005
First paperback edition 2011

A catalogue record for this publication is available from the British Library

ISBN 978-0-521-84800-8 Hardback
ISBN 978-0-521-18777-0 Paperback

Cambridge University Press has no responsibility for the persistence or
accuracy of URLs for external or third-party internet websites referred to in
this publication, and does not guarantee that any content on such websites is,
or will remain, accurate or appropriate.

In Memory of
Lance Corporal George William Gibson
2nd Battalion, Manchester Regiment
Killed in action 24 November 1915
and
Private Wallace Smith
15th Battalion, Cheshire Regiment
Missing in action 19 August 1917

Contents

List of figures	page viii
List of maps	x
List of tables	xi
Acknowledgements	xiii
List of abbreviations	xv

1	Introduction	1
2	Pre-war Liverpool and the Territorial Force	9

Part I Territorial characteristics and the morale of the soldier — 23

3	'Cuff and collar battalions': social change and its impact on the unit	25
4	'Common ties at home and strong county pride': the persistence and importance of county uniformity	57
5	The links with home: communication between the home front and the fighting front during the Great War	89

Part II Command, discipline and the citizen soldier — 119

6	Command and consent in the trenches	121
7	Discipline, punishment and the Territorial ethos	162

Part III Attitudes and experience: the war and its aftermath — 197

8	The experience of active service on the Western Front	199
9	The aftermath of war	242

Bibliography	258
Index	270

Figures

4.1 'The Rose', poem from *Sub Rosa, Being the Magazine of the 55th West Lancashire Division*, June 1917.   page 83
4.2 'The Lancashire Rose', cartoon from *Sub Rosa, Being the Magazine of the 55th West Lancashire Division*, June 1917.   85
5.1 Postcards of the Cloth Hall, Ypres (no date). Postcards are reproduced courtesy of the Trustees of the National Museums Liverpool (King's Regiment Collection, Museum of Liverpool Life).   94
5.2 Arrival of the mail: the Liverpool Scottish receive post from home, 1915. Photograph courtesy of the Imperial War Museum, London (Q49830).   96
5.3 Lord Derby and the 55th Division, during a review by the King of the Belgians, Brussels, 3 January, 1919. Photograph courtesy of the Imperial War Museum (Q3508).   101
5.4 Photographs of the Liverpool Scottish in the Battle of Hooge, published in the *Northern Daily Dispatch* and the *Liverpool Daily Post*, June 1915. Photographs courtesy of the Imperial War Museum (Q49750 and Q49751).   108
6.1 RQMS R. A. S. Macfie. Photograph courtesy of the Imperial War Museum (Q114685).   128
6.2 Captain N. G. Chavasse, Medical Officer of the Liverpool Scottish. Photograph courtesy of the Imperial War Museum (Q67309).   138
6.3 Brigadier General F. J. Duncan. From P. J. Fisher, *Figures and phases of the War 1916–1919* (London: Odhams, 1919).   143
6.4 Major General H. S. Jeudwine. From P. J. Fisher, *Figures and phases of the War 1916–1919* (London: Odhams, 1919).   155

List of figures   ix

7.1 Captain A. Barrett Cardew, Medical Officer of the
    Liverpool Rifles. From P. J. Fisher, *Figures and phases
    of the War 1916–1919* (London: Odhams, 1919).   172
7.2 Military offences tried during wartime in the
    6th Liverpool Rifles, 1915–18.   182
7.3 Offences committed in the 6th Liverpool Rifles,
    1915–19, by month.   183
8.1 Private Walter Mills and Lance Corporal Thomas
    A. Robinson of the Liverpool Scottish in Q2 trench,
    St Eloi, near Ypres, April 1915. Photograph courtesy
    of the Imperial War Museum (Q 49822).   201
8.2 Men of Z Company, Liverpool Scottish, behind the
    lines on 15 June 1915, the day before the Battle of
    Hooge. Photograph courtesy of the Imperial War
    Museum (Q49834).   205
8.3 Guard of the Liverpool Scottish, 7 September 1918.
    Photograph courtesy of Imperial War Museum (Q9458).   237
8.4 Soldier of the Liverpool Rifles, September 1918.
    Photograph courtesy of the Imperial War Museum (Q7065). 238
9.1 55th Divisional Memorial at Givenchy, France
    (John McCartney).   254
9.2 Memorial Hall at Givenchy (John McCartney).   256

Maps

2.1	The social composition of municipal wards in Liverpool, 1914.	*page* 14
4.1	The environs of Liverpool. Map reproduced courtesy of Collins Maps and Atlases.	60
8.1	The Liverpool Scottish attack at Hooge, 16 June 1915.	204
8.2	Battle of the Somme.	212
8.3	The King's (Liverpool) Regiment, 3rd Battle of Ypres, 1917.	220
8.4	German attack at Epéhy, 30 November 1917.	224
8.5	Festubert–Givenchy Sector, 8 April 1918.	229
8.6	The final advance, October–November 1918.	236

Tables

3.1	Chronology of attestation by white-collar men for the Liverpool Scottish Battalion, percentage identifiable, by month	*page* 33
3.2	Social classification of men attesting in the ranks of the Liverpool Scottish Battalion, June–October 1915	33
3.3	Social composition of Number 1 Platoon, A Company, 6th Liverpool Rifles, 1918	36
3.4	Social classification of NCOs serving in Number 1 Platoon, A Company, 6th Liverpool Rifles, 1918	37
3.5	Social classification of NCOs serving in Number 1 Platoon, A Company, 6th Liverpool Rifles, February, May, October 1918	37
3.6	Some characteristics of the military service of the NCOs of Number 1 Platoon, A Company, 6th Liverpool Rifles, 1918, by rank	39
3.7	Social origins of officers in the Liverpool Scottish Battalion, by year commissioned (percentage identifiable)	45
4.1	Percentage of soldiers who died whilst serving in the 1/6th and 1/10th Battalions, King's (Liverpool) Regiment, according to their place of enlistment	61
4.2	Percentage of soldiers who died in fourteen Territorial battalions who enlisted in the unit's home county	66
4.3	Origin of men drafted to the 1/6th Battalion, King's (Liverpool) Regiment, 12 September 1917 to 12 November 1918	68
6.1	Age structure of NCOs serving in Number 1 Platoon, A Company, 6th Liverpool Rifles, 1918, by rank	140
7.1	Court-martial offences committed by a representative sample of infantry battalions that served on the Western Front, 1915–18	173
7.2	Minor offences committed in the 6th Liverpool Rifles, 1915–19	177

7.3 Courts-martial in the 6th Liverpool Rifles and a representative sample of battalions that served on the Western Front, 1915–18 — 186

7.4 Courts-martial in the 6th Liverpool Rifles, 1915–19 — 189

Acknowledgements

During the research and writing of this book I have been fortunate to receive the help of many individuals and organizations. First, I want to thank Jay Winter for his generous help. Without his wise counsel in my first term at Cambridge, this book would never have been written. Whilst he never dictated the course of the study, his encouragement, insight and example have been some of the most important influences on my work.

I am also indebted to John Bourne, Timothy Bowman, Adrian Gregory, Jon Lawrence, Alastair Reid, Gary Sheffield, Dennis Showalter, Andrew Whitmarsh and the anonymous readers of the typescript. I have greatly appreciated their valuable critiques while I was preparing the book for publication. Any errors of fact or judgement are, of course, my own.

Thanks are due to the many helpful archivists and librarians in the Imperial War Museum, Liddle Collection, Liverpool Record Office, Manchester Local History Library, Merseyside Record Office, Public Record Office at the National Archives, University Library, Cambridge, and the Joint Services Command and Staff College Library. I am especially grateful to Dennis Reeves and the late David Evans who opened up the Liverpool Scottish Regimental Museum to me, and to Simon Jones, former curator of the King's Regiment Collection, whose help and friendship were invaluable throughout my time in Liverpool.

For permission to quote from copyright material I am grateful to Liverpool Record Office, the Liverpool Scottish Regimental Museum Trust and the Trustees of the National Museums Liverpool (King's Regiment Collection, Museum of Liverpool Life). I would also like to take this opportunity to thank the Trustees of the Imperial War Museum and the following individual copyright holders for the privilege of consulting and quoting from papers held in their Department of Documents: Mrs W. Wilkinson (W. Evans Papers); Pamela Pehkonen (Macfie Papers); Rose Job (Gordon Papers). Every effort has been made to contact the copyright holders of individual collections, but in a few cases this has not been possible. Permission to reproduce photographs has been kindly granted by the Department of Photographs, Imperial War Museum.

I would like to thank the staff at Cambridge University Press, especially Isabelle Dambricourt, for their patience and help throughout the whole production process. Thanks are also due to Steve Waites and Dan Clayton of the Graphics Department at the Joint Services Command and Staff College, for their painstaking design of the French maps.

Financial support for graduate research was received from the Arts and Humanities Research Board, Board of Graduate Studies, Cambridge (Allen Scholarship), British Federation of Women Graduates, Cambridge Historical Society (travel grant), Girton College, Cambridge (G. M. Gardner Scholarship), Historial de la Grande Guerre, Institute of Historical Research (Scouloudi Fellowship) and the Prince Consort and Thirlwall Fund (travel grant). I am extremely grateful to all institutions concerned.

As a forum for discussion the following seminars and conferences have been helpful in refining my ideas: the War and Society Seminar at the University of Birmingham, the Military History Seminar and Victorian and Edwardian Britain Seminar at the Institute of Historical Research, the Liverpool and the First World War Conference at Merseyside Maritime Museum and the Faces of War Conference at the Royal Air Force Museum. My MA Option students on Advanced Command and Staff Courses 4, 5, 6 and 7 also did more than they realize to challenge and sharpen the ideas in this book.

Support comes in many forms and I have been lucky to have friends from Cambridge, Warwick, Manchester and London who have all listened to my ideas, or, at the very least, humoured me over the past few years. I would like to thank Jeremie Fant, Jason Fensome, Lisa Hull, Edgar Jones, Astrid Elke Kurth, Jenny Macleod, John Phillips, Denise Poynter, Andrew Tweedie, Elliot Vernon and especially Claire Herrick and Sarah Wheatley.

To Robert Foley goes a special acknowledgement. For the past three years he has provided unwavering love and encouragement, not to mention patience when various drafts of the book colonized the living room for the summer. Despite having his own book to finish he has read innumerable drafts, listened to endless ideas and done more than anyone else to make this a better book.

Finally, the greatest debt of gratitude I owe to my parents and my sister who have supported me from the very beginning of the project. For your help, advice, impromptu battlefield tours and much, much more, thank you. I couldn't have done it without you.

Abbreviations

Bde	Brigade
CO	Commanding Officer
CQMS	Company Quartermaster Sergeant
CSM	Company Sergeant Major
DRC	Divisional Reinforcement Camp
DSO	Distinguished Service Order
FGCM	Field General Court Martial
GHQ	General Headquarters
GOC	General Officer Commanding
HMSO	His Majesty's Stationery Office
IWM	Imperial War Museum
KRC	King's Regiment Collection
LRO	Liverpool Record Office
LSM	Liverpool Scottish Regimental Museum Trust
MAL	Maritime Archives and Library, Merseyside Maritime Museum
MC	Military Cross
MLHL	Manchester Local History Library
MLL	Museum of Liverpool Life
MM	Military Medal
MRO	Merseyside Record Office
OC	Officer Commanding
OTC	Officer Training Corps
PRO	National Archives, Public Record Office
RAMC	Royal Army Medical Corps
RMC	Royal Military College
RQMS	Regimental Quartermaster Sergeant
RSM	Regimental Sergeant Major
Sgt	Sergeant
TF	Territorial Force
VC	Victoria Cross

1   Introduction

The First World War drew ordinary British men into an army that by 1918 numbered over 5 million soldiers.¹ Some had volunteered to serve; others had been less willing and were conscripted later in the war. Most had little contact with the military in pre-war days, and before 1914 few would have contemplated participating in war. These men were first and foremost civilians, and this book examines their experience from their initial decision to enlist, through trench warfare on the Western Front, to death, discharge or demobilization at the end of the war. It is concerned with the soldier's relationship both with the army and with home, and examines the extent to which these citizen soldiers maintained their civilian values, attitudes, skills and traditions and applied them to the task of soldiering in the period of the First World War.

The popular image of the British soldier in the First World War is that of a passive victim of the war in general and the military system in particular. On joining the army a soldier supposedly ceased to act as an individual and lost his ability to shape his world. It is an image that has been reinforced by two historiographical traditions and is largely derived from a narrow view of the British soldier presented by the self-selecting literary veterans who wrote the disillusionment literature of the late 1920s and 1930s.²

For some historians, the characteristics of the British 'Tommy' have become synonymous with the qualities of the regular pre-war private soldier. He is credited with being able to withstand great hardship, is

---

[1] HMSO, *Statistics of the military effort of the British Empire during the Great War* (London, 1922), p. 364.
[2] See D. Englander and J. Osborne, 'Jack, Tommy, and Henry Dubb: the armed forces and the working class', *Historical Journal*, 21, 3 (1978), 593–621, and D. Englander, 'Soldiering and identity: reflections on the Great War', *War in History*, 1, 3 (1994), 300–18. Authors of the disillusionment literature included Edmund Blunden, Robert Graves, Wilfred Owen and Siegfried Sassoon. See E. Blunden, *Undertones of war* (London, 1928); R. Graves, *Goodbye to all that* (4th edn, London, 1966); W. Owen, *Poems* (London, 1920); S. Sassoon, *Memoirs of an infantry officer* (London, 1930).

blessed with infinite courage and is believed to have been loyal, submissive and obedient to the end of the conflict.[3] According to this interpretation, ordinary civilians were transformed by army discipline and organization into soldiers who had assimilated the values and ideals of the regular army.[4]

Other historians view the British soldier against a backdrop of social and cultural change. The war is seen as a cataclysmic experience that defied explanation and coloured all that came afterwards. It helped to destroy traditional social and cultural norms and aided the development of new, modernist modes of thinking, marking a watershed in the development of European culture and society.[5]

To these historians, who see the war as destroying traditional beliefs and certainties, the British soldier stands out as a disillusioned figure, caught in the grip of an industrial war. Eric Leed's influential work *No Man's Land* exemplified this interpretation. He argued that pre-war ideals of heroism and self-sacrifice could not sustain the soldier in the face of machine-based slaughter, and he was forced to reject civilian society and retreat into his own unique trench culture based on passivity, fatalism, superstition and, in extreme cases, neurosis.[6] Creating a new defensive identity was seen as the only way for the soldier to survive the war experience.

In recent years the image of the powerless, victimized soldier of the Great War has been undergoing a transformation. It is undeniable that military participation left an imprint on those who experienced it, but there has been a lively debate over the depth of that imprint and its consequences both for the army and for wider society. Many historians have begun to identify more continuities than discontinuities between pre-war civilian society and the war years.[7] It has been argued that soldiers did not internalize regular army values, nor did they create new personalities and develop new values to cope with the experience of

---

[3] See W. Churchill, *The world crisis* (London, 1965 edn), 750; D. Winter, *Death's men: soldiers of the Great War* (London, 1978); A. J. P. Taylor, *An illustrated history of the First World War* (Harmondsworth, 1965).
[4] Winter, *Death's men*, 227–9.
[5] The greatest exponent of this view was P. Fussell, *The Great War and modern memory* (London, 1975). See also M. Eksteins, *Rites of spring: the Great War and the birth of the modern age* (New York, 1989); S. Hynes, *A war imagined: the First World War and English culture* (New York, 1991).
[6] E. Leed, *No Man's Land: combat and identity in World War One* (Cambridge, 1979).
[7] A comprehensive treatment of this theme can be found in J. Winter, *Sites of memory, sites of mourning: the Great War in European cultural history* (Cambridge, 1995). For a wider discussion of historiographical trends, see J. M. Winter, 'Catastrophe and culture: recent trends in the historiography of the First World War', *Journal of Modern History*, 54 (1992), 525–32.

trench warfare.⁸ Soldiers and civilians turned to the traditional and familiar to survive four years of war. In examining the relationship between the soldier and the society from which he was drawn, this study makes a contribution to the debate.

The book centres around the experience of the 1/6th and 1/10th Battalions of the King's Liverpool Regiment, known by the soldiers as the Liverpool Rifles and the Liverpool Scottish.⁹ It is a local study that re-examines some of the familiar historiographical 'truths' about the British experience of the Great War that have previously been analysed at the national level. As Britain was a decentralized nation in 1914 and the horizons of her citizens were profoundly local, it is also important to view war experience from a local perspective. Indeed, questions relating to the identity of the citizen soldier in wartime, his relationship with home and his impact on the command relationship can only be adequately examined at the microlevel.

By examining the history of the soldier and his unit it becomes possible to see what the trajectory of war service must have been like for those who fought. We can identify who the men were, where they came from, where they served and where they went after the war. Moreover, because of the longitudinal nature of the study, we are able to assess how far a unit and its soldiers changed as the war progressed. It is a holistic approach to history that examines not only the soldier himself, but his whole world, both in the trenches and back at home. By studying the soldier in his true context, we can begin to understand his motivations, his attitudes and his reactions to war.

---

⁸ See especially, J. Bourne, 'The British working man in arms', in H. Cecil and P. Liddle (eds.), *Facing Armageddon: the First World War experienced* (London, 1996), 336–52, which considers the impact of working-class society on war; J. G. Fuller, *Troop morale and popular culture in the British and Dominion Armies, 1914–1918* (Oxford, 1990), which examines the transfer of civilian-based popular culture from home to the rear areas of France; G. D. Sheffield, *Leadership in the trenches: officer–man relations, morale and discipline in the British Army in the era of the First World War* (London, 2000), which highlights the fact that the ordinary soldiers were not 'mere passive victims of the war'; J. Bourke, *Dismembering the male: men's bodies, Britain and the Great War* (London, 1996), p. 21, which suggests that 'the gulf between civilians and servicemen was not as wide as some have portrayed' and stresses the importance of personal correspondence; and Englander, 'Soldiering and identity: reflections on the Great War', which constitutes a brief overview of the importance of continuity in the 'make-up and mentality' of British soldiers. For a French perspective see S. Audoin-Rouzeau, *Men at war: national sentiment and trench journalism in France during the First World War* (Oxford, 1992) and L. V. Smith, *Between mutiny and obedience: the case of the French Fifth Infantry Division during World War One* (Princeton, 1994).

⁹ The title of the 1/6th Battalion is also sometimes shortened to 6th Battalion. Second- and third-line battalions of both units were raised later in September and November 1914, but they had different experiences and are only mentioned when their history impinges on the first-line units.

Of course, as no one infantry unit was exactly the same as the next and the experience of a soldier depended, in large measure, on the character and mores of the unit in which he served, the conclusions of a local study are necessarily limited. However, it is precisely because of these diverse experiences that individual unit studies are needed. They can both confirm and refute existing historical conceptions of the First World War and in doing so highlight future areas for investigation.[10]

The reasons that lie behind the type of units chosen for investigation are also important to the study. In August 1914 the British army encompassed three types of infantry battalion: regular, Territorial and Service.[11] On the outbreak of war the regular units comprised the small professional army, and the Territorial Force the reserve. When the mass expansion of the army became necessary, it was undertaken in an *ad hoc* manner. Extra recruits were accepted in the Territorial Force, forming second- and third-line battalions by the end of 1915, but the majority of men were recruited in separate Service battalions locally raised through regular army recruiting channels or by Members of Parliament, prominent local figures and city corporations.[12] The units selected for this study are both first-line Territorial battalions and have been chosen for a number of reasons. First, Territorial experience in wartime has been a relatively neglected topic, saved from anonymity only by the pioneering work of Ian Beckett.[13] The political wrangling that accompanied the birth of the Force has been comprehensively covered, together with its reconstitution as the Territorial Army after the war, but there remain few investigations of wartime Territorials.[14] This

---

[10] This point has been highlighted by both Ian Beckett and Peter Simkins, see I. Beckett, 'Revisiting the old front line', *Stand To: The Journal of the Western Front Association*, 43 (April 1995), 10, and P. Simkins, 'Everyman at war', in B. Bond (ed.), *The First World War and British military history* (Oxford, 1991), 305.

[11] There were also Special Reserve battalions that provided drafts for the Regular units in time of war.

[12] P. Simkins, 'The four armies 1914–1918', in D. Chandler and I. Beckett (eds.), *The Oxford history of the British Army* (Oxford, 1996), 243 and 246.

[13] I. Beckett, 'The Territorial Force', in I. F. W. Beckett and K. Simpson (eds.), *A nation in arms: a social study of the British army in the First World War* (Manchester, 1985), 128–64; I. F. W. Beckett, *The amateur military tradition 1558–1945* (Manchester, 1991). Many individual units published their histories in the aftermath of the war and J. Stirling wrote a book which contained a potted history of each Territorial division, but there was no attempt to write an official history. See J. Stirling, *The Territorial divisions, 1914–1918* (London, 1922).

[14] For an analysis of the birth of the Territorial Force see E. M. Spiers, *The Army and society 1815–1914* (London, 1980), 265–81; Beckett, 'The Territorial Force', 128–30; P. Simkins, *Kitchener's army: the raising of the New Armies, 1914–16* (Manchester, 1988), 10–19; P. Dennis, *The Territorial Army, 1906–1940* (Woodbridge, 1987), *passim*. The case studies that have been completed to date include: a case study of Buckinghamshire units by Beckett in 'The Territorial Force', 148–152; a doctoral thesis on the Leeds Rifles, P. M. Morris, 'Leeds and the amateur military tradition: the Leeds

is a serious omission in the historiography of the war, as the Territorial Force played a significant role in the conflict. During the course of the war 692 Territorial battalions had been in existence compared with 557 New Army and 267 regular or reserve battalions.[15]

Second, first-line Territorial battalions had been established prior to the war and were an expression of the civilian identities of their pre-war members. For example, in 1914 the membership and traditions of the Liverpool Rifles were staunchly middle class, drawn from the business and financial world of their city. The examination of units with established civilian-inspired characteristics and traditions makes it easier to trace continuities and changes in the importance and use of civilian values and skills in wartime.

However, the most important reason for choosing to study the middle-class battalions of the Liverpool Rifles and the Liverpool Scottish is the abundance of personal sources generated by their members. The treasure trove of letters, diaries and memoirs, produced by the whole range of ranks, is a consequence of the socially exclusive nature of the pre-war battalions. Those Territorials who first went to war were highly educated men, familiar with the art of letter writing, and keen to record their experiences in diaries and written accounts. Unsurprisingly, the availability of personal testimony decreases in tandem with the decline in the middle-class character of the Battalions, which occurred as the war progressed.

This has two major implications for the book. First, most beliefs and attitudes expressed in personal sources are those of the provincial middle classes, despite the fact that approximately 40 per cent of the Liverpool Rifles, for example, belonged to the skilled working class in 1918. Secondly, the bulk of the personal sources refer to the years 1914 to 1917.[16] Whilst a number of prolific diarists and letter writers of the 1914 era survived with the Battalions until 1918, only one remained with the Liverpool Scottish to the end of the war. Other, more indirect sources have had to be employed to reconstruct the life of the Battalions in the last years of the war.[17]

As the book relies so heavily on the personal testimony of the soldiers, an assessment of the value of these sources is appropriate. Some of the

---

Rifles and their antecedents, 1859–1918', unpublished PhD thesis, University of Leeds (1983); and K. W. Mitchinson, *Gentlemen and officers: the impact and experience of war on a Territorial Regiment, 1914–1918* (London, 1995).

[15] Beckett, 'The Territorial Force', 132.
[16] For 1918 the Rifles had one memoir and one brief diary whilst the Scottish boasted one letter-writer, two memoirists and the Battalion history.
[17] These included, Battalion diaries, trench magazines, newspaper reports, accounts of actions in Divisional papers and disciplinary statistics calculated from casualties books.

most useful sources are the letters, diaries, and accounts of individual experiences, written as the war unfolded. Whilst official censorship and self-censorship, together with the issue of self-justification, have to be considered, they present a remarkably candid view of the war, particularly from the ranks. The collections vary enormously in size, depending on the inclination of the writer, the length of time he spent at the front and, in the case of letters, the care of relatives in preserving communications.

Collections of letters from individuals such as Robert Scott Macfie that span the entire war are particularly useful. Macfie was a member of a prominent sugar refining family in Liverpool who had been a volunteer in the early years of the century. The Battalion turned a blind eye to his rejoining the Liverpool Scottish as a private at the age of 44, two days after the outbreak of war, and he quickly regained his former post as colour sergeant. Educated at Oundle, Cambridge and Edinburgh, with a passionate interest in gypsy studies,[18] he was something of an eccentric and certainly not a typical colour sergeant, but he was one of the many highly educated men of these Battalions who chose to remain in the ranks for the duration of the war. His acute observations of battalion life and his willingness to express both his feelings, and prevalent attitudes that were in opposition to his own, make his letters a supremely valuable source.

Diaries written at the front are another good source for gauging changing attitudes in relation to experience. The fact that many diaries, including those of Captain McKinnell, Lance Corporal Peppiette and Sergeant Campbell, were sent home after their death in action has meant that the opinions of men who did not survive the war can be included in this analysis.

A more problematic source is that of the memoirs and the piecemeal accounts written post-war. This writing was more self-conscious and prone to omissions, but as with the diaries and letters it is possible, at times, to identify personal prejudices and verify incidents from other sources. The value of the memoir also depends on the motivation of the author, when it was written and whether it was written from memory, or with the aid of diaries and letters. Only one memoir utilized in the thesis was written as late as 1970, but it was useful because the death of the author's contemporaries meant that he felt able to speak more freely about certain topics, including the incidence of self-inflicted wounds and the character of officers.[19]

---

[18] Macfie was secretary and editor of the *Journal of Gypsy Lore* from 1907 to 1914, and was intimately involved with the work of the society after the war. See G. L. Ackerley, 'Memoir of R. A. Scott Macfie', *Journal of Gypsy Lore*, 3rd series, 14 (1935), 20–50.

[19] H. S. Taylor, Reminiscences, LSM, Miscellaneous File T, and H. S. Taylor to Liverpool Scottish Museum, Date unknown, LSM, Miscellaneous File T.

Introduction   7

Most memoirs, however, were written before 1940 and based on wartime diaries and letters.[20] They could be written as a personal or family record,[21] some found their way into the regimental gazettes of their old units,[22] and one was written as a basis for a wider regimental history that never came to fruition.[23] The majority of events were narrated chronologically, dated accurately, and punctuated with extracts from diaries or letters. Certainly those of Sergeant W. G. Bromley and Major S. E. Gordon read as diaries. Only one, a grossly exaggerated but highly entertaining memoir by Basil Rathbone, was published as part of his autobiography in the wake of his Sherlock Holmes success, but even this memoir has some value when corroborated by other sources. Rathbone's claim to have been pinned down in No Man's Land by both the Red Baron and Goering was undoubtedly a product of his theatrical imagination. Nevertheless, the account of his exploits on patrols and raids, for which he received the Military Cross and the admiration of many in the Battalion, was broadly accurate.[24]

Through their diaries, letters and memoirs the soldiers of the Liverpool Territorials have left a record of how ordinary men in uniform thought, felt, suffered and behaved between 1914 and 1919. To assess how far these soldiers retained and utilized their civilian outlook and attitudes through those four years of war, the book has been divided into three sections. The first examines the durability of unit characteristics and the traditions they inspired. It investigates how these traditions, derived from civilian culture, could be both supportive and detrimental to the morale of the soldier at war. The second part looks at how soldiers used rules and conventions of pre-war British society to protect themselves from the excesses of the regular army. It highlights how civilian skills and organization could be harnessed by soldiers to influence the command relationship and the discipline system within a unit and so exert some control over their lives in the army. The final part of the book examines the attitudes of the soldiers who served, to ascertain how far the ideals and aspirations of the men were influenced and changed by the war. It concludes with a short epilogue which highlights the main themes of the book whilst tracing the experience of some of the soldiers and their community as they reintegrated into civilian life and reflected on their achievements and sacrifice in war.

[20] For example, S. E. Gordon, 1917; N. F. Ellison, 1922 (first draft); W. G. Bromley, 1924; E. Herd, 1939; J. S. Handley, c.1950.
[21] S. E. Gordon, Memoir, Gordon Papers, IWM, 77/5/1.
[22] W. G. Bromley, Memoir, LSM, Acc. No. 544.
[23] N. F. Ellison, Diary and Memoir, Ellison Papers, IWM, DS/MISC/49.
[24] B. Rathbone, *In and out of character* (New York, 1962).

Those soldiers who returned home from the Western Front had experienced the alien environment of the trenches as well as long stretches of boredom, punctuated by the fear of battle and the obscenities of agonizing death. Yet most arrived back in their home communities with their civilian identities intact, ready to pick up their lives where they had left off. They were by no means unscathed by their ordeal, but, collectively, they had not become the obedient, passive victims of popular myth. They had remained civilians in uniform for the duration of the war. The ways in which they had been able to shape their own lives when faced by the challenges of army organization, separation from home and family and the fighting itself provide the subject of this book.

2   Pre-war Liverpool and the Territorial Force

The character of a Territorial unit before the Great War was rooted in the civilian life of its part-time soldiers. Its traditions were derived from the social status and values of its members and the locality from which it was recruited. Thus, to understand the characteristics and traditions of the Territorial battalions before and during the war, we must first examine the social and political life of the city from which they came.

On the eve of the Great War, Liverpool was a prosperous commercial centre. Since the late eighteenth century its port had grown in importance and by 1907 it handled one third of British exports and a quarter of the import trade. Liverpool's financial institutions had also gradually increased in stature, with its corn and cotton exchanges, underwriters and insurance companies playing a crucial role in the world economy in 1914.[1]

The port of Liverpool determined the nature of employment available to its inhabitants and thus influenced the social composition and character of the city. It was a city which generated wealth solely through the distribution of goods and celebrated the fact that it had little manufacturing industry of its own.[2] The self-styled second metropolis[3] saw itself as a genteel centre of commerce, unsullied by industrial factories, and asserted its superiority over manufacturing rival Manchester through the popular adage, 'Liverpool gentlemen, Manchester men'.[4]

By 1914 the city of Liverpool was the centre of a much larger conurbation, which had gradually expanded on either side of the River Mersey. It incorporated the shipbuilding and milling centre of Birkenhead, together with the residential suburbs of the Wirral Peninsula to the west, and extended up the commuter line to Southport in the north.

---

[1] R. Muir, *History of Liverpool* (2nd edn, London, 1970), 298.
[2] The main industries in Liverpool were corn milling, tobacco manufacture and sugar refining. Ward Lock and Co., *Liverpool, Birkenhead and New Brighton* (London, 1912), 12.
[3] See *Mitchell's newspaper press directory* (1847), 161, quoted in J. Belchem, '"An accent exceedingly rare": scouse and the inflexion of class', in J. Belchem and N. Kirk (eds.), *Languages of labour* (Aldershot, 1997), 122.
[4] Belchem, '"An accent exceedingly rare"', 102.

Beyond this urban unit, from which the city drew its immediate labour force, lay Liverpool's industrial hinterland. St Helens glass-works and the chemical industries in Widnes received their raw materials and exported their finished products through the port, but Liverpool's importance extended far beyond the hinterland. As the tentacles of its railways had spread across the north-west of England during the nineteenth century, the salt-mines of Cheshire and, most importantly, the manufacturing towns of industrial Lancashire had developed interdependent relationships with the port. Liverpool became vitally important to the region as the gateway to the world economy, assuming a shared leadership role, alongside Manchester, for the county of Lancashire, and neighbouring areas of Cheshire.[5]

The economic and social structure of Liverpool

The old, aristocratic land-owning families, including the Molyneux and the Stanleys, continued to exert an influence over Liverpool at the beginning of the century. The Stanleys, in particular, played an active part in the life of the city, acting as landlords, patrons, politicians and civic representatives, but they were no longer the dominant force. It was the merchants and ship-owners, on whose wealth and industry the city depended, who wielded the most influence over the economy and society of Liverpool in 1914.

The self-made merchant, broker and ship-owning families, established in the first quarter of the nineteenth century, helped to define the physical and psychological character of the city.[6] The distinctive commercial buildings, erected by the merchants and their companies, dominated the skyline. The corn, cotton and stock exchanges were at the heart of the city, whilst the imposing architecture of the Royal Liver Building and the Dock Board Offices framed the 'gateway to Liverpool' from the sea.[7]

The merchant class of Liverpool also epitomized the 'special toughness of the Liverpool fibre' that had developed the port and established commercial prosperity in the face of strong competition from London and Bristol.[8] They were staunch defenders of civic liberties,[9] philanthropists

---

[5] Liverpool became the natural capital for the West Lancashire region, hosting the headquarters of regional organizations. It was no surprise therefore, that the headquarters for the West Lancashire Territorial Association should be located in Liverpool.
[6] These families included the Lairds (shipbuilding), Macfies and Fairries (sugar), Holts (shipping), Fletchers (shipping), Harrisons (steam-ships), Booths (Booth-line shipping) and Pooles (shipping). See B. Orchard, *Liverpool's legion of honour* (Birkenhead, 1893), 22.
[7] Ward Lock and Co., *Guide to Liverpool, Birkenhead and New Brighton*, 9.
[8] The Liverpool Organisation, *Book of Liverpool civic week* (Liverpool, 1928), 8.
[9] *Ibid.*, 9; Belchem, '"An accent exceedingly rare"', 103.

and social leaders,[10] and their commercial success cast Liverpool as a dynamic city of opportunity.

By the early twentieth century the opportunities for individual social and economic advancement had declined markedly, with the amalgamation of smaller businesses to create giant corporations.[11] The decline in the total trade passing through the port had also begun, but these were gradual, long-term trends, which had yet to make an impact on the image of the city.[12] The businesses of the merchants and ship-owners, and increasingly larger corporations, continued to generate wealth and were serviced by a burgeoning financial sector. By 1911, the professional classes in Liverpool accounted for 2.1 per cent of the city's male labour force, whilst 6.9 per cent were engaged in commerce.[13]

The most significant group in the financial sector was the clerks, who had grown steadily in number throughout the nineteenth century.[14] By 1914 Liverpool offered a range of clerical employment, from the routine, characterized by the positions in the department-based offices of the Cunard Shipping Company and the Mersey Docks, to the eminently responsible in the banking and insurance companies.[15]

Wages varied substantially, as did the prestige attached to a clerical job, but in most cases clerks identified with the interests of their employers and viewed themselves as belonging to the middle class. Few clerks were unionized in Liverpool. The National Union of Clerks maintained a low profile in the city, whilst the more popular Liverpool Clerk's Association was little more than a friendly society, being sponsored by business giants in Liverpool.[16] Clerks consistently adhered to values of 'respectability'. Norman Ellison, whose family were clinging to middle-class respectability in the face of financial ruin during the early years of the century, remembered that, 'no matter the state of the family budget, we always had a servant living in to do the household chores in the morning and wear a starched cap and apron in the afternoon to receive

---

[10] See, for example, the Rankin ship-owning family, whose members were well known for their philanthropy and participation in political and civic life (Conservative); also the Rathbones, who operated a ship-owning and merchant business as well as acting as councillors, lord mayors and MPs (Liberal). P. J. Waller, *Democracy and sectarianism: a political and social history of Liverpool 1868–1939* (Liverpool, 1981), 506–7.

[11] J. K. Walton, *Lancashire: a social history 1558–1939* (Manchester, 1987), 319.

[12] G. Anderson, 'The service occupations of nineteenth century Liverpool', in B. L. Anderson and P. J. M. Stoney (eds.), *Commerce, industry and transport: studies in economic change on Merseyside* (Liverpool, 1983), 92.

[13] *Ibid.*, 82 and 86.

[14] Clerks have been identified by Anderson as one of the most important occupational categories in Liverpool, which 'provided the city with much of its character and tone'. *Ibid.*, 88.

[15] *Ibid.*, 88.   [16] Waller, *Democracy and sectarianism*, 6.

visitors'.[17] A preoccupation with outward appearances as well as thrift, self-improvement and self-reliance characterized their lifestyle and set them apart from the artisan class, who often earned similar wages.[18]

The remainder of Liverpool's labour requirements were concentrated at the opposite end of the employment scale. The port needed a large number of unskilled dockers, carters and transport workers in order to function. The dock workers, living in the worst slums of any English city, and suffering from the unskilled, casual nature of their work, added another dimension to the character of Liverpool. The squalor of their living conditions earned Liverpool the dubious title of 'blackspot on the Mersey'.[19]

The peculiarities of the labour market ensured that union membership had traditionally been weak amongst the working class in Liverpool. The absence of an industrial, skilled artisanate class in Liverpool delayed the development of unionization.[20] Nevertheless, by 1911 the poorest manual labourers had begun to make their presence felt. A seamen's strike for improved pay and conditions was backed by a fragile alliance of dock workers, carters and transport workers. The situation escalated into national action and necessitated military intervention and the enrolment of 4000 special constables in Liverpool during August 1911.[21] The strike brought the docks to a standstill and a Strike Committee was established which controlled most transport movements in the city. In response, the government sent regular troops to support the police and maintain order. On 13 August a demonstrating crowd was charged by the police,

---

[17] N. F. Ellison, Memoir 'Early Days 1893–1914', LRO, Unlisted catalogue, item 611.
[18] 'Even when unemployed and in distress, few solicited charitable relief.' Waller, *Democracy and sectarianism*, 6.
[19] Walton, *Lancashire*, 319. It is interesting to note that the 'scouse' image of Liverpool is a twentieth-century construct, a reaction to Liverpool's economic decline which began in earnest during the world-wide depression of the 1930s. The 'scouser' was defined by his quick-witted humour, an image based on the casual, Irish-influenced working class and their strategies for coping with the economic and social difficulties of their city. In recent years two images of the 'scouser' have formed. The first, the 'whinging militant scouser' of the 1980s, whose supposed self-destructive reckless tendencies made Liverpool's decline inevitable. It is accompanied by the image of the 'scally scouser', a roguish character, personifying the easy-going attitude to life derived from seafaring and dockers' traditions and popularly incorporated into comedy series and soap operas. Neither of these representations is illustrative of Liverpool's image in 1914. See Belchem, 'An accent exceedingly rare', 99–119.
[20] The inconsistent nature of dock work, an excess of immigrant labour and, to a lesser extent, sectarian allegiances further hampered attempts to unionize. J. Bohstedt, 'More than one working class: Protestant–Catholic riots in Edwardian Liverpool', in J. Belchem (ed.), *Popular politics, riot and labour* (Liverpool Historical Studies 8, Liverpool, 1992), 203.
[21] Waller, *Democracy and sectarianism*, 249–69, and Bohstedt, 'More than one working class', 212–13.

and a riot ensued in which 200 people were injured and one policeman was killed. Disorder was renewed on 15 August when the prison van transporting those arrested in the previous disturbances was attacked.

Despite the widespread violence, by 19 August the strike had been abandoned. It had been resolved through negotiation between the strike committees and individual employers, but the measures conceded by the ship-owners were minor. Indeed, Richard Holt believed that as a result of the firm attitude of the ship-owners, 'the position of the employers was stronger after the strike than before'.[22] Industrial unrest continued sporadically thereafter, but there were numerous squabbles among the unions' leadership, and action was mostly sectional.[23]

The separation of the poorest dockers and the middle-class clerks of the city was very nearly complete. Different social classes inhabited different worlds in the Liverpool of 1914. Rich commercial magnates had built their homes within the distinctly middle-class southern municipal wards, or migrated to the pleasant residential estates across the Mersey on the Wirral. The dock workers and poorest manual labourers were confined to slum dwellings clustered around the inner wards, close to the hiring stations on the docks,[24] whilst the majority of the salariat lived cheek by jowl with those of lower social status in the suburban quarters of the city. Of the thirty-nine wards in Liverpool, twenty were composed of the working classes, six were exclusively middle-class districts and ten contained a socially diverse population. Three of the older districts, Prince's Park, Granby and Abercromby, contained large mansions interspersed with working-class terraces. The remaining mixed wards had been colonized more recently by estates of terraces and semi-detached housing.[25]

---

[22] Richard Holt was an owner of a large shipping company. Waller, *Democracy and sectarianism*, 257.

[23] *Ibid.*, 262–4.

[24] Belchem, '"An accent exceedingly rare"', 106. See also R. Lawton and C. G. Pooley, 'The social geography of Merseyside in the nineteenth century', Final Report to the Social Science Research Council (Department of Geography, University of Liverpool, 1976).

[25] The districts were classified following the methods used by S. Davies, *Liverpool labour* (Keele, 1996), 211. The 1921 Census was used to calculate these figures because the 1911 Census did not list rooms per person by ward. Most figures provided in the 1911 Census were divided by parish. Davies' figures were calculated from the 1931 Census. However, wards had not changed significantly between 1921 and 1931, the major difference being the development of council housing on the outskirts of the city. Therefore, it is reasonable to assume that Davies' descriptions of the types of housing in mixed wards would have been applicable in 1921 and also 1914, as there was no major development in housing provision between 1914 and 1921 in Liverpool. Other occupational information in Davies, *Liverpool labour*, 206–7, further supports these conclusions. See Map 2.1, showing the Liverpool wards, distinguished according to social class.

14 Citizen Soldiers

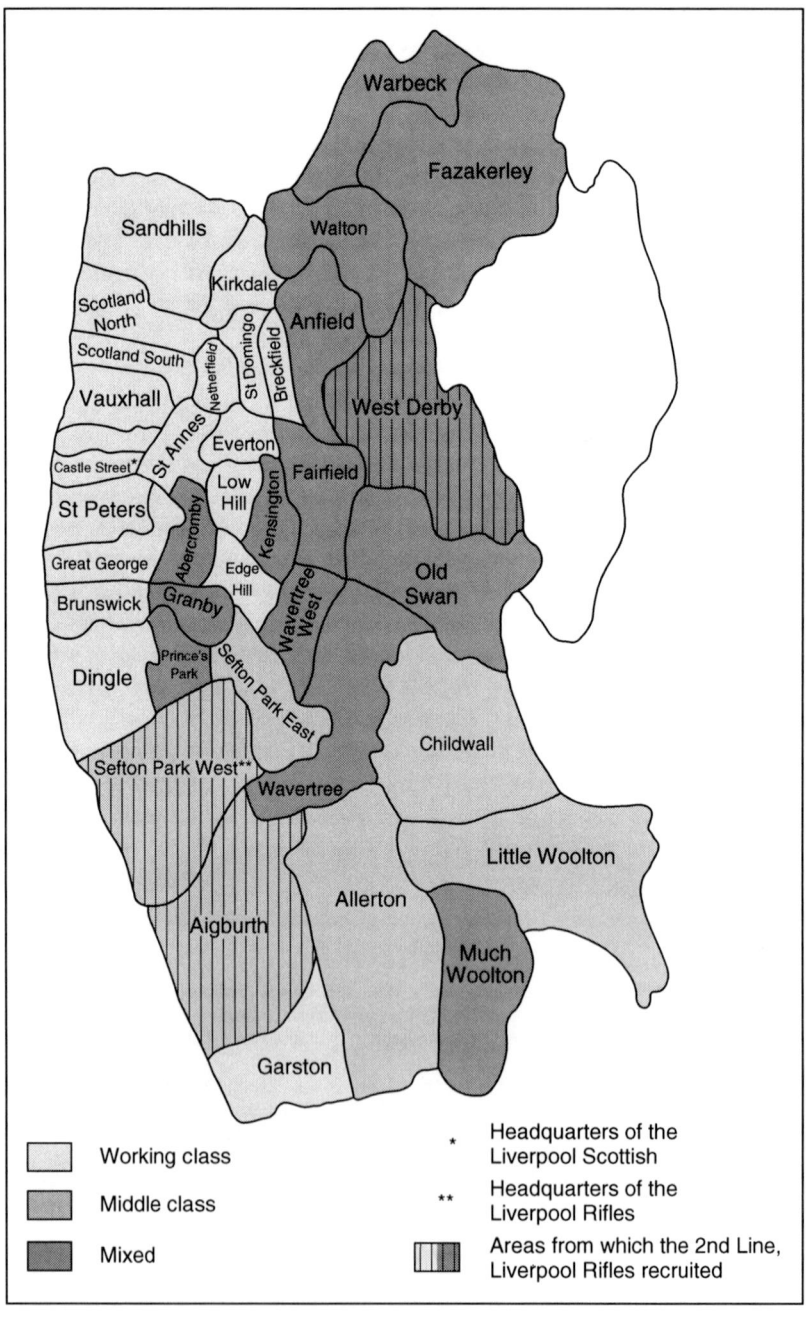

Map 2.1 The social composition of municipal wards in Liverpool, 1914.

The proximity of the middle and lower classes did not foster the development of a strong community based on their immediate locality. In his novel of the Great War, John Brophy described the state of social relations between neighbouring classes. Mr March, an insurance agent, and Mr Foster, a wholesale stationery dealer, were classic caricatures of the lower middle class in Liverpool. They lived in 'a Liverpool suburb, full of rows of fifty year old shabby, but still respectable semi-detached houses ... Many of these abutted on streets of newer, but dingier labourers' cottages. From these habitations of the lowly would occasionally sally forth bands of rough youths ... disturbing the calm of the neighbourhood.'[26] The response of the 'junior clerks and secondary school boys' was to 'give illegal but furious battle to the intruders with varying success'.[27] Thus those of a lower social status, who did not hold the 'respectable' values of the middle class and allowed their 'newer' cottages to become 'dingy', were viewed as 'intruders' and treated as enemies. Whether separated by physical distance, in the case of the more affluent members of the middle class, or by a psychological distance, imposed through differing social values and attitudes, the Liverpolitan middle and lower classes kept apart in 1914.[28]

The historian R. Muir observed in 1907 that it was not only the rich, the 'middling classes' and the poor who lived apart; the poorer elements of the immigrant population also formed self-sustaining communities in specific wards of Liverpool.[29] As a port, Liverpool attracted many immigrants from Wales, Scotland and Ireland, as well as from countries overseas. The Scottish and Welsh retained their identity in Liverpool through founding distinct institutions, rather than relying on residential enclaves. Both used their religion as a focus for their communities, supplemented by cultural societies and organizations.[30] However, as most Scottish and Welsh migrants were attracted by the opportunities for clerks or skilled marine engineers and ship repairers, they lived in neighbourhoods that reflected their social rather than their ethnic status.[31] By contrast, the Catholic Irish, the largest immigrant group, congregated at the bottom of the labour ladder, and lived close to their employment by the docks. Such

---

[26] J. Brophy, *The bitter end* (London, 1928), 24.   [27] *Ibid.*
[28] N. F. Ellison, Memoir 'Early Days 1893–1914', Ellison Papers, LRO, Unlisted catalogue, item 611.
[29] Muir, *History of Liverpool*, 304.
[30] The Scottish founded Presbyterian churches, whilst the Welsh built their own Calvinist chapels. Welsh newspapers were distributed in the city, and the National Eisteddfod was hosted a number of times by Liverpool, whilst the Scottish formed Burns and Caledonian societies. See J. Belchem, 'The peculiarities of Liverpool', in Belchem (ed.), *Popular politics, riot and labour*, 15, and P. H. Williams, *Liverpolitana* (Liverpool, 1971), 19–21.
[31] Belchem, 'The peculiarities of Liverpool', 16.

was their concentration that many of the slum areas were regarded as the province of the Irish.

Liverpool's immigrants brought with them the customs and traditions of their native countries and passed on their values to their children, ensuring the survival of distinctive communities.[32] Nowhere was this more apparent than amongst the Irish, who transferred not only their customs but also their antagonisms to their adopted city.

The sectarian conflict that permeated Liverpool's working class, and led to violence, rioting and border disputes in some working-class wards, began as an internal Irish battle between Catholic and Protestant Irish migrants.[33] John Bohstedt has argued that sectarianism escalated in Liverpool, and spread to other elements of the working class because of specific political and social conditions. In the absence of traditional trade union organizations, which provided 'social services' and 'emotionally satisfying solidarities', the poverty-stricken working class turned to sectarian institutions for emotional and financial support.[34]

Sectarianism and the need for supportive institutions had been astutely exploited by the Tories in Liverpool from the middle of the nineteenth century. They had adopted the Protestant cause, using the rhetoric of 'no popery' to protect the 'marginal privilege' of the Protestant worker, and penetrated the working-class associational culture. By the 1890s, the populist Tory boss Archibald Salvidge had greatly expanded the Working Men's Conservative Association in Liverpool through addressing the political concerns of the Protestant Irish.[35] By contrast, the Liberals had remained aloof from the working class in Liverpool and could not counter the Tory organization. As a result, the Catholic Irish had no champion, were bereft of political and economic protection, and were forced to rely on their own 'ethnic resources'.[36]

Each working-class community thus had a vested interest in supporting its own sectarian institutions, which helped to perpetuate separate communities. Yet this did not mean that all social relations were characterized by conflict. Eric Taplin has emphasized that Catholic and Protestant dockers co-operated well in the workplace, and the few references to the Irish in the diaries and letters of the Rifles and the Scottish were surprisingly favourable.[37] Rifleman Clegg remembered that when the men of

---

[32] Waller notes that the children and grandchildren of Irish-born parents continued to be 'sternly Irishized'. See Waller, *Democracy and sectarianism*, 7.
[33] In 1909 religious parades were utilized by Protestant and Catholic leaders to assert political superiority, and the Protestant demagogue, Pastor George Wise, sparked serious sectarian rioting. Bohstedt, 'More than one working class', 204.
[34] *Ibid.*, 176–88.   [35] *Ibid.*, 184.
[36] See Belchem, 'The peculiarities of Liverpool', 13.   [37] *Ibid.*, 7.

his draft, from the 2/6th Rifles, were paraded before being sent to the front, the 2/8th Irish preceded them on parade, 'and had left behind them a large assembly of friends and relations; these good hearted souls stayed to watch us all off and several of their remarks were marked indelibly on our memories; "stick to the Irish" and "keep your 'earts up and your 'eads down and the Irish will see you through" '.[38] The Irish were still viewed as a separate community by the middle-class members of the Scottish and Rifles, and the 8th Irish Battalion was regarded as the most disruptive in the Regiment, but overt sectarian prejudice was not frequently expressed during the war, and so receives little attention in this book.[39]

In 1914 the people of Liverpool were divided by social class, ethnicity and sectarianism into distinct, although not necessarily mutually exclusive, communities. Each individual held a separate set of allegiances, dictated by his ethnic origin, occupation and religion, and was defined by membership of various institutions and organizations. The six Territorial battalions of the King's (Liverpool) Regiment reflected the stratified and heterogeneous nature of Liverpolitan[40] society by catering for most social and ethnic groupings within the city. The 5th, 7th and 9th Battalions attracted the 'respectable' working class, the 6th Rifles catered for the middle class, and the 10th Scottish and 8th Irish Battalions represented their respective ethnic groups.

These Territorial infantry battalions were part of a long-established tradition of volunteer soldiering in Lancashire. It was the men of Liverpool who raised the first Volunteer battalion in 1859, beginning the permanent revival of the volunteer movement in Britain.[41] By the turn of the century, British auxiliary forces comprising the Volunteers, the Yeomanry and the Militia were in need of reform. The Militia had been recruited by voluntary enlistment since 1852 and, as with the regular army, attracted recruits from the lowest sectors of society; the Yeomanry relied on farming communities and the Volunteers attracted 'respectable' working-class and some middle-class members.[42] These forces were

---

[38] H. Clegg, Memoir, Clegg Papers, IWM, 88/18/1, 21.
[39] There is some evidence to suggest that there were disproportionate numbers of Irish and Catholic soldiers punished by the Rifles in 1918, after absorbing a number of ex-1/8th soldiers, but no diary evidence exists to support this. The absence of sectarian expression may also be due to the fact that the Rifles and the Scottish were composed mainly of the middle and artisan classes to the end of the war, and sectarianism exerted the greatest power in the lowest echelons of Liverpool society.
[40] 'Liverpolitan' was the genteel term used to describe residents of Liverpool in the nineteenth and early twentieth centuries. It was used by the men of the Liverpool Scottish and the Rifles and will be used throughout this book.
[41] T. R. Threlfall, *The history of the King's Liverpool Regiment* (Liverpool, 1915).
[42] I. Beckett, 'The nation in arms, 1914–18', in Beckett and Simpson (eds.), *A nation in arms*, 6.

considered inadequate for their primary role of defending the country and did not constitute a useful framework upon which to expand the army in wartime.[43]

The shock of the Boer War prompted an intense debate over the need for universal military service. Continental powers had all embraced conscription, which was championed by the National Service League from 1902 and recommended by the Norfolk Commission in 1904.[44] Conscription, however, was a politically unacceptable solution in a society based predominantly on consent, and during a period of financial constraint in government. The Secretary of State for War, R. B. Haldane, chose instead to restructure the existing auxiliary forces to form a more efficient second-line army.

The political compromises that accompanied the birth of the Territorial Force and the Special Reserve[45] have been investigated in detail elsewhere.[46] It is sufficient to note here that having originally conceived the Force as a practical expression of the 'nation in arms', Haldane watered down his blueprint for a Territorial army, administered by elected County Associations, which could expand to act as a second reserve to the regular army in time of war.

The idea of County Associations survived, serving to increase the efficiency of the force by separating command and administration, but the elected element was sacrificed to pacify the commanding officers of auxiliary formations.[47] However, the nominated members of the Associations, drawn from universities, employers and sometimes trade unions, did help to broaden representation. They provided the connections and influence that were later to become important to local Territorials in defending the rights of individual units against the War Office.[48]

---

[43] These were the conclusions of the Norfolk Commission in 1904. See Beckett, 'The Territorial Force', 128.
[44] Beckett, 'The nation in arms, 1914–18', 4.
[45] The Special Reserve was formed to provide drafts to Regular units in time of war and attracted recruits from the old Militia units.
[46] P. Simkins, *Kitchener's army: the raising of the New Armies, 1914–16* (Manchester, 1988), 10–17; E. M. Spiers, *Haldane: an army reformer* (Edinburgh, 1980), 92–115, 161–86; E. M. Spiers, *Army and society 1815–1914* (London, 1980), 265–87.
[47] In reducing the ability of County Associations to support cadet corps and other youth groups, Haldane was forced to dilute another key component of his attempt to create a 'nation in arms'. Simkins, *Kitchener's army*, 14–15.
[48] Peter Dennis has emphasized the importance of the County Associations in an article that refers mainly to developments in the 1920s and 1930s. His general remarks, however, are also applicable to the period of the First World War. See P. Dennis, 'The County Associations and the Territorial Army', *Army Quarterly and Defence Journal*, 109, 2 (1979), 210–11.

More importantly, the whole purpose of the Force was altered in the final Parliamentary Bill, by switching its focus to home defence. It was an attempt to appease parliamentary opponents and attract more Volunteers into the new Territorial formations, but as Ian Beckett has shown, this decision was to have crucial repercussions for the role of the Territorials in the Great War.[49]

As a result of the compromises, most new Territorial units were identical to the old Volunteers.[50] The Volunteer battalions of the King's (Liverpool) Regiment were simply numbered differently under the Territorial system, incorporated into a self-sufficient Territorial division, and placed under the auspices of the West Lancashire Territorial Association. The traditions, characteristics and over 70 per cent of the personnel in each unit remained the same.[51] For example, the Second Volunteer Battalion, raised in 1859 from the members of the Liverpool Exchange, became the 6th Liverpool Rifles in 1908 and maintained the tradition of recruiting professional and commercial men.[52] Similarly, the Liverpool Scottish continued to attract members with Scottish ancestry from a middle-class background. The annual subscription fees for both battalions also remained in place.[53]

Given that the new units retained their old character, it is unsurprising that the Territorials attracted recruits for the same myriad reasons as the Volunteers. Young men continued to join up for the 'show', for the uniform, and for the novelty of camp.[54] Forty years and two world wars later, J. S. Handley remembered the excitement generated by the annual camp and acknowledged that 'the rattle of the kettle drums and the shrill clarion of the bugle' continued to thrill.[55]

Sporting and social events were perhaps the greatest recruiting agents, a fact acknowledged by the West Lancashire Recruiting and Discharge Committee in 1913.[56] Indeed, the battalions incorporated many of the features of a pre-war social club. Rugby football, association football, snooker tournaments, concerts and balls featured prominently in the

---

[49] Beckett, 'The Territorial Force', 128.
[50] B. Bond, 'The Territorial Army in peace and war', *History Today*, 16 (March 1966), 159.
[51] *Manchester Guardian*, 7th July 1908.
[52] Cutting from the *Territorial*, undated, in Liverpool Rifles' Association record book, 1933–47, Liverpool Rifles' Association Papers, LRO, MD 162.
[53] *Liverpool Scottish Regimental Gazette*, May 1913, 26.
[54] Hugh Cunningham identified all these motives for the Volunteers. H. Cunningham, *The Volunteer Force* (London, 1975), 103–26.
[55] J. S. Handley, Memoir, Handley Papers, IWM, 92/36/1, 1.
[56] Recruiting and Discharge Committee minute book, May 1913, West Lancashire Territorial and Auxiliary Forces Association, LRO, 356 WES 19/1.

Territorial calendar, alongside the military preoccupation with rifle shooting.[57]

For others, joining the Territorials was a means of asserting their respectability and confirming their social or ethnic identity. Membership of the Rifles, and to a lesser extent the Scottish, readily identified men as middle-class. This could be an important statement, particularly for the 'marginal' men: the clerks and shopkeepers of the lower middle class, struggling to maintain their status on low incomes.[58] These 'class corps', as they were known at the War Office, promoted a relaxed system of discipline,[59] and prized the characteristics of an elite social club as highly as those of an effective military unit.

The Liverpool Scottish Battalion fulfilled a number of additional functions for its Scottish members. Through the public display of Highland uniforms and bagpipes, the celebration of Burns' Night and St Andrew's Day and the adoption of Scottish customs, the unit helped the second- and third-generation Liverpool Scots to maintain some semblance of a Scottish identity.

The Battalion also raised the profile of the Scottish community in Liverpool, affirming their sense of duty and moral integrity. The recruiting literature of the Scottish was particularly adept at exploiting this point in an attempt to gain new members. In May 1913 the Commanding Officer claimed that in a country which 'held the voluntary principle as an ideal', it was the duty of a citizen to join the Territorials to protect hearth and home. He appealed to the pride of the Scottish community to 'uphold the traditions of Scotland and aim at the HIGHEST IDEAL – an efficient Battalion up to strength'.[60]

Whilst the Liverpool Scottish drew many of its members from the Scottish community in Liverpool, it must be remembered that the Battalion's strength was maintained by Englishmen as well as Scotsmen. There were some soldiers who had 'invented' a Scottish grandparent in order to be accepted within the ranks, perhaps influenced by the middle-class cult of the kilt. In the nineteenth century, Queen Victoria's love of the Highlands had popularized the wearing of tartan, and even in 1914 the

---

[57] See *Liverpool Scottish Regimental Gazette*, January to December 1913.
[58] R. N. Price, 'Society, status and jingoism: the social roots of lower middle-class patriotism 1870–1900', in G. Crossick (ed.), *The lower middle class in Britain 1870–1914* (London, 1977), 108.
[59] Ian Beckett has identified this characteristic in the 'class corps' of the London Rifle Brigade and the London Scottish, whilst Patricia Morris has shown that a relaxed discipline system was a feature of the more working-class battalions of the 1/6th, 1/7th and 1/8th Leeds Rifles. Beckett, 'The Territorial Force', p. 144; Morris, 'Leeds and the amateur military tradition', 3.
[60] *Liverpool Scottish Regimental Gazette*, May 1913, 30.

kilt still carried strong associations with royalty.⁶¹ Whatever motivations Englishmen had in joining the Liverpool Scottish, their presence did not dilute its character or alter its significance in the community. By wearing Scottish dress and adopting their customs, these Englishmen helped to perpetuate this symbol of the Scottish community in Liverpool.

Despite the various attractions of the Territorial units, the Force was never popular in pre-war Liverpool. The ridicule they received in the press, the ambivalent stance of many important figures themselves serving in the Territorial Associations⁶² and the increasingly strident tone of the National Service League in 1913 and 1914 did not help the recruitment process.⁶³ The officers and men of each unit performed much of the recruiting work, and battalions were generally constituted from existing networks of friends, family and business associates.⁶⁴

The ledgers of the Recruiting and Discharge Committee of the West Lancashire Territorial Association testify to a serious problem with recruitment and retention. An increasingly sophisticated recruitment strategy was developed by the Committee before 1914. Posters and films were commissioned, recruitment leaflets were printed, and smoking concerts, military parades and military bands at football matches were all organized, to no avail.⁶⁵ Parades and concerts were certainly appreciated by the public at large, but despite selling 5000 copies of their recruiting pamphlet during a church parade in May 1911, the numbers of new recruits in Liverpool remained negligible. The apparent public enthusiasm for military display did not translate into vast numbers of eager recruits.⁶⁶

On the other hand, the Territorials experienced little hostility from any sector of society. The spectacle of the recruiting parades was enjoyed as Sunday afternoon entertainment, and even during the height of the 1911 strike, after regular troops had fired on strikers and rioters, the *Liverpool*

---

[61] Hugh Trevor-Roper, 'The invention of tradition: the Highland tradition of Scotland', in E. Hobsbawm and T. Ranger (eds.), *The invention of tradition* (Cambridge, 1984), 39.
[62] Lord Derby and many other Lord Lieutenants were members of the National Service League. Derby often spoke publicly about the desirability of conscription. See *Liverpool Daily Post*, 21 December 1910.
[63] Spiers, *Army and society 1815–1914*, 280.
[64] S.E. Gordon, Memoir, Gordon Papers, IWM, 77/5/1, 1; J.S. Handley, Memoir, Handley Papers, IWM, 92/36/1, 11; Sergeant M. Cookson to E. Traynor, 20 February 1914, Traynor Papers, KRC, MLL, 1976.5901. This process has been labelled 'social inheritance' by Patricia Morris in her thesis on the Leeds Rifles. Morris, 'Leeds and the amateur military tradition', 3.
[65] Recruiting and Discharge Committee minute book, 1908–1914, West Lancashire Territorial and Auxiliary Forces Association, LRO, 356 WES 19/1.
[66] Recruiting and Discharge Committee minute book, June 1911, West Lancashire Territorial and Auxiliary Forces Association, LRO, 356 WES 19/1.

Daily Post was still able to report that a detachment of Territorials had been cheered on their way to their annual camp.[67] There were just too many other clubs and societies in pre-war Liverpool, which performed similar social functions to the Territorials, and did not require the same degree of commitment.[68]

Yet the recruitment drives and the Sunday parades had not proved entirely fruitless in the years preceding the war. The public profile of the fledgling Force had been raised in Liverpool, and although lacking in recruits, the individual social and ethnic identities of its battalions were well known. On the outbreak of war, men who had avoided military service in peacetime flooded the headquarters of the battalions with which they most closely identified. The recruiting campaigns had come to fruition.

---

[67] *Liverpool Daily Post*, 12 August 1911.

[68] Whilst some men joined for the opportunity to experience Territorial camp, the annual attendance at the fortnight-long camp could also prove an obstacle to recruitment. Many companies made it difficult for their employees to attend, and some discouraged the employment of Territorials. Recruiting and Discharge Committee minute book, 28 May 1913, West Lancashire Territorial and Auxiliary Forces Association, LRO, 356 WES 19/1.

Part I

Territorial characteristics and the morale of the soldier

3   'Cuff and collar battalions': social change
    and its impact on the unit

On the outbreak of war the men of Liverpool clung to their existing social identities and on joining the army exercised their pre-war civilian prejudices and affiliations. The high-status Battalions of the Liverpool Rifles and the Liverpool Scottish performed an important recruitment role by attracting middle-class volunteers to their ranks who had never previously considered joining as alien an institution as the army. In the first years of the war, the elite nature and social homogeneity of the Battalions were perhaps their most distinctive and important features. They were also their most vulnerable. As casualties mounted, and drafts replaced original volunteers, the middle-class composition of the Battalions inevitably diminished. To investigate the loss of such a key Territorial characteristic, we need to establish the extent and timing of social change in both battalions. We will then be in a position to assess the impact of social change on morale and unit traditions to show how soldiers drew on different forms of civilian organization at different times to survive in the trenches.

Middle-class sociability in 1914

The middle class in Liverpool considered themselves a distinct and superior entity in 1914. They defined themselves not only by the nature of their employment and their place of residence, but also by their leisure activities. By joining clubs and societies in accordance with their professions and social status, they helped to reinforce their social position in the city. Sporting institutions, philosophical and literary societies, the University Club, political associations and charitable trusts all competed for a young man's affiliation alongside the Territorials. Most middle-class men patronized a variety of societies, positioned on various rungs of the middle-class ladder. Lieutenant Anderson of the Liverpool Scottish was no exception. He spent his recreational time contributing to four additional organizations: the Birkenhead Dramatic Society, Trinity and Palm Grove Methodist Church, Oxton Cricket Club and Birkenhead Park Rugby

Football Club. His status as a Territorial officer and his membership of the Rugby Club conferred the most social prestige. Nevertheless, his affiliation with all but the Methodist Church clearly identified him as middle class.

Other individuals also featured in the life of multiple societies. Thus, Lieutenant Anderson could expect to play rugby alongside fellow Territorials Lieutenant Cunningham, Lieutenant Renison and Second Lieutenants J. C. Barber and R. C. Lindsay, who were also members of the Birkenhead Park club. Through multiple membership of associations, the middle classes created for themselves an integrated social network.[1]

The middle-class web of sociability was based on a broad social homogeneity, and performed several functions. It constituted an informal business forum, promoted genuine friendships and was used as a middle-class method of expressing their social status and defining their identity. By joining a multitude of clubs with an exclusive reputation, the middle classes could visibly differentiate themselves from other social groupings, and reinforce their own positions in the middle-class hierarchy.

Membership of each club conferred varying degrees of social standing on the individual, and Liverpool's sporting organizations can be used as an illustration. Rugby, golf and rowing, at the pinnacle of the sporting hierarchy, were taught at public and grammar schools and needed a heavy investment in equipment and admission fees. These clubs formed an upper-level social network, mainly confined to the upper echelons of the middle class, from which the pre-war Territorial officers were drawn. Tennis clubs, requiring a lesser financial outlay, attracted a wider social spectrum of players. They were still located within a middle-class sphere and were a point of intersection between upper and lower middle-class networks. The ranks of the Liverpool Scottish and Rifle Battalions also represented a point of intersection, and were of particular importance to the lower strata of the middle class, providing contact with their social superiors and opportunities to establish useful relationships.[2] Whilst the Territorial Force as a whole might be ridiculed in the national press and their efficiency scorned, the criticism did not damage the social statement made by membership of the Rifles and the Scottish, particularly as the units were utilized primarily as social clubs by the men themselves.

Social demarcation through the formal membership of societies was essentially a middle-class preoccupation, but this did not preclude

---

[1] See Liverpool Scottish Officers' Index, Anderson, J.C. Barber, D. Cunningham, R. C. Lindsay, LSM.
[2] R. McKibbin, *Classes and cultures: England 1918–1951* (Oxford, 1998), 88.

working-class participation in the Territorial movement.[3] In fact, the working classes filled three battalions of the Territorial Force in Liverpool, despite their more fluid patterns of sociability, and less circumscribed associations.[4] Although the prestige of the Rifles and the Scottish in Liverpool conferred a degree of social standing on an individual, the members of the 'Scruffy' 5th King's (as they were pejoratively termed by the Liverpool Scots) would not necessarily have preferred to join the Rifles or the Scottish, given an unrestricted choice.[5] Ross McKibbin has suggested that for the middle classes of the 1920s social ease was of paramount importance within a club; so it was for all social ranks who joined the Territorials in 1914.[6]

Social and ethnic unit characteristics in peace and war

The Territorial 'club' offered its members a broad definition of their social status. The following discussion examines this definition and investigates the complex hierarchies and social divisions that manifested themselves within each unit. According to Hugh Cunningham in his social analysis of the Volunteer Force, 'The division between middle and working-class volunteers is one between non-manual and manual occupations.'[7] Many members of the Territorial Force would have supported this definition in 1914. Indeed, members of the 6th Rifles utilized this same division to define their unit. J. S. Handley proudly recalled that the Rifles had been styled the 'cuff and collar' battalion prior to the war.[8]

However, as P. J. Waller has observed, 'The social class ladder did not just contain three rungs, a lower, middle and upper, but an infinite number of levels, each separated with keenly defended marks of station.'[9]

---

[3] See McKibbin for an analysis of the middle-class preoccupation with joining clubs and societies in 1920s Britain: *Classes and cultures*, 87.
[4] Ian Beckett has emphasized the fact that the Territorials were primarily a working-class movement: 'The Territorial Force', 145.
[5] It was likely to be the skilled workers, with regular leisure time, who adhered to 'respectable' values similar to the middle classes, who were attracted to the Territorials. R. Roberts, 'The class structure of the "classic slum"', in P. Joyce (ed.), *Class* (Oxford, 1995), 236–9.
[6] McKibbin, *Classes and cultures*, 95; R. Hoggart, '"Them" and "Us"', in Joyce (ed.), *Class*, 241.
[7] H. Cunningham, *The Volunteer Force* (London, 1975), 33. Robert Roberts has also supported this view in 'The class structure of the "classic slum"', 237.
[8] J. S. Handley, Memoir, Handley Papers, IWM, 92/36/1, 8. The term 'cuff and collar' was used to describe the working dress of those in non-manual employment at the beginning of the twentieth century. This label was still attached to the Rifles as late as 1918. A. Rimmer, interview, 20 December 1998.
[9] P. J. Waller, *Democracy and sectarianism: a political and social history of Liverpool 1868–1939* (Liverpool, 1981), xvii.

This description of social class in general was equally applicable to the middle class within the Territorial units. The civilian rung occupied by a recruit bore a direct correlation to a rung on the ladder of the Territorial military hierarchy. The relative status of Lieutenant Gordon and Rifleman Handley in the peacetime Rifles provides a good example of this. Although born within a year of each other, Gordon had attended the prestigious Rugby School and was a partner in his father's hide brokering firm. Handley, by contrast, had attended the less illustrious Liverpool School of Art and was working as a clerk, albeit in the inner office of a builders' merchants.[10]

It is difficult to describe the interaction between the complex social and military hierarchies in the Battalions from the biographical information that has survived. Occupation, education, membership of sporting and social clubs and the employment of servants were all seen as indicators of social class in the years prior to the Great War, and were utilized by sensitive classification systems.[11] However, comprehensive personal data were never recorded systematically by either Battalion, and such refined systems of differentiation cannot be applied to their recruits.[12] Occupation remains the one consistent variable which can be used to classify the soldiers, and the Registrar General's occupational classification system has been chosen for this purpose.[13]

---

[10] J. S. Handley, Memoir, Handley Papers, IWM, 92/36/1, 1. S. E. Gordon, Memoir, IWM, 77/5/1, 1. Compared to many clerks, Handley had a well-paid and responsible job with promotion prospects. The term 'clerk' as an occupational category covered many different levels of work. The social prestige and wealth of a clerk depended upon his responsibilities and the establishment within which he was working. In general, insurance and banking conferred the greatest prestige, because they offered the best opportunities for promotion.

[11] F. D'Aeth, 'Present tendencies of class differentiation', *Sociological Review*, 2, 4 (October 1910), 269.

[12] Despite D'Aeth's complicated classification, he claimed that society in 1910 fluctuated around two theoretic standards. The first standard contained categories A to C which ranged from what he termed the refuse of society to the 'solid, independent and valuable class in society', the artisans. The second theoretic standard contained classes D to G, the smaller shopkeeper and clerk; the small business class; the professional and administrative class, and the rich. Thus the basic divisions in society were similar to those broad divisions identified by the Registrar General's system, and in some cases the classes correlate, allowing D'Aeth's assessment of the values and social attitudes of an individual class to be utilized.

[13] The 1921 classification has been chosen because it most closely correlates with the attitudes and values of the time. The 1911 classification criteria are less satisfactory than those of 1921 because all white-collar workers were included in social class I. This meant that commercial travellers and clerks were included in the same category as professional men and managing directors of large companies. This was clearly undesirable, as there were clear distinctions between these groups in Liverpolitan society in 1911. Therefore, the 1921 occupational lists which relegate clerks to social class II have

The population was divided into five classes by the Registrar General. Class I represented the upper and middle class, including professional men. Class II was described as an intermediate grade which corresponded to the lower middle class, particularly those connected with the shopkeeping trades and petty clerks. Classes III, IV and V represented the working class: the skilled artisan, the intermediate, partially skilled worker and the unskilled workman respectively.[14]

It is important to realize that the academic categories of the Registrar General were occupational, rather than class categories.[15] Thus, they did not always coincide with the general views on class held by contemporaries. Rifleman Ellison of the Liverpool Rifles claimed his unit contained 'clerks, solicitors, accountants and shop assistants'.[16] Whilst most white-collar occupations, including those of solicitor, accountant and clerk, fitted neatly into the Registrar General's middle-class categories I and II, there were a few aberrations. The shop assistants, identified by Ellison as white collar, were placed in the artisan class III in the Registrar General's scheme. Therefore, we must be careful to ensure that the classification used correlates with contemporary views of social class. With this qualification in mind, all occupational data are classified and interpreted using both methods. The classifications are strengthened when used together. First, the white-collar/manual worker distinction is an important tool, used to describe the broad affinity felt by the white-collar members of the Battalion, defining themselves in opposition to the manual labouring classes. Second, the Registrar General's classification permits a more sensitive interpretation of the social hierarchy within the Battalions.

The Rifles, the most socially homogeneous unit of the two Battalions, had strict entrance requirements. Recruits were selected solely on education, sporting ability and occupation. They did not admit any man lower down the social scale than a clerk, and this selection by social status continued on the outbreak of war.[17] The most prominent and important

---

been used instead. See W. A. Armstrong, 'The use of information about occupation', in E. A. Wrigley (ed.), *Nineteenth century society* (Cambridge, 1972), 200–9, for a more complete discussion of the problems of the 1911 Census categories. See *Registrar General's Decennial Supplement*, Part II, *Occupational mortality, fertility and infant mortality*, 1921, ciii–cxiv, for a list of occupational categories.

[14] See Armstrong, 'The use of information about occupation', 203.

[15] Many scholars have identified the problems associated with this method of classification, highlighting the fact that the social status of the children was determined by the male occupation. However, as we are primarily concerned with the adult male population, this problem is of minor significance. J. M. Winter, 'The decline of mortality in Britain, 1870–1950', in T. Barker and M. Drake (eds.), *Population and society in Britain 1850–1980* (London, 1982), 107.

[16] N. F. Ellison, Diary and Memoir, Ellison Papers, IWM, DS/MISC/49, 7.

[17] N. F. Ellison, Diary and Memoir, August 1914, Ellison Papers, IWM, DS/MISC/49, 2.

defining feature of the Rifles was, therefore, their social exclusivity. It was this reputation that attracted the upper echelons of the middle class to the Battalion on the outbreak of war. The popular belief that the war would be a short and glorious affair meant that it became acceptable for a man of high social status to join the ranks of a socially exclusive unit as a private soldier. Lieutenant Gordon commented upon the new recruits in September 1914, recalling one rifleman who offered his park as a training ground, when their own became too crowded. Gordon continued, 'It was particularly noticeable what a splendid lot of young men we have in our ranks and what a lot of riflemen go off in their private cars when the parades are over.'[18]

These newly enlisted riflemen, who included the offspring of the manager of the Royal Insurance Company and the director of the White Star Shipping Line, were the social equals of the officers and, as such, distorted the social profile of the pre-war Battalion, which had generally maintained officers with civilian positions superior to the men. The anomaly only began to be rectified as those with influential connections wangled commissions, or became casualties, removing them from the unit.

The Liverpool Scottish entry requirements included Scottish ancestry, a non-manual occupation and a 10 shilling admission fee,[19] but this Battalion was not so socially exclusive.[20] It aimed to encourage as many Scottish representatives as possible, although in war, to an even greater extent than in peacetime, the recruit's Scottish background was often tenuous.[21] Although the pride in being a battalion formed from non-manual workers was powerful amongst the Liverpool Scottish, their ethnic identity was also an important defining feature on the eve of war, leading to a more inclusive recruiting policy.

The 10 shilling attestment fee, which was retained through the initial period of recruitment in 1914, may have proved prohibitive for men earning poor or irregular wages. Dock labourers and porters would have found it difficult to pay the required amount.[22] By contrast, artisan wages could be comparable to those earned by the middle classes in Liverpool, and so the fee excluded only the very poorest individuals.

[18] S. E. Gordon, Memoir, September 1914, Gordon Papers, IWM, 77/5/1, 32.
[19] T. W. Wood, Reminiscences, Liddle Collection, T. W. Wood Papers (G. S.)
[20] R. A. S. Macfie to Charlie Macfie, 4 September 1914, Macfie Papers, IWM, Con. Shelf. Sergeant Macfie complained about his semi-literate company orderly corporal, who was unable to write out the Battalion orders for his captain.
[21] W. G. Bromley, Memoir, LSM, Acc. No. 544, 1.
[22] Although dock labourers could earn between 5 and 6 shillings per day, the work was irregular. For other unskilled occupations (appearing in classes IV and V of the Registrar General's classification system), for example railway porters who earned between 16 and 18 shillings per week, the 10 shilling fee was clearly prohibitive. For information

'Cuff and collar battalions'

The attestment levy performed a different function. It ensured that the Scottish attracted recruits who were more likely actively to have chosen the unit for positive reasons, because they identified with the character of the Battalion, rather than blindly drifting into the first unit that required recruits. Similarly, the Scottish accoutrements also served as part of a filtering mechanism. There were men who would not entertain the idea of wearing a kilt, whereas others positively dreamed of donning the Scottish uniform, or felt stirred by the sound of the bagpipes. The power of the kilt as a recruiting tool should not be underestimated, not least because of its alleged effect on women. On joining the Liverpool Scottish, Lance Corporal Peppiette was particularly pleased with his new uniform, remarking that 'all the girls passed on the way seemed interested in my legs and kilt'.[23] Although from the beginning of the war many of the recruits were not Scottish, the Englishmen enthusiastically embraced the romantic image of the Scottish unit and perpetuated the Scottish traditions throughout the war.[24]

Both the Rifles and the Scottish maintained the fortunate position of being able to select recruits for their second-line unit according to their peacetime social criteria when they were given permission to raise another battalion in September 1914. An advertisement for the Rifles in the *Liverpool Daily Post* appealed for recruits from Aigburth, Sefton Park and West Derby,[25] the first two areas being distinctly middle class and the latter having a mixed population.[26] Men who 'knew each other in business and social life' were encouraged to enlist together, following the pre-war practices which had ensured social homogeneity.[27] Their strategy was successful. Captain Wurtzburg, writing the history of the Second Rifles, commented on the attire of the men during their initial training. 'Bowler hats were early discouraged ... some men [were] in the everyday clothes of clerks, some in shooting coats and grey trousers, others in khaki, bought at their own expense.'[28] He was describing the civilian, 'cuff and collar' uniform of the middle class. It was deemed particularly

---

regarding wage levels in Liverpool see F. J. Marquis, *Handbook of employments in Liverpool* (Liverpool, 1916), 218 and 227. The wage levels given in this handbook were collected before the outbreak of war.

[23] E. Peppiette, Diary, 25 June 1916, Peppiette Papers, LSM, Acc. No. 887.
[24] W. G. Bromley remembered that the HQ dugout in the reserve lines was well stocked with whisky to celebrate St Andrew's Day on 30 November 1917. Unfortunately, the Germans attacked in the morning and captured not only the whisky, but also a large percentage of the Battalion. W. G. Bromley, Memoir, LSM, Acc. No. 544, 127.
[25] *Liverpool Daily Post*, 10 September 1914.
[26] See Map 2.1, showing the social composition of municipal wards in Liverpool.
[27] *Liverpool Daily Post*, 10 September 1914.
[28] C. E. Wurtzburg, *History of the 2/6th Battalion, The King's Liverpool Regiment 1914–1919* (London, 1920), 5.

important that the men should be of the same social status as the first line at this juncture in the war, because the Second Battalion was initially expected to be a reserve battalion only, providing drafts for the first-line unit.[29]

Only anecdotal evidence is available to determine the Rifles' initial social composition. The second-line unit continued to furnish the first with men until November 1916, and a third battalion was raised in May 1915 to replenish both, but it is impossible to gauge the social composition of the drafts. Fortunately, the attestment records for the Liverpool Scottish have survived. Their ledgers list attestments between September 1914 and October 1915, and include the occupation of recruits from June 1915.[30]

To place the Scottish attestment figures in perspective, it is necessary to relate them to the social structure of Liverpool. Social classes I and II formed 22 per cent of the male Liverpolitan population of military age in 1911, but accounted for 50 per cent of enlistments in the Scottish between June and October 1915.[31] There was also a significant, although less marked, 9 per cent disparity between the percentage of social class III recruits and their incidence in the general population[32] (see Table 3.2). To what extent this was a result of pre-war selection practices favouring or attracting middle-class candidates is not clear, as well-paid artisan workers, and especially the middle class, have been shown to have had higher enlistment rates throughout Britain.

Jay Winter has highlighted the proportionally higher rates of enlistment amongst the middle classes, but his recruitment statistics refer to the percentage of the pre-war labour force enlisting by sector.[33] There are

[29] It was not until November 1914 that a third-line reserve battalion of the Rifles was raised.
[30] Liverpool Scottish Attestment Book, LSM, Acc. No. 32. The interpretation of this data poses a series of challenges. First, a number of men did not have their occupation recorded on attestment. Others claimed jobs that were either unreadable or unclassifiable. The resulting percentages of attestment by class had to be calculated excluding these men, which may have distorted the results. However, the percentages calculated for white-collar workers attesting per month have shown a significant degree of consistency between June and October, suggesting that the omissions had only a minor effect (see Table 3.1). Second, classification of employment was particularly difficult for those occupations whose labels were applicable to both employer and employee. For example, a tailor who owned his own business would be placed in class II in the Registrar General's scheme, but an employee would be found in class III. In such instances, the recruit has been assigned to the lower category to ensure that the resulting calculation is biased against the conclusions to be drawn, avoiding exaggeration of the argument.
[31] The 1911 Census percentages were calculated from *Census of England and Wales*, 1911, vol. 10, Part II, LXXIX, Table 13 – Occupations (condensed list) of males and females aged 10 years and upwards, 227–9. These percentages are estimates only, because of the difficulty in differentiating social class from the occupational categories given, and apply only to the city of Liverpool and not the surrounding districts.
[32] Thirty-nine per cent of Scottish enlistments were drawn from class III, which constituted 30 per cent of the general population in Liverpool.
[33] J. M. Winter, *The Great War and the British people* (London, 1986), 34.

Table 3.1 *Chronology of attestation by white-collar men for the Liverpool Scottish Battalion, percentage identifiable, by month*

Month	Percentage of classifiable occupations
June 1915	60
July 1915	58
August 1915	56
September 1915	67
October 1915	68

Source: Liverpool Scottish Attestment Book, LSM

Table 3.2 *Social classification of men attesting in the ranks of the Liverpool Scottish Battalion, June–October 1915*

Class	Number	Percentage of all occupations	Percentage of all classifiable occupations	Percentage of Liverpool population
Unknown	141	23	–	2
I	27	4	6	–
II	206	34	44	–
III	185	30	39	–
IV	30	5	6	–
V	25	4	5	–
Middle class (I and II)	233	38	50	22
Artisan (III)	185	30	39	30
Lower class (IV and V)	55	9	11	46

Source: Liverpool Scottish Attestment Book, LSM

no comparable enlistment figures available for individual units, or the British army as a whole, but a tentative comparison can be made with figures computed from the *London County Council Roll of Honour* by Adrian Gregory.[34]

---

[34] A. Gregory, 'Lost generations: the impact of military casualties on Paris, London, and Berlin', in J. Winter and J. L. Robert (eds.), *Capital cities at war: London, Paris, Berlin 1914–1919* (Cambridge, 1997), 79.

Enlistment amongst London County Council employees was estimated to have been 40 per cent non-manual and 60 per cent manual.[35] The Liverpool Scottish clearly had a greater percentage of non-manual workers amongst their recruits between June and October 1915. Numbers of non-manual recruits remained consistently above 50 per cent between June and August and had rocketed to 68 per cent by October (see Table 3.1). However, this comparison must be viewed with caution. Whilst the London roll included employees from a wide range of residential areas and occupations, the London County Council figures were an estimate for the whole war. They incorporated working-class recruits, forced into uniform as a result of conscription, and a large number of ex-regular reservists, recalled to the colours on the outbreak of war.

The Scottish figures provide only a snapshot of their recruitment in 1915. Nevertheless, the percentages are sufficiently high to suggest that before the advent of conscription in January 1916, those enlisting continued to exercise their right to choose the unit with which they most closely identified. The pre-war social characteristics were still considered to be important. Thus, the white-collar tone of the Scottish was maintained, at least until the October cohort of recruits had been trained and dispatched to the front-line Battalion. Most volunteers would have been in the fighting line by August 1916.[36]

The war created consistent employment for those dock labourers who had struggled to make ends meet before 1914.[37] Even so, a strong impulse to join HM Forces existed amongst the unskilled. Lord Derby was forced to form a home-based dockers' battalion to stem the flow of recruits and retain an effective workforce to cope with the increased amount of trade passing through the port. A letter to Derby from the director of Cammell Laird, warning him that his recruiting campaign was causing serious disruption and delay to the production of submarines and naval accessories, provides further evidence that, before conscription, manual workers were joining the army in greater numbers than those found among the Scottish suggest.[38] It appears that those men of lower social status (occupational classes IV and V) actively chose to avoid the Scottish Battalion, probably because of its pre-war social connotations.

---

[35] *Ibid.*, 79.
[36] Random sampling of the Other Ranks Index in the Liverpool Scottish Regimental Museum allowed the attestment date and drafting date to be collated for twenty-four men who joined the Battalion between September 1914 and October 1915.
[37] Peter Dewey has shown that for a few industries, including dock work, enlistment could be inhibited by high wages. P. E. Dewey, 'Military recruiting and the British labour force during the First World War', *Historical Journal*, 27, 1 (March 1984), 218.
[38] Cammell Laird to Lord Derby, October 1915, Derby Papers, LRO, 920 DER (17) 10/2.

The social homogeneity of the Battalions did not last until the end of the war. By December 1916, the diaries and memoirs of both battalions began to record the slow dilution of the middle-class character. Sergeant Handley remembered that after the Somme, 'very few of the peacetime Battalion that we knew were left and after receiving reinforcements, the physique and character was completely changed'.[39]

In both the Scottish and the Rifle Battalions, there was a preoccupation with the physique of recruits. The Liverpool Scottish claimed that they had been selected to form a guard of honour for the funeral of Lord Roberts in November 1914 because of their physique, and the Rifles had advertised for recruits exceeding 5 feet 8 inches in height.[40] The measurement requirements may have been a thinly veiled attempt to filter out smaller, working-class recruits, disadvantaged in height through poor nutrition. The men obviously took a pride in the physical appearance of their Battalions, and Sergeant Handley's disillusioned comments on the calibre of recruits after 1916 suggests that 'physique' and 'character' were inextricably linked in the minds of the middle class.

The introduction of conscription in January 1916 was responsible for destroying the social uniformity of recruits. Whilst the unit preferences of conscripts were marked on their attestation papers, they could only be taken into consideration if the units chosen had vacancies at a particular time.[41] The social profile of a platoon of the Rifles in 1918 can help to illustrate the changes caused by conscription.

Three detailed rolls for a platoon of the Liverpool Rifles still exist.[42] The precise dates of compilation are unknown, although the month can usually be pinpointed. To produce a representative sample for 1918 all rolls have been amalgamated, ensuring that no individual's data are repeated. In addition, the data have been analysed as they appeared in individual rolls. Again, the absence of data constrains the accuracy of the calculations performed, but despite these difficulties the rolls are a valuable and unusually detailed source, of a kind which rarely survives for 1918.

---

[39] J. S. Handley, Memoir, Handley Papers, IWM, 92/36/1, 11.
[40] *Liverpool Daily Post*, 10 September 1914.
[41] That the men were able to express some preference is indicated by the Army Council Instructions of 25 October 1916, which stated, 'In selecting men from Groups to fill the numbers allotted to each corps or unit, those men should first be included who had their original attestation papers marked for, or who when called up have a genuine claim to serve in that corps or unit provided they are suitable for it.' 25 October 1916, Posting recruits who are called up from Class B. Army Reserve, or who come forward for service before being called up, on or after 1 November 1916, Army Council Instructions, PRO, WO 293/5. See also J. Atherton, Narrative of his father's memories, LSM, Miscellaneous File A.
[42] Nominal roll and foot books, 1/6th (Rifle) Bn, King's (Liverpool) Regiment, No. 1 Platoon, A Company, Pegge Papers, MLHL, M198/1/2/1–2.

Table 3.3 *Social composition of Number 1 Platoon, A Company, 6th Liverpool Rifles, 1918*

Class	Percentage of platoon[a]	Percentage of Liverpool population
Middle class (I and II)	38	22
Skilled working class (III)	44	30
Semi-skilled/unskilled (IV and V)	18	46
Unknown	–	2

[a] All percentages are calculated using known occupations only.

Source: W. J. Pegge, Nominal roll and foot books, 1/6th (Rifle) Bn, King's Liverpool Regiment, No. 1 Platoon, A Company, Pegge Papers, MLHL, M198/1/2/1–2; 1911 Census

By 1918, we can see that the white-collar representatives in the platoon had dwindled to 38 per cent, just below that London average of 40 per cent for the whole war.[43] When the figures are analysed more sensitively, however, it is evident that the numbers of soldiers drawn from social groups I, II and III all exceeded their representative proportions in the Liverpolitan population. The middle classes still held a significant stake in the ranks, whereas, at 18 per cent of the platoon, unskilled labourers were dramatically underrepresented (see Table 3.3). The decline in middle-class representation was matched by an increase in the artisan constituent of the platoon. It was never swamped with unskilled labour.

Promotion and the social structure of the platoon in 1918

On closer examination of the rank structure, it is clear that the positions of authority were concentrated in the hands of the middle classes. Amongst the total number of NCOs in the platoon during 1918, 59 per cent came from a non-manual background (see Table 3.4). This percentage was even higher for the first two platoon rolls taken in February and May 1918, when 67 and 69 per cent of their leaders were derived from the middle classes. By October 1918, this high percentage was beginning to

[43] This percentage includes the two middle-class officers of the platoon. Nominal roll and foot books, 1/6th (Rifle) Bn, King's (Liverpool) Regiment, No. 1 Platoon, A Company, Pegge Papers, MLHL, M198/1/2/1–2, and Gregory, 'Lost generations', 79.

Table 3.4 *Social classification of NCOs serving in Number 1 Platoon, A Company, 6th Liverpool Rifles, 1918*

Class[a]	% of lance corporals[b]	% of corporals	% of sergeants	% of NCOs
White collar (I and II)	56	60	63	59
Artisan (III)	33	20	37	32
Intermediate (IV)	11	20	0	9
Unskilled (V)	0	0	0	0

[a] All white-collar occupations in this sample fitted neatly into the Registrar General's categories.
[b] All percentages are calculated using only known occupations.

Source: W. J. Pegge, Nominal roll and foot books, 1/6th (Rifle) Bn, King's (Liverpool) Regiment, No. 1 Platoon, A Company, Pegge Papers, MLHL, M198/1/2/1–2

Table 3.5 *Social classification of NCOs serving in Number 1 Platoon, A Company, 6th Liverpool Rifles, February, May, October 1918*

	Percentage[b]		
Class[a]	Roll 1 February 1918	Roll 2 May 1918	Roll 3 October 1918
White collar (I and II)	67	69	50
Skilled working class (III)	33	23	30
Semi-skilled (IV)	0	8	20
Unskilled (V)	0	0	0

[a] All white-collar occupations in this sample fitted neatly into the Registrar General's categories.
[b] All percentages are calculated using only known occupations.

Source: W. J. Pegge, Nominal roll and foot books, 1/6th (Rifle) Bn, King's (Liverpool) Regiment, No. 1 Platoon, A Company, Pegge Papers, MLHL, M198/1/2/1–2

break down, but it is surely significant that the Rifles were able to sustain such a high degree of middle-class participation throughout the whole command structure of their unit, maintaining a presence even at the lowest levels until the last months of the war (see Table 3.5).

When individual ranks of NCOs for 1918 as a whole are investigated, a subtle pattern of increasing social exclusivity emerges. Table 3.4 indicates that the concentration of white-collar representation increased from 56 per cent amongst lance corporals to 60 per cent for corporals and 63 per cent at the rank of sergeant. To explain the middle-class concentrations in the NCO hierarchy, the promotion procedure operating within the platoon must be considered. There is no literary evidence describing the motivation behind promotion and so any conclusions must be extrapolated from an investigation of promotion patterns.

A complex set of considerations governed the promotion prospects of those in the ranks. External events were the greatest facilitators of promotion. Large-scale attacks, resulting in huge casualties, played a vital role in producing job opportunities for NCOs. Many promotions in 1918 occurred after the Battalion's bloody stand at Givenchy in April (see Table 3.6). Promotion was dependent on circumstance, falling either to those soldiers who survived the attack or to those who had been left on the nucleus.[44] However, few battalions were completely annihilated in any one action, and although casualties were often high, suitable candidates for promotion remained, providing the authorities with a choice. On what grounds was the decision made?

Above all, experience gained under fire was the most precious commodity in the world of the trenches. Of course there were some meteoric rises through the ranks, particularly at the beginning of the war. Lance Corporal Handley became a sergeant after serving an apprenticeship of only two months in France, but this was relatively rare. His promotion followed a heavy casualty toll caused by fighting during the Second Battle of Ypres in April 1915.[45] As the war progressed, the promotion process became a slower procedure, and experience counted. On average, it took nine months' service in the trenches to be promoted lance corporal[46] and thirty-two months to reach the rank of sergeant[47] (see Table 3.6).

---

[44] A 'nucleus' of soldiers remained at the transport lines during a major attack. It provided a basic complement of personnel from which to rebuild the Battalion in the event of large casualties.
[45] 1/6th Battalion, King's (Liverpool) Regiment Casualty Book 1, KRC, MLL, 58.83.537a–b.
[46] Percentage calculated from known details in Nominal roll and foot books, 1/6th (Rifle) Bn, King's (Liverpool) Regiment, No. 1 Platoon, A Company, Pegge Papers, MLHL, M198/1/2/1–2. See Table 3.6.
[47] Percentage calculated from known details in Nominal roll and foot books, 1/6th (Rifle) Bn, The King's (Liverpool) Regiment, No. 1 Platoon, A Company, Pegge Papers, MLHL, M198/1/2/1–2. See sergeants McKnight, Tilley, Jennings and Davies in Table 3.6.

Table 3.6 *Some characteristics of the military service of the NCOs of Number 1 Platoon, A Company, 6th Liverpool Rifles, 1918, by rank*

Final rank in 1918	Name	Age	Occupation	Social class	Date joined Rifles	Unit of origin	Date of promotion Lcpl	Cpl	Sergeant	Date left Rifles	Medal	Date of medal
LCpl	Wright, J.	22	Electrician	3	1/18	1/8th	Inherited[a]			3/18		
LCpl	Jones, C. N.	24	Carpenter	3	1/18	1/8th	9/18	2/19		End		
LCpl	Morris, T.	20	Clerk	2	12/17	18th	Inherited			End		
LCpl	Harrison, H.	23	Carter	4	12/17	18th	9/18			End		
LCpl	Speedie, A.	32	Farmer	2	12/17	18th	Inherited			4/18 d		
LCpl	Barrow, T.	19	Miller	3	4/16	6th	10/17			4/18 w		
LCpl	Bradley, L.	18			4/18	6th	5/18			9/18 w		
LCpl	Holt	24	Butcher	2	4/18	6th	7/18			End	MM	3/16
LCpl	Evans, H.	32	Clerk	2	5/16	6th	7/17			4/18 d		
LCpl	Gascoigne, F.		Clerk	2	Original	6th	12/15			End	MM	9/18
Cpl	Nicholls, J. R.	20	Clerk	2	2/17	6th	7/18	9/18		End		
Cpl	Farris, F. E.	19	Teacher	2	3/18	52nd		1/18		End		
Cpl	Kelly, S.	22	Clerk	2	5/16	6th	8/17	4/18		Left?	DCM	5/18
Cpl	Hulme, J. S.	32	Plasterer	3	5/17	19th	8/17	6/18		9/18 d		
Cpl	Elston, T.	19	Horseman	4	9/17	2/9th	4/18	9/18		End		
Sgt	Canning, D.								Inherited	End		
Sgt	Cliff, R.	29	Woodwork machinist	3	1/18	1/5th				End	MM	12/17
Sgt	Matthews, W. H.	32							4/18	End		
Sgt	McKnight, A.	26	Weaver	3	7/17	1/9th	9/17	9/17	6/18		MM	4/18
Sgt	Smith, J. W.		Clerk	2				4/18	4/18	6/18 d		
Sgt	Tilley, J.	24	Clerk	2	Original	6th	Original	11/17	4/18	5/18 hos		

Table 3.6 (cont.)

Final rank in 1918	Name	Age	Occupation	Social class	Date joined Rifles	Unit of origin	Date of promotion Lcpl	Date of promotion Cpl	Date of promotion Sergeant	Date left Rifles	Medal	Date of medal
Sgt	Jennings, E.		Baker	2	Original	6th	5/15	7/17	5/18			
SSgt	Geekie, W.		Gunsmith	3							MID	5/18
Sgt	Davy, S. F.	26	Picture dealer	2	Original				Original	8/18 w		
CQMS	Davies, H. T.				Original	6th		Original	5/18			
CSM	Andrews, A. E.	25	Salesman	2					9/18	End		

'Original' indicates a soldier who was serving with the Rifles when they first arrived in France during February 1915.
'Inherited' indicates that the NCO joined A Company with his rank.
d, died; DCM, Distinguished Conduct Medal; hos, hospitalized; MID, Mentioned in Dispatches; MM, Military Medal; w, wounded.

Source: W. J Pegge, Nominal roll and foot books, 1/6th (Rifle) Bn, King's Liverpool Regiment, No. 1 Platoon, A Company, Pegge Papers, MLHL, M198/1/2/1

'Cuff and collar battalions' 41

It was logical that those who had experienced the greatest variety of fighting conditions would be those who had served in the trenches the longest. It was often their tenacity, care and skill, as well as good fortune, that had contributed to their survival, and equipped them for the duties of an NCO. It was also inevitable, given the social uniformity of the Rifles in late 1915, that the sergeants would be predominately middle class. Thus, it was not necessarily social prescription that ensured the prevalence of middle-class NCOs. It may merely have been a result of the initial social biases inherent in the Rifles' recruiting campaigns.[48]

On the other hand, it is probable that the Battalions actively attempted to retain a hierarchy based on the civilian social structure. To promote soldiers from lower classes above the middle-class elements of a platoon would have been a subversion of the social order, an anathema to those pre-war soldiers who joined the Rifles. A high standard of literacy was also desirable for some NCO posts, particularly that of the sergeant. Returns had to be completed and there were written orders to be sent and received, and it was the middle classes that had the requisite educational background to complete these tasks. A survey of battlefield accounts, written by all NCOs in the Rifles following the Third Battle of Ypres, provides further evidence to suggest that NCOs were selected for their standard of education. Only three accounts out of a total of forty were marred by grammatical errors.[49]

It is also apparent that the men from social class III who achieved the rank of sergeant over the heads of class II candidates were exceptional characters within the platoon. All three had been awarded the Military Medal, or had been Mentioned in Dispatches, which may have acted as stepping-stones to their elevated positions. Sergeant A. McKnight, for example, was awarded his Military Medal in April 1918, and was promoted the following June (see Table 3.6). It was generally accepted that medals did not necessarily indicate bravery or ability, for they could glorify irresponsibility and rash behaviour, or result from the self-promotion of a unit by its battalion commander.[50] However, the fact that the battalion was the ultimate arbiter of awards means that medals can be used as a rough guide to the value commanding officers placed on the men under their command.

---

[48] Unfortunately there are no comparable sources against which to test this hypothesis.
[49] 55th Divisional Narratives 31 July–1 August 1917, Records of the 55th (West Lancashire) Division, LRO, File 52A, 356 FIF 4/1/158–1/224.
[50] Medals could often indicate irresponsibility. The desire of a scout sergeant in the 2/6th Rifle Battalion to win a decoration almost cost the lives of an entire patrol. A. Rimmer, interview, 20 December 1998. For further discussion on the debatable value of medals see Lieutenant Colonel D. D. Farmer VC, MSM, Autobiography, LSM, Officers Miscellaneous File, 17.

The lower classes (IV and V) did attain a degree of representation in the power structure of the platoon, but it was marginal. Of the twenty-two NCOs serving in Number 1 Platoon during 1918, 32 per cent were from class III and 9 per cent from class IV. The artisan strata consistently provided more candidates for promotion than the labouring classes until the end of the conflict. This can be explained, in part, by the small percentage of classes IV and V in the platoon as a whole, but their promotion rate was low, even when their small presence in the ranks is taken into consideration (see Tables 3.3 and 3.4).

An impoverished background was not an insurmountable barrier to promotion, nor did middle-class status confer an automatic right to high rank. The patterns of advancement among the members of the platoon suggest that ability, experience and a willingness to accept responsibility were taken into account. We must remember that class did not always determine the desire for promotion. There were some middle-class men who refused to accept the mantle of authority. Others, such as H. C. Eccles, a cotton broker in civilian life, rejected their NCO status. Eccles reverted to being a rifleman at his own request in December 1917, after serving sixteen months as a lance corporal.[51] It was possible for carters to become corporals, whilst those of higher civilian status remained riflemen, but it was unusual. The platoon hierarchy mirrored that of civilian Liverpool, the middle classes retaining control over the positions of authority. To see this trend exemplified, we must now turn to the social structure of the officer class.

The officer caste

The first officers of the Rifles and the Scottish were the sons of religious, civic and business leaders of the city. Their privileged education and subsequent employment placed them in class I of the Registrar General's classification system and set them apart from the lower middle-class shopkeepers, clerks and white-collar employees who formed the greater part of the other ranks.

The death of Second Lieutenant Norman Mather of the Liverpool Scottish in August 1915 received wide coverage because he was the son of the Lord Mayor of Liverpool,[52] and the deaths of two brothers from the

---

[51] Service record of H. C. Eccles, 1/6th Battalion King's (Liverpool) Regiment Casualty Book 1, KRC, MLL, 58.83.537 a–b, and H. C. Eccles, Diary, 29 December 1917, H. C. Eccles Papers, Liddle Collection (G.S.). Frustratingly, Eccles does not provide a reason for giving up his stripe. He merely records the fact in his diary, but his transfer to the signal section may have been influential in his demotion.

[52] Newspaper cutting dated August 1916, Newspaper Cuttings Scrapbook, LSM, 77.

Dickinson family were reported in *The Times*, their father being a JP for the Lancashire County.[53] The Battalion could also claim the son of the bishop of Liverpool as its own medical officer until August 1917 and artistic flair was present amongst the Scottish in the form of Lieutenant Barnish. His work as the architect for the imposing Royal Liver buildings, which came to dominate the docks of Liverpool, was perhaps one of the most significant contributions to the Liverpolitan landscape for decades.[54]

All these officers in the Scottish had attended elite public schools and the majority had attended university. As a result of their privileged education, many were technically proficient at sport. Between 1914 and 1916 the Liverpool Scottish could boast at least seven rugby football internationals, as well as two former rugby captains of England and Scotland. Lieutenant F. H. Turner had captained the Scottish rugby football team and held fifteen caps for Scotland. He had been educated at Sedbergh and Trinity College, Oxford. Lieutenant P. D. Kendall had captained the England side, held three caps for England and had played forty-five matches for Cheshire. He had been educated at Tonbridge and Trinity Hall, Cambridge. These two men were destined to be buried side by side in a churchyard near Ypres.[55]

On leaving for France, the Liverpool Rifles had a similar complement of officers to the Scottish, with four captains and two lieutenants from Liverpool College, the leading public school in the area, and one officer from the Liverpool Institute. Of the other officers whose educational background could be traced, two were educated at Marlborough and two at Sedbergh, and the remaining five had attended Rugby, Oundle, Repton, Charterhouse and Winchester.[56]

Officers in the pre-war Territorial Force were often recruited from junior sections of the OTC or, before its establishment, the cadet corps attached to public schools. Whilst Territorial officers were not required to have the landed gentry background of the professional officers, the militaristic training they had received at school, and the advantage of their common social and sporting background, invested with notions of 'Christian manliness', meant that they loosely conformed to the 'gentlemanly' ideal of the professional officer.[57] As previously noted, it was the

---

[53] Liverpool Scottish Officers' Index, A. P. Dickinson, LSM.
[54] Liverpool Scottish Officers' Index, L. Barnish, LSM.
[55] E. Sewell, *Rugby football internationals roll of honour* (London, 1919), 78 and 212.
[56] Educational background was derived from J. Naylor, *Lancashire biographies* (London, 1917) and A. Haig-Brown, *The OTC and the Great War* (London, 1915), Appendix II.
[57] For a description of a pre-war professional officer and his ideals see K. Simpson, 'The Officers', in Beckett and Simpson (eds.), *A nation in arms*, 68. For discussions on 'Christian manliness' and the public school ethos see J. O. Springhall, *Youth, empire and society* (London, 1977).

merchant elite that was of most significance within Liverpool. Its members moved in the same social circles as the remaining aristocratic families of Lancashire and Cheshire and it was natural that the city's battalions should draw their officers from its own influential families.

On the outbreak of war, recruitment continued to be aimed at public school products, maintaining a socially homogeneous officer corps. Whether this policy was maintained throughout the war is less clear. The surviving evidence is sparse and any conclusions are impressionistic.

Seven officers who received their commissions with the Rifles during the war were recorded in the *Liverpool Scroll of Fame*.[58] Six out of the seven officers had attended public school, suggesting that the majority of officers continued to belong to social class I at the pinnacle of the Liverpolitan social hierarchy. Seven officers of the Rifles do not form a representative sample, but the broad conclusions can be tested against a more systematic study of the Liverpool Scottish officers.

A sample of ninety-two Scottish officers was constructed by selecting every tenth officer from an alphabetical card index found in the Liverpool Scottish Regimental Museum.[59] Formed over a period of thirty years from relatives' enquiries to the Museum, the card index contains biographical information gained from each query, together with supplementary information drawn from Museum records. It appears to be a relatively representative sample of the officers who served in the Liverpool Scottish as it is not confined to those officers who were either members of the old comrades association, or those who actively sought to have their memoirs or diaries preserved. Rather, it is dependent on the more random actions of families seeking or donating information about their relatives.

However, an examination of the sample taken from the index suggests that there are interpretative difficulties arising from the collation of the material. The biographical information provided for the officers commissioned between 1908 and 1916 is more detailed than that recorded for those commissioned in 1917 and 1918. For example, it is not possible to determine the social status of an officer in 75 per cent of the cases in 1917 and in 64 per cent of the cases in 1918. An index reliant on relatives providing information is inherently inconsistent, as some families could recall more details than others. In addition, the documents held by the Museum concentrate on those men who enlisted, or were commissioned,

---

[58] G. Thompson, *Liverpool Scroll of Fame*, Part I, *Commissioned Officers*, (Liverpool, 1920), 42, 122, 159, 181.

[59] Where the officer chosen had not served in the First World War, the next card was selected. However, as the majority of the index was devoted to officers from the 1914–18 conflict, this happened infrequently. See Liverpool Scottish Officers' Index, LSM.

Table 3.7 *Social origins of officers in the Liverpool Scottish Battalion, by year commissioned (percentage identifiable)*

Year	Social class			
	I	I/II	II	III
1914	88	12	0	0
1915	79	16	0	5
1916	100	0	0	0
1917	60	20	20	0
1918	75	25	0	0

Source: A random selection of officers from the Liverpool Scottish officers' index, LSM

prior to or during the early stages of the war. It was these men who had remained in contact with their old battalion after the cessation of hostilities, and who formed the old comrades associations. Thus, it was easier to supplement the biographical details for officers from the 1914, 1915 and 1916 cohorts.

Despite its faults, the sample has generated a valuable guide to the social status of the officers of the Liverpool Scottish between 1914 and 1918. Table 3.7 shows that the impressionistic findings for the Liverpool Rifles are borne out by the results of the Scottish. The social status of the officers remained relatively constant to 1918, with a brief dip in the percentage of those commissioned from a class I background occurring in 1917. This trend may have continued in a downward spiral in other Territorial battalions, including the Rifles, but the Scottish were rescued by the amalgamation with their second line in 1918. The second line had seen little fighting, and consequently had more personnel who had been recruited in earlier, more stringent times.

The one aberration in the figures was the officer with a class III background, commissioned in 1915. This is easily explained as an exceptional case. Sergeant Farmer was a regular soldier who had been awarded the VC in the Boer War. His courage and intelligence gained him a commission, and after the war he became a beer salesman, and thus had moved up the social pyramid into the ranks of the lower middle class.[60]

---

[60] Liverpool Scottish Officers' Index, D. D. Farmer, LSM.

Collective statistics based on the demobilization of industrial groups have shown that by the end of the war one third of British army officers had been professionals, students and teachers in civilian life. It is difficult to determine the precise social class of officers in remaining occupational groups, but there is sufficient detail to suggest that there had been a broad and fundamental change in the social and educational background of the officer corps by the end of the war. By 1918, many more officers were drawn from the lower middle class, than from the gentry who had traditionally supplied regular candidates.[61]

When compared with the army as a whole, the change in social composition of the officer corps does not appear to have been as significant for the Liverpool Territorials. Indeed, diaries and memoirs do not indicate deterioration in the social status of newly commissioned officers to the Liverpool Scottish or the Liverpool Rifles. One explanation may be that the social gulf between the urban elite and the urban lower middle class was smaller than the gulf that existed between a member of the gentry and, for example, a railway clerk. The changes in the social composition of the officer corps were less marked in Territorial battalions and thus warranted fewer comments than may have been the case in a regular unit. A more convincing explanation for the smooth incorporation of the lower middle class into the Territorial officer caste, however, is the fact that they were so few in number (see Table 3.7). Territorial officers of the Rifles and the Scottish continued to be drawn from the sons of the Liverpool elite and remained a homogeneous group throughout the war.

Internal promotion accounted for 58 per cent of all officer acquisitions and, because there were a large number of middle-class men in the ranks at the beginning of the war, the Scottish had a large supply of potential candidates to maintain the social status of the officer pool.[62] Having a vociferous commanding officer, keen to support internal promotion, was also valuable in maintaining the social status of officer drafts. Colonel Davidson wrote to his brigade commander complaining about replacement officers who had been attached to his Battalion from the 16th King's (Liverpool) Regiment in September 1915. He concluded, 'The result of having officers from other regiments permanently on the strength of this unit will be to block the appointment of our own officers and will be detrimental to the best interests of the Battalion.'[63] Another letter on the

---

[61] Simpson, 'The Officers', 88.
[62] Percentage calculated from a random selection of eighty-eight officers from the Liverpool Scottish Officers' Index, LSM.
[63] O.C. 1st Battalion Liverpool Scottish to G.O.C. 9th Infantry Brigade, 2/9/15, Uncatalogued Scrapbook, LSM.

'Cuff and collar battalions' 47

same subject was addressed to Lord Derby, describing the way in which Davidson had handled the situation and appealing for help from the West Lancashire Territorial Association.

> One who arrived in our kit was easily dealt with as I sent him back two minutes after his graceful descent from the wagon that brought them up. Did you ever hear of such damn impertinence? ... I have stated that I am sure the West Lancs. Division knows nothing of the matter and it is here that you can help me. Can you see Parkes and find out whether there is any way in which the Association can help us. We ought to have sufficient influence if we apply to the proper quarters.[64]

Finally in a letter to Colonel Blair,[65] Davidson described the outcome of his complaints: 'It seems to have fared well until it reached the 2nd Army. At the worst I take it that the joke will not be repeated.'[66] The 'joke' was not to be repeated, at least in the short term. Lieutenant Colonel Fairrie, the commanding officer of the 3/10th Liverpool Scottish, ensured that the officer vacancies in the first-line Battalion were filled by men he had vetted.[67]

By 1916 the system for selecting officers for temporary commissions had been formalized. A candidate had to be recommended by his commanding officer and undergo four months of training with an officer cadet battalion before commissioning.[68] There was no guarantee a newly commissioned officer would be returned to his original unit, but the Territorials were fortunate in having an established Association, which, despite the restrictions on its power imposed by the government, could still exert some influence over issues such as commissions. This, together with the existence of officers such as Fairrie, who had served in the Territorials and Volunteers for many years and had an intimate knowledge of administrative military machinery, gave the Territorial units in Liverpool more control over their officer personnel than those units raised on the outbreak of war.

The importance of social homogeneity in wartime

The social composition of each battalion changed continuously throughout the war. Each major change in personnel affected social relations within

---

[64] Lieutenant Colonel J. R. Davidson to Lord Derby, undated, Derby Papers, LRO, 920 DER (17) 26/1, May–September 1915.
[65] Colonel Blair was a former Commanding Officer of the Scottish who was serving at the Liverpool Scottish depot in Liverpool in 1915.
[66] Lieutenant Colonel J. R. Davidson to Colonel Blair, 18/9/15, Uncatalogued Scrapbook, Liverpool, LSM.
[67] Lieutenant Colonel J. R. Davidson to Lord Derby, undated, Derby Papers, LRO, 920 DER (17) 26/1, May–September 1915.
[68] See Simpson, 'The Officers', 80.

a unit, creating distinct problems and new benefits for the efficiency and cohesion of the Battalion. This section investigates the impact of social change within each unit, and assesses the importance of social homogeneity to the Rifles and the Scottish.

The pre-war social profile of these Territorial units reflected the civilian social hierarchy of the middle classes. The officers were drawn from class I, and the other ranks were derived mainly from the white-collar sectors of classes II and III, although, particularly in the Scottish Battalion, the social mix in the ranks was less prescriptive than this suggests. On the outbreak of war, both Battalions saw men of high social status enlisting as privates, which immediately placed strain on the hierarchical relationships within each unit.

Stanley Gordon, a lieutenant during the training period in August 1914, remembered the initial confusion caused by a large number of upper middle-class men in the ranks. His memoir related a typical story from the beginning of the war. Whilst relaxing in the officers' mess the adjutant of the 6th Rifles was informed that there was a 'gentleman' to see him. 'The adjutant, thinking that it was possibly the Brigade Major, jumped up and went to the door of the hut. His demeanour then rapidly changed and he said, 'Gentleman indeed! I call him a corporal and a damned dirty one too!'[69]

Civilian standing was no longer commensurate with military authority within the Battalion, but the Territorials did not entirely relinquish their civilian status. Sergeant Macfie's experience is a good example of the compromise that ensued. Active in the elevated business, academic and social circles in Liverpool, Macfie was viewed as ideal officer material. Yet he consistently rejected offers of a commission. On rejoining the Battalion in August 1914, Macfie immediately rose to his old rank of colour sergeant, but his standing in civilian life entitled him to privileges not normally afforded a sergeant. Breaches of military convention were often overlooked, as was his virulent criticism directed against some officers. A characteristic outburst was recorded in a letter to his father explaining why he had refused to accept a commission. 'I don't feel anxious to lounge about an officers' mess with a lot of idle and rather incompetent people ... It is not a time when honour and dignity should be taken into consideration.' Similar comments continued for the duration of the war, and were never censored.[70] To cope with a subverted hierarchy, officers in the Territorials found it necessary to allow concessions towards high-status other ranks. The tradition of a lenient discipline system and relaxed

[69] S. E. Gordon, Memoir, Gordon Papers, IWM, 77/6/1, 32.
[70] R. A. S. Macfie to father, 30 August 1914, Macfie Papers, IWM, Con. Shelf.

'Cuff and collar battalions' 49

relations between ranks, formed as a result of the social homogeneity of the pre-war Battalion, became an even greater asset in the early years of the war.[71]

The concentration of middle-class men in the ranks also had other repercussions for the operation and efficiency of the Battalion. Their levels of education and civilian employment were cited as causes for the high rate of illness suffered by the Liverpool Scottish in the first months of the war. Captain McKinnell believed that the educated men of his unit had a more 'varied imagination upon which to draw',[72] whilst Dr Chavasse advanced an alternative explanation, claiming that the sickness of his charges was a direct result of so many of them having been clerks. As such, they had to acclimatize both to their new outdoor life and to the wearing of a draughty kilt.[73]

In general, the civilian occupations of the middle classes did not equip soldiers for life in the field. Although often intelligent and quick to learn, most middle-class commercial men lacked practical skills on enlistment. For example, Stanley Gordon, the transport officer for the Rifles on mobilization, bemoaned the fact that few of his men had experience with horses. This was a serious problem for the transport section, whose mobility was entirely dependent on these animals.[74]

The Liverpool Scottish fared better than the Rifles at the beginning of the war, having attracted men with a range of occupations. Their commanding officer, as chief engineer to Liverpool water board, was able to use his civilian expertise when draining trenches, and their small artisan contingent proved their worth, constructing dugouts and designing innovative stretchers.[75]

As the war progressed through 1915, the prime officer and NCO material languishing in the ranks began to voice discontent. The experience of the Second Battle of Ypres in April led to the realization that the war was to be a long and bloody enterprise. As a result, many men of high social status began to re-evaluate their rash decision to enlist in the ranks, and the opportunities for promotion increasingly could not match the demand.

---

[71] See chapter 7 for a detailed analysis.
[72] B. McKinnell, *The diary of Bryden McKinnell, Liverpool Scottish* (Liverpool, 1919), 4 December 1914.
[73] N. G. Chavasse to E. J. Chavasse, 27 September 1914, quoted in A. Clayton, *Chavasse: double V.C.* (Barnsley, 1992), 63.
[74] S. E. Gordon, Memoir, Gordon Papers, IWM, 77/5/1, 28.
[75] A patent for a new type of short folding stretcher was awarded to W. E. Pinnington in 1915. Pinnington had been an apprentice carpenter in civilian life. Liverpool Scottish Other Ranks' Index, W. E. Pinnington, LSM.

Lieutenant Gordon recalled that the commander of the Third Army had congratulated his Battalion on providing so many candidates for commission.[76] However, many of these men were destined to remain candidates only, as their aspirations were sacrificed to the needs of the war. The Territorial battalions had become an essential part of the force at Kitchener's disposal by early 1915, and it made sense to maintain the Territorials as coherent fighting units whilst the New Armies were being trained. According to Major Gordon, there was a total absence of drafts in the Rifles between March and August 1915, during which time they had to replenish their ranks with men returning from hospital. This is consistent with the Battalion War Diary, which listed only ten other ranks arriving during this period.[77] Under these conditions the Battalion could not afford to lose any men through promotion.

Private Ellison later remembered his feelings during this period. He was resentful that Kitchener's Army was 'full of inexperienced youths with commissions'; he believed that the battle-hardened men of his Battalion would have been eminently more suitable. In November 1915 Ellison asked his company commander to recommend him for a commission. At the same time his father offered to 'pull some strings' in England. Ellison surmised that the wrong strings were pulled, as he did not acquire a commission.[78] Rifleman Eccles had a similar experience. He first applied for a commission in August 1915, but by March 1916 had not been accepted. Captain Westby offered to intervene on his behalf, but was unsuccessful. Eccles spent the rest of his war as a rifleman and lance corporal.[79]

The promotion situation was not as severe in the Scottish unit and similar experiences were not recorded in their diaries and memoirs. Throughout 1915, the Scottish received more reinforcements from their second and third lines than the Rifles, permitting eligible candidates to take up their commissions elsewhere. The Scottish also suffered their first bloodbath in June 1915, which created many vacancies at all levels in the Battalion. Casualties sent to Britain were frequently offered officer training on recovery, and their replacements, although still from social class II, were no longer from the upper echelons of the middle class.[80] The pre-war social contours of the unit were re-established at an earlier

---

[76] S. E. Gordon, Memoir, Gordon Papers, IWM, 77/5/1, 32.
[77] S. E. Gordon, Memoir, Gordon Papers, IWM, 77/5/1, 144 and 216, and 1/6th Battalion King's (Liverpool) Regiment War Diary, March–August 1915, KRC, MLL, 58.83.501.
[78] N. F. Ellison, Memoir and War Diary, November 1915, Ellison Papers, IWM, DS/MISC/49, 70.
[79] H. C. Eccles, Diary, 29 December 1917, H. C. Eccles Papers, Liddle Collection (G.S.).
[80] Liverpool Scottish Officers' Index, LSM.

point than in the Rifles, who had to wait until after the bloodletting on the Somme.

Despite the resentments that a socially homogeneous background could cause, social uniformity was a Territorial characteristic considered important to both Battalions in the first years of the war. It helped to motivate the men in the trenches, promoted social cohesion and generated a local support network, based on established civilian friendships.

Both pre-war members and those men who joined the Rifles or the Scottish on the outbreak of war had chosen their unit because they felt an affinity with its characteristics and practices. Most middle-class men wanted to serve with people to whom they could immediately relate, and social uniformity helped to foster an immediate degree of cohesion within the unit. The young men who fought in the early years of the war were bound together by shared motivations that sprang from a common background and value system.

Many soldiers subscribed to the belief that they had a duty to uphold the honour of Liverpool and to deliver their country from the threat of German hegemony in Europe.[81] There was also the need to safeguard the power and authority of the middle class in Liverpool from both external and internal threats. 'I wonder how you all are and pray that you should be spared the horrors of losing your positions',[82] wrote Private Francis to his family in 1914. As leaders of Liverpolitan society the middle class had most to lose in the event of an invasion, and Francis was one of many middle-class soldiers fighting to preserve his status and position.

At the same time, mass military participation by many different sectors of Liverpolitan society ensured there was a need for the middle classes to assert their social leadership and retain their reputation at home through displaying courage on the battlefield. The ways in which this was achieved are described elsewhere in the book. It is sufficient to note here that the desire to prove themselves in battle was an important and near universal source of motivation for the men of both Battalions during the first six months of 1915.

Support systems, based on civilian social and ethnic networks, also played a vital role in sustaining the soldiers in the trenches. Not all soldiers who served with the Rifles and the Scottish in the first years of the war had been pre-war Territorials, but most had participated in the middle-class clubs and societies of Liverpool. Thus, the majority of each Battalion was, at the very least, acquainted, and shared similar civilian

---

[81] N. Chavasse to father, 5 September 1914, quoted in Clayton, *Chavasse: double V.C.*, 61.
[82] *Liverpool Echo*, undated cutting, Private Francis to family in J. Bedford, With the Liverpool Scottish, Scrapbook 1, LSM, Acc. No. 476.

loyalties and interests. Many more soldiers had closer family ties, being related by blood or marriage,[83] whilst others had long histories of friendship stretching back into childhood.[84]

For a number of Liverpool Scots, culled from large Presbyterian congregations, there was also the support of their church community. In some cases, the congregation appeared to have been transposed directly into the trenches. J. G. Colthart Moffat, a sergeant in the Liverpool Scottish, was also a church elder at St Andrew's Presbyterian Church. The men under his control in the Company were also the men he watched over in civilian life. Colour Sergeant Macfie observed the value of this relationship and described the situation to his father: 'Moffat, (the sergeant I mentioned) knows about many of their homes. He is a church elder or something and looks after his men somewhat as a parson looks after his parish.'[85] It is true that civilian rivalries and arguments as well as friendships could be transferred to the trenches, making life uncomfortable for some, but the evidence from both Territorial Battalions suggests that close civilian ties were more often comforting and familiar, providing practical and emotional support to men disorientated by war.

The value of primary group membership in motivating and sustaining soldiers has been noted by many historians and sociologists.[86] The idea that soldiers fight because of the development of a fierce loyalty to the members of a group has much validity. In the Rifles and the Scottish, this type of bonding was most apparent in the early years of the war, and was based on their existing civilian social networks. Most relationships, even among the successive volunteer drafts, were based on civilian experience and friendship, and were strengthened, but not forged, in the heat of battle.[87]

The beginning of 1917 marked a watershed in the minds of many of the commentators who had been fighting since the units arrived on the continent.[88] The slow trickle of conscripts, who had not been selected

---

[83] Some of the many families which populated the Liverpool Scottish included the two Turnbull brothers, and the three Nethercott brothers. See newspaper cuttings, 1914, T. D. Fisher Papers, Liddle Collection (G.S.) Miscell. F10.

[84] For example, the friendship between J. S. Handley and Jimmy Armstrong had begun during their studies at Liverpool School of Art: J. S. Handley, Memoir, Handley Papers, IWM, 92/36/1, 10–11.

[85] R. A. S. Macfie to father, 25 August 1914, Macfie Papers, IWM, Con. Shelf.

[86] See S. L. A. Marshall, *Men against fire: the problem of battle command in future war* (New York, 1947); M. Janowitz and E. Shils, 'Cohesion and disintegration in the Wehrmacht in World War II', *Public Opinion Quarterly*, 12 (Summer 1948), 280–315; J. Bourne, *Britain and the Great War, 1914–1918* (London, 1989), 220.

[87] See, for example, the close friendship between Private Herd and his sergeant: E. Herd, Memoir, November 1915, KRC, MLL, Herd Papers, 1981.850.

[88] See, for example, J. S. Handley, Memoir, Handley Papers, IWM, 92/36/1, 11.

using strict social and ethnic criteria, began to have an impact, and veterans began to pronounce unfavourably on new drafts, suggesting that the physical and social character of each unit was undergoing a fundamental change.[89]

In reality, there were still many men of middle-class origin in the ranks in 1917, and it was to be many months before the middle classes were outnumbered. Soldiers who had been evacuated sick and wounded during the early years of the war returned in 1917 and 1918,[90] alongside a significant number of middle-class conscripts, who sometimes had established family connections with the units.[91] Thus, the vestiges of a pre-war middle-class network remained through 1917, a point that was highlighted by Sergeant Burden, a shipping clerk in civilian life. In September 1917 he wrote to his girlfriend: 'This is a little world. A chap out of our office was killed a day or two ago and a chap told me that he was that chap's young lady's brother.'[92]

Yet social change had certainly begun in 1917. After the Somme, veterans mourned the wholesale loss of close personal friends, and foresaw the slow disintegration of their tight social networks that had sustained them thus far. The kinds of friendship that had been nurtured in civilian life and cemented through the initial experience of war were hard to replicate on a large scale, even if survivors were prepared to risk further emotional trauma by forming new relationships. John Bourne reminds us that whilst membership of a primary group made the exigencies of war easier to bear, it also made loss more devastating, and the change in the social status of a large number of recruits ensured that their social networks could not be renewed in the same way.[93]

---

[89] J. S. Handley, Memoir, Handley Papers, IWM, 92/36/1, 11.

[90] Many men of the Liverpool Rifles have two embarkation dates in the casualty books. One of the many men who returned to the Battalion after injury was J. F. Kneale. Kneale served with the Rifles from May 1915 to August 1916 when he was wounded in the foot. He returned in February 1917 and served until October of that year, when he left the unit as a candidate for commission. 1/6th Battalion King's (Liverpool) Regiment Casualty Books 1–2, KRC, MLL, 58.83.537a–b. Further evidence for this is provided in the *Greenjacket*, which claimed that 'We were many times more fortunate than some units, for repeatedly those members of the 6th who had been wounded returned to the Battalion instead of being dissipated in miscellaneous drafts all over the British Army in France': *Greenjacket*, July 1927.

[91] For example, Ted Heatley first arrived in the Rifles in August 1917. His father had been a drill instructor for the unit in pre-war days. J. A. Burden to E. Robinson, 5 August 1917, J. A. Burden Letters, LSM, Acc. No. 1122.

[92] J. A. Burden to E. Robinson, 19 September 1917, J. A. Burden Letters, LSM, Acc. No. 1122.

[93] Bourne, *Britain and the Great War*, 221. See also Bourke, *Dismembering the male*, 170.

For many middle-class men in the Battalions, both veteran and newly arrived conscript, the friendship patterns, of localized, supportive, primary groups, began to change. Instead, middle-class Territorials came to rely on friendships with individuals from the same social background. As Audoin-Rouzeau has observed amongst French soldiers, the men of the Rifles and the Scottish remained attached to their social origins, and found it difficult to relate to men of a different class.[94]

Eric Peppiette, a university librarian in civilian life, was a Derbyite who encountered this problem when he first entered the army. Shocked by the rough habits and lewd behaviour of many of his fellow recruits, he turned to his diary and letter writing for support.[95] However, on arrival in France in July 1916, it is evident that he had made a firm friend who hailed from a similar background.[96] Private Warry's friendships also followed a similar, exclusive pattern. On 9 March 1917 he wrote in his diary that his friend Bert Wylie had been attached to the Lewis Gun Section, and that Smith was now his pal. By 26 May 1917, Smith was in hospital with diphtheria and Johnstone from Chester was his replacement. All Warry's friends shared a similar social background.[97]

This change in friendship patterns did not necessarily mean that comradeship lost its significance within the Battalions in the latter years of the war. It is likely that the working-class privates formed their own primary support groups as they increased in number,[98] and the middle classes simply changed their pattern of comradeship to accommodate changed circumstances.[99] What this evidence does call into question is the prevalent belief that primary group loyalty was the key motivating force for soldiers at the end of the war. The support and motivation the primary group could offer to a soldier was dependent on his social background relative to his fellow warriors, and the length of time that group had been in existence. For many soldiers, encouragement and assistance had to be sought elsewhere.

Ironically, the breakdown in social homogeneity that some of the middle-class men deplored may have averted serious unrest developing in the Rifles. After the bloodletting on the Somme, the Rifles were able to

---

[94] Audoin-Rouzeau, *Men at war 1914–1918*, 50.
[95] E. Peppiette, Diary, 29 April 1916, Peppiette Papers, LSM, Acc. No. 887. A 'Derbyite' was a soldier who had volunteered to serve under Lord Derby's Scheme in November 1915 and was subsequently called up.
[96] E. Peppiette, Diary, 5 August 1916, Peppiette Papers, LSM, Acc. No. 887.
[97] G. Warry, Diary, 9 March 1917 and 26 May 1917, Warry Papers, IWM, 96/12/1.
[98] Unfortunately this cannot be verified because of the dearth of working-class sources for both Battalions.
[99] This pattern of close personal relationships is similar to that identified by Audoin-Rouzeau: *Men at war 1914–1918*, 50.

promote their aspiring middle-class candidates and dispel the simmering discontent of earlier years. The artisan background of many of the new conscripts ensured that they had fewer opportunities and therefore fewer expectations of gaining commissions, as generally only middle-class men were considered. The middle-class men who remained as private soldiers in 1918 had generally stayed in that position by choice. Social stability had been restored.[100]

The social structure of both units began to resemble the familiar hierarchy of civilian society. In 1918 Sergeant Macfie was more likely to find his ex-employees in the drafts to the Liverpool Scottish, than his social equals.[101] Yet as Lieutenant Pegge's evidence suggests, despite the dissolution of the general social uniformity, the middle-class survivors of earlier years remained concentrated in key positions of authority throughout the final year of war.[102] It was these experienced soldiers, particularly the senior NCOs, who provided a much-needed degree of continuity within the Battalions. Through initiating each new draft, these veterans ensured that the unit traditions of a relaxed discipline system and informal command relations, influenced by the initial social exclusivity of each Battalion, continued, albeit in modified forms, to the end of the war.[103]

Conclusion

When the middle-class men of the Territorials joined the army before and during 1914 their choice of unit was governed by its social character. They wanted to serve with their friends in a socially homogeneous unit. This social uniformity provided a number of vital advantages for the Territorial units in the first years of the war. Primarily, it allowed groups of civilian friends to fight together in the trenches. Pre-war friendships provided reassurance and the familiarity of home in uncertain times, and because the men instinctively trusted one another their friendships were

---

[100] For a discussion on social stability see Bourne, 'The British working man in arms', 349–50.
[101] R. A. S. Macfie to Charlie Macfie, 8 March 1918, Macfie Papers, IWM, Con. Shelf.
[102] See Tables 3.4 and 3.5. Gary Sheffield has also shown that there was a degree of continuity in the ranks of the 22nd Kensingtons throughout the war. 'A very good type of Londoner and a very good type of colonial: officer–man relations and discipline in the 22nd Royal Fusiliers, 1914–18', in B. Bond et al., 'Look to your front': studies in the First World War by the British Commission for Military History (Staplehurst, 1999), 142. K. W. Mitchinson has arrived at similar conclusions for the London Rifle Brigade, Gentlemen and officers, 14. Patricia Morris also suggests that traditions were handed down to new drafts in the Leeds Rifles, although she does not examine the processes by which this occurred. Morris, 'Leeds and the amateur military tradition', 993.
[103] Greenjacket, July 1927.

also instrumental in binding inexperienced units together when facing their first terrifying and demanding ordeals.

Social homogeneity inevitably began to break down by 1917, but social background remained important to the men. As individuals, they clung to the prejudices and affinities learned in civilian life, and the experience of the trenches did not make friendship across the chasm of social class any more attractive. Social status remained as much of a barrier to social integration in the army as it had proved in pre-war Liverpool. The close-knit support network of the first years in the trenches was never renewed and soldiers had to look elsewhere for psychological support.

Yet social homogeneity had been a mixed blessing for the Territorials, and its breakdown had positive as well as negative consequences for the morale of the soldier. It had been useful to pre-war Territorials to whom attending Battalion meetings had been a leisure activity. Social uniformity had created a comfortable atmosphere in which men could enjoy themselves. Soldiering in wartime was a different proposition. The Battalion was now their workplace, and the middle-class soldier was not used to a socially homogeneous working environment which offered few promotional opportunities.

Thus the change in the social composition of the Battalions was fortuitous. The influx of working-class recruits meant that middle-class soldiers could now be promoted out of the unit or concentrated in key positions of responsibility. Moreover, those that remained were able to perpetuate the traditions of a relaxed discipline system and more informal command relations, creating a working environment that in social hierarchy and management relations was more closely allied to the civilian workplace than that provided by either regular army or pre-war Territorial organization.

4   'Common ties at home and strong county pride': the persistence and importance of county uniformity

Localism was a key feature of British society before the Great War. In 1914 Britain was decentralized, both administratively and culturally. Differing dialects, customs, entertainment and occupations defined towns, counties and regions, endowing each with distinguishable characteristics. The central state wielded relatively little influence over the lives of the general public, whilst the local authorities, together with voluntary institutions, maintained the infrastructure of the county and regulated everyday life. Most people lived their lives at the local level. Their aspirations, expectations and connections were limited to the local and their loyalties were tied to village, town and county through their interaction and familiarity with civic institutions and their membership of community clubs and associations.[1]

Territorial soldiers, drawn from the local community, also shared the local outlook. If social exclusivity was the primary Territorial characteristic in the pre-war era, localism came a close second. Recruitment techniques and the need for convenient access to drill halls and social facilities ensured that recruits were drawn from a finite area and localism was a part of battalion life that was taken for granted.[2] In the first months following the outbreak of war, local patriotism also played an important role in drawing men to join Territorial and New Army units. Others have described how local patriotism and even local rivalries helped to motivate new soldiers during their training in Britain, supported them through their first experiences of action abroad, but disappeared as a force after the slaughter of the Somme.[3] In this chapter, we look again at the persistence and importance of local uniformity in units to explain how

---

[1] See R. Colls, *Identity of England* (Oxford, 2002), 225–8; J. Winter, 'Popular culture in wartime Britain', in A. Roshwald and R. Stites (eds.), *European culture in the Great War: the arts, entertainment and propaganda 1914–1918* (Cambridge, 1999), 330.
[2] Lieutenant Colonel The Honourable Sidney Peel, DSO, MP, 'The Territorial Force', *Army Quarterly*, 1, 1 (1920–21), 36.
[3] Simkins, *Kitchener's army*, 208–9.

58   Territorial characteristics and morale

local loyalties were of value to both the soldiers and the army throughout the course of the Great War.

The persistence of localism in Territorial units

The received historiography maintains that there was a conscious nationalization of the British army between 1916 and 1918. It is generally accepted that in 1914 most Territorial units drew their membership from their local recruiting area, but that as the war progressed the local character of units was vulnerable to dilution. In the wake of large casualties men were drafted to the battalions which required reinforcements most urgently, irrespective of the regional origin of the draft.[4] This has been viewed as a policy which performed a dual function, enabling the quick reconstitution of badly mauled battalions whilst addressing governmental concern over the effect of mass, localized bereavement on the home front.[5]

Whilst it is undeniable that many soldiers fought in units having little or no connection with their home area, the experience of both the Liverpool Scottish and the Liverpool Rifles does not support the idea of a nationalization of the British army; rather, it suggests that a broad regional homogeneity, centred on the county of Lancashire, was sustained in both units until 1918.

The evidence used to investigate changing local uniformity is derived from *Soldiers died in the Great War*, which provides a list of the soldiers, by battalion, who died during the conflict.[6] In most cases the places of residence and enlistment are recorded, which allows the regional origin of the men to be identified.[7]

---

[4] Beckett, 'The Territorial Force', 147.
[5] Advocates of this idea include J. Fuller, *Troop morale and popular culture in the British and Dominion Armies* (Oxford, 1990), 43–4; P. Simkins, 'British divisions in the hundred days', in P. Griffith (ed.), *British fighting methods in the Great War* (London, 1996), 59; J. C. Dunn, *The war the infantry knew* (2nd edn, London, 1987), 245; and F. W. Perry, *The commonwealth armies: manpower and organisation in two world wars* (Manchester, 1988), 20.
[6] War Office, *Soldiers died in the Great War* (vol. 13, London 1920).
[7] This source must be used with caution as the figures derived from the data represent only those men from the units who were killed in action or died of wounds or sickness, and so the percentages calculated may not be representative of a whole battalion. However, both the Scottish and the Rifle Battalions were scrupulous in ensuring that each company spent the same amount of time in the line, and the companies of the Liverpool Scottish even shared the time spent in the most dangerous areas of the trenches during some tours. Thus, the casualties were unlikely to be concentrated in specific companies and were probably representative of the Battalion. A platoon roll from the 6th Rifles in 1918 provides further corroborative evidence. Fifty-two per cent of Number 3 Platoon hailed from Liverpool, suggesting that, if anything, *Soldiers died in the Great War* underestimates local homogeneity in the Battalion. For these reasons, the statistics gained from *Soldiers died in the Great War* have been used to suggest trends for the whole Battalion.

Place of enlistment provided the best category of data to represent the regional affiliations of the men, partly because it provided the most consistent dataset from *Soldiers died in the Great War*, but also because it most accurately reflected their sense of civic identification. There would have been many reasons for enlisting in Liverpool.[8] Desire to join a battalion with their friends, siblings or colleagues was the usual motivation. Men were also drawn by a sense of duty to protect their home area, or by a desire for adventure. In most cases the men would have enlisted in the area in which they lived, or, less frequently, in an area with which they felt most affinity, often the city in which they were born and raised. Indeed, some men travelled from as far afield as Canada and Australia to enlist in Liverpool.[9]

Until 1916 and the introduction of conscription, each volunteer could, within reason, choose the battalion he joined, and although some men joined regiments outside their home area to avoid, for example, height restrictions, most men chose to serve in a unit connected with their home district. Thus, the place of enlistment provides a clear indication of the number of men in each unit with close links to the city of Liverpool.

For the purposes of this analysis, areas of enlistment have been divided into three generic categories. The first represents the pre-war recruiting area of a unit. For the Liverpool Territorials this encompassed Liverpool and her dormitory areas, the dormitory areas being those districts adjacent to the city in which a large number of commuters resided.[10] The areas included Birkenhead, Claughton, Heswall, Wallasey, Liscard, New Brighton, New Ferry, Bebington, Hoylake, Bromborough, West Kirby and Eastham, all on the west bank of the Mersey, and Blundellsands, Formby, Birkdale and Southport, which were situated on the coast to the north of Liverpool. All these areas had well-established transport networks with the city, which had encouraged commuting.[11] The second category incorporates the pre-war recruiting area and the county with which it was associated. In the case of the Liverpool Territorials the county was Lancashire. The third category is the broadest and sweeps up all other soldiers who enlisted in the rest of Britain. The results are displayed in Table 4.1.

Table 4.1 shows that close local ties did decrease as the war progressed. High percentages of the Battalions' dead hailed from Liverpool until the

---

[8] For a discussion of reasons for enlisting in wartime, see J. M. Osborne, *The voluntary recruiting movement in Britain, 1914–16* (London, 1982) and Simkins, *Kitchener's army*, 49–104.
[9] See Liverpool Scottish Other Ranks' Index, LSM.
[10] See Map 4.1.
[11] Ward Lock and Co., *A guide to Liverpool and Birkenhead*, 43, 124–30.

Map 4.1 The environs of Liverpool.

end of 1917, but in 1918 there was a sharp decline, which happened to a greater extent in the Liverpool Rifles than in the Scottish. The explanation for this may be found in the amalgamation of the first- and second-line Battalions in February 1918. The 2/10th Battalion, formed in 1915, had seen little fighting and as such would have contained many Liverpool men when it amalgamated with its first-line unit.[12] By contrast, the 1/6th and 2/6th Rifle Battalions remained fighting independently for the remainder of the war and so had to obtain reinforcements from other, less locally homogeneous sources in 1918.

Given that only 42 per cent of those killed in the 6th Rifles in 1918 came from Liverpool, the statistics appear to support the idea that the territorial character of units decreased during the war. However, if we widen our conception of territorial character, and broaden the investigation to include the county, we can see that the percentages calculated are

---

[12] The Battalion arrived in France in February 1917. Its first major action was the Third Battle of Ypres, in which it played a supporting role as a reserve battalion and sustained relatively minor casualties.

Table 4.1 *Percentage of soldiers who died whilst serving in the 1/6th and 1/10th Battalions, King's (Liverpool) Regiment, according to their place of enlistment*

a. Liverpool, dormitory areas

	% of soldiers died who enlisted in Liverpool and dormitory areas				
Battalion	1914	1915	1916	1917	1918
6th	100	100	98.5	67	42
10th	100	96.5	84	73	68

b. Liverpool, dormitory areas, Lancashire

	% of soldiers died who enlisted in Liverpool, dormitory areas and Lancashire				
Battalion	1914	1915	1916	1917	1918
6th	100	100	100	83	70
10th	100	100	92.5	91	87

c. Other areas of Britain

	% of soldiers died who enlisted in other areas of Britain				
Battalion	1914	1915	1916	1917	1918
6th	0	0	0	17	30
10th	0	0	7.5	9	13

Source: Statistics derived from War Office, *Soldiers died in the Great War* (vol. 13, London, 1920)

significantly different. Table 4.1 also shows that 70 per cent of the 6th Battalion's dead in 1918 came from the county of Lancashire, compared with 87 per cent of the Liverpool Scottish. Both units have surprisingly high percentages of men who originate from the same county, suggesting that even if they were not being reinforced by men from their traditional recruiting areas, they were at least gaining drafts of Lancastrian origin to the end of the war.

Other historians have used *Soldiers died in the Great War* to calculate some very different results. Ian Beckett, for example, has constructed a convincing thesis, based largely on the experience of Buckinghamshire units, which suggests that their local specificity was destroyed during the war. Indeed, for one unit, the 1/1st Royal Buckinghamshire Hussars, he calculates that the loss of their local character began as early as 1916.[13] This divergence in the statistics for Liverpool and Buckinghamshire units requires explanation. Why did the Liverpool Territorials retain their broad

[13] Beckett, 'The Territorial Force', 147–51.

regional affiliation and the Buckinghamshires see the disintegration of their territorial characteristics over the course of the war? Were the Liverpool battalions an aberration in wartime Britain, or does their experience indicate a broader trend applicable to other units? To answer these questions we need to examine the recruitment, drafting and amalgamation policies that operated within the British army between 1914 and 1918.

Recruiting the reserves

Of paramount importance in retaining county homogeneity within units was the way in which men were recruited. In 1915 each regular, Service and Territorial battalion had its own regimental reserves, recruited directly from its locality.[14] In September 1914 regiments had been given permission to raise second-line units for all existing Territorial battalions, and by May 1915 third-line units were in existence. The second-line units of both the 10th Liverpool Scottish and the 6th Liverpool Rifles provided initial drafts to their respective first-line Battalions abroad. The 2/10th Battalion, for example, provided 600 men in four drafts, between November 1914 and May 1915.[15] After February 1916 this practice ceased, the second lines being used as viable units in their own right, first to guard areas of importance on the south coast, and later to fight in France. The responsibility for the provision of drafts for both the first and second lines passed to the third-line Battalion.

With the introduction of conscription, the regimental reserves of the Territorial and Service battalions were unable to cope with the large numbers of recruits. Moreover, the recruiting authorities were facing a further problem. They needed to devise a system which would provide 'a large reservoir from which drafts could in an emergency be sent to any infantry battalion'.[16] The solution was the establishment of the Training Reserve, a new, flexible organization designed to receive, train and dispatch recruits to regiments abroad.[17] It is the organization of this Training Reserve that has convinced historians of the existence of a deliberate attempt to nationalize the army.

Yet a close examination of official publications from the time suggests that nationalization was remote from the true aims of the authorities. In

---

[14] E. A. James, *British regiments in the First World War* (2nd edn, London, 1976), Appendix iii to part II, 129.
[15] A. M. McGilchrist, *The Liverpool Scottish* (Liverpool, 1930), 259.
[16] War Office, *Organization and training of the New Armies*, Part 2 (London, 1917), 5.
[17] See James, *British regiments in the First World War*, 129.

'Common ties at home and strong county pride' 63

addition to providing a flexible reservoir of drafts to be used in an emergency with minimal difficulties, the War Office was keen to 'interfere as little as possible with the Territorial and Regimental traditions to which so much importance is justly attached'.[18] Thus, after September 1916, Britain continued to be divided into seven regional Commands for the purposes of military administration, which in turn were divided into regimental recruiting areas,[19] and all regiments retained their regimental reserve battalions.[20]

On being called up, new recruits were posted to the regimental reserve units until they reached full strength. As the Army Council Instructions explained:

All general service recruits raised in an area and allotted to infantry will be appointed to the regiment affiliated to that area, and posted to a reserve battalion, Regular or TF, of that regiment so long as there are vacancies in the establishment of the Regimental reserves; surplus recruits in any area will then be allotted to other regiments in the same Command which have insufficient recruits in their area to fill the regimental reserves.[21]

As was the case before conscription, it was considered desirable that each area of a Command should supply recruits to specific regiments. When this was impractical, recruits could be assigned to a finite number of units within the wider Command, but would often still be allocated to a unit raised in the same county or district. Whilst the very specific localized recruiting to individual battalions could no longer be sustained, the general posting policy for new recruits was based on the regimental system, tied to local areas. Thus the regimental reserves for the King's (Liverpool) Regiment were likely to be composed of Lancashire men.

After all regimental reserves in a Command had been filled, surplus recruits were then assigned to the Training Reserve which provided drafts to front-line units if the regimental reserves were unable to provide sufficient numbers of trained men.[22] Basil Williams, in his book *Raising*

---

[18] War Office, *Organization and training*, 5.
[19] Britain was divided into Scottish Command (1 and 2), Western Command (3 and 4), Northern Command (5A, 5B and 6), Southern Command (7 and 8), Eastern Command (9) and London District.
[20] The 10th Liverpool Scottish retained its own reserve, and the third lines of the 5th and 6th Battalions amalgamated as a reserve battalion from September 1916.
[21] Army Council Instructions, 2020, 25 October 1916, Posting recruits who are called up from Class B. Army Reserve, or who come forward for service before being called up, on or after 1 November 1916, Army Council Instructions, PRO, WO 293/5.
[22] James, *British regiments in the First World War*, 129; B. Williams, *Raising and training the New Armies* (London, 1918), 126–30; and Army Council Instructions: 1528, 6 August 1916, Formation of a 'Training Reserve' and 2020, 25 October 1916, Posting recruits who are called up from Class B. Army Reserve, or who come forward for service before

and training the New Armies, explains that county uniformity could often be maintained even within Training Reserve Battalions. The Training Reserve was organized by each separate Command and their supply of men was 'kept up by recruits drawn from the whole area of the Command to which the brigades may be affiliated', and while the Training Reserve Battalions had no direct regimental connection, they were, in practice, used to provide drafts for 'a certain definite number of regiments'.[23]

The battalions of the King's (Liverpool) Regiment were helped in maintaining their county uniformity by the geographic structure of Western Command. The Command was divided into two administrative areas. The first (Area 3) was comprised of Lancashire, Cumberland and Westmorland, and the second (Area 4) covered Cheshire, Wales and Shropshire. If the Training Reserve Brigades serving the Liverpool Regiment drew their men from Area 3 of the Command, this would ensure that their supply of recruits remained Lancastrian; the other two counties, being sparsely populated, would have yielded few men.[24]

It was possibly the geographical composition of the seven recruiting areas in Great Britain that had the greatest influence on county homogeneity within battalions and can help to explain the differences between the Liverpool and Buckinghamshire Territorials. Whilst Lancashire dominated Western Command, other commands were composed of a greater number of counties, more sparsely populated. Buckinghamshire's section of Southern Command (Area 7) was formed from the six counties of Warwickshire, Worcestershire, Oxfordshire, Buckinghamshire, Herefordshire and Berkshire and the city of Bristol, with populations of different sizes. As the majority of recruits for the Command were drawn from the Birmingham Recruiting Area, Warwickshire battalions would have retained a large proportion of local men, but the same would not be true for those from Buckinghamshire, at the lower end of the population scale.[25] Out of necessity, Buckinghamshire battalions would have received men from all six counties.

being called up, on or after 1 November 1916, Army Council Instructions, PRO, WO 293/5. It should also be noted that the drafts trained within the Training Reserve were transferred to the regimental reserves of the battalion to which they were to be drafted, in order to finish their military training and be dispatched to the front. See Perry, *The Commonwealth armies*, 20, and Army Council Instructions, 1800, 15 September 1916, Procedure re: drafts from Training Reserve Battalions, Army Council Instructions, PRO, WO 293/5.

[23] Williams, *Raising and training the New Armies*, 131. Williams was a captain in the Territorial Artillery from 1915 and a major on the General Staff 1918–19. *Who was who 1941–1950* (vol. 4, London, 1952), 1236–7.

[24] For Command Areas see Consolidated Recruitment Tables, PRO, NATS/1/400.

[25] On 12 February 1916, 94 per cent of recruits raised in Western Command (Area 3) were from Lancashire. By contrast, Buckinghamshire and Oxfordshire raised only 12 per cent of

In general, the boundaries of the Commands corresponded roughly with local and county borders, and those living within each Command felt a sense of regional identity. For a minority of counties in Southern Command this was not the case. Bristol, Buckinghamshire and Warwickshire were very different entities which had been forced into one Command. They lacked the local loyalties that bound the various parts of Lancashire together.

On 1 November 1917 recruiting powers passed from the Army Council to the Ministry of National Service.[26] Under this new organization the recruiting areas were redrawn, utilizing regional boundaries. Among the more significant changes was a new North Western Recruiting Area comprising Lancashire and Cheshire only. Wales now stood alone, and Cumberland and Westmorland passed over to the Northern Recruiting Area. More cohesive sets of East Midland and West Midland counties were formed and Bristol was added to the South Western district. The only area that once again failed to cohere was that incorporating Buckinghamshire. The county now became one of ten in the East Anglian Region, alongside Essex, Bedfordshire, Hertfordshire, Huntingdonshire, Cambridgeshire, Norfolk, Suffolk, Berkshire and Oxfordshire.[27] As the recruits for the Training Reserve could be drawn from the whole area of a Command from September 1916 onwards, it follows that the greater the number of counties in a Command or Recruiting Area, the greater the potential for the disintegration of county homogeneity – a hypothesis borne out by the experience of the Buckinghamshire battalions.

And so we turn to the relative populations of the individual counties themselves. Lancashire, a large district, littered with urban conurbations, had a population of 1,739,320 in 1911. Buckinghamshire, being small and rural, had only 219,551 people living within its boundaries.[28] It is not

---

Southern Command's (Area 7) total, the county of Warwickshire providing 55 per cent. See Numbers of recruits raised in each recruiting area for week ending 12 February 1916, London, PRO, NATS/1/401. Similarly, on 25 June 1918, 70 per cent of recruits raised in the North Western Recruiting Area were from Lancashire, whereas only 7 per cent of recruits raised in the East Anglian region were from Oxfordshire and Buckinghamshire. See Numbers of recruits (classified grade 1) dispatched to Army Reception Depots, Naval Authorities or IDC on 25 June 1918, PRO, NATS/1/401.

[26] See Press Communiqué re: Ministry of National Service transferring powers of the Army Council, PRO, NATS/1/868.
[27] See Consolidated Tables, PRO, NATS/1/401.
[28] The population figures quoted here refer to the total population living within the administrative boundaries of each county, and not solely to the number of men of fighting age. They are merely a crude index to show the difference in scale between the two populations. *Census of England and Wales, 1911, Index to the population tables* (London, 1913), vol. 5.

Table 4.2 *Percentage of soldiers who died in fourteen Territorial battalions who enlisted in the unit's home county*

Battalion (and recruiting area)	1915	1916	1917	1918
6th Liverpools (Liverpool, d. areas, Lancashire)	100	100	83	70
10th Liverpools (Liverpool, d. areas, Lancashire)	100	92.5	91	87
1/1st Buckinghamshires (Buckinghamshire)	64	77	46	39
1/4th Ox. and Bucks. (Oxfordshire)	91	86	57	46
1/7th West Yorkshire (Yorkshire)	98	94	76	71
1/8th Leeds (Yorkshire)	97	89	72	67
1/6th Manchesters (Lancashire)	100	100	100	88
1/8th Manchesters (Lancashire)	99.5	100	98	82
1/7th Warwickshires (Warwickshire)	100	91	56	61
1/5th Gloucesters (Gloucestershire)	89	74	52	43
1/6th Gloucesters (Gloucestershire)	–	98	60	61
1/4th Wiltshires (Wiltshire)	89	89	93	53
1/5th Norfolks (Norfolk)	99	100	91	76
1/4th Berkshires (Berkshire)	94	89	60	62

Source: Statistics derived from War Office, *Soldiers died in the Great War*, vols. 11, 13, 14, 19, 33, 47, 52, 58 and 59 (London, 1920). All battalions selected spent a proportion of their career serving on the Western Front.

surprising that, even from the beginning of the war, the Liverpool units contained higher percentages of men from their county, compared with the Buckinghamshire units, which had relatively low percentages of men from their traditional recruiting areas (see Table 4.2). Whilst Liverpool had more units to supply, raising five times more Territorial battalions than Buckinghamshire, as well as having a greater number of men in reserved occupations, its reservoir of recruits was infinitely larger. This ensured that the erosion of county homogeneity in the Liverpolitan battalions took longer and was less successful than in the Buckinghamshire units.

Drafting the reinforcements

The recruitment strategies in Britain centred on the regiment and promoted county uniformity in most regimental and training reserve battalions, but this alone did not guarantee county homogeneity in units at the front. Equally important were the drafting procedures. In previous conflicts, drafts to front-line battalions had been found from within the wider regiment, but historians believe that this type of drafting system collapsed during the First World War under the sheer weight of casualties.[29] However, for the Liverpool Territorials to preserve their regional character throughout the war it follows that their drafts must have been consistently drawn from some locally homogeneous source, if not a regiment then at least a regional Command.

Any investigation of the drafting system relies heavily on the evidence provided by the casualty books of the Liverpool Rifles, which list the unit of origin of all major drafts to the Battalion during the latter years of the war.[30] The casualty books show that between 12 September 1917 and 12 November 1918 there were 1433 men drafted to the Battalion in a series of large drafts. Seventy-nine per cent of the drafts were from various battalions of the King's (Liverpool) Regiment (see Table 4.3).

It is significant that such a large percentage of the drafts came from the Liverpool Regiment, particularly as many battalions of the Regiment served in different divisions. For example, whilst the first-line Territorial battalions served in the 55th West Lancashire Division from January 1916 until the cessation of hostilities, the 1st regular Battalion served in the 6th Brigade, Second Division, the 13th Service Battalion served in the 3rd Division, and the 17th and 19th Battalions served in the 30th Division until June 1918. Thus there was no obvious divisional link between the drafts, suggesting that regimental connection was the most important factor in determining the drafting of men, even as late as 1918.

Indeed, Lieutenant General Sir Nevil Macready, who served as the Adjutant General at the War Office between 1916 and 1918, also stressed the importance of the regiment in drafting. In his memoirs, Macready explained the method of drafting employed in 1916:

What actually happens is that France indents us for the number of men required per battalion and we send them out by *regiments*. That is to say, we may send out to

---

[29] H. Strachan, *The politics of the British Army* (Oxford, 1997), 207.
[30] 1/6th Battalion King's (Liverpool) Regiment Casualty Books 1–3, KRC, MLL, 58.83.537a–b. The first two books contain the service records of most casualties between 1915 and 1917 and are entered alphabetically. This method of recording casualties makes it difficult to identify which man arrived with which draft. However, the third casualty book dispenses with the alphabetical organization and lists each new man in chronological order as he joined the first line of the 6th Battalion between September 1917 and the end of the war. It is therefore feasible to analyse the numbers of men in drafts and the units from which the drafts were transferred. Nevertheless, the draft lists in the third book are not complete. They exclude men returning to the Battalion from hospital or after being attached to another unit. The return of soldiers in these categories would have been recorded under their original service record entry in books 1 or 2. As those who served with the Liverpool Rifles in the early years of the war were more likely to have had connections with Liverpool and Lancashire, it follows that the numbers of Lancastrians joining the Battalion between September 1917 and October 1918 will be underestimated in any calculations.

Table 4.3 *Origin of men drafted to the 1/6th Battalion, King's (Liverpool) Regiment, 12 September 1917 to 12 November 1918*

Type of draft	Battalion	Number of men drafted
King's Liverpool Regiment		
Regular battalions	1st Battalion	26
	4th Battalion	11
Territorial battalions	1/5th Battalion	11
	2/5th Battalion	16
	1/6th Battalion	186
	2/6th Battalion	16
	1/7th Battalion	31
	2/7th Battalion	14
	1/8th Battalion	248
	2/8th Battalion	1
	1/9th Battalion	39
	3rd West Lancs. RE	1
Service battalions	11th Battalion	3
	12th Battalion	49
	13th Battalion	46
	17th Battalion	65
	18th Battalion	206
	19th Battalion	4
	20th Battalion	12
	25th Battalion	17
	26th Battalion	26
Graduated battalions	51st Battalion	21
	52nd Battalion	81
Drafts from other regiments		
	229 Infantry Battalion	72
	225 Infantry Battalion	5
	Labour Corps	1
	10th Lincoln	10
	8th North Staffords	10
	2/6th North Staffords	22
	2/6th South Staffords	11
	1/4th Leicesters	1
	11th East Lancashires	39
	1st Sherwood Foresters	3
	52nd Sherwood Foresters	100
	51st Welsh	29

Source: Statistics derived from 1/6th Battalion King's (Liverpool) Regiment Casualty Book 3, KRC, MLL, 58.83.537a–b

France 1000 men belonging to one regiment and when they arrive in France they are drafted to such battalions of that regiment as are likely to require to be made up to full strength at once in conformity with the plans of the General Staff.[31]

It must be noted that Macready also acknowledged that in a war of massive casualties regimental drafting was not always possible. In some instances, only nationality, rather than county affiliation, could be taken into account.[32] This was particularly true for the smaller regiments. It is understandable that the King's (Liverpool) Regiment, which boasted some forty battalions, should have had much greater scope to juggle its manpower requirements than the Oxfordshire and Buckinghamshire Light Infantry composed of only sixteen battalions. For this reason it was less likely that individual Liverpool battalions would be forced to accept drafts from another regiment and almost inevitable that a Buckinghamshire battalion would have to integrate foreign reinforcements.

When we examine Table 4.3 we see that even battalions belonging to as large a regiment as the King's Liverpools were forced to accept drafts from other regiments. The 6th Rifles' casualty book shows that 21 per cent of the Battalion's drafts were derived from units with no affiliation to their parent regiment. However, the timing of these drafts is significant: they were added to the Liverpool Rifles after it had suffered very heavy casualties. The drafts from the 10th Lincolns, 8th North Staffordshires, 2/6th North Staffordshires, 2/6th South Staffordshires, 1/4th Leicesters and 229 Infantry Battalion arrived on 12 and 13 September 1917, after the Battalion had suffered 251 casualties during the first phase of the Third Battle of Ypres (31 July–2 August). As the Battalion was expected to participate in an attack on 18 September, rapid reinforcement was necessary. Between September 1917 and April 1918 only three men from 229 Infantry Brigade and thirty-nine men from the 11th East Lancashires were drafted to the Liverpool Rifles. The remainder of the drafts were from the King's (Liverpool) Regiment.[33]

The second influx of 'foreign' drafts was absorbed by the Liverpool Rifles between 17 and 21 April 1918. One hundred men from the 52nd Nottinghamshire and Derbyshire Regiment (Sherwoods) and twenty-nine men from the 51st Welsh Regiment were drafted as reinforcements to replace the 197 men lost during the defence of Givenchy between 9 and 15 April 1918. As in September, the Battalion did not have a long period

---

[31] General the Rt Hon. Sir Nevil Macready, *Annals of an active life* (2 vols., London, 1924), 257.
[32] *Ibid.*
[33] For an analysis of how outsiders integrated into units see chapters 6 and 7. 1/6th Battalion King's (Liverpool) Regiment Casualty Book 3, KRC, MLL, 58.83.537a–b; 1/6th Battalion King's (Liverpool) Regiment War Diary, KRC, MLL, 58.83.501.

of time in which to reinforce. They were needed back in the trenches on 27 April at Festubert. It appears, therefore, that under such circumstances the Battalion had to accept drafts from other regiments.[34]

From April 1918 to the Armistice, the Battalion was more fortunate in that it only accepted drafts from the King's (Liverpool) Regiment, despite suffering 205 casualties in June and 103 in September, and having virtually no time to reinforce.[35] Thus, it may be the case that it was only during times of great stress along the whole British front that the policy of matching drafts to units of their parent regiment broke down. This policy is also reflected in the drafting records of the 10th Liverpool Scottish Battalion for 1916. A roll of men who were attached to other units indicates that 147 were sent to the 9th King's (Liverpool) Battalion, twenty-three to the 5th Battalion and 200 to the 13th Battalion.[36] Only forty-nine men were sent to the 21st Manchesters, and these men were needed urgently because of the high casualty toll, resulting from a raid in June which left the Manchesters too weak to perform their role in the Somme Offensive on 1 July.[37]

The experience of the Liverpool Territorials suggests that the battle experience of a unit was also an important factor affecting the local composition of a unit. Where possible, regimental drafts were matched to their parent battalions in the front line, but during major offensives, when casualties were high and drafts at a premium, the regional composition of reinforcements for specific units could not be guaranteed. They would often be dictated by the availability of drafts from home, the number of other units of a regiment competing for reinforcements, the magnitude of the replacements needed and the urgency with which a unit was required back in the trenches. Some units were simply unluckier than others in both the number and the timing of their casualties.

A final influence on the drafting system was highlighted by Ian Macpherson, the Under Secretary of State for War, who explained the power politicians could wield with regard to the drafting procedure. In November 1917 he told the House of Commons that he had received letters of complaint about the drafting system from Territorial battalions raised in his own constituency. He had complained to the authorities

---

[34] For an analysis of how outsiders integrated into units see chapters 6 and 7. 1/6th Battalion King's (Liverpool) Regiment Casualty Book 3, KRC, MLL, 58.83.537a–b; 1/6th Battalion King's (Liverpool) Regiment War Diary, KRC, MLL, 58.83.501.

[35] For an analysis of how outsiders integrated into units see chapters 6 and 7. 1/6th Battalion King's (Liverpool) Regiment Casualty Book 3, KRC, MLL, 58.83.537a–b; 1/6th Battalion King's (Liverpool) Regiment War Diary, KRC, MLL, 58.83.501.

[36] Draft Book, 10th Liverpool Scottish, King's (Liverpool) Regiment, 1914–16, LSM, Acc. No. 19.

[37] Old Comrades Committee, *The 21st Battalion of the Manchester Regiment: a history* (Manchester, 1934), 10.

as an ordinary MP and they had done their best to draft men to regiments with which they identified.[38] The Liverpool Territorials possessed an even more powerful ally. Edward George Villers Stanley, 17th earl of Derby, was intimately connected with the recruiting process in Liverpool, being the chairman of the West Lancashire Territorial Association and the driving force behind the raising of the numerous Service battalions in Lancashire. At the same time, Derby was also a national figure. In 1915 he was appointed as Director General of Recruiting, progressing to Under Secretary of State for War in June 1916 and Secretary of State for War from December 1916. He finished his war as the British Ambassador to France. In all these various roles, Derby wielded great power amongst the politicians and military commanders of his day, counting many of the most influential amongst his personal friends.[39]

Derby was one of the last great examples of the patrician culture in action. He was anxious to protect the interests of his men and was not reticent in demanding favours. In September 1915, Derby urged Kitchener to keep his units 'as Lancashire as possible'.[40] He was also instrumental in establishing a Lancashire company of the Inns of Court Officer Training Corps which guaranteed a steady supply of Lancashire officers for Lancashire regiments.[41]

Derby maintained contact with the generals commanding the Lancashire formations. He corresponded unofficially with General Sir Ian Hamilton during the Gallipoli campaign in an attempt to replenish Lancashire brigades with Lancashire men.[42] He also communicated with Major General H. S. Jeudwine of the 55th West Lancashire Division, who shared his views on the value of county homogeneity. The link between the two men was strengthened by the appointment of Major Milner, Derby's school friend and former director of his household, as Jeudwine's aide de camp. It was suggested in Parliament that 'sloppy staff work' was a key factor causing the transfer of men to alien regiments.[43] An active policy in the 55th West Lancashire Division to promote regional feeling and uniformity, emanating from the Divisional Commander and

---

[38] *Hansard, Parliamentary Debates*, 5th Series, XCVII, Wood, Fox and MacPherson, November 1917, 1565. Ian MacPherson was MP for Ross and Cromarty.

[39] R. S. Churchill, *Lord Derby, King of Lancashire* (London, 1959).

[40] K. Grieves, 'Lord Derby in Liverpool; military recruitment and dock labour', paper given at Liverpool and the First World War Conference, Merseyside Maritime Museum, Liverpool, 21 November 1998.

[41] Derby to Lieutenant General Sir F. Robb, 6 August 1915, Derby Papers, LRO, 920 DER (17) 26/4.

[42] K. Grieves, 'Lord Derby in Liverpool; military recruitment and dock labour'.

[43] *Hansard, Parliamentary Debates*, 5th Series, XCVII, Wood, Fox and MacPherson, November 1917, 1558.

backed by senior staff officers, would have ensured that 'sloppy staff work' was kept to a minimum.

The Buckinghamshire battalions lacked similar influential champions. Their Territorial Association, led by Colonel Lord Cottesloe, remained impotent in the face of amalgamations.[44] Cottesloe, although a former Assistant Secretary to the Secretary of State for War between 1900 and 1903, no longer wielded influence in government or the army in the same way as Lord Derby. However, whilst individual personalities, civilian and military, undoubtedly made a difference, they alone could not personally alter the destinations of hundreds of thousands of drafts. The county homogeneity of the Liverpool battalions could not have been maintained without the necessary administrative structure to recruit and guide Lancashire men to Lancashire units.

Unit amalgamations

The final factor affecting county homogeneity in battalions was unit amalgamation. Whilst there were a number of amalgamations between 1915 and 1917, the greatest number took place between January and March 1918 when each division in France was reduced from twelve battalions to nine in response to the manpower shortage. Those disbanded were often privately raised units such as the Pals battalions or second-line Territorial units.[45] Amalgamations usually occurred between battalions of the same regiment, and this was certainly the case for the Liverpool Territorials.[46] The 6th Rifles absorbed men from a number of second-line units of the Liverpool Territorials, whilst the Liverpool Scottish were even more fortunate to absorb their own second-line battalion, thus renewing not only their regional character, but some of their social characteristics as well. All King's Territorials remained in the King's Regiment, which undoubtedly helped to sustain county homogeneity in the remaining battalions.

Other units were not so fortunate. Ian Beckett documented a number of amalgamations that caused deep resentment amongst the troops. He cites parliamentary debates in which the amalgamation and disbandment of Territorial units is lamented,[47] and there is no doubt that the Territorial

---

[44] Beckett., 'The Territorial Force', 149.
[45] See Perry, *The commonwealth armies*, 28. Second-line Territorial units were a logical choice for disbandment, as often they had less front-line experience than their first-line counterparts.
[46] HQ Directorate of Organization 1914–18, AG2 Drafts and Reliefs, PRO, WO162/6, 130.
[47] See *Hansard, Parliamentary Debates*, 5th Series, LXXII, Rolleston and Tennant, 28 June 1915, 1474, LXXIII, MacCallum and Tennant, 15 July 1915, 994–5, XCIV, Allen and MacPherson, 11 June 1917, 626.

battalions suffered a disproportionate number of amalgamations throughout the war. This treatment rankled to such an extent amongst the Territorial leadership that it was to colour all post-war discussions about the future role of the Territorials.[48]

There was undoubtedly dissatisfaction amongst Territorial soldiers regarding the methods of drafting and amalgamation of battalions. Complaints arrived at the War Office through military channels, directly through letters from soldiers or their families and through Parliamentary Questions.[49] Yet the majority of these complaints had more to do with the loss of battalion integrity than with concerns about the decline in local homogeneity within units. Although battalions belonged to the same regiment they were often very individualistic, possessing different traditions and different social characteristics. Soldiers were always going to be dissatisfied if they were posted to battalions with which they were unfamiliar, and similarly, battalions were disgruntled when first receiving drafts who possessed different social backgrounds and were imbued with different traditions. This was particularly true for the early Territorial soldiers who had enlisted prior to the Military Service Acts in 1916 and who had signed up on the condition that they would not be transferred to another unit without their permission.[50]

However, the system that recruited, drafted and amalgamated soldiers was not the arbitrary or dysfunctional process that has been described in previous studies.[51] Although nationalizing the recruitment and drafting processes would have made life much easier at the War Office, there was a recognition that localism was a very powerful force that needed to be conserved where possible. In 1917, the Under Secretary of State for War, Ian MacPherson, explained the government position. He told the House of Commons: 'I am perfectly convinced that it was the Territorial instinct before the war and for a long time after, which gave this country the power which it has and which inspires its troops to gallantry ... if transfers have taken place it has been for one reason only, because of the urgent necessity of military exigencies at the front.'[52]

---

[48] Beckett., 'The Territorial Force', 138.
[49] HQ Directorate of Organization 1914–18, AG2 Drafts and Reliefs, PRO, WO162/6, 131–2.
[50] See chapter 6.
[51] Beckett, 'The Territorial Force', 147; Fuller, *Troop morale and popular culture*, 43–4; Perry, *The commonwealth armies*, 20; Strachan, *The politics of the British Army*, 207.
[52] *Hansard, Parliamentary Debates*, 5th Series, XCVII, Wood, Fox and MacPherson, November 1917, 1565. This contradicts the belief of Captain Dunn, P. Simkins and J. Fuller that the authorities were actively attempting to draft men to units which were unconnected to their area of origin.

How far local and county uniformity could be maintained within Territorial battalions depended on many factors, including the size and population of the county of origin and the experience of the battalion, but as Table 4.2 indicates, the majority of Territorial units across the country followed the pattern of the Liverpool battalions and retained their county affiliation to the end of the war.

The importance of county homogeneity to Territorial units

Ian MacPherson was correct to identify the importance of the Territorial instinct as a motivational and cohesive force within the army. Localism had been a key part of the Territorial psyche for many years, and the pre-war Force had been recruited on the assumption that each battalion would defend its home area in the event of an invasion of Britain. Indeed, much of the training of the Liverpool Scottish was devoted to the protection of their seaport.[53] Haldane's grand hopes to use the Territorial Force as a means of expanding and reinforcing the regular army overseas had been diminished by successive political compromises.[54] The Force was sold to the public in 1908 as a home defence force, and it was to this idea that the members subscribed.

At battalion level, recruitment tactics reflected the sense of responsibility felt towards local defence, which permeated Territorial thinking before 1914. A father wrote to congratulate his son on joining the Liverpool Scottish: 'Your sister says she does not want her garden trampled over by a foreigner and looks to you to take your share in protecting it. Her hyacinths are doing splendidly.'[55] This lighthearted letter was published in the *Liverpool Scottish Regimental Gazette* with the serious aim of stimulating recruiting, suggesting that, in the opinion of battalion command, the protection of the home was a strong motivating factor encouraging enlistment.

The men too viewed their function purely as the protection of the local. The invitation to take up the voluntary Imperial Service Obligation to serve overseas was eschewed by most pre-war Territorials.[56] If they were motivated by any sense of duty at all, it was the notion of home defence

---

[53] *Liverpool Scottish Regimental Gazette*, January 1913.
[54] Beckett, 'The Territorial Force in the Great War', in P. H. Liddle (ed.), *Home fires and foreign field: British social and military experience in the First World War* (London, 1985), 21; E. M. Spiers, *Haldane: an army reformer* (Edinburgh, 1980), 92–115.
[55] *Liverpool Scottish Regimental Gazette*, July 1912.
[56] Beckett, 'The Territorial Force', in Beckett and Simpson (eds.), *A nation in arms*, 129.

that was uppermost in the Territorial temperament, and remained a potent feature of Territorialism throughout the conflict.

On the outbreak of war, the attachment to the concept of home defence became a double-edged sword: it both promoted and inhibited the formation of effective Territorial units. Many men needed to be persuaded forcefully to volunteer for foreign service. Some refused to serve abroad and were replaced by new volunteers, and a minority of men enlisted for home service only.[57] This Territorial tradition, interpreted narrowly, allowed men to opt out of overseas service until the Military Service Act of January 1916, causing disruption and discontent amongst the battalions preparing to fight abroad.

Other men viewed the concept of home defence in a wider context. Private Francis, serving with the Liverpool Scottish in Belgium, believed strongly that he was helping to prevent an invasion of Liverpool. The belief sustained him when crouching, knee deep in a waterlogged trench, for hours at a time. After one such episode he wrote to his family, 'Christmas will be upon us before I write again. I know you will feel a little low spirited, but think of the homeless Belgians. When I remember we are protecting our homes from the same fate I could bear all the ... discomforts cheerfully.'[58]

The idea of local men fighting side by side in local regiments to defend their local area was invested with enormous power. It was connected with a fundamental desire to protect their home, and by association their local community, city and county, helping to reinforce the determination to fight to the end of the conflict.

Volunteering was also an expression of civic loyalty.[59] Despite Liverpool's torturous social problems, many men regarded their home city with great affection and were proud of its achievements in the commercial and shipping spheres. Whilst soldiers identified most strongly with their homes, families and immediate localities, the local community was inevitably linked to the wider city. For the previous sixty years Victorian identity builders, in the form of city aldermen, had been at work in Liverpool, creating a sense of place.[60] The imposing commercial architecture was supplemented by grand public buildings, museums, galleries and libraries which, together with local newspapers and sporting teams, came to represent the city of Liverpool.[61] As most soldiers had

---

[57] McGilchrist, *The Liverpool Scottish*, 14.
[58] Undated cutting from *Liverpool Echo*, December 1914, Private Francis to family in J. Bedford, With the Liverpool Scottish, Scrapbook 1, LSM, Acc. No. 476.
[59] Peel, 'The Territorial Force', 48.
[60] Colls, *Identity of England*, 226.
[61] Ward Lock and Co., *A guide to Liverpool and Birkenhead*, 2–11.

grown to adulthood on the banks of the Mersey, Liverpool, the place and its reputation, had become an integral part of their identity. Indeed, as previously noted, men living as far afield as Canada and Australia felt compelled to return to the city of their birth to enlist.[62] When men went to war to protect their city, it was not an abstract construct they were defending. The threat to Liverpool represented a threat not only to their families, their livelihood and their positions, but to their whole sense of being. It is thus understandable that civic pride, which helped to encapsulate these feelings, was important to the soldiers at the front.

A sense of the wider county was also discernible in 1914.[63] Since their revival as a physical location in the 1880s, counties had increased in importance. It was not only the army that was organized on a county basis, but constabularies and even some unions. County histories were rewritten, county antiquarian societies were established and county cricket and rugby were played.[64]

Liverpool, as the leading port and commercial centre in the county of Lancashire, imported raw materials to be processed by its satellites and exported their finished products. A symbiotic relationship existed between the Lancashire towns and their capital. Together they had raised their county to national prominence during the Industrial Revolution, gaining disproportionate power and influence within Britain, and around the world. At a regional level, in 1914 Lancastrian cities were rivals and defined themselves in opposition to each other. Indeed, in prizing commerce over industry, Liverpool sat apart from the rest of Lancashire. But at the national level, towns and cities of the county were united by a common antipathy towards southern England, whose monopolistic commercial practices were resented and perceived as a threat to Lancashire's position.[65] This national rivalry, as well as the developments in county organization and institutions, had ensured that Lancashire was viewed as a meaningful concept by the Territorials of the Great War. It is not surprising that, for most Lancastrians, strong identification with their home town or city could also be accompanied by pride in their county.[66]

---

[62] Liverpool Scottish Other Ranks' Index, LSM.
[63] Peel, 'The Territorial Force', 48.
[64] Colls, *Identity of England*, 226.
[65] The Liverpool Organisation, *Book of Liverpool civic week*, 8; Belchem, '"An accent exceedingly rare"', 108.
[66] J. K. Walton and L. Castells have suggested that the north-west region failed to form its own identity because of the disparate industries and societal structures that existed in Lancashire towns. As a result of this, they argue that only civic and national loyalties were motivating factors in the Great War. The following evidence in this chapter challenges Walton's interpretation, suggesting that pride in and identification with town, county and nation were all-important to the Liverpool Territorials. See J. K. Walton and L. Castells,

The first advantage that military units gained from civic or county homogeneity was therefore motivational, but there were other benefits too. Localism could help to enhance fighting performance by facilitating the establishment of mutual trust within individual units and within component parts of a formation. Mutual trust and confidence within the rank and file of a unit as well as between leaders and led were essential in trench warfare, which often required the devolution of tactical control and the exercise of initiative at the lowest levels.[67] Addressing a parliamentary audience in 1917, the Under Secretary of State for War claimed that, 'There is no doubt that a man who is fighting with men of his own unit ... is a far better fighter than a man who is placed haphazard under the command of an officer he has never heard of, or in association with men whose instincts and views are entirely different and apart.'[68]

Given the marked regional differences in dialect and attitudes that existed in 1914, these observations are unsurprising. Local homogeneity provided a strong base on which to build mutual confidence to produce effective units. Men who came from the same area, at the very least shared an interest in their home town and in many cases a similar outlook. A letter sent to the *Liverpool Echo* by Private Johnson of the Liverpool Scottish highlights the importance of this rapport. He wrote: 'It is wonderful what a lot of Liverpools one meets in the Service ... a red cross man will see the shoulder plate and ask you can you do with a pint of Cains? Or as happened this morning someone will shout, "how is Everton going to do this year?"'[69]

The insidious parochialism, described by Peter Simkins in his book on the raising of the New Armies,[70] was not recorded to the same extent amongst the Liverpolitan Territorials. However, his examples warn us that civic and particularly county homogeneity could foster rivalry and exclusion, as well as cohesion. Certainly, a common regional background did not guarantee automatic acceptance for the officers of the Liverpool Pals who were attached to the Liverpool Scottish in September 1915.[71] Similarly, individual units of the Pals and Territorials did not always see

---

'Contrasting identities: north-west England and the Basque Country, 1840–1936', and E. Royle, 'Regions and identities', both in E. Royle (ed.), *Issues of regional identity in honour of John Marshall* (Manchester, 1998), 45–77 and 1–14.

[67] See chapter 6.
[68] *Hansard, Parliamentary Debates*, 5th Series, XCVII, Wood, Fox and MacPherson, November 1917, 1565.
[69] Undated cutting from *Liverpool Echo*, December 1914, Private Tom Johnston, Liverpool Scottish, in J. Bedford, With the Liverpool Scottish, Scrapbook 1, LSM, Acc. No. 476.
[70] Simkins, *Kitchener's army*, 208–9.
[71] Lieutenant Colonel Davidson, as previously described, wrote angry letters to the High Command over the attachment of Liverpool Pals officers to his Battalion. See J. R. Davidson to Colonel Blair, 18/9/15, in uncatalogued scrapbook, LSM.

eye to eye. Some Service battalions had been trained by 'dugout' regular officers and NCOs, which facilitated identification with regular rather than Territorial units, and the Territorials' pre-war reputation for inefficiency did not help the bonding process.[72] Major McGilchrist remembered:

> There was a great deal of stupid jealousy in the earlier stages of the war between the Territorials and Kitchener's Army. Those Territorials who had borne the brunt of the first winter looked upon themselves as being almost in the veteran class, [and] resented the superior air which some members of Kitchener's Army affected ... Kitchener's Army, on the other hand, were horrified at the indignity of being taught their job by mere Territorials and were not very willing pupils. One of them made the mistake in an estaminet one night, of dropping a disparaging remark to a Lincoln about the Liverpool Scottish ... The Lincoln warned him to be careful of what he said about the 'Lincolnshire' Scottish, and emphasising his point with a bottle, temporarily reduced the strength of the 12th Manchesters by one.[73]

The Liverpool Scottish had fought alongside six regular battalions, including the Lincolnshires, for nine months and had slowly gained their respect, which explains the vociferous response of the Lincoln.

The problems between Service and Territorial battalions were solved, to some extent, by the formation of the 55th (West Lancashire) Territorial Division in January 1916. Although many of the subsequent drafts to the Territorials came from Pals units, the majority of hostile comments were restricted to the months following the arrival of the Service battalions in France. The animosity was superficial and short-lived, generated by the inevitable initial jostling for military position and public recognition.

Intimate jokes and references to Liverpool abounded in both Battalions during the war. The Rifles recreated Liverpool city centre in the small village of Vaux during October 1915. 'The officers you will find billeted in the Angel and they look out on a very doubtful Exchange Flags. Then there is Dale Street leading to Abercromby Square and a manure heap that would make the original blush.'[74] This was no random allocation of street names; they closely mirrored the layout of Liverpool's commercial centre. In November 1917, labelling of billets and trenches was still in evidence, with the Brigade Headquarters of the Liverpool Scottish being known as the Adelphi.[75] All names had one thing in common: they described universally known landmarks of the city, with which all

---

[72] Beckett, 'The Territorial Force', 129 and 140.
[73] McGilchrist, *The Liverpool Scottish*, 52.
[74] N. F. Ellison to mother and father, 7 October 1915, Ellison Papers, IWM, DS/MISC/49; see also S. E. Gordon, Memoir, 12 October 1915, Gordon Papers, IWM, 77/5/1, 144.
[75] W. G. Bromley, Memoir, November 1917, Bromley Papers, LSM, Acc. No. 544. The Adelphi was a famous hotel in Liverpool city centre.

members were familiar. The names also reflected general norms within Liverpool, and were allocated according to the social connotations they engendered, the brigade headquarters being designated, perhaps a little facetiously, as the most exclusive hotel the city could offer.

It was not only the landscape that was described in terms of home; the experience of the trenches was also expressed in terms of mundane activities connected with Liverpool. Private Taylor remembered his first surprise of the salient: 'it reminded me of being a commuter to Exchange Station in Liverpool on my way to the Cunard Offices';[76] and Sergeant Macfie described his Battalion's return from the trenches in December 1914 in similar terms: 'We do not walk erect, or step out with a soldier like stride. We slouch along at the rate you would walk down Bold Street if you were half an hour early for your train ... many are lame and we would make a terribly depressing picture.'[77]

These practices kept the memory of Liverpool alive, but they were more than simply a reminder of home. They allowed the Territorials to assert their civilian identity through using civilian labels in a military setting. More importantly, perhaps, they also constituted a coping mechanism for dealing with the strangeness of the trenches, and the often confusing contrast between front and rear. In the changing world of the battalion, where death was random and certainty had evaporated, there was a need to describe the experience using comprehensible metaphors. To describe France in terms of Liverpool landmarks helped to normalize their environment.

The mechanism worked on one level by rendering the strange familiar. If wartime experiences and landscape could be described in terms of home, then they did not appear so alien. Familiarity was comforting and reduced the impact of frightening or depressing periods abroad. When a Lancashire Hussar rode past a Liverpool Scot in the winter of 1914 yelling, 'Good lads. It's a bit colder here than Sefton Park isn't it?'[78] he was understating the bone-chilling weather conditions. The middle-class men of the Liverpool Scottish were experiencing their first gruelling winter in stinking trenches, remembered afterwards as the worst of the war, causing many frostbite casualties and utter misery amongst the rank and file. The reference to windswept Sefton Park, another familiar feature of the Liverpool landscape, somehow made the situation more bearable.

[76] H. S. Taylor, Memoir, Liddle Collection (G. S.), 30.
[77] R. A. S. Macfie to sister, 26 December 1914, Macfie Papers, IWM, Con. Shelf.
[78] Undated cutting from *Liverpool Echo*, December 1914, in J. Bedford, With the Liverpool Scottish, Scrapbook 1, LSM, Acc. No. 476.

As the war progressed, the social and local composition of the battalions changed and instinctive understanding between soldiers became even more important to the effectiveness of a unit. Whilst the first generation of Territorials had learned to trust each other during months on the training grounds of Britain, drafts and veterans had to find ways to rebuild the cohesion of their unit quickly to resume their place in the line. A shared local identity was a place to begin. By 1917 the common point of reference had expanded to the county. Thus, whilst references to Liverpool were current within the Battalions to the end of the war, other, more inclusive, representations of the county were also employed to perform similar functions to the civic labelling.

Blackpool provided a popular reference point, well known to most members of both Battalions, as either their home town, their training camp or a holiday destination.[79] Private Campbell described the feelings of his fellow soldiers as they marched back from an attack in 1916: 'The sign of sand on the roads seemed to herald the sea and reminded the boys of Blackpool.'[80] Further reminders were placed in their canteen at Gouy in the form of 'large posters of Blackpool exhibiting pleasure and sunshine' to 'create as much comfort as possible'.[81]

Lord Derby acted as another symbol of home to many men. He had close personal relationships with many officers' families, being part of the same social network, but his near universal appeal was generated by his civic, county and Territorial roles in civilian life. As a former Lord Mayor of Liverpool, as a landowner and thus landlord for large tracts of land throughout Lancashire, as the chairman of the West Lancashire Territorial Association, and through his personal direction of recruiting campaigns in the county, he was a recognizable figure to the men. More than just a figurehead, Derby was a man who involved himself practically with the welfare of the men and was appreciated for his efforts.[82] He was not, of course, universally accepted, but the fact that his visits to the front were favourably recorded in the diaries of officers and men, conscripts and volunteers alike, suggests that his potency both as a regional figure and as a link with home was strong amongst the men.[83]

The value of county loyalty for promoting cohesion, fostering fighting spirit and developing pride in military formations was also recognized by those in authority. County identity was to be used as the citizen soldier's

---

[79] J. K. Walton, *Lancashire: a social history* (Manchester, 1987), 295.
[80] W. H. Campbell, Diary, 16 July 1916, LSM, Acc. No. 484.
[81] W. H. Campbell, Diary, 19 August 1916, LSM, Acc. No. 484.
[82] S. E. Gordon, Memoir, 10 August 1914, Gordon Papers, IWM, 77/5/1, 22.
[83] See chapter 5 for the importance of links with home.

equivalent of regimental loyalty. Major General Jeudwine, commanding the 55th West Lancashire Division, sought to reinforce and thus capitalize on the latent regional feeling existing in his command, through the use of more abstract images than those which had emerged from the ranks.

For example, the rose of Lancaster was adopted as a divisional badge in 1916. An ancient symbol of the region, the rose came to be omnipresent, being used as an identification mark on guns and on transport and as a badge sewn on the shoulder of every member. From June 1918 it was imprinted on metal plaques, which were placed on the graves of all the dead of the Division, and it furnished the Divisional Concert Party with their name, the Red Roses.[84] Jeudwine claimed, 'so great was the pride in the badge that no more dreaded a punishment could be awarded for slackness ... than to order the individual to remove the rose from his shoulders or the unit to erase it from its transport',[85] the implication being that the absence of the rose was a badge of shame and an indication that they had failed not only their division, but also their county and their families.

We ought to treat this statement as self-congratulatory. Whilst Jeudwine's assertions undoubtedly contained elements of truth, in reality the badge was not always easy to acquire, and loyalty to the symbol was exaggerated. Theoretically, the shoulder badges were provided free of charge from Divisional funds[86] and distributed through canteens, but in March 1918 they were still difficult to obtain. Sergeant Macfie remembered bitterly the stinging reprimand issued to the Quartermasters' departments in 166th Brigade over the absence of divisional badges at an inspection. In this instance, the rose of Lancaster served to generate ill-feeling, rather than fostering *esprit de corps*.[87]

Nevertheless, Jeudwine's faith in the motivating power of the rose was not entirely misplaced. It was not simply a symbol imposed from above, but one that was accepted and utilized by the rank and file in imaginative ways. The badge inspired Lieutenant Wall of the 275th West Lancashire Brigade to compose a poem. The last line of the final verse, 'We win or die

---

[84] Lieutenant General H. S. Jeudwine, General information on the adoption of the red rose of Lancaster as the Divisional symbol, Records of the 55th (West Lancashire) Division, 1914–19, LRO, 356 FIF 54/5; Clayton, *Chavasse*, 177.

[85] Lieutenant General H. S. Jeudwine, General information on the adoption of the red rose of Lancaster as the divisional symbol, Records of the 55th (West Lancashire) Division, 1914–19, LRO, 356 FIF 54/5.

[86] Lecture on operations at Givenchy–Festubert, 9 April 1918; notes regarding General Sir Hugh Jeudwine's Lecture, RMC Sandhurst, 1928, Records of the 55th (West Lancashire) Division, LRO, 356 FIF 54/5, 23.

[87] R. A. S. Macfie, Order from Brigadier General Kentish, 166 Brigade, to Os. C. Coys and T.O.I/C Hdqrs Q.M., 23/3/1918, Macfie Papers, IWM, Con. Shelf.

who wear the rose of Lancaster', was adopted as the divisional motto. The poem struck a chord with those at the front and at home alike, and appeared in Liverpolitan newspapers, in the 55th Divisional Magazine and, most significantly, in the obituaries of those killed in action.[88] Sergeant Macfie, originally hostile to the idea of transferring to the 55th Division, was decorating his billet with the divisional rose by November 1917. He explained to his brother, 'For external and possibly internal decoration I have, with my nail scissors and a piece of tin, made a fine stencil of our divisional sign, the red rose of Lancaster.'[89] If the symbol of the rose had not been important to Macfie, it is unlikely that he would have expended time and energy producing a stencil.

In August 1918 a mother sent a letter to Major General Jeudwine asking for returning wounded to be drafted back into the 55th Division. It suggested that for families and soldiers, the rose had successfully amalgamated divisional and county pride. She wrote,

> To many it is perhaps immaterial where and with whom they fight, but our boys are very proud of their division, recruited as it has been from warehouse, office and dockside of our town ... You have done so much for the men who have served under you and to perpetuate the memory of our dear lads who have fallen, that I feel sure if it is in your power you will also grant to them this great privilege and honour they crave, to serve again under you and once again fight, and if God so wills it die, side by side, still wearing their Red Rose.[90]

This letter was found amongst Jeudwine's papers, and for good reason; it vindicated his decision to cultivate county feeling in his division. Yet it was a genuine letter, which suggests that an affinity for the home area remained strong in the Division to the end of the war.

Jeudwine did not rely solely on stamping symbols on his Division to harness regional feeling. *Sub Rosa*, the 55th Divisional Magazine was launched in June 1917. Its content was heavily influenced by the staff officers at Divisional Headquarters, where the selection of articles and editing took place. As fostering county pride was tantamount to official policy in the Division, submissions relating to Lancashire may have been given priority. Certainly, a large proportion of the articles published were regionally specific.[91]

---

[88] Newspaper cuttings scrapbook, LSM, Acc. No. 14.
[89] R. A. S. Macfie to Charlie Macfie, 16 November 1917, Macfie Papers, IWM, Con. Shelf.
[90] Letter from unknown mother to Major General H. S. Jeudwine, 28 August 1918, Records of the 55th (West Lancashire) Division LRO, 356 FIF 45.
[91] One third of the articles published in the Divisional Magazine of June 1918 were connected with Lancashire.

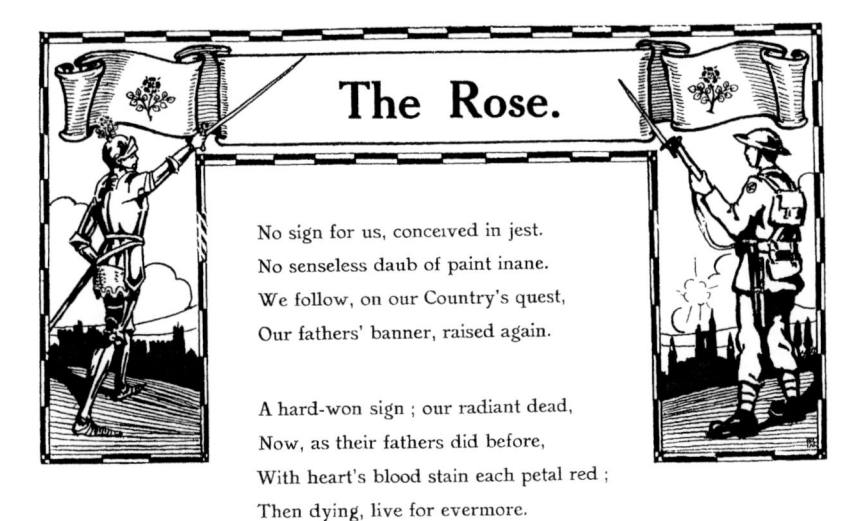

The Rose.

No sign for us, conceived in jest.
No senseless daub of paint inane.
We follow, on our Country's quest,
Our fathers' banner, raised again.

A hard-won sign ; our radiant dead,
Now, as their fathers did before,
With heart's blood stain each petal red ;
Then dying, live for evermore.

A gentle sign ; it's grim behest
To beckon like some towering spire
To heights where Freedom flaunts as crest
The Rose of fighting Lancashire.

Figure 4.1 'The Rose', poem from *Sub Rosa, Being the Magazine of the 55th West Lancashire Division*, June 1917.

The magazine contributions with a Lancashire flavour took three major forms: regional history conveyed through poetry, Lancashire tales written in dialect and cartoons.

In June 1917, a poem entitled *The Rose*, appeared in the magazine:

> No sign for us conceived in jest,
> No senseless daub of paint inane,
> We follow, on our country's quest,
> Our fathers' banner raised again.[92]

If we look at the illustrations at the top of the poem (Figure 4.1), we see that on the left there is a figure dressed in armour, reaching out with his sword towards a contemporary figure in battle dress on the right. A clear

---

[92] *Sub Rosa, Being the Magazine of the 55th West Lancashire Division*, June 1917.

visual link was being made between past and present conflicts. The same theme was elucidated more clearly by another poem in the 1918 edition:

> When Princes fought for England's crown,
> The house that won the most renown,
> And struck the sullen Yorkist down,
> Was Lancaster
>
> And blood red emblem stricken sore,
> Yet steeped her pallid foe in gore,
> Still stands for England evermore,
> And Lancaster
>
> Now England's blood like water flows,
> Full many a lusty German knows,
> We win or die who wear the rose of Lancaster.[93]

The poems evoked a sense of pride in Lancashire's past history by regurgitating the old story of the part played by Lancastrians in the instigation of the Tudors on the English throne. In doing so, they linked the duty and bravery shown in the Wars of the Roses with the deeds being performed by the 55th Division in the current war. As a new Territorial formation, the 55th West Lancashire Division had no catalogue of glamorous military honours won in previous, more exotic conflicts, such as those vaunted by regular units. Instead, its soldiers turned naturally to their civilian roots and regional history for a tradition to inspire loyalty.

The 'blood red emblem' was the rose which symbolized that history and acted as a link between the centuries, but it was more than just an emblem of tradition sewn to the shoulder. It had multiple, contemporary meanings for the people of the county. A woman's head emerging from the centre of a flower, sketched by an artist of the Division, was a good example of this, providing a more tangible, female interpretation of the 'Lancashire rose'[94] (see Figure 4.2).

Popularized in the nineteenth century through local magazines, dialect prose with a humorous theme began to be widely read throughout Lancashire.[95] The dialect prose appearing in the Divisional Magazines was similar in style to its civilian forerunners, evoking memories of Lancashire through the familiarity of the genre, its tone and content. The phraseology and pronunciation were specific to Lancashire and would have been very familiar to all those who lived in the region,

---

[93] *Sub Rosa, Being the Magazine of the 55th West Lancashire Division*, June 1918.
[94] *Sub Rosa, Being the Magazine of the 55th West Lancashire Division*, June 1917.
[95] M. Beetham, '"Healthy reading": the periodical press in late Victorian Manchester', in A. Kidd, *Manchester in the late nineteenth century* (Manchester, 1990), 167–87.

Figure 4.2 'The Lancashire Rose', cartoon from *Sub Rosa, Being the Magazine of the 55th West Lancashire Division*, June 1917.

irrespective of whether they spoke with a marked accent. Indeed, the Liverpolitan accent had more in common with that spoken in surrounding parts of Lancashire in 1914 than it does today.[96] Some stories were set in the county and revolved around familiar characters such as the Lancashire farmer, and the characters were often saddled with Lancashire names, Cobblethwaite being a favourite.[97] Others relied on the Lancastrian tradition of humour. An Owd Lancashire Tale is a good example. A mouse drowning in a vat of ale persuaded a cat to rescue him, promising that, in return, he would submit and consent to be eaten. Once out of the vat, the mouse escaped to his hole.

'Nay coom. Coom now, fair doos. Tha said if ah poo'd thee out ah wur hae thee. Now didn't ta? Fair doos now. Tha said ah could hae thee.'
'Aye ah know,' says th' mouse backin a bit further into 'is 'ole, 'but tha knows that a chap'll say owt an, what's moor, e'll promise owt, when he's i'liquor'[98]

The mischievous humour of the story would have struck a chord with most Lancastrians. Whilst humour permeated most trench newspapers, and has been identified as a predominately British trait,[99] it was a specific Lancastrian form of wit that was being celebrated. The wry, ironic humour, which often relied upon a knowledge of local habits and customs, also appeared outside the confines of the Divisional Magazine. A local newspaper carried a letter from a rifleman under the heading 'Local humour': 'Some fellows try to be funny, as witness the board outside number 22. The sniper's chateau they have called it. Our last trench by the way was called Lord Street and the orderly room dug-out had a wooden sign, "no hawkers; no circulars"; also "Tradesmen's entrance" on the back of it.'[100] Locally based humour and understatement were used by men in all ranks and were employed as another survival mechanism to diffuse both the boredom and the horror of life in the front line.[101]

We cannot easily judge the influence of this semi-official magazine within the Battalions. Circulation figures do not exist, nor do comments on its contents appear in the diaries and memoirs. It is obvious that the whole magazine was an exercise in propaganda. The articles were designed to be humorous, uplifting and familiar, reminding men of their duty and cementing resolve, and in the 1918 edition it was admitted

[96] See Belchem, '"An accent exceedingly rare"', 107.
[97] *Sub Rosa, Being the Magazine of the 55th West Lancashire Division,* June 1918.
[98] *Sub Rosa, Being the Magazine of the 55th West Lancashire Division,* June 1917.
[99] Fuller, *Troop morale and popular culture,* 34.
[100] Undated newspaper article, *c.* 1916, in Liverpool Rifles' Association record book, 1933–47, Liverpool Rifles' Association Papers, LRO, MD 162.
[101] See Fuller, *Troop morale and popular culture,* 32 for the importance of the music hall tradition as a sustaining force for the men in France.

'Common ties at home and strong county pride' 87

that censorship had taken place as 'some contributions were deemed unsuitable for publication'.[102] Nevertheless, we must remember that all articles originated from fighting units, and that the diversity of the images presented, including representations of rural and urban, industrial and commerical Lancashire, suggests that they expressed the views of a number of different authors.[103] Thus, it seems likely that identification with their county remained important to troops of the 55th Division to the end of the conflict. Fed up with the war they may have been by 1918, but many had not lost their affinity with home, or their original motivation for fighting.

In a lecture at Sandhurst in 1928, Lieutenant General Jeudwine claimed that his Division had two key advantages derived from its Territorial nature, 'common ties at home and strong county pride'.[104] Was this stress on county homogeneity justified? Jeudwine certainly thought so. He instigated numerous measures to enhance county pride, the most successful being the symbolic rose that fired many imaginations within the Division. As the Divisional Magazines have shown, it could conjure up different images of home for different people and still retain the power to motivate, support and unite. The varying motivations behind the soldiers' affinity and pride for their county were less important than the fact that a common county sentiment existed.

Whilst Jeudwine exaggerated the intensity of county identification for the benefit of his Sandhurst audience, he had nevertheless correctly identified a key Territorial trait. County homogeneity was valued by all sectors of society, from the government and families on the home front, to the Army Command and soldiers in the trenches. As the stream of casualties became a torrent, and replacements diluted other distinctive characteristics, county homogeneity became one of the most enduring features of the Liverpool Territorials.

Conclusion

Between 1914 and 1918 there had been no conscious nationalization of the British army. Neither was its recruitment and drafting system so overwhelmed by the pressures of modern warfare that it ceased to function and dispersed men to units in a random fashion. Far from a perfect

---

[102] *Sub Rosa, Being the Magazine of the 55th West Lancashire Division,* June 1918.
[103] *Sub Rosa, Being the Magazine of the 55th West Lancashire Division,* June 1917 and June 1918.
[104] Lecture on operations at Givenchy–Festubert, 9 April 1918; notes regarding General Sir Hugh Jeudwine's Lecture, RMC Sandhurst, 1928, Records of the 55th (West Lancashire) Division, LRO, 356 FIF 54/5, 26.

solution, the system nevertheless represented an important compromise between the desire of the soldiers to serve with those with whom they identified and the unpredictable manpower needs of the army in the field. The War Office could not respect unit integrity and guarantee that a soldier would always serve in the battalion in which he had enlisted, but, where possible, a broad regional homogeneity within units was their aim.

The experience of the Liverpool Territorials serves to illustrate how and why the War Office developed the drafting and recruitment compromise, despite the logistical difficulties it posed for its officials and despite the fact that local homogeneity could prove detrimental to morale and efficiency as well as reinforcing it. The advantages conferred by local and county homogeneity far outweighed the problems generated. Each Territorial battalion began the war as a cohesive unit, with its soldiers bound together through close local links and motivated by a shared desire to protect their homes and families. Inevitably, those tight community ties could not be sustained in the face of mass casualties and by 1918 were no longer a key feature of battalion life. However, they had been replaced by a broader county identity that performed similar motivational and cohesive functions. County uniformity could be used to stimulate pride in a formation and provide common ground from which to rebuild units decimated in battle, thus helping to sustain the morale of the soldier through the last years of war.

5 The links with home: communication between the home front and the fighting front during the Great War

The traditional view of relations between home and fighting front maintains that the links between soldiers and their communities in Britain were tenuous. Civilians remained largely ignorant of the nature of the war, retaining a glamorized, idealistic impression of the fighting.[1] This view contends that the ignorance of civilians arose as a result of the twin evils of censorship and propaganda. Censorship prevented civilians from comprehending the physical hardships borne by the troops, the mental trauma induced by the experience of battle, and the scale and manner of death during attacks. Propaganda was believed to have inculcated a vicious hatred of the enemy in the civilian population, in opposition to the soldier's supposed brotherly attitude to his opponent, and misrepresented the views of the troops, claiming that they were consistently happy to attack, whatever the conditions. The propagation of these falsehoods, it has been argued, caused soldiers to become disillusioned with those at home, to retreat into their own trench culture and to become alienated from civilian life.[2]

The consensus surrounding this 'alienation thesis' is now under attack.[3] A number of historians have asserted that remarkably truthful accounts about the nature of the fighting were transmitted to the home front and that the image of the disenchanted soldier, betrayed by civilian society, is largely a myth.[4] The wartime experience of the Liverpool

---

[1] C. Haste, *Keep the home fires burning* (London, 1977), 31. Other proponents of this argument include P. Knightley, *The first casualty* (London, 1978); M. L. Sanders and P. Taylor, *British propaganda during the First World War* (London, 1982); G. Messinger, *British propaganda and the state in the First World War* (Manchester, 1992); P. Buitenhuis, *The Great War of words* (London, 1989).
[2] See Leed, *No Man's Land*, 193.
[3] See Bourke, *Dismembering the male*; N. Hiley, 'You can't believe a word you read', *Newspaper History*, 1994; Winter, *Sites of memory, sites of mourning*, 36; Englander, 'Soldiering and identity', 300–18. For the French perspective see Audoin-Rouzeau, *Men at war*.
[4] Bourke, *Dismembering the male*, 20; E. F. Schneider, 'What Britons were told about the war in the trenches, 1914–1918', unpublished DPhil thesis, University of Oxford (1997).

89

Territorials, to whom home was all important, supports the revisionist interpretation of wartime relations between soldiers and civilians. Symbols and images of city and county had the power to motivate, to entertain, to support and to unite. The memory of home made life more bearable and the fighting more meaningful for the Territorials in the trenches. Given the strength of this attachment, it is not surprising that the soldiers sought to maintain links with the communities they were trying to protect and to which they hoped to return. Using three main sources of communication available to the Liverpool Territorials – letters, leave and newspaper reports – we can investigate the strength of these links between home front and fighting front and how they sustained a community separated by war.[5]

Letters and leave

The letters sent from the front were censored by the military authorities. The officers' mail was censored at the base and the men's correspondence was censored by their officers. Yet, despite these official procedures, much of the censorship was subjective and often derisory. Whilst the warnings issued in the *Field Service Regulations*[6] may have inhibited some men from expressing their true feelings at first, most soon came to realize that their officers were faced with mountains of mail to check, and it was possible to write what they wanted, within reason. Lieutenant Turner wrote to his mother on 1 June 1915 that he had just censored 300 letters during that evening.[7] It is inconceivable that even the most diligent officer would have found time to scour 300 communications.

The official duty of a censor was to remove specific information concerning casualty and armament figures, and place and battalion names that could be of military use to the enemy. As most men heeded the advice to avoid quoting any explicit logistical information, the officers had few obvious targets to censor. They also had the authority to censor any

---

[5] It has not been possible to examine all available sources of communication between front and home front. Communication through film and visual media has not been covered here, but this has already been examined in N. Reeves, *Official British film propaganda in the First World War* (London, 1986); N. Reeves, 'Through the eye of the camera: contemporary cinema audiences and their experience of war in the film, Battle of the Somme', in H. Cecil and P. Liddle (eds.), *Facing Armageddon: the First World War experienced* (London, 1996), 780–98; J. Carmichael, *First World War photographers* (London, 1989); N. Hiley, 'Making war: the British news media and government control, 1914–1916', unpublished PhD thesis, Open University (1985).

[6] War Office, *Field Service Regulations, part II, 1913* (London, 1913), Section 100, 131.

[7] Lieutenant W. S. Turner to mother, 1 June 1915, Turner Papers, KRC, MLL, 1973.163.5.

disclosure that was damaging to morale, but this was left to the discretion of the individual officer.

Sergeant Macfie's letters indicate that the conscientiousness and pedantry of the individual censor were very important. Whilst he was with the Liverpool Scottish Battalion, his letters home were never once censored, although he often wrote detailed reports of unit actions. During some weeks in hospital, away from the Battalion, however, Macfie experienced a different attitude from the military authorities. Despite having little military information to impart, his letters became very difficult to read, a significant proportion of the words having been obliterated by the censor's pencil.[8]

It is possible that the relaxed approach taken by Territorial units towards discipline extended to the practice of censorship, and other units may have experienced a more rigorous regime. Even if this was the case, there were ways in which a soldier could bypass regimental censorship altogether and communicate more freely with home. Letters could be sent via wounded soldiers, or posted in Britain by comrades returning home on leave. The men were also allowed to write one letter a month which was enclosed in a green envelope and censored only at the base.[9] Such envelopes allowed the men to reveal as much about their lives as possible, without being subject to the scrutiny of their own officers. Indeed, as David Englander reminds us, the authorities surveyed service correspondence in an attempt to gauge the mood of the troops, and if this strategy was to be successful the soldier had to have some scope for expressing his feelings.[10]

The surviving letters, written by the members of the two Battalions to their families, are remote from anodyne products of a censorship system; they are perhaps the most illuminating sources regarding the lives, attitudes and feelings of the men in the trenches. The men saw little reason to conceal the truth about the detail of their lives and were remarkably candid in their letters, enabling the families to construct a realistic picture of front-line experience.

The nature and circumstances of death in the trenches were frequently described. Private Douglas wrote to his father about the death of an officer on 14 January 1915: 'I had just turned round to speak to my pal when I heard a splash and pore [sic] Lieutenant Turner was lying dead at the bottom of the trench in a pool of water and mud. The bullet had gone clean through his head, chewing out his brains.'[11] Many other letters

---

[8] R. A. S. Macfie to Lewis Paton, 20 January 1915, Macfie Papers, IWM, Con. Shelf.
[9] J. A. Burden, Letters 1916–17, LSM, Acc. No. 1122.
[10] Englander, 'Soldiering and identity', 308.
[11] P. Douglas to father, 15 January 1915, Douglas Papers, IWM, 66/274/1.

describing the physical conditions in the trenches also arrived in Liverpool in the first months of service. Between November 1914 and May 1915, the knee-high mud, the exhausting carrying parties, the dead Frenchmen they encountered who had become integral parts of the trench wall, the intense cold and the inadequate food were all related to those at home.[12]

During this period, the first deaths in the units, the weather conditions and the gruelling work appeared to be dominant themes in the letters: 'Just fancy', wrote Sergeant W. J. Boulton to his mother in December 1914, 'standing up to your waist in cold mud, unable to move. If you straighten yourself up, half a dozen shots come whizzing round your head.'[13] As a result of these conditions, by 9 January 1915, Sergeant Macfie informed his father that 'The men are fed up with Belgium and are very homesick.'[14] By May 1915 the weather and the condition of the trenches had improved, and with it the mood of the Liverpool Scottish. Macfie wrote home describing his delightful trench, situated in a wood, which was 'full of nightingales, cuckoos, glow-worms and flowers'. He explained that 'there could be no greater contrast than the appearance of our men in January and now'.[15]

The mental strain and boredom imposed by living under shellfire were also described by the soldiers. Rifleman Ellison of the Liverpool Rifles wrote of his need to escape the unrelieved tension after forty-five consecutive days under fire in trenches and dugouts. His contemplation of the free nature of a skylark singing in the vicinity of his trench caused him, in contrast to his belligerent attitude of a few weeks earlier, to reflect despondently on his situation in a letter to his father: 'No doubt it is a highly scientific proposition to hurl a cwt of steel 5 miles and blow a man to bloody fragments, but just on the moment, this cheeky little bird rather blurs my appreciation of the triomphal [sic] onward march of civilisation.'[16]

When the Liverpool Rifles moved to a different part of the line, Ellison's view of the war changed again. The 6th Battalion became part of the Third Army support troops, which provided the soldiers with a much-needed break from trench warfare. Ellison himself was assigned the task of supplying the Third Army with coal, which provided him with a

---

[12] P. Douglas to mother and father, 6 January 1915, Douglas Papers, IWM, 66/274/1; Letters published in newspapers in J. Bedford, LSM, Acc. No. 476.
[13] W. J. Boulton to mother, 21 December 1914, in J. Bedford, With the Liverpool Scottish, Scrapbook 1, LSM, Acc. No. 476.
[14] R. A. S. Macfie to father, 9 January 1915, Macfie Papers, IWM, Con. Shelf.
[15] R. A. S. Macfie to father, 17 May 1915, Macfie Papers, IWM, Con. Shelf.
[16] N. F. Ellison to parents, 3 July 1915, Ellison Papers, IWM, DS/Misc/49, 53.

degree of freedom he relished. His correspondence again became infused with positive images of the war.[17]

The role of a soldier within the battalion also determined his experience of warfare, and consequently influenced the content of his letters home. Cooks, transport men, storekeepers and cobblers rarely saw continuous front-line service, although their duties took them briefly into the line. Private S. P. Moulton of the Liverpool Scottish noted an improvement in his meals, once he was transferred to the transport lines as a groom,[18] and Private Herd realized that his life as a stretcher bearer was much less monotonous than life in the company. His duties were more varied, as he was systematically rotated between the dressing station and the trenches.[19]

It appears that the views of the war sent home to Liverpool were dependent on the conditions in the trenches, the nature of duties in which the Battalion was involved and the position of the correspondent within that Battalion. The attitudes expressed by individuals were constantly changing, influenced by their immediate experiences. Few soldiers completely rejected the war and its objectives, but equally few were constantly cheerful, accepting the war without question. The evidence contained in the letters to their families, above all, portrayed the human face of war. They presented a more nuanced interpretation of life at the front than the proponents of the alienation thesis acknowledge.

We cannot ignore the fact that there were some soldiers who did not possess either the literacy or the inclination to convey their thoughts and feelings to their families. Many men were content to send monosyllabic postcards to their loved ones. However, these too, depending on their illustration, could transmit messages about the nature of the war. Popular series of French and Belgian postcards depicted photographs of familiar towns before and during the conflict, and were found amongst the papers of many men from both Battalions. Typical postcards purchased by Private Herd exhibited the Cloth Hall in Ypres before and after shelling (see Figure 5.1). These postcards avoided conveying the full horror of the war, through the depiction of damaged buildings rather than dwelling on the suffering of damaged human beings, but it did not require a vivid imagination to realize that houses were not the only targets for the enemy's shells.[20] If a shell could demolish a building, it was equally capable of rendering a soldier an unrecognizable pulp.

---

[17] N. F. Ellison to parents, September 1915, Ellison Papers, IWM, DS/Misc/49.
[18] S. P. Moulton, Diary, LSM, Miscellaneous File M, Acc. No. 760/7.
[19] E. Herd, Diary, April 1916, Herd Papers, KRC, MLL, 1981.850.
[20] This point was made with regard to the drawings of Muirhead Bone by K. Grieves: 'War correspondents and conducting officers on the Western Front', in Cecil and Liddle (eds.), *Facing Armageddon*, 726.

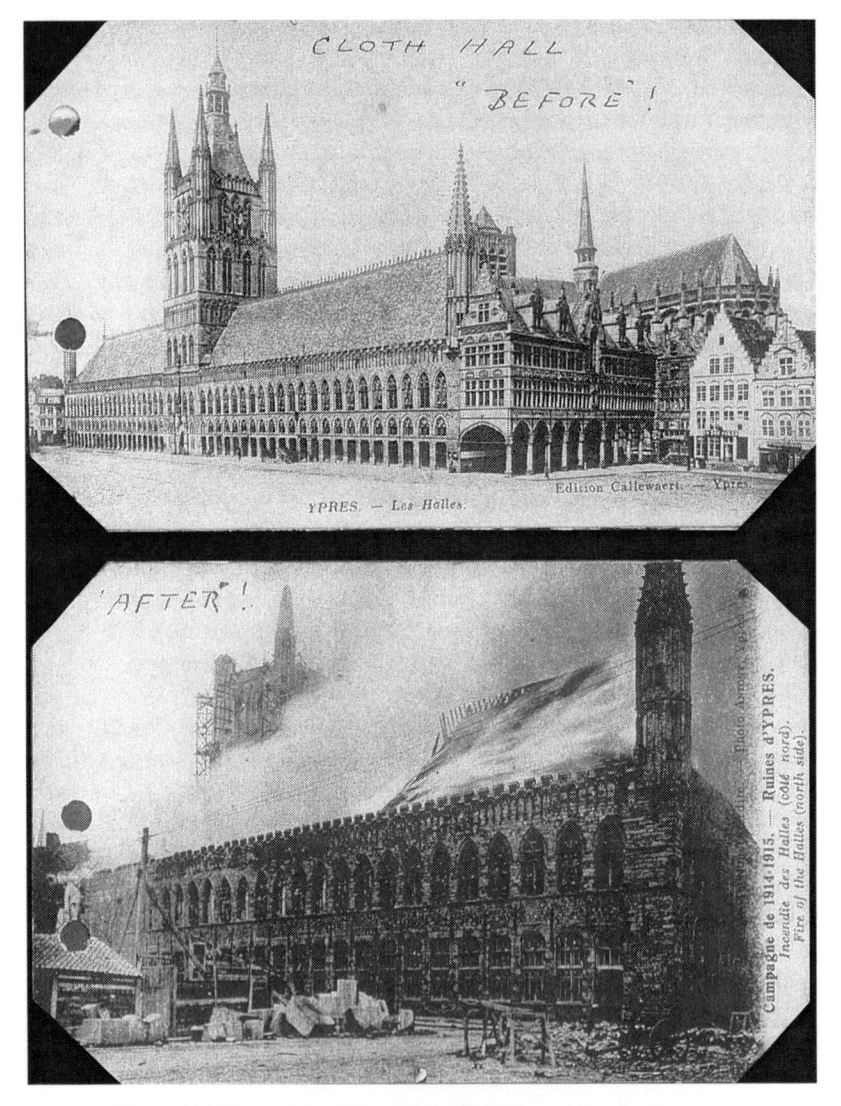

Figure 5.1 Postcards of the Cloth Hall, Ypres (no date).

The issue of self-censorship must also be taken into account. Some men did not want to worry their families unnecessarily, and so their letters were either exceedingly brief or contained sanitized descriptions of their conditions. Sergeant Burden, for example, refused to give his fiancée details of his exploits in the Third Battle of Ypres, because he did not want her to worry for his safety.[21]

Yet despite the undoubted prevalence of self-censorship, the majority of families, waiting for news of their relatives, understood the progress of the war from the soldier's point of view. Personal information was disseminated amongst networks of friends and family, and if an individual soldier was reticent about his experiences his comrades' communications often provided his family with a more detailed understanding of the war. Letters were often passed to different branches of an extended family, or read aloud at the breakfast table. They sometimes reached a quite different audience from that which the correspondent had envisaged. Herbert Malleson described the reaction of his son to a letter written by Sergeant Macfie:

> I read aloud your letter and lo! When I came to your story of the tragedy of the Liverpool Scottish, my small boy aged seven suddenly disappeared under the table and sounds of sobbing could be heard ... When he had finished he quietly slipped back into his chair again and solemnly proceeded with his breakfast. No words were said. He has just done his little bit, in memory of your comrades.[22]

Just as civilians expressed a close interest in the life of the men at the front, so soldiers wanted news of home. Letters from home updating soldiers on the minutiae of family and local life were eagerly awaited by troops in the trenches. The exchange of letters constituted a dialogue between home and front in which both parties were equal participants.

Despite the fact that few letters to men in the field survive, it is possible to deduce the topics of discussion from the soldiers' replies. The Reverend Coop, for example, enquired about his wife's 'sale of work', gave advice on the hiring of a housekeeper and expressed concern about his daughter starting school.[23] Coop did not surrender his role as a husband and parent on joining the army. He maintained his interest in the domestic activities of home life and offered advice and support to his wife. Although he was in France, his influence in the family unit continued. Letters sent from Sergeant Macfie to his father took, on average, four days to arrive. Assuming this was the norm, advice given by men at the front would not be irrelevant by the time it reached the recipient

---

[21] J. A. Burden to E. Robinson, September 1917, LSM, Acc. No. 1122.
[22] Herbert Malleson to R. A. S. Macfie, 29 July 1915, Macfie Papers, IWM, Con. Shelf. The 'tragedy' to which Malleson referred was the attack of the Liverpool Scottish at Hooge, 16 June 1915, in which a large percentage of the unit were casualties.
[23] Reverend J. O. Coop to wife, 13 January 1916, 25 January 1916, 6 February 1916, 25 October 1916, IWM, 87/56/1.

Figure 5.2 Arrival of the mail: the Liverpool Scottish receive post from home, 1915.

at home, helping to reinforce family bonds and maintain effective communication.[24]

Tangible material contact was also maintained through the sending and receiving of parcels. The family at home reacted to the men's descriptions of their meagre rations and the intense cold endured in winter by dispatching food and clothing parcels, often to the financial detriment of the remaining family members. The men too sent parcels home, in some cases presents of Belgian lace or children's toys. More commonly, it was the soldiers' dirty laundry that crossed the English Channel to Liverpool. As Sergeant Macfie appreciatively commented to his brother: 'A very modern war isn't it? When one can send one's dirty washing home to be washed.'[25]

The parcels achieved more than alleviating the physical wants of the men. They were an expression of concern for the soldiers, and as such, their significance cannot be overestimated. 'The fact that I am remembered kindly by my relatives, as proved by the welcome arrival of parcels,

---

[24] R. A. S. Macfie's father helpfully noted the date of receipt at the head of all letters. The time frame of four days is only applicable to those who served on the Western Front. The time taken from other theatres of war would necessarily have been longer.

[25] R. A. S. Macfie to brother, 3 July 1915, Macfie Papers, IWM, Con. Shelf.

is comforting to a degree that you can scarcely conceive',[26] wrote a sergeant on receipt of a parcel from his aunt. The parcels were 'proof' that those at home had not forgotten the men at the front and that their efforts were appreciated.

It is evident that the army never became the sole provider for these citizen soldiers at the front. The family maintained its traditional role of providing practical and emotional support for its members, whether fighting at the front or remaining in Liverpool. Most men survived in the trenches in part through the support of their relatives, and equally the interest and advice transmitted to their families was greatly valued by those at home. Thus there was a powerful incentive to maintain a strong familial link between front and home front during the war.

The family was not the only institution that provided emotional and material support, and in which the Territorials maintained a stake. Business, social, cultural and civic organizations also sustained regular contact with their members fighting abroad. As with the family, contact was sustained through written correspondence and parcels. Most organizations had special collections to enable them to send gifts to their members at the front. Many businesses and institutions went further, including soldiers' letters in their monthly publications. In doing so, they were propagating the views from the front to a wider audience than just the family, and allowing soldiers to maintain links with their wider civilian circle.[27]

Progress, the Lever Brothers newsletter, carried a series of extracts from the diary of an ex-employee, Private H. L. Leaton of the Liverpool Scottish. In contrast to the family letters, the diary was more guarded. He did not elaborate on his first introduction to shellfire, and merely stated that he would tell those at home if his life was spared, but his account provided a comprehensive description of the monotony of life in and out of the trenches.[28]

Church magazines also carried letters from soldiers, whilst some institutions initiated specific, wartime publications. The Crescent Congregational Church in Liverpool created a newsletter named *Young Crescent*. It aimed 'to provide an interchange of experiences between

---

[26] R. A. S. Macfie to aunt, 11 February 1915, Macfie Papers, IWM, Con. Shelf; see also P. Douglas to father, 18 December 1914, Douglas Papers, IWM, 66/243/1.

[27] See Records of the *Liverpool Daily Post and Echo*, Minute Book, LRO, 331 GRA 4/1; Lever Brothers, *Progress*, 1914–19; *Liverpool News*, 1916, League of welldoers, 1856–1986, MRO, 364 LWD 23/1/84; *Our Church News*, 1915–19, MRO, Provincial and church records, 285 TRI 13/3; *Young Crescent*, 1915–19; *Caldian*, school magazine, 1918, LSM, Acc. No. 411.

[28] Lever Brothers, *Progress*, May–July 1915.

those at home and those whose services are required by King and Country', and was designed to appeal both to soldiers and to civilians.[29] Articles, church events, poetry, cartoons and letters formed the substance of the magazine. Contributions were included from all members of the congregation, and by February 1916 a large readership had been established, with 350 copies alone being sent overseas each month.[30] Those with no direct connection with the church were also influenced by the magazine, as Mrs J. Williams emphasized in 1917: 'One or two friends of mine who are not connected with the Crescent look forward to each number keenly, and feel they know many of the lads whose adventures they follow each month.'[31]

The *Young Crescent* was an excellent example of a communication network established to fulfil the specific needs of a community separated by war. It was the congregation, scattered throughout the world, that determined the content of the magazine, and therefore the messages they wished to be transmitted about their experience of the war. Although, again, less graphic than personal letters, the communications still expressed complex emotions engendered by the war. The incongruity of an all-loving God and the destruction of war was often discussed, and feelings induced by bereavement disclosed. Men wrote to express their sympathy to the relatives of those killed. Poetry, describing the character of the deceased and the sacrifice made, also became a regular feature of the newsletter, which helped relatives come to terms with the death. Thus, at one level the *Young Crescent* constituted a support network for the bereaved.

The attraction of the magazine for the men in the forces lay in the humorous articles, cartoons and poetry describing church events and civilian life. Reading the *Young Crescent* provided an opportunity for the men to return in their mind to the familiar civilian world, and briefly forget the hardships and difficulties of army life.

That the soldiers retained their importance in the civilian world, portrayed in the *Young Crescent*, was reinforced by the messages from the home front. They followed a formula which involved stressing how much the men were missed, socially and practically. They were constantly looking forward to the end of the war, when the men would return and once again help with the organization of church activities. The choir, the swimming, rambling and athletics societies and the committee

---

[29] *Young Crescent*, church newsletter, July 1915.
[30] *Young Crescent*, church newsletter, February 1916. *Young Crescent* also encouraged three other Congregational churches to produce similar magazines during the war.
[31] *Young Crescent*, church newsletter, January 1917.

responsible for the preparation of free breakfasts for the poor all expressed their need for the men to return.[32]

Other elements of the formula included praising the courage and endurance of the soldiers, and ensuring that those fighting abroad felt appreciated. The soldiers returned the compliments. John Moir's Christmas message in December 1917 exhorted his fellow soldiers: 'Encourage the folk at home who are struggling with the burden of the church by your frequent letters to the *Young Crescent Mag.* and they in turn will strengthen us with their prayers.' Others praised the mothers: 'Bravo to them all – they are heroines every inch. We chaps out here cannot fully realise what troubles and trials they must have while we are away.'[33] The men at the front appreciated the difficulties faced by those at home and praised their continuing efforts. Through the magazine, each soldier was able to continue to play a role in the life of the church.

On the second Sunday of the month a roll of honour service was held at the church. During the service the name of each Crescent member serving with the forces was read out. Such personalization of the service ensured that the soldier was remembered as an individual within the church community. Mrs Thompson described her experience of the regular ceremonies in April 1917: 'I attend the Roll of Honour Services and the prayers of our minister always bring me nearer to my boy and all the boys as their names are called out.'[34]

The service provided comfort for those families concerned for their loved ones, and was seen as another link between those members of the community at home and those fighting abroad. This idea was reinforced by the invitation to all members overseas to mingle their prayers with those at home. Soldiers were also encouraged to send requests for favourite hymns, so that they might feel that they had taken some constructive part in the service.[35]

A similar publication to the *Young Crescent* was produced at the civic level by the Lord Mayor of Liverpool.[36] Bulletins regarding Liverpool's charitable contribution to the war effort introduced the magazine. The intention was to assure those fighting that the home front was actively supporting the war effort. Important figures from all sectors of the community also included short appreciative messages to the men at the front, in addition to the usual comic articles, cartoons and stories of Liverpool

---

[32] *Young Crescent*, church newsletters, 1915–18.
[33] *Young Crescent*, church newsletter, June 1916.
[34] *Young Crescent*, church newsletter, April 1917.
[35] *Young Crescent*, church newsletters, 1917.
[36] *Liverpool News*, Christmas edn 1916, League of welldoers, 1856–1986, MRO, 364 LWD 23/1/84.

life. Again, the pamphlet was intended to be read by all Liverpool's citizens, whether at home or temporarily abroad, and represented official, civic recognition of all contributions by Liverpolitans to the war effort. In the pamphlet, Sir Edward Russell, editor of the *Liverpool Daily Post*, stressed the value of mutual understanding:

> Comradeship is one of the great joys and benefits of life. In every heart-whole imagination it defies distance and surmounts separation ... Our Christmas messages are to bring Liverpool Comrades at home and abroad nearer still together ... And when this grievous trouble shall have passed, there will be much to remember and to tell our children how those Liverpool men who fought and those who worked at home were true to each other.[37]

Telegrams sent from civic leaders, such as Lord Derby, to divisional and battalion commanders also provided civic recognition of the achievements of a unit. They were communicated to the men through Battalion Orders and Divisional Parades.[38] Such parades were occasionally graced by the civic representative in person. Although they would have appeared remote, they were valued as a symbol of the appreciation of Liverpool, and their visits were always reported in diaries and letters.[39]

Private citizens too made the journey to the rear areas in France. Miss Whitson, matron of the Liverpool Merchants Mobile Hospital, commandeered the Hôtel des Anglais in Paris Plage for the use of visiting family and friends of wounded officers.[40] Relatives were permitted to travel to France, not only to be with a dying husband or son, but also to comfort him before a major operation, such as an amputation.[41] Wounded men were able to relate their experiences of life in the front line and in hospital. Their wounds also provided grim visual evidence of the effects of shell and machine gun fire. Such experiences could not fail to impress upon the relatives the butchery involved in war.

Although the government was prepared, in theory, to reimburse those too poor to pay for their travel expenses, in practice the bureaucracy involved ensured that it was only those who had the opportunity and private means who could afford to make the journey.[42] Similarly, it was only those

---

[37] *Liverpool News*, Christmas edn 1916, League of welldoers, 1856–1986, MRO, 364 LWD 23/1/84, 11.
[38] After their defence of Givenchy in April 1918, the 55th Division received telegrams from Lord Derby and the General Secretary of the Liverpool Prisoners of War Flag Day Committee. *55th Division at Givenchy*, pamphlet, MLHL, W. J. Pegge Papers, M198/6/5.
[39] J. O. Coop, Letters, Coop Papers, IWM, 87/56/1; N. F. Ellison to parents, February 1916, Ellison Papers, IWM, DS/Misc/49, 67.
[40] Matron Whitson, Diary, 16 September 1915, LSM, Acc. No. 1104.
[41] Matron Whitson, Diary, 25 September 1916, LSM, Acc. No. 1104.
[42] See Winter, *Sites of memory, sites of mourning*, 33–4.

Figure 5.3 Lord Derby and the 55th Division, during a review by the King of the Belgians, Brussels, 3 January 1919.

privileged families who possessed a telephone who could speak to their loved ones during the long periods of separation. The families of most other ranks had to wait until the soldier returned home, either hospitalized or on leave.

Leave was infrequent, approximately once a year, but the men spent their time visiting as many people as possible, including the families of those friends left behind in the trenches.[43] Most soldiers were not reticent in communicating their experiences. Corporal W. M. Lyon, for example, warned his parents: 'We shall have quite a lot of experiences to relate when we get back, so you can reserve a few nights around the fire for this event.'[44] He was not an isolated case. From subsequent cryptic references in their letters home, it was evident that the Liverpool Territorials had revealed much about the war to their families and friends at their various social and sporting clubs.[45]

---

[43] Private Eccles visited his friend's parents and Sergeant Macfie's batman visited the Macfie sugar plant and was entertained by the family. See H. C. Eccles, Diary, 13 June 1917, H. C. Eccles Papers, Liddle Collection (G.S.); R. A. S. Macfie to Sheila Macfie, 5 January 1918, Macfie Papers, IWM, Con. Shelf.

[44] Corporal W. M. Lyon to parents, cutting from the *Liverpool Echo* in A. Bryans Scrapbook, LSM, Acc. No. 545.

[45] See Reverend J. O. Coop, Letters, 25 January 1916, IWM, 87/56/1.

From 1917 both government and military leaders were becoming increasingly worried about this opportunity for communication between home and front which bypassed all elements of censorship.[46] The effectiveness of this method of communication was highlighted by the collapse of the 55th Division in the face of a determined enemy attack near Cambrai in November 1917. Despite official attempts to diminish the significance of the disaster, it did not take long for the true nature of the situation to be understood in Liverpool. Appendix 'L' of the Court of Enquiry into failures at Cambrai addressed the problem of 'rumours'. These were apparently spread:

> not merely by newspapers and members of parliament, but also through the medium of 400,000 officers and men who have proceeded backwards and forwards on leave during the past two months. The most prolific propagators of baseless stories are the wounded. Moreover, they get home before the telegrams, and rapidly spread the foolish notion that if they had been in charge of the conduct of the operations, things would have been very different.[47]

The proposed remedy for this was interesting. The commanders accepted that they could not prevent the men from talking to their families and friends and proposed to counter future rumours with short semi-official stories of battles to be issued as soon as possible after the event, together with improved briefings for newspaper reporters. The appendix concluded: 'The effect of the present inadequate means of conveying history and rumours to the public at home is that the Battle of CAMBRAI has by now come to be regarded as a German success, instead of a British victory.'[48] It is clear from this evidence that the British public, faced with believing an 'official' story, or one communicated by their friends and relatives at the front, chose the latter. The views of civilians and soldiers, however inaccurate they might be, remained remarkably similar throughout the war.

The families of Territorial soldiers had an extra advantage over most New Army battalions in their attempt to garner information concerning their men at the front. Whilst most families relied on the, admittedly efficient, local gossip and the newspapers for information, the established

---

[46] Englander, 'Soldiering and identity', 313.
[47] 'Comments and suggestions concerning rumours by a member of the court', Appendix 'L' of the Court of Enquiry on the action fought south of Cambrai on November 30th 1917, 29 January 1918, Records of the 55th (West Lancashire) Division, 1914–19, LRO, 356 FIF 50/6/146. The member in question was Lieutenant General Ivor Maxse.
[48] 'Comments and suggestions concerning rumours by a member of the court', Appendix 'L' of the Court of Enquiry on the action fought south of Cambrai on November 30th 1917, 29 January 1918, Records of the 55th (West Lancashire) Division, 1914–19, LRO, 356 FIF 50/6/147.

Territorial network in Liverpool disseminated information about their battalions to a wide range of families. This was particularly important in the aftermath of serious battles, when the fate of many men remained unknown. For example, Sergeant Macfie produced an account of the Battle of Hooge, including a breakdown of the fate of all casualties in his company, which could be obtained from the Battalion Headquarters in Liverpool on the condition it would not be transmitted to the press.[49] The bishop of Liverpool also circulated an account of the battle written by his son, the Medical Officer attached to the Liverpool Scottish. It also named those killed and injured in the Hooge action.[50]

Specific Territorial memorial services were also organized throughout the war, and were well attended by both ex and serving soldiers, as well as relatives of Territorial troops.[51] These services performed two functions that helped to bind front and home front together. First, they were an excellent opportunity for the interchange of information between soldiers and civilians, but they were also a necessary gesture of solidarity: the front and the home front united in their grief for those who had died and in acknowledging the continuing sacrifice in the trenches.

'Can't believe a word you read': newspaper reporting in the Great War[52]

Printed sources formed another link between the front and the home front during the Great War. The history of the King's (Liverpool) Regiment was published in 1915, and contained information concerning recent engagements of the Territorial Battalions, complete with letters describing conditions at the front.[53] Poetry was also published by a member of the Liverpool Scottish, E. I. M. McClymont. He had four poems published in *Soldier poets: more songs by the fighting men*. His subjects of loss and longing for home presented the reader with familiar themes, expressed through more elevated language.[54]

More widely read were the newspapers. It is from these publications that historians, advocating the existence of an unbridgeable gap between front and home front, have formulated their ideas. They have begun with

---

[49] R. A. S. Macfie, Casualties at the Battle of Hooge, KRC, MLL, 4.315.
[50] Chavasse Papers, Letter to father, June 1915, LSM, Officers Miscellaneous File.
[51] J. G. C. Moffat, Scrapbook, Miscellaneous File M, LSM, Acc. No. 199.
[52] C. E. Montague, *Disenchantment* (London, 1922), 98. According to Montague, this phrase had become a catchphrase of the British army.
[53] T. R. Threlfall, *The history of the King's (Liverpool) Regiment* (Liverpool, 1915).
[54] E. I. M. McClymont, in *Soldier poets: more songs by the fighting men* (2nd Series, London, 1918), 45–7.

the assumption that information regarding the war was scarce on the home front between 1914 and 1918 and have consequently examined the effectiveness of the machinery of censorship. The Press Bureau (a body established to censor communications to newspapers from overseas and to disseminate information to the press) and the mechanics of the censorship rules have been investigated in detail.

Having established the Press Bureau was ineffective, other theories have been developed to explain the supposed lack of detailed war news. Colin Lovelace argues that although the Press Bureau wielded very little power, the editors and foreign correspondents exercised strict self-censorship. Journalists believed that it was their patriotic duty to suppress technical information that might assist the enemy in the prosecution of their war effort.[55] A. G. Marquis argues on a similar line, suggesting that the censorship of news was a result of informal government control. Editors, newspaper owners and leading politicians all belonged to the same social network and did not want to risk being ostracized from this elite group through failure to exercise patriotic censorship. It has been suggested that the loyalty of the newspapers was finally sealed by incorporating the Press Lords into the official structure of the propaganda machine, with appointments being bestowed on Lord Beaverbrook and Lord Northcliffe.[56]

It is surprising that these historians have not examined in depth the content of the newspapers they discuss. Their studies provide little evidence of the way in which the censorship laws they describe were interpreted by editors and affected articles appearing in print.[57] Their arguments are also based almost exclusively on evidence culled from the national press. With the exception of the *Manchester Guardian*, which in its circulation and reputation was the equal of the major daily newspapers, all the newspapers studied were national papers. Thus

---

[55] C. Lovelace, 'British press censorship during the First World War', in G. Boyce (ed.), *Newspaper history: from the 17th century to the present day* (London, 1978), 307–19.
[56] A. G. Marquis, 'Words as weapons', *Journal of Contemporary History*, 13 (1978), 476–80, 485. This form of control was used to secure political support for the government, rather than to prevent the publication of descriptions of conditions on the Western Front. Riddell, the powerful editor of the *News of the World*, recorded in his diary a conversation he had with Lloyd George in May 1918, during which it was decided to offer Alan Jeans, the chief proprietor of the *Liverpool Daily Post*, a knighthood to end the hostility of the paper towards the government. J. M. McEwen (ed.), *The Riddell diaries* (London, 1986), 12 May 1918.
[57] T. Rose, *Aspects of political censorship, 1914–18* (Hull, 1995) is an exception. However, she examines the content of the newspapers only with respect to strikes and the Russian Revolution. For another limited exception see S. Badsey and P. Taylor, 'Images of battle: the press, propaganda and Passchendaele', in P. H. Liddle (ed.), *Passchendaele in Perspective: the third battle of Ypres* (London, 1997).

the authors have not explored the significance of the highly influential local press.[58]

The local press in Liverpool consisted of the Liberal *Liverpool Daily Post* and *Liverpool Echo*, which were balanced by the Conservative *Liverpool Express*, the *Liverpool Courier* and the northern edition of the *Daily Dispatch*.[59] A close examination of the newspaper reports in these five papers will be used to assess the picture of the war provided by the local press.

During the first months of the war the army was hostile towards the press, and official information was scarce.[60] All types of newspapers, local and national, had three major sources of official information: official dispatches from the commander in chief, the so-called 'eyewitness' articles written by an army officer based at GHQ, and the enemy newspapers. From May 1915, five foreign correspondents had official permission to roam around the front, accompanied by their army minders, who also acted as their censors.[61] Each source of information provided a daily article in the newspapers, alongside home journalists' strategic assessments of the war. This news was supplemented by more personal features. The 'In Memoriam' messages filled several columns a day, whilst particularly prominent in the local press were communications from soldiers at the front, and rolls of honour, listing deaths, wounds and decorations of those serving, often accompanied by photographs and biographical information. Using the Liverpool Scottish and their first action at the Battle of Hooge, we can begin to investigate the ways in which local and national newspapers utilized their sources of information to present different images of the war at the local and national levels.

---

[58] John Bourne has already highlighted this issue using examples from the *Barnsley Chronicle* and the *Northampton Daily Chronicle* in J. Bourne, *Britain and the Great War* (London, 1989), 206. According to A.P. Wadsworth, 'Newspaper circulations, 1800–1954', *Transactions of the Manchester Statistical Society* (1954–5), 1–40, if a provincial town in 1914 had two morning newspapers their daily circulation was, on average, 35,000 copies. If this figure is added to an estimate of the circulation of two evening papers, we get a total circulation figure of 92,000 copies. Although we cannot claim that the circulation figures were directly proportional to the influence wielded by the papers, it would be irresponsible to ignore publications with a circulation of this magnitude.

[59] The *Liverpool Daily Post* circulated in Liverpool, Lancashire, Cheshire, Derbyshire, Staffordshire and Wales, whilst the *Liverpool Echo* had an 'immense circulation in the Provinces'. The *Liverpool Courier* circulated throughout Lancashire, Cheshire, Derbyshire, Shropshire, Yorkshire, North Wales and the Isle of Man, and the *Liverpool Evening Express* covered Liverpool, south-west Lancashire, Birkenhead, Cheshire and North Wales. They all had Fleet Street offices. Sell's Ltd, *Sell's world press* (London, 1919).

[60] P. Gibbs, *Realities of war* (London, 1920), v.

[61] Grieves, 'War correspondents and conducting officers', 719–21.

The action which took place at Hooge on 16 June 1915 was the first major attack undertaken by the Liverpool Scottish, and is described in detail later in the book. Designed to be a relatively minor operation, with the aim of pinning down German reserves to aid major British and French attacks to the south, the battle was a bloodbath. The Liverpool Scottish suffered 400 casualties. It had entered the battle 542 strong.[62]

The first reports of Hooge appeared in the national papers on 17 June 1915. The information given was very brief and was derived from a German report which stated, 'The English succeeded near Ypres in slightly pushing back our positions north of the lake and village of Bellewaarde.'[63] The next reports appeared in *The Times* and the *Liverpool Courier*, and consisted of a report from their special correspondent, H. M. Macartney. He did not exaggerate the gains of the battle, describing it as successful but 'local in effect'.[64] The final report was that of 'eyewitness' at GHQ.[65] This too appeared in both the national and the local press. Again, this report did not exaggerate the victory gained, but failed to acknowledge the huge casualty list. It concentrated on the demoralization of the prisoners taken, the supposedly accurate shelling performed by the British artillery, and the individual acts of bravery displayed by the various units and individuals who took part in the action.[66] 'Our next line had swept forward in another glorious rush and had reached the German trench almost on the heels of the first line', claimed 'eyewitness'.[67] It was a typical description of the Battle of Hooge, which, in common with the other officially sanctioned reports, contained no impressions of the conditions of the battle.

To obtain more detailed information, editors had to turn to a different source, that of personal letters and interviews. In this enterprise the local newspapers were more successful than the national papers. The national newspapers lacked the direct connections which the local press maintained with the battalions from their respective cities. Men wrote and families sent in letters to their local paper more readily than to the national press, and correspondents interviewed the wounded in English hospitals. As previously discussed, the censorship of such material was

[62] McGilchrist, *The Liverpool Scottish*, 48.
[63] *Daily Mirror, Manchester Guardian, The Times*, 17 June 1915.
[64] *The Times, Liverpool Courier*, 18 June 1915.
[65] 'Eyewitness' was a regular official communiqué, written by a Regular officer at GHQ, which disseminated war news. The practice was abandoned in 1916 and instead war correspondents were used. See Grieves 'War correspondents and conducting officers', 720.
[66] *Manchester Guardian*, 22 June 1915; *Liverpool Daily Post*, 23 June 1915.
[67] *Manchester Guardian*, 22 June 1915; *Liverpool Daily Post*, 23 June 1915.

minimal, permitting graphic descriptions of battle to be transmitted to the newspapers.

The audience for whom the journalists were writing must also be considered. The local papers were able to carry greater details of individual battles because they had the freedom to concentrate solely on one or two local battalions. The specific, unit-based articles that sold local newspapers were, however, not suitable for national papers, which had to appeal to a wider audience and provide a greater variety of news. Consideration of their audience, rather than a strict adherence to the censorship rules, may have led the national papers to print fewer letters.

The accounts of the Battle of Hooge provided by the participants differed in terms of the quality of description. They were by no means entirely accurate and often gave a very partial view of the battle. However, when read as a whole, they provided a comprehensive and balanced narrative of events.

The accounts related by the men were heroic in tone, and conveyed the excitement they had felt during combat, making them compulsive reading. Private Fyfe's article is a case in point. 'There could be nothing finer than this attack of our infantry, as, led by officers, they charged stubbornly and steadily right into the teeth of hell.'[68] This heroic description of the troops was followed by a description of the fate of some of those heroes. Fyfe did not spare the feelings of the public. 'Many of our fellows had their heads blown clean off and others were simply smashed to red fragments.'[69] In his report Fyfe was keen to stress the bravery of the Liverpool Scottish, but the glamour of war was noticeably absent. This attitude towards the war was prevalent in many of the accounts. There were few who did not stress the huge losses incurred by the Battalion, alongside their depictions of courage.

Some reports on the battle dispensed with the descriptions of heroism altogether. Private Izzett wrote to his father: 'We took the trenches alright and stuck to them, but we lost heavily whilst doing so. I don't remember it very clearly, in fact I could remember nothing but shells and heaps of dead men.'[70]

In contrast to the national papers, even the headlines of the local papers acknowledged the terrible losses. In the first account by the *Liverpool Daily Post*, there were four introductory headlines to the article, arranged in the following order, 'A Glorious Charge, Liverpool Scots in Action, Storming German Trenches, Casualties among Officers.'[71] Two days

---

[68] *Liverpool Echo*, 21 June 1915, Private Fyfe.
[69] *Liverpool Echo*, 21 June 1915, Private Fyfe.
[70] *Liverpool Daily Post*, 23 June 1915, Private Douglas Izzett.
[71] *Liverpool Daily Post*, 21 June 1915.

Figure 5.4 Photographs of the Liverpool Scottish in the Battle of Hooge, published in the *Northern Daily Dispatch* and the *Liverpool Daily Post*, June 1915. They were taken by Private F. A. Fyfe while lying wounded in No Man's Land.

later, the ordering of the headlines had changed: 'Charge of the Scottish, Battalion Losses, More Thrilling Stories.' As the obituaries flooded into the newspaper offices, it became apparent that the attack had been costly and this was reflected in the headlines.

Photographs of the attack were also published. Although the taking of unofficial photographs in France was regarded as an offence by the military authorities, this did not deter certain members of the Liverpool Scottish. Private Fyfe, a photo-journalist in civilian life, smuggled a vest pocket camera, previously used for police court work, to the front. It was secreted in a bandolier by removing two cartridge clips.[72] His picture of the battle scene, taken whilst he was lying wounded, relayed images to the home front of dead soldiers and the debris and desolation of No Man's Land. It was published in several papers and reinforced the dual message of the heroism of the Liverpool Scots and the confusion and brutality of battle (see Figure 5.4).

---

[72] *Liverpool Echo*, 12 February 1963.

Figure 5.4 (cont.)

These articles from 1915 challenge the myth that civilians were ignorant of the conditions and consequences of battle. Few people reading the articles from the local papers could have failed to register the enormous cost in lives of the Battle of Hooge. Nor could they have harboured any notions of a glamorous war when the descriptions of the battlefield evoked images of horror.[73] Yet the opinions of the civilians remain difficult to quantify. How can we gauge the real civilian reaction to the Battle of Hooge?

The 'In Memoriam' messages placed in the *Liverpool Daily Post* a year later, on 16 June 1916, may go some way to providing an answer. These messages indicated that the majority of the families and friends of the victims had rejected any notions of a glorious war. They took consolation in the belief that their men had sacrificed their lives for the sake of their country. The concept of duty and of honour appeared in many of the messages.[74] However, despite the headlines such as 'A Glorious Charge'

---

[73] Geoffrey Moorhouse has used the *Bury Times* as a major source for his book *Hell's foundations: a town, its myths and Gallipoli* (London, 1992). Although he does not discuss the role of the local newspaper in the town, the passages quoted support the argument that graphic descriptions of battle were published in the local papers. Similarly some of the books in the Pals series contain detailed local newspaper reports. See, for example, L. Milner, *Leeds Pals* (Barnsley, 1991), 150–62.

[74] A quarter of the forty-one messages contained references to duty and honour.

that had been emblazoned in the newspapers a year previously, there was no glorification of the Charge by the relatives. Of the forty-one messages, only one mother referred to her son being 'killed in the glorious charge'. The grieving relatives had absorbed the underlying message of the brutality of war that had been embedded in the majority of letters and newspaper reports of 1915. The civilians of Liverpool, at least, cannot be reconciled with the 'bewildered' ignorant civilians other historians have depicted.[75]

Of course, there were some elements of the battle which were exaggerated or left undisclosed. Private Fyfe's claim that the Germans suffered more casualties than the British was patently untrue, and the excessive concentration on the German prisoners captured ensured that the public received the impression that the enemy had suffered heavy losses.[76] These inaccuracies are likely to have been a result of the combatants' partial view of the battle, rather than a deliberate attempt to deceive. All the authors of the exaggerated reports were wounded early in the battle, when Germans were indeed fleeing from the first line of trenches. If lightly wounded, these men were given the responsibility of escorting the prisoners behind the lines, thus their accounts inevitably mentioned the German prisoners.

A more conscious manipulation of the story was the omission from all newspaper coverage of the British artillery shelling their own men. It is possible that some correspondents were not aware of the fact. Diary entries of Private Herd, for example, also do not mention the artillery at all.[77] However, many private letters to families refer to friendly fire, so it is likely that any mention of this incident was either censored by the editors or withheld by the men and their families in the first place. The men were keen to promote a heroic image of their battalion within Liverpool, and the fact that many casualties had been caused by the Battalion advancing too far, too quickly, did not reflect well on the discipline of their unit. Yet, despite these omissions and exaggerations, the remainder of the Hooge narratives, published in the local newspapers, were all consistent with other sources, including diaries, reminiscences and unpublished letters. Thus, it appears that the soldiers had been remarkably candid in their descriptions of, and feelings towards, the battle.

As the war progressed and more Liverpolitan battalions became engaged in the fighting, it became increasingly difficult for even the local newspapers to cover the activities of individual battalions, particularly when many were fighting in the same action. The content of the

---

[75] Haste, *Keep the home fires burning*, 31.   [76] *Liverpool Echo*, 21 June 1915.
[77] E. Herd, Diary, 16 June 1915, Herd Papers, KRC, MLL, 1981.850.

national and local papers began to converge. Letters from the men at the front became less prominent in the provincial dailies as the role of the special newspaper correspondent evolved.

The special correspondent for the *Liverpool Daily Post*, Philip Gibbs, was shared with the *Daily Chronicle*. However, Gibbs managed to preserve the local angle and frequently emphasized the role of Liverpolitan units in major offensives.[78] The life of the Lancashire Territorials, both in and out of the line, was reported in special articles throughout the war.[79] For example, many Liverpolitan men were interviewed after their actions in the Third Battle of Ypres in August and September 1917.[80] Gibbs' stories highlighted the human cost of taking pillboxes that had not been adequately destroyed by artillery, and described the gruesome deaths of the enemy: 'Their dead bodies were mixed with tons of mud and wreckage ... Here and there you could see a few sticking out of the mud and sometimes you would come on a mud bespattered face with two glazed eyes staring at you from the muddy waste.'[81] That Gibbs concentrated on the fate of the enemy did not detract from the impact of the article or blind civilians to the similar fate of the Liverpolitan soldiers, whose names subsequently adorned the rolls of honour in the newspapers.

The defence of Givenchy, where the 55th Division held back a determined enemy attack, also received wide coverage in the local and national press, in part because it was one of the few success stories emerging from the Western Front after the German Offensives in March and April 1918. The papers heaped praise on the Division. 'Lancashires' stand', 'How the 55th Division excelled', read the headlines of the *Liverpool Daily Post* on 11 April 1918. Yet again, the agonies of battle were not ignored, with the action being described by Gibbs as 'grim fighting in a bad corner of hell'.[82]

In his book, *Battles of the Somme*, Gibbs acknowledged that he did not tell the whole truth about the war,[83] but this was true for all who tried to explain the experience of combat. As an artillery officer commented, after reading his own attempt to describe an artillery bombardment, 'I suppose, that the whole thing defies description.'[84] Those at home could never truly understand what it was like to live and fight in the trenches.

---

[78] *Liverpool Daily Post*, 21 September 1917; 22 April 1918.
[79] Articles included 'What the Terriers have done in the War', *Liverpool Courier*, 7 May 1915; 'Poppies and crosses', *Liverpool Echo*, 1 October 1917.
[80] *Liverpool Daily Post*, 22 July 1917; 4 August 1917.
[81] *Liverpool Daily Post*, 7 August 1917.   [82] *Liverpool Daily Post*, 11 April 1918.
[83] P. Gibbs, *Battles of the Somme* (London, 1917), 17.   [84] *The Times*, 19 August 1916.

Perhaps, however, this was unnecessary. C. E. Montague, a press censor himself, made an important point in a letter to his wife in September 1917:

> Of course just as in ordinary life one does not go out of the way to describe details of a friend's death by cancer ... so one does not keep harping on details of incised, contused or lacerated wounds ... But why should one? One assumes that every adult knows for himself that death by bayonet or shell wounds cannot be a pleasant experience or sight.[85]

Those on the home front did not need graphic description to realize the hideous nature of battle. For both sides, letters and newspapers provided escape and comfort, and for this reason they did not want their newspapers feeding them a diet of unrelieved horror.

Common to all reporting throughout the war was an absence of military criticism. The failure of the artillery at Hooge was not communicated in the press, and the Liverpool newspapers did not dwell on the reverse at Cambrai in November 1917. Whilst there was some criticism of generalship, it was largely confined to those comments made by MPs in the House of Commons,[86] and there was no criticism of the performance of the 55th Division.[87]

The civilians were aware, from reading personal letters and talking to soldiers returning from the front, that the men did not always agree with the ways in which the war was being fought. However, the reasons behind the absence of criticism in the newspapers were understood and accepted by both soldiers and civilians. They were aware of such omissions when reading the papers.[88] In December 1917, Mr Perry Robinson, the special correspondent of the *Liverpool Echo*, explained the unofficial rules governing newspaper reporting in wartime. He was concerned that the reading public were too sceptical of the newspapers, and urged them that 'reading between the lines' was not always necessary. Whilst admitting that he was careful to say nothing that would encourage the enemy or depress the men, he claimed: 'our dispatches are vastly more truthful

---

[85] O. Elton, *C. E. Montague: a memoir* (London, 1929), 193–4.
[86] *Liverpool Daily Post*, 13 December 1917.
[87] *Liverpool Daily Post*, 28 December 1917. A number of gruesome stories regarding the work of the Liverpools and the Cheshires at Cambrai were published, but there was no criticism of the 55th Division.
[88] Keith Grieves has suggested that, despite his book entitled *Disenchantment*, C. E. Montague, one of the GHQ press censors, acknowledged the necessity of propagating a high level of falsehood in the interests of successful surprise attacks. He commented that Montague's tolerance of falsehood was higher than might at first be thought. The same holds true for the soldiers and civilians of Liverpool. 'War correspondents and conducting officers', 731.

than the public gives them credit for'.[89] The civilians in Liverpool were an informed and distrustful audience; they were not easily manipulated by the press or by those in authority.

If censorship remained low-key and omissions were understood as a necessity, did propaganda, the other strand in the alienation thesis, antagonize the men at the front? Newspapers could be charged with alienating soldiers through their constant denigration of the enemy, characterizing the German soldier as variously weak, inhuman, evil and barbarous. Undoubtedly, civilian newspapers pedalled this type of propaganda from the beginning of the war, but it did not create a rift in outlook between home front and fighting front. Clumsy atrocity stories did not turn the civilians of Liverpool into rabid xenophobes. They had access to many additional sources of information with which to assess the veracity of the stories, and did not believe everything they read. Nor did the soldiers consistently feel a sense of comradeship and community solidarity with the opposing enemy. The 55th Divisional Magazine, in both its 1917 and 1918 editions, carried contributions from the ranks that expressed a deep-seated contempt for their enemy.[90] Soldiers were equally capable of accepting and even initiating crude stereotypes and anti-German propaganda to be found in the civilian newspapers.

Both at home and at the front, the way in which the enemy was viewed altered according to his behaviour, rather than simply being led by newspaper opinion. The first chlorine gas attacks at Ypres in 1915 left the men of the Liverpool Rifles with a fierce hatred for their enemy who was not following the rules of warfare. Gradually, this hatred subsided, and when faced by Saxons on the Somme, a mutual agreement to 'live and let live' was arranged. In November 1915, Macfie wrote to his father, 'the men seem to be on excellent terms with the enemy ... they say that our bombers in the listening post ... sit on their parapet and sings songs to the Germans who take their part in the concert ... yesterday they apologised for the Prussian artillery'.[91] Families and friends on the home front were kept well informed of the soldiers' fluctuating attitudes towards the enemy.

Sometimes the reporting of an enemy action would touch both soldiers and civilians simultaneously. The sinking of the liner the *Lusitania* in May 1915 provoked strong responses from the Liverpool Scottish and the

---

[89] *Liverpool Echo*, 7 December 1917, 4. Philip Gibbs claimed in his book, *Realities of war*, that as the war progressed the censor 'allowed nearly all but criticism, protest and the figures of loss', v.

[90] *Sub Rosa: Being the Magazine of the 55th West Lancashire Division*, June 1917 and June 1918.

[91] R. A. S. Macfie to father, 15 November 1915, Macfie Papers, IWM, Con. Shelf.

civilian community in Liverpool. The *Lusitania* story was a propagandist's dream, and was used to denigrate the enemy throughout the world, with newspaper headlines such as that of the *Daily Mirror* reading, 'Sea murderers toll of 30 little babies.'[92]

Irrespective of the emotive reporting, the *Lusitania* held a special significance for the people of Liverpool. The *Lusitania* was the pride of the Cunard shipping line, a Liverpool-based company, whose employees were well represented in both Liverpool Battalions. On her maiden voyage in 1907, 200,000 Liverpolitans had lined the waterfront to see her depart. She won the Blue Riband for Britain at the expense of Germany, and reigned supreme on the transatlantic crossings until 1914.[93] The *Lusitania* became the symbol of the success and power of the city, and the people of Liverpool felt the attack personally. Their responses – the civilian looting of the unfortunate German businesses in Liverpool and the enthusiastic attack by the Liverpool Scottish a month later at Hooge – were executed with equal venom. Although other factors, including the death of comrades and the desire to prove themselves as an effective battalion in their first major attack, also promoted the savage bayoneting of dazed Germans by some members of the Liverpool Scottish, their war cry of 'remember the *Lusitania*',[94] as they rose from their trenches, indicated that they also had a strong desire to avenge the sinking of the ship.

Another key way in which newspapers were supposed to have alienated the soldier was by misrepresenting the feelings and attitudes of the British Tommy. Soldiers were portrayed as constantly cheerful, whatever the conditions in which they found themselves.[95] The civilians of Liverpool, on the other hand, knew from personal letters that the men could be angry, depressed, scared, anxious and sometimes happy.[96] That they understood the difficulties faced by the men was indicated in Annie Stock's contribution to the *Young Crescent* in April 1916: 'It must be a splendid thing for you to have such strong support from your church while you are away, and I feel sure it must make you strong, courageous and true in moments when you are tempted to give way.'[97] The significance of her message lay in the acknowledgement that there was a temptation to 'give way' which had to be resisted. This message was

---

[92] *Daily Mirror*, 10 May 1915.
[93] P. Young and J. Bellen (eds.), *Whitbread book of Scouseology, 1900–1987*, vol. 2, *Merseyside life* (Liverpool, 1987), 6.
[94] Threlfall, *The history of the King's (Liverpool) Regiment*, 178.
[95] Robb, *British culture and the First World War*, 125.
[96] The changing mood of the Battalions over the whole war is discussed in chapter 8.
[97] *Young Crescent*, church newsletter, April 1916.

reinforced by the Reverend William McNeill in an article on the importance of maintaining a positive outlook, in the *Trinity Presbyterian Church Magazine*: 'Do you suppose that the hope and courage of the men at the front so manifest in their letters came to them from the skies as they cross the channel to the continent? Not a bit of it. They are the product of discipline.'[98] McNeill referred to a personal discipline of the spirit, which was, he claimed, something for which one had to struggle. The noncombatants, remaining in Liverpool, had not been indoctrinated by the cheerful propaganda of the newspapers.

It is evident that local newspapers formed a vital link between the home and fighting fronts. The men used the newspapers as another mechanism of communicating with their friends and family and with the wider community. A soldier, whose letter was subsequently published in the *Liverpool Courier*, wrote to his friend advising him to watch the newspapers as the Liverpool Scottish were about to make a name for themselves.[99] Other soldiers sent home newspaper cuttings of photographs pertinent to their situation. The *Daily Mail* carried a photograph on 13 August 1917 in which a dugout Sergeant Macfie had occupied on the first day of the Third Battle of Ypres was depicted.[100]

The local newspapers were used as a forum, through which soldiers could present their ideas to a wide audience. Private Fyfe's account of the Battle of Hooge was published in at least three newspapers: his own paper, the *Daily Dispatch*, on 20 June; the *Liverpool Echo* on 21 June; and the *Liverpool Courier* a day later. Fyfe succeeded in acquiring the largest possible circulation of his Battalion's exploits, informing the home front about the nature of the war, and gaining recognition for his unit. Public recognition was particularly important to those fighting for home in the trenches, as one soldier explained: 'It cheers us up to know that while we have been doing our bit, the people of the old town have had us in their thoughts.'[101]

Some men were not averse to presenting their own distortions to raise their profile at home, usually exaggerating the activities of their battalion during a particularly boring period in the trenches, and of course men did not all concur in their views of battle and living conditions. Members of the same battalion sent letters to the newspapers, attacking each other's point of view.[102] However, through their letters, the men at the front were

---

[98] *Our Church News*, 7 May 1916, MRO, Provincial and church records, 285 TRI 13/3.
[99] *Liverpool Courier*, 22 June 1915.
[100] Macfie Papers, IWM, Con. Shelf.   [101] *Liverpool Courier*, 7 March 1916.
[102] See *Liverpool Echo*, 17 December 1914; *Liverpool Daily Post*, 5 February 1915; B. McKinnell, *The Diary of Bryden McKinnell, Liverpool Scottish* (Liverpool, 1919), 40.

exerting control over the messages which the newspapers were communicating to their home community. This was an empowering rather than an alienating experience.

It is therefore difficult to believe that the soldiers were alienated by the content of the newspapers in which they had affected the material published. Although an article appeared in the 55th Divisional Magazine, in which the newspaper editor Horatio Bottomley, thinly disguised as 'Halario Bounderby',[103] was caricatured, the men valued their contact with home provided by the newspapers and, significantly, never criticized the local papers.

The men in the trenches had constant access to both local and national papers. They too were reliant on the newspapers for the comprehensive picture of the conflict.[104] Thus, the soldiers and civilians of Liverpool were party to the same information regarding the war and the home front, which helped to promote understanding of each other's situations, rather than widening the knowledge gap between combatants and non-combatants.

That some men suffered a sense of alienation from civilian life on returning home on leave or discharge cannot be denied. Such feelings were articulated on both sides by literary figures, including Siegfried Sassoon and Erich Maria Remarque, but were never held universally. For most men, the major sources of dissatisfaction were specific figures, including shirkers, profiteers and politicians. Sergeant Macfie was critical of those civilians who were on strike in March 1915:

> I object to all these extravagant demands for rise of wages and strikes, while men [in the trenches] are living miserably for 1/- a day ... In my opinion all strikers should be given the alternative between enlistment and the hangman's rope.[105]

Private Ellison expressed disgust for the businessmen he met when on leave, who, whilst complaining of the restrictions the war imposed, were rapidly accumulating profit through arms manufacture.[106] *Sub Rosa*, the 55th Divisional Magazine, also devoted column space to articles attacking politicians. The author of one feature observed an MP being given a

---

[103] *Sub Rosa: Being the Magazine of the 55th West Lancashire Division*, June 1918.
[104] Sergeant Macfie claimed that the newspapers were distributed free in such abundance that he was able to cancel his orders placed with newspapers in England. The only type of paper missing was a picture paper, such as the *Sphere*. See Hiley, 'You can't believe a word you read', 95, for an indication of the importance of the national papers to the men at the front, and 96–7 for estimates of circulation figures for the British national press in France.
[105] R. A. S. Macfie to brother, 31 March 1915, Macfie Papers, IWM, Con. Shelf.
[106] N. F. Ellison, Diary and Memoir, November 1915, Ellison Papers, IWM, DS/MISC/49, 75.

tour of the safe area behind the line, and commented that on his return to England the MP would 'let off more gas than the old Boche has since the war began. And I'm not sure which does the most harm.'[107] The men objected to politicians, who did not experience the true nature of the fighting yet pompously expounded their views on the war to the public in Britain. The soldiers at the front could be angered by actions taken or views held by civilians in Britain, but their criticisms and feelings of frustration were rarely directed at the home front as a whole. Their major grievances were directed at small, discrete sectors of the population. Dissatisfaction with politicians, newspaper editors and profiteers did not serve to alienate soldiers from their friends, family or home community.

Conclusion

At the level of the family, the local community and civic circles, soldiers and civilians went to extraordinary lengths to maintain contact with each other. Through a variety of communication channels, including the three basic links of letters, leave and the press, the soldiers transmitted images of the war as they saw it, whilst in return civilians sent news from home to the trenches. Local and, later in the war, county homogeneity helped to support these links. Soldiers on leave could disseminate information to families of those still serving in the trenches, and on returning to the front could impart the latest news from the home town. For their part, newspapers carrying stories of local battalions retained their relevance to the end of the war, particularly as Liverpool's dailies had a wide circulation, including the counties of Lancashire and Cheshire.

The interchange of information and views played a vital role in maintaining the morale of the men in the trenches. It provided acknowledgement of the soldiers' sacrifice, promoted mutual understanding of the hardships and difficulties experienced both at home and at the front, and fostered a common perspective on the conflict. The Territorials may have been serving in the army, but they remained an integral part of their families and pre-war social circle; the worlds of the soldier and the civilian remained closely linked for the duration of the Great War.

---

[107] *Sub Rosa: Being the Magazine of the 55th West Lancashire Division,* June 1918.

Part II

Command, discipline and the citizen soldier

6   Command and consent in the trenches

In the years before 1914 British society had attained a remarkable degree of cohesion, despite the obvious inequalities that existed between the social classes in the realms of education, wealth and influence.[1] It was a hierarchical society based on consent and mutual agreement, rather than on coercion. The repressive mechanisms maintained by the state were very weak. The judiciary, although staffed by the upper classes, remained independent, and the government had no standing army with which to impose its views. Moreover, although electoral rights were confined to the better off, those lower down the social scale enjoyed the freedom to express their opinions, and there were labour laws that allowed for collective bargaining.[2] Neither the government nor the employers were free to impose their authority on those below them in the social pyramid. Employers and employees, leaders and led, recognized they were part of a reciprocal relationship. Those in authority received deference only when they fulfilled their obligations to their workforce. At all levels of society, boundaries defining acceptable behaviour were set and bargaining over contentious issues took place within these parameters.[3]

The pre-war regular army also relied on an unspoken bargain between officers and other ranks to operate, but the nature of the bargain was different from that brokered in civilian society. The lower ranks were kept in a position of extreme dependence and social relations within the army were underpinned by a punitive disciplinary system.[4] Drawn from the poorest, most marginalized sectors of society, the recruits to the regular army were typically young, unemployed slum dwellers with little education.[5]

---

[1] A. J. Reid, *Social classes and social relations in Britain 1850–1914* (Cambridge, 1992), 34.
[2] *Ibid.*, 35–6. The 1911 strike in Liverpool and the subsequent settlements are indicative of the scope for negotiation between employers and employees in Liverpool before the Great War.
[3] Bourne, 'The British working man in arms' 344. Sheffield, *Leadership in the trenches*, 71–2.
[4] Bourne, 'The British working man in arms', 337. Sheffield, *Leadership in the trenches*, 12.
[5] E. M. Spiers, 'The regular army in 1914', in Beckett and Simpson, *A nation in arms*, 44, and W. J. Reader, *At duty's call* (Manchester, 1988), 6.

These soldiers often served for long periods abroad, policing the Empire. Distanced from civilian life, soldiers became psychologically and practically dependent on their regiment. It provided a substitute family and a focus for loyalty, as well as catering for their immediate day-to-day needs.[6] In return, soldiers were expected to be unquestioningly obedient to their officers and fiercely loyal to their unit and its traditions. Punishment for non-conformity was harsh and uncompromising.[7]

It is not surprising that the average volunteer, who differed from his regular counterpart in social status, educational standard and aspirations, was not prepared to serve under such an oppressive regular army regime. As we have seen in previous chapters, the Liverpool Territorials were men who retained a stake in civilian society and carried their civilian expectations and attitudes with them when they joined their unit. In the same way as the French soldiers in Leonard V. Smith's study recognized and negotiated a social contract with military authorities, the men of the Liverpool Territorials expected those in authority to respect their status as citizen soldiers. Both armies reflected the political organization of their respective societies. For the French, the legitimacy of the army resided in the Republic, which through popular sovereignty was responsible to all its citizens, including those in the trenches. This gave their soldiers the moral authority to negotiate with their commanders.[8] British citizen soldiers lacked the formal constitutional rights of the French, but their experience of a pre-war society based primarily on consent meant that they too expected decision-making in the army to involve a degree of consultation and bargaining. The rules and conventions of pre-war society, as well as their own skills and abilities, were employed to help shape their lives in uniform. The myriad ways in which they did so will be examined in this chapter and the next.

Volunteering

The belief that men were owed certain rights and privileges, even when serving in the army, was reinforced by their perception of the act of volunteering. Volunteering in itself was an example of consensual democracy in action. Whilst men were prepared to volunteer to defend the country in times of national danger, Britain could avoid maintaining

---

[6] Bourne, 'The British working man in arms', 337.
[7] This portrayal of the regular army is undoubtedly simplistic and further research may reveal that the regular soldier too had more scope for the expression of his views than we have hitherto realized. However, more individual studies of regular units are needed to investigate this theme.
[8] Smith, *Between mutiny and obedience*, 193.

a large, expensive and potentially oppressive standing army.[9] The small regular army, dispersed throughout the Empire, posed little threat to the lower echelons of society, and the Territorials were not expected to suppress any internal disturbance.[10]

The steadfast resistance to the introduction of conscription, and the general attachment to volunteering as a concept, provide an indication of the general abhorrence of compulsion in British society.[11] The Territorial handbook explained the importance of volunteering in no uncertain terms: 'Universal service as it prevails in the great military states demands so close a grip of the state on the individual, so rigid a mechanism for collecting yearly levies, that it would affect our domestic life and our existing social system most profoundly.'[12] This sentiment was felt so strongly, by both Liberal politicians and the general public, that it was 1916 before conscription was imposed.[13] Volunteering allowed the British to maintain 'freedom' abroad, whilst retaining freedoms at home. As one middle-class lance corporal put it: 'They have swept with their unconscripted legions all over the world and planted the flag of Britain in every land, and in every land it has stood as a symbol of freedom. It is this sense of strength and fair play that has made the British nation and the soldier unite in times of stress.'[14]

On the outbreak of the Great War, therefore, the government was reliant on its citizens voluntarily enlisting in the army or, in the case of serving Territorials, volunteering to fight abroad. The rush to the colours, particularly in late August and September 1914, indicated that the tradition of volunteering was alive and well. Whilst volunteering was regarded as a duty, it was a duty that civilians chose to perform. By contrast, men in continental countries that practised conscription did not have the same

---

[9] Before the war Britain and her colonial interests were defended by the Royal Navy, the small regular army and the Indian army. These forces provided an economic and politically safe solution to the defence of British strategic interests until 1914. See A. Gregory, 'Lost generations' in Winter and Robert, *Capital cities at war*, 66.

[10] Their terms of engagement stated that, 'Officers and men of the Territorial Force are not liable to be called out as a military body in aid of the civil power in the preservation of peace.' War Office, *Service in the Territorial Force: terms and conditions* (London, 1912), 4.

[11] Of course the conscription debate and the structure of the pre-war armed forces was more complicated than this and was also informed by the naval tradition, financial considerations and the needs of the Empire which could not be effectively policed through short-term conscription. Beckett, 'The nation in arms', 4 and E. M. Spiers, 'The regular army in 1914', in Beckett and Simpson (eds.), *A nation in arms*, 39.

[12] War Office, *Rights and duties of Territorial soldiers* (London, 1912), 86.

[13] See R. J. Q. Adams and P. P. Poirier, *The conscription controversy in Great Britain, 1900–1918* (London, 1987).

[14] A. Bryans, Are the Britons phlegmatic?, 4 June 1915, Bryans scrapbook, LSM, Acc. No. 484.

option. Thus, the British volunteer made a personal decision to sacrifice his home comforts, his job and in some cases his life.

This was never an easy decision to make, particularly where dependants were involved. Sergeant Macfie felt the weight of responsibility when urging the men of his company to volunteer for overseas service. He wrote to his father: 'Some of them were in pitiable circumstances – quite young lads without parents who support a family of younger brothers and sisters, recently married boys with a little baby and fellows who have aged parents beyond work, who will be left alone. They were pathetically anxious to go, but anxious about their dependants too and I felt it was a very heavy responsibility to urge that it was their duty.'[15] It was this level of personal sacrifice that required those in authority to acknowledge the efforts of the Territorials and respond to their grievances. The willingness to fight was an extension of the agreements brokered in civilian society and could not be taken for granted.

In 1908 the volunteering tradition had been codified with the establishment of the Territorial Force. The formal terms and conditions constituted a compromise between the architects of the Force and its members. They conferred privileges on the pre-war Territorials, many of which were successfully defended until 1916, although they were not extended to volunteers in other formations. The Territorial soldier was guaranteed the right to serve with the unit he joined and was not liable to serve outside the United Kingdom.[16] This meant that Territorial battalions could not be used as feeder units for the regulars, nor were they required to fight abroad without 60 per cent of the battalion assenting. These privileges were jealously defended by County Associations and their supporters in parliament.[17]

The right to serve with the unit of their choice was a privilege which posed logistical difficulties for the army, but which survived beyond 1915. An attempt to force the Territorials to sign away their right failed in the wake of parliamentary opposition and an immediate decline in recruitment.[18] Lord Derby was particularly concerned with the plummeting numbers of enlistments, prompting his protest that the action was 'murdering recruiting' in Lancashire.[19] Until the Military Service Acts of 1916 standardized the terms and conditions of all recruits, removed the right to resist transfer and compelled men to serve, potential volunteers had the power to shape army regulations through declining to enlist.

---

[15] R. A. S. Macfie to father, 25 August 1914, Macfie Papers, IWM, Con. Shelf.
[16] War Office, *Service in the Territorial Force: terms and conditions* (London, 1912), 2–4.
[17] See chapter 4. [18] Beckett, 'The Territorial Force', 136.
[19] Churchill, *Lord Derby, King of Lancashire*, 185–6.

After May 1916 this avenue of protest was closed, but the tradition of balancing civilian desires against military and governmental requirements did not die with the Military Service Acts. The War Office was forced to keep units regionally homogeneous throughout the war, largely in response to soldiers' demands,[20] while separation allowances, rent restrictions, deferral of debt payments, and disability and widows' pensions were expected as a right, whatever the fiscal demands placed on government by the war.[21] Although the Territorials relinquished some of their formal constitutional rights under wartime conditions, in general the government was not permitted to abdicate its responsibilities towards its citizen soldiers. Indeed, at the end of the war the authorities were forced to amend their demobilization plans to allow those who had served longest to be released first, instead of demobilizing in accordance with industrial need.[22]

Conditions of service: rights and responsibilities in the Liverpool Territorials

At the beginning of the war the Territorials were not afraid to exercise their rights if they felt that the authorities were not affording them proper consideration. Many men in the Liverpool Rifles persistently declined to take the Imperial Service Obligation. On 10 August 1914 their Colonel appealed to their sense of duty, which was followed by an impassioned speech from Lord Derby on 26 August. James Handley remained unmoved by the efforts of his superiors, later remarking, 'Lord Derby at church parade pleaded hard for volunteers for foreign service. He did not convert me.'[23] Handley had joined the Force in 1912, one of the minority for whom patriotism was a primary motivating factor. However, his first experience of active service was not a happy one. His company was left single-handedly to wind up the annual camp whilst the rest of the Battalion returned to Liverpool. Handley and his comrades perceived this as grossly unfair, which contributed to their decision to resist the call to overseas service.

Financial considerations were also an inhibiting factor for the middle-class men of the Liverpool Rifles. 'Some of the older, married NCOs came forward and said that their life insurance polices would not hold good if they went on campaign abroad ... the question of insurance policies was eventually arranged by Lord Derby taking up the question

---

[20] See chapter 4. [21] Englander, 'Soldiering and identity', 314.
[22] A. Rothstein, *The soldiers' strikes of 1919* (London, 1980), 98–9.
[23] J. S. Handley, Memoir, Handley Papers, IWM, 92/36/1, 5.

with the government.'[24] This was one of many demands which the state had to meet before the men were prepared to volunteer to serve abroad.

The Liverpool Scottish had similar problems gaining the minimum number of overseas volunteers required for the unit to be deployed as an independent battalion. A number of pre-war soldiers were barred from serving abroad by age restrictions,[25] but there were many others who had serious misgivings about volunteering for overseas service. Macfie wrote to his father of the canvassing that was employed to persuade the men to volunteer: 'Today the colonel (rather a silly old ass) appealed for more and each man was asked individually. At the end we were still 70 below the minimum ... Moffat, an old sergeant of mine, and I went round the company and got 20 more from E company alone in about 10 minutes.'[26] Whilst a certain amount of bullying took place, it was, in the end, the right of a Territorial to refuse to serve abroad, and the men were aware that it was their personal decision.

Not only did individual Territorials utilize their rights on the outbreak of war; the battalions were also given some leeway to negotiate the terms of their deployment. The Rifles, having acquired the requisite number of volunteers to serve abroad, turned down the opportunity of being stationed in Egypt in September 1914.[27] A similar opportunity was rejected by the Scottish.[28] Egypt was viewed as a side-show, and the Battalions, wanting to take part in the main fight, held out for a place in the line in France. Whilst this was not the experience of all Territorial units, many of whom undertook to relieve regular units in the outposts of the Empire,[29] it is clear that some Territorials could exploit their privileged volunteer status to determine when and where they fought in the initial months of the war.

Until 1916, Territorials could return home 'time expired' if they had completed their pre-war contract and served their supplementary wartime 'buckshee' year. Such men were encouraged to re-enlist with the promise of a month's furlough in Britain and a bounty payment. Records of time-expired men do not exist, but a number of soldiers in both the Scottish and the Rifles took advantage of the opportunity. For some it was

---

[24] S. E. Gordon, Memoir, Gordon Papers, IWM, 77/5/1, 22.
[25] In general, men of the Territorial Force had to be aged between 19 and 41 to serve overseas. In some cases the Battalion turned a blind eye to men serving over the upper age limit. Those discovered to be underage on active service were placed in a non-combatant role, or were returned to the feeder battalions in England.
[26] R. A. S. Macfie to father, 25 August 1914, Macfie Papers, IWM, Con. Shelf.
[27] S. E. Gordon, Memoir, Gordon Papers, IWM, 77/5/1, 16.
[28] N. G. Chavasse to F. J. Chavasse, in Clayton, *Chavasse*, 59.
[29] Beckett, 'The Territorial Force', 134–5.

age or ill health that informed the decision to leave,[30] but for others it became a statement of dissatisfaction with the inequities of the army system. In March 1916, Sergeant Macfie described the response of his supply section to an incompetent Brigade Headquarters: 'Small mistakes are made frequently and the list sent seems designed to protect the staff from responsibility rather than to assist the men who must unpack the goods ... this caused feelings of discontent in the Battalion which is causing to the Battalion the loss of two of its oldest CQMS, among them Gillespie, a man whose sterling worth and integrity it would be impertinence to praise.'[31] Gillespie had experienced enough and escaped to Liverpool, time expired.

Other men simply felt that by serving for a year or more in France they had fulfilled their moral obligation and could honourably pass on the responsibility to those who had not yet had a taste of the fighting. After particularly arduous experiences, this was often the prevailing view in the whole unit, whether or not the men were due to be sent home time-expired. Macfie described to his father, in January 1915, the dark mood of his Battalion,

They say no more Territorials are to leave Britain and that we cannot expect strengthening drafts of men. If so, what will they do with the remnant of us? Probably employ us in fatigues at the base, but the men are hoping fervently to be sent home. When they get home, (if they do) they will immediately want to come out again, but in the meantime they are 'fed up' with Belgium and very homesick.[32]

Again, after the Battle of Hooge in June 1915, there was a strong feeling that the Battalion had done its duty and was owed a break from the trenches. Sergeant Bromley recalled the attitude of the men at that time: 'After Hooge the men felt that they had done their bit and wanted to go home, or at least be put on communication lines. They had had their moment of glory and were quite prepared to let someone else take over, at least for a while.'[33] It was not possible at the time for commanders to accede to the wishes of the men in the Scottish. The New Armies were only partially trained and there were no replacements. However, the feelings of the men could not be ignored, and all members of the Battalion were granted a clear six days' leave in England, in recognition

---

[30] S. E. Gordon, Memoir, Gordon Papers, IWM, 77/5/1, 86.
[31] R. A. S. Macfie, Army Book Ration Report, 16 March 1916, Macfie Papers, LSM, Acc. No. 315, 20.
[32] R. A. S. Macfie to father, 9 January 1915, Macfie Papers, IWM, Con. Shelf.
[33] W. G. Bromley, Memoir, LSM, Acc. No. 544, 55. See also E. Herd, Diary, 26 June 1915, Herd Papers, KRC, MLL, 1981.850, 22.

Figure 6.1 RQMS R. A. S. Macfie.

of their ordeal at Hooge. This was an unprecedented move, widely attributed by the men to Lord Derby's skill in negotiation.[34]

It was the illusive concept of 'fairness' that lay at the heart of the unwritten contract between the authorities and the soldiers. Whilst the Territorials would have preferred a break from the trenches, they understood that the military authorities were grappling with a dangerous manpower shortage, and under the circumstances six days' leave was a fair compromise.

This did not mean that such compromises produced immediate acquiescence and stifled all discontent. In the aftermath of Hooge, leave proved problematic to arrange, given the Battalion's continuing responsibilities in the trenches. It began on 11 July, but the Battalion was forced to return to the trenches on the 14th, which caused great consternation among the survivors. Macfie recorded that: 'The men went to the trenches with bad grace ... They argue that some may be killed before they have been home and that it would not be fair! Consequently they are behaving with exemplary caution.'[35] If the authorities were unwilling to safeguard the lives of the survivors until they had been granted leave, then those survivors were unwilling to take any unnecessary risks on behalf of the authorities.

For the Rifles different issues, including a lack of promotion, provoked discontent which rumbled away until the Battle of the Somme.[36] Again, it was the 'unfairness' of the situation that grated on the middle-class Territorials. They resented being deprived of opportunities, whilst promotion in the Service battalions was plentiful. Private Ellison recalled later that, 'It seemed grossly unfair at the time and we said hard and bitter things about the nebulous "they" who controlled our lives from London.'[37] Underlying the vociferous discontent, however, was a realization that, though regrettable, their sacrifice was necessary for the successful prosecution of the war effort. Ellison's post-war assessment of the pre-Somme period concluded magnanimously, 'So the first lines of our Territorial Regiments were sacrificed through the exigencies of war. Let us not blame anybody; they volunteered for a nasty job and did it.'[38]

Each battalion harboured specific, sometimes unique grievances. Lack of opportunity was a middle-class preoccupation which would have affected

---

[34] W. G. Bromley, Memoir, LSM, Acc. No. 544, 53. After the Somme and Passchendaele the men were given the opportunity of visiting the seaside channel resorts in France.
[35] R. A. S. Macfie to Sheila Macfie, 19 July 1915, Macfie Papers, IWM, Con. Shelf. See also E. Herd, Diary, 14 July 1915, Herd Papers, KRC, MLL, 1981.850, 25.
[36] See chapter 3 for a full discussion.
[37] N. F. Ellison, Diary and Memoir, Ellison Papers, IWM, DS/MISC/49, 70.
[38] N. F. Ellison, Diary and Memoir, Ellison Papers, IWM, DS/MISC/49, 70.

only a minority of units in 1915. Similarly, few Territorial or New Army units had borne the burden of the early fighting of 1915 or could claim the battle experience of the Liverpool Scottish. What was considered fair or unfair by a unit could be interpreted differently according to their wartime experience and the civilian expectations and social status of its members.

Conscription and the concept of fair play

The act of volunteering endowed the recruit with a sense of pride that helped to boost morale in the trenches and often lasted a lifetime. Conversely, it also promoted a degree of intolerance towards those who had not joined the volunteering 'club'. Volunteering had always been an essential component of Territorial values, but by 1916 it had acquired a heightened significance. Fair play not only was demanded from the military authorities, it was also expected of the wider society. Those soldiers who had shirked their moral duty in waiting for compulsion were viewed as having placed an unfair burden on those who had volunteered, and there was a suspicion that some may have profited financially from war work.[39] Anyone who had breached the rules of fair play was liable to be treated with hostility. This had implications for the way in which conscripts integrated into battalions and raises questions about the extent to which conscripts were able to accept the traditions of their host units and assimilate their behaviour.

For the British, the label 'conscript' became a term of denigration which evoked the image of an untrustworthy and inefficient soldier. These concerns about the willingness and fighting spirit of conscripts were endorsed at the grass roots level by Sergeant Macfie writing home in March 1917: 'We have a lot of conscripts now. The old mob used to try to do as much as possible as well as they could. These unwilling soldiers do as little as they may and as badly as they dare ... I hope to have the pleasure of making the lives of these unpatriotic jellyfish a misery to them.'[40] Similarly, the regimental historian of the Liverpool Scottish recalled one conscript who had the audacity to complain that his tea was cold. The Company Sergeant Major's reply, 'No wonder my lad, it's been waiting for you for two years',[41] was made in jest, but the underlying contempt was unmistakable.

---

[39] Profiteering, whether on a large scale by industrial magnates, or on a personal level, was viewed with distaste. See J. Robert, 'The image of the profiteer', in Winter and Robert (eds.), *Capital cities at war*, 104–33.
[40] R. A. S. Macfie to Charlie Macfie, 31 March 1917, Macfie Papers, IWM, Con. Shelf.
[41] McGilchrist, *The Liverpool Scottish 1900–1919*, 262.

Yet conscripts were by no means a homogeneous group.[42] Whilst some soldiers, like Macfie, dismissed them *en masse*, distinctions were often made between true older conscripts, 18-year-old conscripts and Derbyites.[43] Derbyites were those soldiers who had voluntarily attested their willingness to fight under the Derby Scheme, which ran from October to December 1915. They were to be called up when required, single men first. The scheme was intended to provide a mechanism for balancing the needs of industry and the army, whilst avoiding the element of compulsion inherent in conscription.[44]

By January 1916 the last ditch attempt to prolong volunteering had clearly failed. Too few single men had attested, and so the first Military Service Act was passed in January 1916 authorizing the conscription of single men. In May, conscription was extended to all men between the ages of 18 and 41.[45] Most single Derbyites were called up between January and May 1916 and formed many of the reinforcements after the Battle of the Somme. Conscripts filtered through a few months later, and although the majority of them were pressed men, some were boys who had turned 18 during the war and volunteered before they were called up. From September 1916 onwards a draft to a unit would have contained a mixture of Derbyites, 'volunteer' conscripts and pressed men. Thus the term 'conscript' encompassed a variety of recruits with different backgrounds and motivations.

Investigation of this theme has been difficult. The conscript diaries that survive for the Liverpool Territorials are few and far between, but do reflect the diversity of recruits. The first was written by Eric Peppiette, a Derbyite called up in February 1916, another was produced by Gerald Warry, a conscript who had volunteered early in 1916 to serve from his 19th birthday the following June, and the third diary, of Private Lorimer, chronicled the life of a true conscript who joined his battalion in July 1917.[46]

The Derbyites were not regarded as having quite the same integrity as the volunteers. They had postponed joining the army, and in some cases had not chosen their unit. Nevertheless, they had volunteered to serve of their own free will, in contrast to the conscripts who had to be forced.

---

[42] I. Beckett, 'The real unknown army: British conscripts 1916–1919', in J.J. Becker and S. Audoin-Rouzeau (eds.), *Les sociétés européennes et la Guerre de 1914–1918* (Paris, 1990), 346.
[43] H. Clegg, Memoir, Clegg Papers, IWM, 88/18/1, 66.
[44] J. M. Bourne, *Britain and the Great War 1914–1918* (London, 1989), 121.
[45] Beckett, 'The nation in arms', 14.
[46] E. Peppiette Papers, LSM, Acc. No. 887; Warry Papers IWM, 96/12/1; J.W. Lorimer Papers, LSM, Acc. No. 794.

It was the 'true' conscripts who received the greatest opprobrium of the volunteers. Surprisingly, the surviving diaries present a rosy picture of the smooth integration of conscript drafts, and a willingness to accept the status quo of the battalions, suggesting that successful integration into the battalions was the norm. Clearly, not all volunteers were hostile to the incoming conscripts. Rather than ostracizing new drafts, senior members of the battalions often made a conspicuous effort to help them settle into the unit.[47] We know that the senior members of the battalion were usually those who had worked their way up through the ranks, and had often served from the early days of the conflict.[48] They were invaluable in teaching new additions the rules of survival and the traditions of the battalions.[49]

It should not, perhaps, be too surprising that conscripts were quietly assimilated into the battalions. They were products of the same society and used to the same rules in civilian life, thus they were keen to adopt the volunteer attitude that demanded concessions from the authorities in return for co-operation. Moreover, their general attitudes towards the war were often similar to those of the volunteers.[50] They too saw the war as merely an interlude in their lives,[51] were concerned about loved ones at home, and retained a healthy disrespect for excessive military discipline.[52] Of course, the specific issues over which the soldiers negotiated, and in some cases the ways in which they negotiated, changed over the course of the war. For example, at the end of the war, Sergeant Bromley was surprised to find that the Liverpool Scottish Battalion was being run almost according to trade union rules. Everybody had a set job, with restricted hours.[53] Although this happened after the end of hostilities, such an arrangement would have been unthinkable in the middle-class Battalion of pre-war days. However, this change had to do more with a shift in the social composition of the unit than with the influx of conscripts. Men naturally turned to the form of negotiation most familiar

---

[47] G. Warry, Diary, 30 November 1916, Warry Papers, IWM, 96/12/1, 5.
[48] See chapters 3 and 8.
[49] R. A. S. Macfie to Charlie Macfie, 13 March 1917, Macfie Papers, IWM, Con. Shelf. See also J. Atherton, Narrative of his father's memories, LSM, Miscellaneous File A, 7–10. Corporal Forbes of the Liverpool Scottish had served since 1914. In November 1917 he was still teaching new conscripts basic survival skills. Whilst this second-hand memoir is of limited value, it reinforces the first-hand accounts.
[50] Janet Watson has also noted a similarity between volunteer and conscript attitudes towards the war: *Fighting different wars* (Cambridge, 2004), 27.
[51] E. Peppiette Papers, LSM, Acc. No. 887; Warry Papers IWM, 96/12/1.
[52] J. W. Lorimer Papers, LSM, Acc. No. 794.
[53] W. G. Bromley, Memoir, LSM, Acc. No. 544.

to them in civilian life, and for the working class trade unions were, increasingly, a feature of the workplace.

Other studies have suggested that conscripts did not adversely affect the fighting performance of a unit.[54] This evidence from the Liverpool Territorials suggests that their social behaviour too was similar to that of the volunteers. In general, conscripts and volunteers alike expected to receive certain rights and privileges in return for their military service, and if the issue was deemed important enough they were prepared to negotiate for a solution they considered 'fair'.

The limits of military duty

As well as negotiating over their basic conditions of service, the men were able to influence the level of violence on their section of the front. As Len Smith has shown for the French 5th Division, it was the men who decided what was militarily feasible in any given situation and this determined the extent to which they were prepared to follow orders from above.[55]

The men in the trenches were certainly prepared to sustain casualties to achieve worthwhile objectives. Major Gordon's assessment of a 1916 raid concluded that, 'the losses amongst the NCOs and men were not out of proportion to the results obtained'.[56] But useless slaughter was not to be tolerated. If the men felt themselves to have been abandoned to their fate by their commanders, then surrender, the most dramatic end to the negotiation process, ensued. Accounts of surrender, although coloured by a desire to exonerate, suggest that rapid calculations were made based on the possibility of rescue through counter-attack or artillery support, as well as the usefulness of the resistance. Surrender was not entirely a function of lowered morale, although mood could influence the calculations made, and it did not necessarily mean that a man had abandoned hope of his country winning the war. Men such as Corporal Evans, who surrendered in preference to being massacred on 30 November 1917, were not cowed by the experience. As they marched under guard to a station, the men discreetly shredded letters and other evidence that they thought might prove useful to the enemy.[57]

Similar calculations characterized decision-making during periods of trench warfare. Instances of 'live and let live', a process by which tacit truces were established with the enemy, appeared in diaries from time to

---

[54] Sheffield, *Leadership in the trenches*, 183.
[55] Smith, *Between mutiny and obedience, passim*.
[56] S. E. Gordon, Memoir, January 1916, Gordon Papers, IWM, 77/5/1, 171.
[57] W. Evans, Account of Capture, Evans Papers, IWM, Con. Shelf, 7.

time.[58] For example, when the 6th Rifles occupied the village of Vaux in 1915, the agreement with the enemy opposite to abstain from shelling arose because both sides held cliff tops that overlooked the other's village. In No Man's Land below, however, vigorous patrol fighting continued, a clear indication that the men were prepared to use violence if it served a useful purpose.[59]

Whilst Smith is right to suggest that the soldiers took a functional approach to military aggression, he does not always investigate the complex reasoning behind decision-making. Military utility was important, but not the only criterion to be considered. Revenge and recognition also had their part to play. Consider the evaluation of the Battle of Hooge by the Liverpool Scottish. They recognized that it had been a failure in terms of the ground captured and the men lost, but considered it a triumph because their bravery in the face of carnage had won a name for themselves amongst both the regular army and the citizens of Liverpool. It had been a primary objective to 'prove themselves as Terriers and men'[60] before the Battle, and psychological achievement could be as, if not more, important than the material objectives gained.

The mechanics of the bargaining process: leadership and the command relationship

The command relationship in a regular battalion was based on a structured, paternalistic hierarchy, designed to impose order on the chaos of the battlefield and unruly elements of the unit. At the pinnacle of the hierarchy, the Commanding Officer of the Battalion communicated the orders and regulations to the men at the base of the pyramid via officers and NCOs at company, platoon and section levels.[61] In this regular model those at the bottom obeyed those above them because of a stylized paternalistic exchange in which obedience was given in return for a leader providing a courageous example and attending to the needs of his men before his own. Theoretically, this system ensured that the orders issued at the top of the command chain would be executed unchanged by privates in the field.[62]

---

[58] This concept was first described by T. Ashworth in *Trench Warfare, 1914–1918: the live and let live system* (London, 1980).
[59] N. F. Ellison, Diary and Memoir, Ellison Papers, IWM, DS/MISC/49, 60.
[60] B. McKinnell, *Diary of Bryden McKinnell Liverpool Scottish* (Liverpool, 1919), 14 June 1915.
[61] There were four companies, sixteen platoons and sixty-four sections in a battalion. In general, a company held 240 men, a platoon had sixty and a section fifteen.
[62] War Office, *Standing Orders of an infantry battalion* (London, 1917).

Many historians have accepted this model of the command relationship at face value. They have assumed that the model provided a template for all British formations during the war and thus have criticized the British command system on the grounds that it was inflexible and crushed independent thought, leaving those at the end of the chain in a childlike state with little freedom to innovate.[63] This interpretation of the British military command chain has some merit, but is too simplistic. It ignores both the pre-war discussions within the British army over the nature of the command relationship and the reality of its wartime operation in both Territorial and Service battalions.

As early as the 1890s the nature of the command relationship was already being discussed within the British army. Looking ahead to future wars involving temporary, volunteer soldiers, G. F. R. Henderson, a British military intellectual, suggested that the 'habits and prejudices of civil life will have to be considered in their discipline and instruction and officers will have to recognize that troops without the traditional instincts and training of the regular soldiers require a different handling from that which they have been accustomed to employ'.[64] Henderson believed that in future conflicts it would be necessary to harness the education and initiative present amongst the citizen soldiers in the ranks.

Whilst the regular army had generally been able to avoid addressing contentious issues such as delegating authority downwards, or changing training regimes to promote initiative in the years before the war,[65] the

[63] One of the leading proponents of this argument is T. Travers. In his book *The killing ground*, he argued that the mindset of the Edwardian army ensured that the criticism of superiors did not occur and this affected communication throughout the army structure, although it must be acknowledged that Travers' main focus was the flawed relationships between Haig, GHQ and Army GOCs. Martin van Creveld has further emphasized the disastrous legacy of the peacetime structure of the British army, which sought to regulate every aspect of a soldier's life. He also stressed the importance of the ideas of the structured battlefield and centralization of command to British commanders, and compared them unfavourably with their German counterparts. M. van Creveld, *Command in war* (Cambridge, 1985). However, as John Bourne has highlighted, command, leadership and tactical developments have been neglected at corps, divisional and brigade level, making the assessment of the character and success of the British command system difficult. The publication of Bourne's chapter, 'British generals in the First World War', in G. D. Sheffield (ed.), *Leadership and command, the Anglo-American experience since 1861* (London, 1997), has begun to address this gap in the historiography, alongside more general works which stress the extent to which the British army understood the necessity of decentralization. See R. Bryson, 'The once and future army', in Bond et al. (eds.), *'Look to your front'*, 34–6, and Griffith, *Battle tactics of the Western Front*, 22.

[64] G. F. R. Henderson, *The science of war*, ed. N. Malcolm (London, 1906), 310.

[65] Gary Sheffield has suggested that attitudes towards discipline and the officer–man relationship in the regular army may have been more complex than we have previously realized. However, in general, the army was seen as possessing a rigidly hierarchical approach. See Sheffield, *Leadership in the trenches*, 23.

Territorial Force had been forced to consider the needs of its citizen soldiers, coming to similar conclusions to those of Henderson. Both before and during the war a greater degree of consultation had to be introduced into the command relationship, creating a more relaxed atmosphere in battalions, and a greater degree of open discussion over important issues. Initiative was seen as something to be harnessed in the lower ranks of the Territorial Force and the formal punitive discipline system was a tool to be applied only *in extremis*. To be sure, Territorial battalions did not always get the balance right, but there was certainly an awareness that citizen soldiers had different skills and expectations from the average regular recruit and to ignore these facts could have serious consequences for the morale and discipline of units.[66] If we examine what was expected of leaders within the Liverpool Territorials we can begin to appreciate how the command relationship worked in units of citizen soldiers.

For the battalions of the Rifles and the Scottish, composed almost exclusively of men with high social status in 1914, the difficulties of accommodating citizen soldiers were acute. The middle-class rankers were used to being at the top end of the hierarchy, exercising paternalism rather than being on the receiving end, and allowances had to be made for this in the first two years of the war.

At the beginning of the war, officers and sergeants were denied the opportunity of fulfilling the traditional duties of the regular army officer in caring for the practical needs of their men. They did not need to supplement the diet and clothing of their subordinates, as the other ranks turned to their wealthy families at home to send out endless parcels. Sergeant Robert Scott Macfie, for example, was forced to bestow gifts of clothing sent out by his family on regular troops serving alongside his Battalion, rather than on the men under his command.[67] From 1915 onwards, the units were also inundated with gifts from charitable organizations in Liverpool.[68] The role of the officers in this respect was redundant.

Those in authority had to look for other ways to demonstrate their concern for the practical welfare of the men. Sergeant Macfie found the issue of inconsistent pay an area in which he could demonstrate a caring attitude. In the First World War a soldier's pay was often delayed, with errors in calculation caused by poor administration in Britain. Recognizing this fact, Sergeant Macfie appealed to Captain Rae, then the adjutant of the 3/10th Liverpool Scottish at Oswestry, to protect the interests of the men on foreign service. He wrote:

---

[66] Peel, 'The Territorial Force', 41.
[67] R. A. S. Macfie to Jenny Paton, 4 March 1915, Macfie Papers, IWM, Con. Shelf.
[68] R. A. S. Macfie to father, 6 May 1916, Macfie Papers, IWM, Con. Shelf.

Men at the front do not have time nor the ability to check their pay and rely on the paymaster. I do not mean to accuse the paymaster of any deliberate attempt to cheat soldiers. But I do assert as a truth to which every NCO who has dealings with them can testify, that the state of continuous confusion that reigns in this office is a scandal that would not be tolerated in any bank.[69]

Rae sent a CQMS from the Reserve Battalion to the paymaster's office at Preston every month to check for inaccuracies.[70]

In the first few years of the war the Medical Officer was the one figure who was in a unique position to look after the physical well-being of the men in both Battalions, without appearing patronizing. He had a difficult and ambiguous role, being expected both to protect the health of the men, and to police the sick parade to keep as many soldiers as possible in the fighting line.[71] Some doctors undoubtedly failed to strike the right balance, but the Liverpool Scottish were fortunate to have an exceptional Medical Officer.

Lieutenant, later Captain Chavasse, took his responsibilities very seriously. Not only did he treat the inevitable casualties; he safeguarded the health of the Battalion by organizing a laundry wherever possible and instigated a regime to prevent trench foot. Private Warry remembered that, 'At some time during the day we had to each go to the stretcher bearers' dugout in the trenches and have our feet rubbed with whale oil to prevent frostbite and we were given dry socks if required.'[72] The experimental prophylactic regimes could, however, go too far. 'At one time he had a brain wave and persuaded the Colonel to allow the experiment of rubbing the men's feet with the rum ration and giving them hot cocoa to drink. The experiment was short-lived. Possibly there was risk of mutiny.'[73] There was a limit to what the men would accept, even from the 'Doc'.

Chavasse also had a sixth sense for identifying men who were about to break down. Vulnerable men were removed for 'rest' in fatigue companies behind the lines, a practice which was instituted as early as Spring 1915.[74] By contrast, malingerers and shirkers were dealt with very severely. The

---

[69] R. A. S. Macfie to Captain G. B. L. Rae, 14 November 1916, Macfie Papers, IWM, Con. Shelf.

[70] Captain G. B. L. Rae to R. A. S. Macfie, 17 November 1916, Macfie Papers, IWM, Con. Shelf.

[71] For an analysis of the tension between the different roles a Medical Officer was expected to perform in the Great War, see C. E. J. Herrick, 'The broken soldier: the bonesetter and the medical profession', in Bertrand Taithe and Tim Thornton (eds.), *War* (Stroud, 1998), 184.

[72] G. Warry, Diary (post-war addition to diary), Warry Papers, IWM, 96/12/1, 6.

[73] E. Herd, Diary (post-war note, 1939), Herd Papers, KRC, MLL, 1981.850, 51.

[74] R. A. S. Macfie to Charlie Macfie, 30 January 1915, Macfie Papers, IWM, Con. Shelf.

Figure 6.2 Captain N. G. Chavasse, MC, VC and Bar, RAMC, Medical Officer of the Liverpool Scottish.

treatment of a Gordon Highlander, who had shot himself in the leg on his way up to an attack at Sanctuary Wood, sent a clear message to the men who witnessed his treatment. 'When the Doctor heard that the wound was self-inflicted he poured iodine into it. The shrieks of the poor man were awful. Dr Chavasse was absolutely the finest man I have ever met in my life ... but if he had any suspicion that a man was malingering ... his sympathy rapidly evaporated.'[75]

At a psychological level, some officers and senior NCOs were able to provide emotional support in a form that did not offend the sensibilities of the middle-class rankers. In many cases this worked simply because of the age differential. In 1914 only 34 per cent of the officers of the Liverpool Scottish were under the age of 24, whereas in September 1914, this cohort accounted for 62 per cent of new other ranks, and it had risen to 71 per cent by November 1914.[76] Older officers and sergeants found the paternalistic relationship a natural one.[77] They became 'father' or 'uncle' figures for the younger soldiers, and because of the close pre-war civilian relationships among men of the Territorials, those in authority had often promised families at home to look after their sons.[78] The Liverpool Scottish tradition of Presbyterian church elders attaining sergeant's rank also meant that sergeants were older than those under their control. They had their civilian moral authority to bolster their position in their companies and pre-war experience of a paternalistic, pastoral role.[79] These two factors ensured that the command relationship worked better than might have been expected for the middle-class battalions until social homogeneity broke down at the end of 1916, and the more comfortable civilian-style social hierarchy was restored.

Courageous leadership was another key quality regular soldiers required from their officers as part of the paternalistic/deferential exchange.[80] The ranks of the Liverpool Territorials also required their officers to display

---

[75] W. G. Bromley, Memoir, LSM, Acc. No. 544, 56–7. See also *Sunday Graphic and Sunday News*, 5 November 1933.
[76] Officer percentage calculated from a random sample of officers in Liverpool Scottish index. Recruitment figures calculated from Liverpool Scottish Attestment Book, LSM, Acc. No. 32.
[77] This was also the case for some of the officers of the 22nd Royal Fusiliers. G. Sheffield, 'A very good type of Londoner and a very good type of colonial: officer–man relations and discipline in the 22nd Royal Fusiliers, 1914–18', in Bond *et al.* (eds.), *'Look to your front'*, 141.
[78] P. Douglas to parents, 15 February 1915, Douglas Papers, IWM, 66/274/1. This trend of older NCOs could still be discerned in A Company of the Liverpool Rifles in 1918 (see Table 6.1).
[79] *Liverpool Scottish Regimental Association Gazette*, June 1932, vol. 2.
[80] Sheffield, 'Officer–man relations, discipline and morale in the British Army of the Great War', 419.

Table 6.1 *Age structure of NCOs serving in Number 1 Platoon, A Company, 6th Liverpool Rifles, 1918, by rank*

Age group	% of lance corporals	% of corporals	% of sergeants
18–19	22	22	0
20–24	56	56	16.5
25–29	0	0	67
30–34	22	22	16.5

Source: W. J. Pegge, Nominal roll and foot books, 1/6th (Rifle) Bn, King's (Liverpool) Regiment, No. 1 Platoon, A Company, Pegge Papers, MLHL, M198/1/2/1–2

leadership ability and courage, but their expectations were, arguably, set higher than in regular battalions. The absence of a clearly defined social class barrier between the officers and other ranks meant that the leadership of both the Rifles and the Scottish was under constant scrutiny. There were many men in the ranks with the necessary credentials, equally capable of performing a leadership role. This meant that those in authority had to meet high standards before they were accepted by their men.

Some officers lived up to these high standards. Captain Turner was well respected for his calm manner under fire. On his death in January 1915 the company requested that his brother, newly arrived from England, should be posted to them.[81] Similarly, W. G. Bromley, a private at the time, remembered the actions of the officers during their sojourn on Slaughter Hill, April 1915: 'During all this time the shells were dropping all around and it seemed as if we were simply waiting for death ... The officers, and in particular Sergeant Jones, turned out to be trumps and acted with an utter disregard for danger, walking about, giving assistance to the wounded and cheering up the men generally.'[82]

For newly arrived and inexperienced officers, however, the demanding environment could pose almost insurmountable difficulties. Such officers were regularly ridiculed or even ignored if less than able. One captain's 'ridiculous habit of going about in the trenches in an almost crouching position ... drew ribald remarks when observed by some of the old sweats'.[83] His reputation as a rugby international did not compensate for his unease in the trenches.

[81] Turner Papers, Letters and newspaper cuttings, KRC, MLL, 1973.163.5.
[82] W. G. Bromley, Memoir, LSM, Acc. No. 544, 35.
[83] H. S. Taylor to Liverpool Scottish Regimental Museum Trust, Date unknown, LSM, Folio 2.

Sergeant Bromley questioned the judgement of his new platoon officer on a number of occasions during July and August 1916. He recalled ignoring a dangerous order given by the young Second Lieutenant. 'The officer said "Why the hell don't you lead on as ordered?" By this time I was feeling pretty fed up and not considering or caring for the consequences said "it is suicidal to take the men over the crossroads until the next salvo is past. And when you have been out here as long as I have, you will perhaps know something of the game."'[84] Bromley suffered no punishment for this outburst, but the officer did not learn from his mistakes.

By the time the Liverpool Scottish took their place in the line for their part in the Somme Offensive, Bromley had made a decision to eschew the formal leadership structure of the platoon. He described the actions of his officer prior to the battle: 'He marched along at a terrific pace, eyes glaring ... His actions throughout the march were so peculiar and unnatural that I made up my mind that I would not follow him blindly in the attack but use my own discretion to a certain extent.'[85] It proved a wise choice. As soon as the officer went over the top he made a beeline for the German trenches, keen to get at the enemy, but having forgotten about his responsibility to the rest of the platoon. He was never seen again. The average educated Territorial in the ranks did not become an unthinking automaton on joining the army and obedience was often conditional on the character and experience of those issuing the orders.

Finally, for the command relationship to work effectively a degree of loyalty had to be displayed by both parties. Officers expected the men to be loyal to their unit and by association to their leaders. Pride in the battalion had been the basis of the regular regimental system.[86] The Territorial brand, based on social and regional pride, was no less potent, endowing many men with the strength to continue fighting under appalling conditions. Conversely, the men expected loyalty and support from their commanders, and when this was not forthcoming there were serious consequences for discipline and morale.

Brigadier Kentish, commanding 166th Brigade, was continually clashing with his Battalion commanders over trivialities,[87] but he overstepped the

---

[84] W. G. Bromley, Memoir, LSM, Acc. No. 544, 83.
[85] W. G. Bromley, Memoir, LSM, Acc. No. 544, 84.
[86] This was certainly the case for the Second Scottish Rifles at the Battle of Neuve Chappelle. See J. Baynes, *Morale, a study of men and courage: the Second Scottish Rifles at the Battle of Neuve Chappelle, 1915* (London, 1967), 253.
[87] 166th Bde. Letter No. AQ100/23, 23 March 1918, Macfie Papers, IWM, Con. Shelf. Battalion commanders and all quartermasters' staff were officially reprimanded for the men being deficient of wound stripes and various badges.

mark in February 1918 when his Headquarters failed to send an instruction to the Liverpool Scottish and then allowed the Battalion to take the punishment for this oversight from the Divisional Commander. 'X Company's feelings were rather those of the small boy who is whipped for something his elder brother had done, while the elder brother looks on with his hands in his pockets.'[88] The Scottish could not tolerate this injustice and the Battalion Commander sacrificed his command by taking up the matter with Jeudwine. His removal became inevitable given the strained relations that ensued between Battalion and Brigade. Kentish had failed to exercise the loyalty expected of him, which generated ill feeling for many months following the incident.

Brigadier General F. J. Duncan, commanding 165th Brigade, was another domineering character. His attitude was that of an uncompromising regular, keen to mould the Territorials into a regular-style brigade. As Major Gordon observed, 'General Duncan undoubtedly did not like Territorials at first and was inclined to consider them as mere civilians.'[89] Again the approach created much tension within the Brigade, particularly as the Territorials did not prove malleable. However, Duncan had one saving grace; he remained loyal to his battalions and stood up for his people against outsiders.[90]

The men recognized this quality and reciprocated: 'After our raid in November 1916 the raiding party, when visited by the Staff Captain with the congratulatory telegrams, insistently inquired "But what does the Brigadier think about it?"'[91] Gradually both sides came to respect each other and even his catch phrases – 'eat well, sleep well and work well, but no time for loafing'[92] – became proverbial in the 6th Rifles, although one suspects more in jest than in practice. Duncan, for his part, showed his attachment to his men very publicly after an engagement during the Battle of the Somme. Sergeant Handley later described his actions: 'Brigadier Duncan, that hard stern soldier whom we feared stood by the roadside taking the "salute" ... as we turned our heads we saw him standing erect, his right arm raised in salute and – tears streaming down his face – ... barely a quarter of his men returned.'[93]

So the Territorials required their leaders to fulfil some, although by no means all, of the requirements traditionally demanded by regular

---

[88] McGilchrist, *The Liverpool Scottish*, 163.
[89] S. E. Gordon, Memoir, 15 May 1916, Gordon Papers, IWM, 77/5/1, 265.
[90] S. E. Gordon, Memoir, January 1916, Gordon Papers, IWM, 77/5/1, 146.
[91] S. E. Gordon, Memoir, April 1917, Gordon Papers, IWM, 77/5/1, 265.
[92] S. E. Gordon, Memoir, April 1917, Gordon Papers, IWM, 77/5/1, 265. See also Figure 6.3.
[93] J. S. Handley, Memoir, Handley Papers, IWM, 92/36/1, 11.

Command and consent in the trenches 143

PHASES OF THE WAR:—2. Gen. D——n finds a man doing dam-all.

Figure 6.3 'General Duncan finds a man doing d–n all': Brigadier General F.J. Duncan, DSO, commanding 165th Brigade and Lieutenant G. B. Birkett, Liverpool Rifles.

soldiers, but the exchange was certainly not the traditional one. As Henderson had identified years before the war, to lead citizen soldiers successfully not only required a willingness to provide a courageous example and attend to the basic needs of the men, it also necessitated a willingness to listen to those citizen soldiers and to make an effort to understand and respond to their multifarious concerns. First and foremost of these was their need to maintain those close links with home that were described in the previous chapter.

Unlike the regulars, Territorial soldiers had families, jobs and interests that were unconnected with the military. Alternative interests gave the Territorials different attitudes towards the war compared with the regular soldiers whose regiment was both the spiritual and the physical home. There was a general understanding within both Battalions and the wider Division that their members were citizen soldiers with responsibilities to their families as well as to the state. A man constantly worried about affairs at home did not make an efficient soldier, and it was to ensure military effectiveness, as well as in the spirit of humanitarian compromise, that a number of measures were instituted to alleviate some of the separation anxiety suffered by soldiers.

Whilst the Liverpool Territorials never disappeared *en masse* to keep up with work on the farm (as was the practice of some Territorials in 1915),[94] their officers were granted extended leave to attend to financial and domestic arrangements. Lieutenant Hughes was called home for 'business purposes' in January 1916, after having served seven months in France. He was transferred to the home establishment and did not return to the trenches until November of the same year.[95] This practice was established throughout the British army in early 1918 in the form of substitution leave. 'Officers and men who either had two years continuous service in the line, or were suffering from strain, or even for very urgent private reasons, were allowed, if recommended by their CO, to return to England for six months ... their places being filled by others of the same rank from the draft finding units at home.'[96]

In the Rifles individual problems were often regarded sympathetically, and in extreme cases men could be kept out of the firing line. On returning from compassionate leave in January 1916, Private Ellison explained to his CSM and Company Commander that his mother was dead, his father was seriously ill and that it was looking increasingly likely that he would soon have the responsibility of two young sisters to support. In recognition of his situation, Ellison was allotted the less risky jobs. He became a company storeman delivering rations and mail and remained at the Battalion transport lines during both Somme attacks in 1916.[97]

Y Company of the Liverpool Scottish also attempted to mitigate the effects of family separation from the beginning of the war, this time through helping those suffering at home. Sergeants Macfie and Colthart Moffat were able to draw up a short list of families who might be in immediate distress and a longer roll of those who would be in distress if their relation was killed or incapacitated. They appealed to family and friends at home to assist the families on the lists where necessary.[98] Obviously this sort of informal support system worked most effectively at the beginning of the war, when many of the families knew each other personally, the sergeants were familiar with the background of their men,

---

[94] Bourke, *Dismembering the male*, 149.
[95] S.E. Gordon, Memoir, January 1916, Gordon Papers, IWM, 77/5/1, 144; 1/6th Battalion King's (Liverpool) Regiment Casualty Book 1, KRC, MLL, 58.83.537a–b; D. D. Farmer, quartermaster of the Second Battalion of the Liverpool Scottish, was also granted time away from the Battalion in 1916 to nurse his sick wife. He returned in time to serve overseas in February 1917.
[96] McGilchrist, *The Liverpool Scottish*, 159.
[97] N. F. Ellison, Diary and Memoir, Ellison Papers, IWM, DS/MISC/49, *passim*.
[98] R. A. S. Macfie to father, November 1914, Macfie Papers, IWM, Con. Shelf.

and the innovators remained with the Battalion. It was later in the conflict that the more formal, institutionalized Territorial network came into its own.

The Territorial network was composed of past and present personalities well known to both families at home and men at the front. These personalities were either too old or medically unfit to fight, but supported the Battalions on the home front, through attending to the requirements of the Battalion, administering the funds raised and liaising with families. They were helped in these tasks by the established Battalion depots in Fraser Street and Warwick Street, which provided convenient bases from which to support those in need. Lieutenant Colonel G. A. Blair was the linchpin of the Liverpool Scottish depot's war effort. Having relinquished command of the Battalion in November 1914, he was put in charge of the depot, where he was noted for the 'scrupulous attention he paid to the claims made upon him by the relatives and friends of the men who were serving overseas'.[99]

Territorials also demanded that their leaders respect battalion traditions. These could range from practical traditions of uniform, drill and saluting, to unspoken attitudes regarding discipline and inter-rank relations that affected the way in which the unit was run. Chief among these traditions was the stubborn duration mentality of the men, an attitude which came to be shared by volunteers and conscripts alike. In a post-war article Sergeant Moffat explained the prevailing outlook of the wartime Liverpool Scottish. 'There is never a lad who turns to volunteering as willingly as an old British volunteer. He does not shirk his duty, but greets his demob with smiles. Demob he calls liberation.'[100] Whilst some men were more eager to join the war than others, most saw their wartime rank as temporary and were keen to leave the army at the conclusion of the conflict. Indeed, after August 1914 all Territorials joined for the duration of hostilities only.

By contrast, though the regulars were also volunteer soldiers, the army was their career. Their performance in war determined their promotion during and, very importantly, after the end of the conflict. As a result, regular soldiers, and particularly regular officers, could be more constrained to follow the rulebook to the letter and consequently rarely effected a complete integration into the more relaxed life of a Territorial unit. Sergeant Macfie, for example, voiced his indignation over the matter of his morale-boosting cooking competition, which was designed to entertain the Battalion and improve the culinary skills of the cooks. In a letter to his sister he wrote, 'The CO has sanctioned the competition and

---

[99] McGilchrist, *The Liverpool Scottish*, 266.
[100] *Hornsley Journal*, 23 October 1925, A. Moffat, Liverpool Scottish.

deleted all the best paragraphs from the rules in case the general should see them and stop his promotion. Professional soldiers are dreadful cowards morally.'[101] The CO was D. C. D. Munro of the 1st Battalion, Gordon Highlanders, who had joined the Liverpool Scottish four months earlier in March 1918. A year later, it was evident that he had failed to gain the trust of the Territorials, still being described as a 'stranger' in February 1919.[102]

The traditions and individuality of units rendered some officers rank outsiders and a disregarding of those traditions could cause serious discontent which undermined their own authority. The experience of Lieutenant Colonel Drew illustrates this point. Drew caused much disquiet on taking command of the Liverpool Scottish when he criticized their discipline and attempted to dictate the way in which they should wear their kilts. The collective discontent was expressed by the RSM, who, after a particularly heavy encounter with the rum bottle, voiced his feelings outside Drew's tent. After much discussion, the RSM retained his rank and discipline continued in a similar vein. To his credit, the Commanding Officer realized that it was not possible to impose a regular-style regime on the Battalion.

Another officer defeated by Territorial tradition was Captain Jaeger. Sergeant Bromley related that Jaeger 'caused amusement and cursing by expecting all NCOs and men to salute him in the trenches. Usual procedure was just to stand to attention, but being new from England and evidently determined to make the Territorial Force more proficient, this was not sufficient for him. Needless to say his expectations were not realised.'[103] The Liverpool Scottish had a succession of Commanding Officers, some sympathetic to Territorial traits, others favouring a harsher, regular approach, but no officer, not even a Commanding Officer, could impose his methods at the expense of Territorial tradition.

We should be careful, however, not to take this argument too far. Territorial traditions were seen as something to be defended, but if a Commanding Officer had a valid point the Territorials would, grudgingly, admit the need for changes. The first inspection by Brigadier General Duncan was affectionately remembered after the war in the Rifles' journal: 'our new Brigadier was not long in inspecting his units. Months of fighting had rubbed the polish off us, and in regard to smartness there was

---

[101] R. A. S. Macfie to Sheila Macfie, 7 June 1918, Macfie Papers, IWM, Con. Shelf.
[102] R. A. S. Macfie to Jack Macfie, 26 February 1919, Macfie Papers, IWM, Con. Shelf. Major Gordon also remembered a Regular officer, Lieutenant V. G. Hardy, who failed to fit in with the 6th Rifles' Territorial ways. S. E. Gordon, Memoir, 26 August 1915, Gordon Papers, IWM, 77/5/1, 142.
[103] W. G. Bromley, Memoir, April 1916 and October 1917, Acc. No. 544, 76 and 88.

a good deal to be desired. For instance, when the machine-gun limber was inspected the place which should have been devoted to ammunition was found to contain a gumboot and an old sock.'[104] There was a general acknowledgement amongst the rank and file that the Battalion needed to improve its performance and deserved the tirade it received from Duncan.[105]

The mechanics of the bargaining process: initiative and the command relationship

The Territorials were fortunate in their Divisional Commander, Major General Hugh Sandham Jeudwine, who proved responsive to the needs of Territorial troops and helped set the tone for the whole Division. So convinced was he of the qualities of citizen soldiers that he defended his junior ranks in print against criticism of their performance at Cambrai, and enthusiastically accepted the position of Director-General Territorial Army post-war.[106] The men of the Liverpool Territorials may have criticized their Divisional Commander over planning failures, particularly in regard to the Somme (1916), but they could not fault him on his methods of motivation and leadership.[107] Jeudwine was sensitive to the importance of Territorial characteristics. He was perceptive enough to harness regional identity to achieve military ends and valued the Territorials' capacity to act on their own initiative, an aptitude developed in civilian life.

In part, encouraging initiative in his subordinates was a logical response to the problems facing a divisional commander in the First World War. It was realized from an early stage that 'troops once committed to the attack must act on their own initiative'.[108] Orders passed down the line from higher formations, and conversely, situation reports from the front line, were rarely relevant by the time they arrived because of the technical limitations of communication.[109] In May 1917 Jeudwine indicated that he was well aware of the difficulties of his position, writing to Brigadier General Stockwell that, 'It is impossible for any book or any person to lay down the methods by which every possible situation that

---

[104] *Greenjacket*, July 1926.
[105] S. E. Gordon, Memoir, Gordon Papers, IWM, 77/5/1, 146.
[106] Bourne, 'British generals in the First World War', 103.
[107] R. A. S. Macfie to A. M. McGilchrist, 11 December 1928, LSM, Miscellaneous File M.
[108] Orders to Brigades, 55th (West Lancashire) Division No. 122 (G) 1 February 1916, Records of the 55th (West Lancashire) Division 1914–19, LRO, 356 FIF 13/2/671.
[109] J. Terraine, *The Great War* (Ware, 1997), xi; Bourne, 'British generals in the First World War', 105.

can be encountered in war should be met. All that can be done, or should be attempted, is to lay down principles and leave to the military knowledge and experience of commanders the selection of suitable methods.'[110] It was clear that responsibility for decision-making had to be devolved downwards.

Tactical responsibility was officially handed to the platoon commander through the GHQ training pamphlets SS135 of December 1916 and SS143 issued in May 1917, which marked the platoon as the basic unit of infantry tactics.[111] In his pamphlet entitled *Training principles* issued in December 1916, Major General Jeudwine emphasized the importance of the platoon to his Division:

> It must be impressed on all platoon leaders that each one of them now has a 'self contained command' and that this war has been said to be a platoon commander's war. It is within the power of each one of them to influence to a great extent the course of an action by his knowledge, resolution and courage. Every means possible must be employed to develop the character and the initiative of these leaders.[112]

In keeping with the ever-increasing devolution of tactical control, platoon commanders, in turn, were encouraged to cultivate their section commanders.[113] Major Rae's course notes for Commanding Officers stressed their importance as unit leaders, and the importance of training understudies to be able to exercise initiative on the battlefield.[114]

Developing initiative at the very lowest levels of command became a priority within the 55th Divisional training programme. This evidence contradicts the argument that the command structure of the British army stifled enterprise and self-reliance in the ranks. On the contrary, Major General Jeudwine recognized that many of his soldiers had held responsible positions in civilian life that required independent thought and problem-solving skills. By devolving decision-making down the chain of command he was able to harness their skills and experience to enhance tactical performance on the battlefield.

---

[110] Major General H. S. Jeudwine to Brigadier General Stockwell, 1st May 1917, Records of the 55th (West Lancashire) Division, LRO, 356 FIF 14/2/796.

[111] A. Whitmarsh, 'The development of infantry tactics in the British 12th (Eastern) Division, 1915–1918', *Stand To. The Journal of the Western Front Association*, 48 (January 1997), 30.

[112] H. S. Jeudwine, Training Principles, 55th Division (G 104), 8 December 1916, Records of the 55th (West Lancashire) Division, 1914–19, LRO, 356 FIF 13/2/642-3.

[113] Second Lieutenants were nominally in charge of platoons, but in general it was the sergeants who were more influential in controlling the men. Corporals commanded sections. See Griffith, *Battle tactics*, 22.

[114] G. L. Rae, Commanding Officer Course Notes, 3 April 1917, LSM, Miscellaneous File R.

The mechanics of the bargaining process: communication and the operation of command and consent

Recognizing the need to devolve decision-making and understanding that citizen soldiers demanded leaders who were responsive to their needs was only the first step in commanding citizen soldiers effectively. Unambiguous communication at all levels within a unit was essential to address these issues. For example, front-line soldiers had to be allowed to express their views to ensure that those issuing the orders were well informed of their outlook. Having listened, the leaders at each level of command had a duty to act upon the ideas emanating from below and to adjust their vision of what was possible. The resultant orders had to be justified in a way that would satisfy the men that their commanders held similar perspectives to their own. The consequences of a breakdown in communication, leading to divergent aims and expectations, were exhibited on a grand scale by the French mutinies of 1917.[115] Moreover, as the war progressed and responsibility was devolved down the chain of command, the men in the ranks had to be entrusted with more intelligence information to enable them to make sensible judgements without reference to higher authority. A breakdown of communication in this area could have catastrophic results for all types of military action.

Major General Jeudwine was fortunate to be building upon an adaptable Territorial command and communication system. The tradition of relaxed relations and inter-rank discussion in the Territorials eased the development of a complex network of communication channels and ensured that information passed upwards as well as downwards. Traditionally orders were delivered through the hierarchical rank system. Written orders, training instructions, and situation and intelligence reports passed up and down the rank structure and remained the most important methods of communication between front and rear, together with verbal commands passed along the field telephone system during static periods of trench warfare. In his attempt to garner additional information, Jeudwine also began to augment the feedback mechanisms within his Division. Some were additions to the existing hierarchy, others bypassed the traditional rank structure altogether, and some were initiated by those at the bottom of the military pyramid, transmitting information to all levels of the command structure.

---

[115] See Smith, *Between mutiny and obedience*.

Written communication

Most soldiers had an opinion on the manner in which the war was fought and organized. A minority put their ideas down on paper to send up the line of command. W. E. Pinnington's design for a new type of stretcher, for example, was championed by Captain Chavasse, who authorized its experimental construction. The stretcher was then shown to the ADMS and Divisional General, who gave orders for it to be produced by the Brigade workshops.[116]

Another member of the Liverpool Scottish, Private W. H. Campbell, was a budding tactician who devised a scheme for machine gun fire control. On 11 October 1916 he recorded the fate of his idea: 'Explained my scheme to Mr Buchanan [his company captain]. Accepted favourably. Red tape difficulty to overcome ... Colonel accepts my scheme. Good outlook!'[117]

Submitting written suggestions up the chain of command could result in the adoption of ideas generated from below, but it was a method of communication that was probably class specific. It relied on well-educated men in the ranks with the ability and inclination to express themselves on paper. Campbell, a draughtsman in civilian life, was motivated by a desire to secure some kind of promotion for himself. The willingness of junior officers to listen, and refer promising ideas up the chain of command, was also pivotal, and facilitated in Territorial units by the relaxed relations promoted by social homogeneity.

Even so, an idea took time to be passed through the ranks, and there were many opportunities for rejection at various levels of command before it reached the level at which it had influence. By the Third Battle of Ypres Jeudwine was beginning to appreciate the value of the views from the trenches, and was unwilling to wait for them to trickle up the chain of command. He commissioned his own battle narratives in the wake of 31 July 1917, thus forging a direct link with those in the front line. All junior officers, NCOs and, where section commanders had not survived, privates were expected to provide a narrative of events from their own perspective. Each man was to 'add his remarks as to any lessons learnt from his experiences'.[118] The instructions sent to the battalions were clear: 'A copy of each narrative to be sent to Divisional Headquarters as soon as possible with any comments that higher commanders may

---

[116] Patent application by W. E. Pinnington for short trench stretcher, 30 September 1915, LSM, Miscellaneous File P.
[117] W. H. Campbell, Diary, 11 October 1916, LSM, Acc. No. 484.
[118] Lieutenant Colonel T. Rose Price, General Staff, 55th Division to O.C. Battalions, 3 August 1917, Records of the 55th (West Lancashire) Division, 1914–19, LRO, 356 FIF 2/1/232.

wish to make, but without alteration or co-ordination of narrative.'[119] Jeudwine was keen to elicit the unadulterated views from the firing line, indicating that he was genuinely interested in utilizing their opinions.

The men responded according to their capabilities and individual agendas. Some used the opportunity for self-glorification; the majority produced a chronological account, listing successes and failures alongside descriptions of the terrain and the condition of the enemy and his defences. A few went as far as suggesting remedies to the difficulties faced. Collectively, the narratives highlighted the agonizing, bone-chilling weather conditions and their adverse effect on the men, the criminal delay in relief and reinforcement, and the problems of advancing in wave formation in poor visibility. The confusion caused by the mixing of waves and even battalions was detailed in almost every narrative.[120]

The adjustments made to the tactics to be used in the next attack in September were an attempt to address the concerns of the men. In a secret memorandum the lessons to be learned from the August fighting were outlined. The wave system was to be abandoned, with the men advancing in small columns in artillery formation, giving them more flexibility and freedom to deal with fortified strong points. In addition, reserves were to be brought closer to the front for ease of communication and rapid deployment during the battle.[121]

These alterations were not, of course, a panacea and the defects of the amended tactics littered the narratives after the September attacks. Rather than losing contact with each other, the men were now 'too bunched up all the time and that caused a lot of casualties as it made good targets'.[122] The rifle grenades and bombs were ineffective against pillboxes and there was a need for more snipers on the flanks to keep the enemy in their strong points.[123] The Lewis gunners also suffered a high casualty rate, and Lance Corporal Levey felt that they should have

---

[119] Lieutenant Colonel T. Rose Price, General Staff, 55th Division to O.C. Battalions, 3 August 1917, Records of the 55th (West Lancashire) Division, 1914–19, LRO, 356 FIF 2/1/232.
[120] 6th Liverpool Rifles, 55th Divisional Narratives, July 31–August 1 1917, Records of the 55th (West Lancashire) Division, LRO, File 52A, 356 FIF 4/1/158–1/224.
[121] Modifications required in our attack formations to meet the enemy's present system of defence. Fifth Army Memorandum, 24 August 1917, Records of the 55th (West Lancashire) Division, LRO, 356 FIF 14/2/801.
[122] Lance Corporal J. Levey, Corporal H. Gobie, B Company, 6th Liverpool Rifles, 55th Divisional Narratives, 20 September 1917, Records of the 55th (West Lancashire) Division, LRO, File 52A, 356 FIF 4/1/976, 983.
[123] Lance Corporal A. Arcles and Lance Corporal L. Kenny, Corporal H. Gobie, B Company, 6th Liverpool Rifles, 55th Divisional Narratives, July 31–August 1 1917, Records of the 55th (West Lancashire) Division, LRO, File 52A, 356 FIF 4/1/977–8, 983.

gone over behind the Battalion.[124] Nevertheless, the narratives in general were more positive than those of August. Consider Lance Corporal Lee's contribution, for example: 'There is no doubt that concrete emplacements and shelters for the enemy are their only means of safety and these can easily be overcome by flanking parties dashing forward by short rushes ... this last affair of the 20th has proved that with determination our infantry can overcome any obstacles put in their way by the enemy.'[125]

The practice of collecting narratives became institutionalized after the Third Battle of Ypres, helping Jeudwine to re-evaluate and refine his tactical thinking. It is difficult to judge the influence Jeudwine was able to exert over the general evolution of British tactics, but he certainly mixed with key players in the army structure. In December 1917 he was invited to contribute a pamphlet on defensive tactics alongside Colonel J. E. Edmonds and Brigadier General C. N. McMullen,[126] and although this was never published, the ideas developed there contributed directly to the success of the stand of the 55th Division at Givenchy. The plans, sketches and narrative of the Battle of Givenchy were subsequently circulated to other divisions as an example of good defensive practice.[127] Thus, the men of the 55th Division could be said to have helped indirectly to shape the tactical thinking of the British army as a whole.

Another way of canvassing the opinion of the ranks was to tap into the trench journal movement that had originated in the trenches.[128] The material used in the magazine of the 55th Division was tame when compared with the more open protests found in the *Peronne Gazette*, a publication read by the Liverpool Scottish, but admittedly produced after the end of hostilities.[129] The *Gazette* was much more vociferous in its criticism of the authorities, but in many ways what was left out of the Divisional magazine was more significant than what was published. Contributions were to be sent to Divisional Headquarters, anonymously if desired, allowing the men to vent their feelings without the fear

---

[124] Lance Corporal J. Levey, B Company, 6th Liverpool Rifles, 55th Divisional Narratives, 20 September 1917, Records of the 55th (West Lancashire) Division, LRO, File 52A, 356 FIF 4/1/158–1/976.

[125] Lance Corporal A. Lee, A Company, 6th Liverpool Rifles, 55th Divisional Narratives, 20 September 1917, Records of the 55th (West Lancashire) Division, LRO, File 52A, 356 FIF 4/1/985–7.

[126] Samuels, *Command or control?*, 203.

[127] Lecture on operations at Givenchy–Festubert, 9 April 1918; notes regarding General Sir Hugh Jeudwine's Lecture, RMC Sandhurst, 1928, Records of the 55th (West Lancashire) Division, LRO, 356 FIF 54/5.

[128] See Fuller, *Troop morale and popular culture*.

[129] *Peronne Gazette*, February 1919.

of retribution. That some offerings were 'unprintable', as admitted in the preface to the 1918 edition, suggests that Divisional Command were receiving a comprehensive view of the mood of the men, and not merely flattering eyewash.[130]

Verbal communication

The conference and the lecture became increasingly important as tactical control was devolved. As Jeudwine pointed out to his battalion commanders in 1918: 'COs must talk to their officers, who in turn must talk to their men. A large number of officers do not talk half enough to their subordinates. This is very necessary as the individual man is going to win or lose the fight and that depends a lot on what he is made by his officers and knowing what we are at.'[131]

There was a proliferation of conferences and lectures after December 1916 which were primarily used as tools of instruction, to ensure that all ranks, down to the private, understood the ideas and objectives of the High Command. They could be delivered at parades, through training schools, at formally convened conferences and informally in the trenches. The commanders set the agenda, often delivering a monologue on their forthcoming plans, but there was also an attempt to gauge the views of the men. The reaction of the other ranks after a parade address could provide the commander with an inkling of their attitudes,[132] but the real forum for discussion could be found in the conference and the trench lecture.[133] The outcome of such meetings was not a foregone conclusion, as Major Gordon explained: 'many conferences were held without anything definite resulting, but at any rate it provided a definite scheme for units to train for operations'.[134] The negotiating process took time to yield results, but there was a genuine desire both to inspire the men with confidence in their orders and to canvass their opinions.[135]

---

[130] *Sub Rosa: Being the Magazine of the 55th West Lancashire Division*, June 1918.
[131] Notes on Divisional Conference, 28 June 1918, Records of the 55th (West Lancashire) Division, 1914–19, LRO, 356 FIF 48/2/72.
[132] H. S. Taylor, Reminiscences, LSM, Miscellaneous File T, 9.
[133] A 1918 pamphlet on training for defence stressed the importance of trench lectures which would 'stimulate interest and make them (the NCOs and men) more able intelligently to carry out the orders they may receive in battle'. Training for defence, 55th Divisional Memorandum, 12 February 1918, Records of the 55th (West Lancashire) Division, 1914–19, LRO, 356 FIF 14/2/805.
[134] S. E. Gordon, Memoir, April 1917, Gordon Papers, IWM, 77/5/1, 264.
[135] On a grander scale, an official educational scheme was instituted to bolster morale in March 1918. The aim was to provide lectures and discussions on citizenship to shape the attitudes of the soldiers and ensure that they had reasons to fight, although the scheme

154   Command, discipline and the citizen soldier

Another of Jeudwine's supplements to the hierarchical feedback system was the instigation of Brigade Liaison Officers. These officers were to report directly to Jeudwine on events taking place at Brigade and Battalion Headquarters during battles. They were intended not to be spies but rather to 'communicate the Brigadier's views to the Divisional Commander and will personally bring to him views impossible or difficult to send by wire'. Safeguards were built into the system in order to ensure that the Brigade was comfortable with their Liaison Officer. Jeudwine promised that, 'Should the Liaison Officer be found to be lacking in tact, or to be unable to work with the Brigade Staff, a report to this effect will be submitted to Divisional Headquarters by the Brigadier and he will be changed'.[136]

During periods of static warfare, the Divisional and Brigade commanders preferred to visit the trenches in person. It is a misconception that all generals remained in grand châteaux, safe behind the line, as touted by the middle-class war poets.[137] John Bourne has shown that a number of generals were killed in the front line,[138] a point reflected in Lieutenant McClymont's parody of Sassoon's *The General*.

> Good morning, good morning the General said
> As he passed down the line with a wound in his head
> Now we knew he was wounded by the way that he bled
> And when he got to the base the poor bugger was dead.[139]

Though the inspections could prove wearying for the men, especially when they had been working all night,[140] they did provide an opportunity for bypassing the official command structure and gaining the views of the other ranks. Touring the trenches was approached in different ways according to the personality of the commander. Brigadier Duncan had the annoying habit of wandering the trenches of 165th Brigade incognito, his rank hidden by an old trench coat.[141] Jeudwine, on the other hand,

---

had barely been given a chance to develop before the war ended. See S. P. Mackenzie, *Politics and military morale: current affairs and citizenship education in the British Army, 1914–50* (Oxford, 1992).

[136] H. S. Jeudwine, Training Principles, 55th Division (G 104)), 8 December 1916, Records of the 55th (West Lancashire) Division, 1914–19, LRO, 356 FIF 13/2/649–50.

[137] See for example, S. Sassoon, 'Base details,' and 'The General', in *Siegfried Sassoon: the war poems*, ed. R. Hart-Davis (London, 1983), 60 and 67.

[138] Bourne, 'British generals in the First World War', 100. See also F. Davies and G. Maddocks, *Bloody Red Tabs: General Officer casualties of the Great War 1914–1918* (London, 1995).

[139] E. I. M. McClymont, untitled poem, LSM, Miscellaneous File M.

[140] 'They find fault with everything and you have to walk round with them; they completely forgetting that we have been working all night and have just turned in': McKinnell, *The Liverpool Scottish*, 92.

[141] *Liverpool Scottish Regimental Association Gazette*, March 1933, 13.

PHASES OF THE WAR:—1. Tabs on the Warpath (Wind Vert.).

Figure 6.4 'Tabs on the warpath': Major General Sir H. S. Jeudwine, KCB, commanding the 55th West Lancashire Division with a staff officer and Major M. H. Milner, ADC.

made regular, official visits, darting about his trenches and questioning the men (see Figure 6.4).

Front-line Territorials were not averse to correcting any misapprehensions held by those with higher rank. In February 1916, Brigadier General Wilkinson Green of 166th Brigade was enquiring about the effect of British shelling on the German garrisons in the front line. 'Captain Davidson in his drawling tone said "Oh yes, I saw the caretaker and his dog running out of the strong point when the shelling commenced." The Brigadier was intensely annoyed at being so easily taken in. It was well known that the Germans held the trenches there with the very minimum of garrison.'[142]

The soldiers in the trenches, however, were not content to wait to be consulted. Through individual and collective representations they initiated discussion within the Battalion and helped to resolve disagreements. The tradition of relaxed relations again aided communication, permitting the men to appeal directly to the authority figure who had the power to solve the problem. In the early months of the war, Sergeant

[142] W. G. Bromley, Memoir, LSM, Acc. No. 544, 72.

Macfie received a very polite delegation, requesting that existing friendship groups should be respected when allocating commanders to sections,[143] and Sergeant Bromley received a similar deputation in 1916 with the aim of unseating an unpopular platoon corporal.[144]

Individual confrontations also took place. Sergeant Bromley felt aggrieved at being chastised during a route march, in front of the whole Battalion, for something that was not his responsibility. Boiling with rage, he obtained an audience with his Commanding Officer to discuss the matter. Lieutenant Colonel Macdonald had the grace to admit his error, which gained Bromley's admiration, for 'he could very easily have given me a further ticking off for daring to broach the subject'.[145]

Bromley's testimony shows that the men were aware that their appeals would not always be successful. Leaders could choose to accept or reject appeals from below, depending on the possible repercussions. For example, Macfie refused to rearrange his sections, giving 'a reply worthy of Asquith',[146] but Bromley was more amenable to the complaints of his men, recommending the offending corporal for a course of instruction, as he felt that the discontent was having an effect on the whole platoon. The men could not expect their superiors to institute everything they demanded, and this was accepted as part and parcel of the process of negotiation, but at the same time, the leaders could not dismiss all requests out of hand.

More informal methods of communication open to the men included grousing, a regular army favourite, and protest through humorous acts in concert parties. In the Liverpool Scottish, the entertainment was generally run by an egalitarian committee, which encompassed all ranks. The company representatives on the committee in July 1917 included a second lieutenant, two sergeants and a lance corporal.[147] The concerts organized were not imposed by the leadership and drew on the musical and dramatic talents of the Battalion. They encouraged, among other events, a risqué limerick competition, providing ample opportunity for the men to air their grievances. Again, the leadership was able to assess the strength of feeling in the unit and choose the appropriate response.

---

[143] R. A. S. Macfie to Charlie Macfie, 1 September 1914, Macfie Papers, IWM, Con. Shelf.
[144] W. G. Bromley, Memoir, LSM, Acc. No. 544, 77.
[145] W. G. Bromley, Memoir, LSM, 122.
[146] R. A. S. Macfie to Charlie Macfie, 1 September 1914, Macfie Papers, IWM, Con. Shelf.
[147] Papers relating to the Battalion Eisteddfod and beer garden, 14 July 1917, LSM, Miscellaneous File M.

Sabotage and disruption

A soldier's conduct was perhaps his most expressive and powerful form of communication, over which he retained ultimate control. He could choose to obey his commanders, suggesting that he broadly accepted their objectives and behaviour, or he could disrupt and disobey. At a personal level the men often marked out their status in the trenches through their actions. A sergeant of the Liverpool Scottish indicated his displeasure at a new officer commandeering his dugout by knocking down a stove carefully constructed by the officer's batman. It was a clear signal to the officer to respect the privileges of the sergeant. No words were exchanged, but the officer heeded the warning and nothing further was heard of the matter.[148]

Malingering was another indicator of disenchantment in the ranks that infected volunteers and conscripts alike. It could be an individual, generalized protest against the war, such as that expressed by Jack Lorimer. His carefully devised strategy, blending malingering with volunteering for specialized training courses, contrived to keep him out of the trenches for five months in 1918.[149] However, Lorimer's penchant for 'swinging the lead' passed apparently unnoticed by his immediate commanders. As an individual his impact was negligible, but malingering *en masse* was much more effective in alerting the authorities to discontent in the ranks. In November 1914 Macfie was sceptical of the high proportion of his company claiming to be sick, and he wrote to his sister about his suspicions: 'It is difficult for them to dry their clothes; kilts hold an awful lot of water. The result is that we had 20 sick yesterday and 16 today ... I think the real "complaint" was that they did not like to put on their wet clothes.'[150] It can be no coincidence that shortly afterwards the Medical Officer went to great lengths to establish a laundry replete with drying room.

Equally blatant were the messages conveyed by the speed and efficiency with which tasks were completed. There is no evidence that trade union inspired 'go slows' were actively orchestrated in either Battalion, but despite middle-class hostility to union techniques, there was, at times, obvious inactivity in the face of orders from above. In 1915 Major General Aylmer Haldane complained bitterly about the performance of the Liverpool Scottish,[151] and again in 1918 Jeudwine was to complain

---

[148] W. G. Bromley, Memoir, LSM, Acc. No. 544, 122.
[149] J. W. Lorimer, Diary, LSM, Acc. No. 794.
[150] R. A. S. Macfie to Sheila Macfie, 15 November 1914, Macfie Papers, IWM, Con. Shelf.
[151] Haldane MSS; NLS MS 20248, ff.145, 373, in E. Spiers, 'The Scottish soldier at war', in Liddle and Cecil (eds.), *Facing Armageddon*, 321.

repeatedly about the lack of defensive digging being completed in the trenches[152] and the inconsistency of patrolling.[153] The higher command was acutely aware of this sabotage threatening the success of their plans. In some cases they were forced to capitulate to the men. The conscientiousness of patrolling remained patchy throughout the Division during the latter period of 1918.[154] Jeudwine did little to rectify this, beyond periodically reiterating his demands at conferences. On other issues, Jeudwine was more forceful, responding with explanation and justification. The men were reminded that pick and shovel work secured their own safety, and aerial photographs of the more advanced enemy trenchworks were sent down to Brigade Headquarters in an effort to motivate.[155]

Disruption and sabotage proved to be a universally effective method of communication. It was perhaps the only method that did not rely on a high standard of literacy and could be practised by all men, whatever their social background. As such, it provided valuable information about the collective mood and aims of the ranks, but the method of communication yielded by far the most difficult information to interpret.[156] Many acts of defiance were prompted by complex underlying grievances, which were impossible to discern from crude action. It took a perceptive commander, who understood the mentality of his men, to be able to identify correctly the causes of disaffection in the ranks and amend his policies to accommodate the views from below.

Communication with civilian authority

The Liverpool Territorials utilized the full range of opportunities available to communicate with those above them in the military hierarchy, but when senior commanders proved unresponsive or ignored their needs, the Territorials also had recourse to civilian authority. The links that were maintained with leaders at home provided formations with another locus

---

[152] 55th Divisional instruction to Brigadiers, 55th Divisional Headquarters, 4 May 1918, Records of the 55th (West Lancashire) Division, 1914–19, LRO, 356 FIF 11/1/602.
[153] Notes on Divisional Conference, 28 June 1918, Records of the 55th (West Lancashire) Division, 1914–19, LRO, 356 FIF 48/2/72.
[154] Indeed, Lieutenant Basil Rathbone fabricated many of his patrol reports during May to September 1918. Rathbone, *In and out of character*, 2.
[155] 55th Divisional instruction to Brigadiers, 55th Divisional Headquarters, 4 May 1918, Records of the 55th (West Lancashire) Division, 1914–19, LRO, 356 FIF 11/1/602.
[156] J. Brent Wilson has identified indexes based on the incidence of sickness, trench foot and indiscipline that were established to chart the reliability and morale of divisions and corps. See J. Brent Wilson, 'The morale and discipline of the British Expeditionary Force', Unpublished MA dissertation, University of New Brunswick, 1978, 28–9.

of power to which they could appeal. It gave them greater scope for addressing their grievances and increased their protection against the military machine.

The older Territorials, serving at the depots and in the drafting battalions, were representatives of the old and powerful Liverpool families who had led the volunteering movement since the late Victorian era.[157] With their excellent personal contacts, they were able to secure recognition and help for their first-line units and their families, backed up by the influential civilian and military members of the West Lancashire Territorial Association, which included Lord Derby. From the Divisional Commander downwards, the Liverpool Territorials shamelessly exploited their local links, a process made easier by the persistence of regional homogeneity. Thus, Jeudwine both appealed to and received help from Lord Derby in exonerating the 55th Division in the aftermath of the Cambrai débâcle.[158] Lower down the chain of command, Lieutenant Colonel Davidson, on finding that his protest against having officers of 16th Liverpools foisted on the Liverpool Scottish without adequate reason had been rejected at army level, expressed his dissatisfaction to Lieutenant Colonel Blair at the Battalion depot. Blair mobilized the Territorial Association, and for the rest of the war the Scottish had more control over the origin of their officers.[159]

The concentration of the upper middle classes in the Rifles and the Scottish ensured that, at least at the start of the war, both officers and men at Battalion level had influential contacts in Liverpool, and the ability to get their voice heard. These were the landed families and the business leaders who had personal relationships with politicians, civic dignitaries and military commanders.

The Rifles contained men such as Captain Brocklehurst from a prominent ship-owning family, and Captain J. Phillips, Secretary of the Liverpool Stock Exchange as well as the offspring of the manager of the Royal Insurance Company and the director of the White Star Shipping Line. Within the Liverpool Scottish the Macfies, the Grahams (sugar refiners) and the Buchanans (millers), who were linked through marriage to Lord Russell of Liverpool, were among the many business families that

---

[157] Liverpool Scottish Officers' Index, LSM.
[158] Jeudwine's sensitive letter was hand-delivered by Major Milner, his ADC and a former employee of Derby. He played on the Territorial connection to enlist Derby's help: 'In the circumstances I have no-one else to appeal to and your Territorial connection with the Division gives me confidence in doing so.' Jeudwine to Derby, 3 January 1918, Records of the 55th (West Lancashire) Division, 1914–19, LRO, 356 FIF 44/6/15.
[159] Lieutenant Colonel J. R. Davidson to Colonel Blair, 18 September 1915, Uncatalogued Scrapbook, LSM.

had helped to found the Scottish Battalion in 1901, and continued to be represented during the Great War. Both Battalions were also well represented in the civic sphere, incorporating the progeny of Alderman H. Carruthers JP, Alderman B. Cain, Mayor of Bootle, Arthur Mather, Lord Mayor of Liverpool, F.J. Chavasse, bishop of Liverpool, and J. Laybourne, Chief Constable of Chester.[160] There were also the journalists within both Battalions who had the direct contacts in the newspaper industry through which to express their views,[161] and of course, the men had the right to voice their concerns to their MPs or the War Office.

All soldiers had the right to communicate with civilian authorities whilst serving in the trenches. During the war there were many exchanges documented in *Hansard* debating the rights of individual battalions,[162] and a routine part of War Office responsibility involved dealing with complaints regarding the treatment of soldiers, the dispatch of drafts, the medically unfit and the underage. Indeed, the War Office received thousands of queries from the relatives or friends of serving soldiers.[163] Yet we must not forget that the middle-class Battalions of the Rifles and the Scottish had more opportunities than most for influencing the civilian and military authorities in Britain. The numerous soldiers that could count Lord Derby as a friend and the educated eloquence of the rankers set the Battalions apart. Communication with leaders at home was perhaps of more significance to middle-class battalions than to working-class units, drawn from a wider geographical area.

Conclusion

The middle-class Territorials of 1914–15 arrived in the trenches keen to do their duty, but with a strong conviction about the nature of their rights and responsibilities as volunteer soldiers. They possessed the necessary education and civilian contacts to negotiate effectively within their formations, and clung to a sense of self-worth and civilian importance that gave them the confidence to challenge those above them.

The initial social homogeneity of both Battalions, as in pre-war times, necessitated relaxed relationships between the ranks and their

---

[160] Liverpool Scottish Officers' Index and Liverpool Scottish Other Ranks' Index, LSM; Thompson, *Liverpool Scroll of Fame*.
[161] Journalists included: Private F. Fyfe, *Daily Dispatch*; Sergeant W. Houghton, *Liverpool Daily Post* and *Echo* (Manager of the Llandudno office); Sergeant Lamont, *Liverpool Daily Post*; Private H. Cooper, *Daily Dispatch*; Private W. Lavin, *Daily Dispatch*.
[162] See Beckett, 'The Territorial Force', in Beckett and Simpson (eds.), *A nation in arms*, 156–8.
[163] Staff Duties, miscellaneous, Directorate of Organisation, PRO, WO 162/6, 131–2.

commanders. Whilst this promoted effective communication of original ideas, there was a darker side. The paternalistic–deferential exchange was directly threatened, with tensions created by the frustrating lack of promotion opportunities in 1915 and the conspicuous competence of senior NCOs, compared with some junior officers.

After 1916, as the social composition of the Battalions changed, the paternalistic–deferential relationship became easier to operate. The officers remained predominately upper middle class, the majority of middle-class privates of 1914–15 had either been commissioned or had risen through the ranks to positions of responsibility, and the new working-class recruits were more familiar with the deferential role assigned to them.

Despite the change in social composition, new recruits accepted the traditional framework of the battalions. The Territorial legacy of relaxed relations and clear communication persisted to the end of the war, encouraged by platoon reorganization, the devolution of responsibility down the chain of command, and the increasing desire of senior commanders to canvass the ideas and attitudes of the men in the trenches.

Of course the command framework was imperfect, personality clashes impeded negotiation, and it would be wrong to exaggerate the extent to which the private soldier was able to communicate with the general. Nevertheless, the Liverpool Territorial in the trenches had more opportunities to communicate and negotiate at Battalion and even Brigade or Divisional level than the traditional top-down hierarchical model allows. It was this practical involvement in negotiation, whether over tactics or over basic rights and responsibilities, which gave the men a sense of control, and helped to perpetuate their consent to the continuation of the war.

7 Discipline, punishment and the Territorial ethos

Territorial battalions in the First World War favoured a relaxed approach to discipline.[1] They preferred to motivate their men through positive, civilian-inspired strategies, rather than enforcing behaviour by the threat of punishment. Yet they were still military units and their personnel subject to military law. In contrast to most occupations in civilian life, those serving in the army were being asked to risk their lives on a daily basis. Under these circumstances, many commanders, including those of the Territorial Force, saw the punitive sanctions of the disciplinary system as an important tool to help ensure compliance.

Most historical analysis of the British army's disciplinary system has concentrated exclusively on capital courts-martial.[2] Books such as *Shot at dawn*[3] have captured the popular imagination, and fuelled recent campaigns to obtain a parliamentary pardon for those executed.[4] Research of this genre, which focuses on wartime executions to the exclusion of other, less dramatic, disciplinary strategies, paints a picture of a discipline system that was harsh and inflexible. For the unfortunate men executed, the system was indeed brutal, but their experience needs to be considered in context. Whilst the generals considered executions to be a necessary deterrent amidst the unprecedented slaughter of the war,[5] only 346 men had their death sentences confirmed. They formed only 11.23% of all men sentenced to death by courts-martial, and 0.006% of the British

---

[1] Beckett, 'The Territorial Force', 144.
[2] See A. Babington, *For the sake of example* (London, 1983); L. Sellers, *For God's sake, shoot straight* (London, 1995); G. Oram, *Worthless men: race eugenics and the death penalty in the British Army during the First World War* (London, 1998); G. Oram, *Death sentences passed by military courts of the British Army 1914–1924* (London, 1998).
[3] J. Putkowski and J. Sykes, *Shot at dawn* (Barnsley, 1989); *Shot at dawn* detailed, occasionally inaccurately, the background to each capital court-martial and the identity of the accused.
[4] For a summary of the activities of the campaign for pardons, see J. Peaty, 'Capital courts-martial during the Great War', in Bond *et al.* (eds.), *'Look to your front'* (Staplehurst, 1999), 89–91.
[5] Babington, *For the sake of example*, 191.

army as a whole.⁶ Clearly, the resort to capital courts-martial occurred only in a minority of cases.

An examination of the wider disciplinary framework has been hampered by a shortage of available historical sources.⁷ Nevertheless, a number of studies have begun to broaden the discussion of disciplinary strategies used by the British army and its allies during the First World War.⁸ In particular, Gary Sheffield and Timothy Bowman have both highlighted the fact that the disciplinary system was not used in a uniform manner. Often, the type of unit affected the nature of its disciplinary record.⁹ The following investigation of the punishment regime operating in the Liverpool Rifles supports this view. Despite the rules and punishments prescribed by the official manuals, the application of military discipline within the Rifles was most often dictated by its character, traditions and experience. Punitive sanctions were undoubtedly used to highlight unacceptable behaviour and deter its recurrence by the offender or his comrades, but the nature and severity of the punishment itself could become the subject of negotiation.

The power to impose sanctions on a soldier was governed by the *King's Regulations* and the *Manual of military law*. The rules they contained were little more than guidelines that set maximum sentences and detailed general punishment procedures. It was left to the battalion commander and his subordinates to determine how an offence should be tried and the type of punishment awarded. From time to time, generals would order specific punishments for prevalent crimes, but even then, the system relied on the company and battalion commanders reporting incidents, and to the end of the war it was regimental officers, in negotiation with their men, who determined the disciplinary regime of a battalion.

The Commanding Officer was a key figure in setting the disciplinary tone of a unit. For the most serious offences, men were referred to a court-martial

---

[6] Peaty, 'Capital courts-martial', 91.
[7] Until recently, court-martial documents had been withheld by the Public Record Office. Today, only basic courts-martial indices, capital court-martial transcripts, and some court-martial records in officers' personal files survive. I am grateful to Timothy Bowman for advice on this point.
[8] D. Englander, 'Mutinies and military morale', in Strachan (ed.), *The Oxford illustrated history of the First World War*; Englander and Osborne, 'Jack, Tommy and Henry Dubb'; Sheffield, *Leadership in the trenches*; G. Sheffield, *The Redcaps: a history of the Royal Military Police and its antecedents from the Middle Ages to the Gulf War* (London, 1994); C. Pugsley, *On the fringe of hell: New Zealanders and military discipline in the First World War* (London, 1991); Timothy Bowman, *Irish Regiments in the Great War: discipline and morale* (Manchester, 2003); Wilson, 'The morale and discipline of the British Expeditionary Force, 1914–1918'.
[9] Sheffield, *Leadership in the trenches*, 28; Bowman, *Irish Regiments*, 7; G. Oram, *Military executions during World War One* (Basingstoke, 2003), 169.

for punishment, but the Commanding Officer was permitted to try soldiers for a total of twenty-three military offences.[10] Sanctions were divided into summary punishments – detention,[11] fines,[12] deductions from pay,[13] field punishment[14] and minor punishments – confinement to barracks, punishment drill, extra guards or piquets, admonition.[15] A Commanding Officer of a battalion could award all these punishments to a private soldier, but was only able to admonish, reprimand, severely reprimand and reduce the rank of an NCO until 1917, when field punishment was permitted below the rank of sergeant.[16] Most offences, particularly those that required minor punishments, were dealt with by the company commander, a delegation that was enshrined in the *King's Regulations*.[17] Thus, company commanders could be granted considerable autonomy to manage the discipline of their men.

The way in which the British system of discipline was codified allowed for a degree of flexibility in its administration. The punitive code was viewed as a set of adaptable instructions which enabled company commanders and the Commanding Officer to take into account the circumstances of an offence, the past conduct of an offender and the wider disciplinary requirements of

---

[10] These included neglecting to obey any general or other orders, absence without leave, drunkenness, striking or using or offering violence to any person, and conduct to the prejudice of good order and military discipline. War Office, *Field Service Regulations*, Part II, *Organisation and administration* (reprinted with amendments to October 1914, London, 1914), 135–7.

[11] The CO could award any time up to 168 hours for any period of absence from one to seven days. Above this, he could only award one day's detention for each day's absence. E. Harry, *From crime to court martial: a simplified rendering and index of those parts of the 'Manual of military law' and 'King's Regulations' which deal with a soldier's offences and punishments* (London, 1918), 20.

[12] Fines can only be imposed for drunkenness and are fixed by *King's Regulations* K.R.512 and *Manual of military law*, 419. Harry, *From crime to court martial*, 13.

[13] Forfeiture of pay and field punishment could only be awarded on active service.

[14] Field punishment was designed as an alternative to imprisonment on active service. The punishment was divided into two categories, One and Two. Field Punishment Number One consisted of continuous labouring duties and could take place with the Battalion. The prisoner could be kept in iron fetters or handcuffs during his imprisonment, and tied to a wheel or fixed object for two hours a day in three out of any four consecutive days, up to a total of twenty-one days in all. Field Punishment Number Two comprised similar treatment, but without the threat of being shackled to a fixed object. See Babington, *For the sake of example*, 89.

[15] For distinction between summary and minor punishments see Harry, *From crime to court martial*, 25.

[16] The CO could award up to twenty-eight days field punishment to a private soldier only, until the law was changed to encompass NCOs in 1917. A court-martial could award up to three months. See Pugsley, *On the fringe of Hell*, 92, and S. T. Banning, *Military law made easy* (Gale and Polden's military series, London, 1917, 11th edn), 18.

[17] 'A CO is authorized to grant a large measure of discretionary power to Company etc. Commanders to dispose of any offence which he himself may deal.' War Office, *King's Regulations and orders for the Army 1912* (reprinted with amendments published in Army Orders up to 1 August 1914, London, 1914), 484 (3).

their unit, when choosing a form of punishment.[18] The punishment regime of a battalion was thus influenced more by the traditions of the pre-war unit and the attitudes and expectations of the men and junior officers in the trenches, than by the views of the generals. As the social composition of the Liverpool Rifles changed and the progress of the war affected attitudes, the application of the punitive code became an important area of negotiation within a battalion and helped to define most clearly what both the officers and the men deemed to be acceptable behaviour at any given point in time.

Historians have already noted that harsh punitive sanctions, deemed essential in controlling the regular army, never achieved the same importance among the Territorials. In peacetime, the social homogeneity of members and the strong socializing purpose of units meant that the Territorials had to maintain a more relaxed punitive regime to ensure the retention of personnel.[19] The Rifles were no exception to the rule. Their civilian, middle-class code of honour and self-respect compensated for a lack of formal military discipline and inspired more inventive, unofficial sanctions which harnessed their need to uphold an unblemished reputation. For example, during field training in 1903 a soldier in the Liverpool Scottish falling out of a march was given a ticket that stated '——was unable to keep up',[20] a method equally as effective as regular-style punishments of parades and drills.

In 1914 this more relaxed discipline regime, supplemented by punishments tailored to the social status of the men, was firmly entrenched as part of Territorial tradition. To investigate whether this system continued to operate throughout the Great War we need to turn to the punishment records contained within the casualty books of the Rifles, and the centralized court-martial ledgers of the Judge Advocate General's Office.

Before examining the punishment statistics, some consideration should be given to the character of these sources and the problems inherent in their manipulation. The centralized court-martial ledgers list the name, unit and rank of the defendant, offence committed, date of trial and the outcome.[21] These details have been entered into a database for a representative sample of battalions by Tim Bowman as part of

---

[18] During all trials, at all levels of the Battalion, the conduct sheet of the offender was read out as part of the procedure. G. B. L. Rae, Notes from lecture on military law, 12 October 1915, Miscellaneous File R, LSM.
[19] See Beckett, 'The Territorial Force', 144.
[20] Liverpool Scottish scrapbook 1902–6, R. A. S. Macfie Papers, LSM, Acc. No. 306.
[21] Ledger books of Field General Courts-Martial, 1915–19, PRO, WO 213/1–24. The Rifles' court-martial statistics were drawn from their casualty books and checked against the centralized ledgers held at the National Archives. The records matched in all but three cases.

his doctoral thesis.[22] The database has been utilized in this study to compare courts-martial in the Rifles with those in other battalions and to draw some general conclusions about Territorial behaviour.[23]

As already highlighted, courts-martial were but one level of the discipline system. Whereas previous historians have been limited to examining the court-martial stage, the Rifles' casualty books also list summary punishments awarded by the Commanding Officer, allowing the investigation of Battalion-level punishments. Unfortunately, those offences dealt with by company commanders were not deemed sufficiently serious to warrant an entry in the casualty books, which reduces some of the conclusions in the following analysis to conjecture. One of the main difficulties caused by the omission of company punishments centres on the fact that we cannot verify whether the absence of an offence in a particular year was a reflection of the good behaviour of the men or a result of company commanders assuming the responsibility of punishing the offence. Nevertheless, much can be deduced from these punishment data. The relative threat to the Battalion posed by minor offences can be assessed and the incidence of more serious cases that always required court-martial or summary punishment can be investigated.[24]

Drawing data from the casualty books, rather than the centralized court-martial ledgers, has an additional advantage. When a man joined the Battalion, his name, embarkation date, previous unit and date he arrived in the field were entered in the casualty book. His subsequent service details were updated when he was ill, injured or punished.[25] These service

---

[22] Bowman, 'The discipline and morale of the British Expeditionary Force', 730–48. Bowman chose a representative set of battalions to compare with his Irish units, with a bias towards the 'Celtic fringe'. In choosing battalions from Bowman's selection, I have tried to counteract this. Whilst the choice may be far from perfect, time constraints prevented the construction of a separate representative sample, and so clear are the trends that emerge from the data, it is probable that they are broadly typical.

[23] The statistics provided in *General Annual Reports of the British Army (including the Territorial Force) for the period from 1 October 1913 to 30 September 1919*, Accounts and Papers, Cmd. 1193 (London, 1921) and *Statistics of the military effort of the British Empire* (London, 1922), 643–9 refer to the whole of the British army, including dominion forces, serving abroad on all fronts. Any comparison with the Rifles would be hampered by the fact that there is no reliable figure for the total number of men serving abroad between 1914 and 1920, nor would a detailed comparison be fair, particularly regarding individual offences, as patterns of offending differed according to the front, the branch of service and even nationality.

[24] For example, we can be fairly certain that all cases of desertion and long-term absence would be tried by court-martial or by the Commanding Officer; therefore the incidence of the offences, the way they were handled within the Battalion and the threat they posed to the cohesion of the unit can be assessed accurately.

[25] 1/6th Battalion King's (Liverpool) Regiment Casualty Books 1–3, KRC, MLL, 58.83.537a–b.

Discipline, punishment and the Territorial ethos 167

records provide significant information regarding a soldier's wartime experience, and, used in conjunction with a roll for Number 1 Platoon of A Company, help to build up a comprehensive picture of offenders.[26]

Between February 1915 and March 1919, 176 soldiers were tried by the Commanding Officer and courts-martial were invoked forty-two times amongst a population of 5000 soldiers who served abroad with the 1/6th Liverpool Rifles.[27] Thus, when considering the offences punished within the Battalion, it must be remembered that the soldiers who committed military crime constituted a tiny minority and, in many cases, the numbers of individual offences recorded in the casualty books are too small to be meaningful. Therefore, only the most important and prevalent offences are discussed below.

Quitting or sleeping on a post

All cases of sleeping on or leaving a post, in the front or support lines, were referred to court-martial, but the few offences that took place in camp, behind the lines, were treated more leniently and punished by the Commanding Officer. Six men were court-martialled for sleeping and three for quitting their post. Rifleman J. Williams was the first man to leave his post in March 1917, followed by two more offenders in 1918. The first rifleman fell asleep on duty in July 1916 and was followed by a further five on 26 October 1917.[28] In the case of the October offenders, all men had fought in the Rifles' final action during the Third Battle of Ypres, barely a month before, and although the Battalion had been moved to a quiet sector, the men were overstretched, holding an extended line without adequate reinforcements.[29]

These two types of offence were different in intent. Leaving a post was a deliberate act, whereas sleeping on a post was perhaps more involuntary, an

---

[26] Number 1 Platoon, A Company, nominal roll and foot book, 1918, W. J. Pegge Papers, MLHL, M198/1/2/1.
[27] 1/6th Battalion King's (Liverpool) Regiment Casualty Books 1–3, KRC, MLL, 58.83.537a–b, and Ledger books of Field General Courts-Martial, 1915–19, PRO, WO 213/1–24. It should be noted that all offenders in the Rifles were tried by Field General Court-Martial. This type of court was permitted only on active service, required three officers, including the president of the court, who was to hold the rank of captain or above. Any death sentence passed had to be reached unanimously. Other types of court-martial included the General Court-Martial, which had to consist of at least five officers and was usually utilized for the trials of officers. See Babington, *For the sake of example*, 12 and Oram, *Worthless men*, 34.
[28] 1/6th Battalion King's (Liverpool) Regiment Casualty Books 2–3, KRC, MLL, 58.83.537a–b.
[29] 1/6th King's (Liverpool) Regiment Battalion War Diary, October 1917, KRC, MLL, 58.83.537 a–b.

understandable product of exhaustion, induced by previous experience. Both offences, however, presented the same threats to the Battalion in the trenches. There was the physical risk to the security of the unit and psychological repercussions for the Battalion as a whole. For a unit to function effectively, as Major General Jeudwine never tired of reminding his men, there had to be strong mutual trust.[30] It follows, therefore, that any action that threatened that trust had to be punished severely via court-martial.

Rifleman Costin, the first to fall asleep at his post, received an initial sentence, confirmed by Brigadier General Duncan, of death by being shot. His sentence was later commuted to six months' imprisonment with hard labour (suspended). The five offenders in 1917 each received five years' penal servitude (suspended).[31] The punishments were similar for those abandoning their posts and ranged from ten years' penal servitude, later commuted to two years' imprisonment with hard labour, to six months' imprisonment with hard labour commuted to fifty-six days' Field Punishment Number One.[32] Punishments determined by court-martial were not directly influenced by the Battalion, but in general the presiding officers were drawn from the defendant's own brigade or division and so did represent current attitudes within the wider formations. Such harsh punishments indicate the seriousness with which these offences were regarded and suggest that intent to commit the crime was not taken into consideration; it was the potential consequence of the crime that was the determining factor.

Desertion and absence

Absence from the Battalion could take many forms, overstaying leave, absence without leave and desertion being regarded as the most serious. The relative incidence of all types of absence increased as the war progressed, culminating most dramatically after the Armistice.

---

[30] Lecture on operations at Givenchy–Festubert, 9 April 1918; notes regarding General Sir Hugh Jeudwine's lecture, RMC, Sandhurst, 1928, Records of the 55th West Lancashire Division, 1914–19, LRO, 356 FIF 54/5, 23.

[31] The Suspension of Sentences Act, passed in 1915, allowed a convicted soldier to return to his unit, thus conserving manpower stocks, and ensuring that offenders did not gain respite from the front. The sentence of a soldier was reviewed at a later date and his behaviour in the intervening period would be taken into consideration. Good conduct could win the remission of the sentence; poor behaviour could result in imprisonment. A recalcitrant offender could damage the cohesion of a unit and, despite a manpower shortage, such men had to be removed, but for the majority of soldiers the suspended sentence proved an incentive to conform. For details of the Act, see Babington, *For the sake of example*, 22.

[32] 1/6th Battalion King's (Liverpool) Regiment Casualty Books 2–3, KRC, MLL, 58.83.537a–b.

Overstaying leave did not occur, or at least was not punished by the Commanding Officer of the Liverpool Rifles, until after the Battle of the Somme. On 9 November 1916 the first soldier was punished, followed by four in 1917, twelve before the Armistice in 1918 and four post-war. None merited a court-martial.[33]

Rifleman Ellison remembered the temptation of overstaying his leave during the Christmas of 1915, but his desire to maintain a clean conduct sheet propelled him back across the Channel on Christmas Day.[34] After the bloody experience of the Somme, and the realization that luck could not hold forever, men with exemplary service began to overstay their leave. Sergeant J. S. Handley, an original, pre-war member of the Battalion, initiated the trend and was closely followed by two further men who had fought since February 1915.[35]

Men of all ranks judged that the benefits of spending a few more days with their family were worth the punishment they received on returning to the Battalion. For this reason, the deterrence factor had to be increased from the forfeiting of one day's pay in 1916 to ten days' Field Punishment Number Two with deprivation of twenty-eight days' pay or the removal of a lance stripe, and at its harshest, twenty-eight days' Field Punishment Number One at various points in 1918.[36] It is significant that the punishments did not rise uniformly over time, but increased sharply during periods when manpower was at a premium.

Absence without leave could be punished by the Commanding Officer or referred to court-martial, depending on the seriousness of the offence. During hostilities, Colonel McKaig was responsible for court-martialling only one man for absence. Two courts-martial took place at Etaples in 1917, but not at the instigation of the Rifles commander, and were, in any case, ill judged. The offender was subsequently declared insane and evacuated to England. Where possible, absence was dealt with inside the Battalion, despite a dramatic increase in incidence during 1918, which could have provoked a spate of courts-martial in a less lenient unit.[37]

---

[33] 1/6th Battalion King's (Liverpool) Regiment Casualty Books 1–3, KRC, MLL, 58.83.537a–b.
[34] N. F. Ellison, Memoir, Ellison Papers, IWM, DS/MISC/49, 76.
[35] 1/6th Battalion King's (Liverpool) Regiment Casualty Books 1–2, KRC, MLL, 58.83.537a–b.
[36] 1/6th Battalion King's (Liverpool) Regiment Casualty Books 1–3, KRC, MLL, 58.83.537a–b.
[37] 1/6th Battalion King's (Liverpool) Regiment Casualty Books 1–3, KRC, MLL, 58.83.537a–b. Offences of absence without leave, punished by the Commanding Officer, increased from four between 1915 and 1917 to thirteen in the first eleven months of 1918.

Unlike those who overstayed their leave, absenteeism on active service was often repeated or combined with other offences. The offenders were almost exclusively conscript riflemen, the majority having been transferred to the Rifles piecemeal from other battalions. In the first eleven months of 1918, six out of thirteen men tried by the Commanding Officer for absence without leave committed multiple offences, ranging from drunkenness to further periods of absence, and two men were sent for court-martial. Such evidence suggests that absence without leave was an offence perpetrated by those who had failed to fit into the unit and consequently lacked an adequate support network.[38]

The punishments inflicted by the Battalion Commander for absence varied according to the past conduct of the offender, his length of absence and the timing of his absconding. Nevertheless, a pattern similar to that of overstaying leave emerged. Those few volunteers who offended in the early years of the war were absent for less than twenty-four hours, and were deprived of a few days' pay, unless they were unfortunate enough to be apprehended by the military police. As the war progressed, the sentences generally became harsher, in part because the length of absences increased and also because the manpower shortage was more acute. Even in 1918, however, there was still room for discrimination. Field Punishment Number One was reserved for persistent offenders or for those men who absented themselves during or immediately before a trench tour.[39]

Compared with absence, its infinitely more serious cousin, desertion, occurred rarely in the Battalion. Indeed, Colonel McKaig resorted to the charge only once during the war (although two men of the 6th Rifles were court-martialled for the offence at Etaples).[40] The refusal to accuse men of desertion was a prime example of a Commanding Officer framing charges to manipulate the disciplinary code in the way he deemed most appropriate. Military law stated that a man could be automatically charged with desertion after an absence of twenty-one days, but there was scope to brand a man a deserter who was apprehended sooner, if his actions suggested an intent to avoid a particular duty, or abandon his duties permanently.[41] According to these rules, Rifleman Williams

---

[38] Christopher Pugsley has also identified the fact that loners in New Zealand units were more likely to be tried by capital court-martial. Pugsley, *On the fringe of Hell*, 297.

[39] 1/6th Battalion King's (Liverpool) Regiment Casualty Books 1–3, KRC, MLL, 58.83.537a–b.

[40] 1/6th Battalion King's (Liverpool) Regiment Casualty Books 1–3, KRC, MLL, 58.83.537a–b; Ledger books of Field General Courts-Martial, 1915–1919, PRO, WO 213/1–24.

[41] Adjutant General's Branch of the Staff General Headquarters, S. S412b. Circular memorandum on courts-martial for use on active service, 1918, 13. Quoted in Pugsley, *On the fringe of Hell*, 313.

should have been charged with desertion. He absconded from the Battalion on 14 August 1918, the day before the Battalion returned to the front-line trenches at Festubert, and yet he was court-martialled for absence.

Williams received a gruelling ninety days' Field Punishment Number One to atone for his actions, a harsh punishment by any standard, but he was fortunate when compared to his comrade Rifleman G. Wallace who had defected from an Infantry Brigade depot at Etaples two weeks earlier. Wallace was initially sentenced to death for desertion on 26 September 1918. On 13 October the death sentence was commuted to five years' penal servitude and he was committed to military prison. He finally returned to the Battalion under a suspended sentence in February 1919.[42]

After the Armistice, desertion and absence were the only offences referred for courts-martial in the Rifles. The authorities feared the men would lose their resolve to serve in the army at a time when there was an imperative need to retain men. A peace treaty had yet to be signed, occupation troops were required for Germany and soldiers became increasingly restless, resorting to strikes and protests in base areas.[43] Although the death sentence was not utilized, the punishments remained harsh after the war, with many offenders now being committed to military prison.[44]

Malingering and self-inflicted wounding

Malingering and self-inflicted wounds represented the most severe threat to the integrity of the Rifles. From the beginning of the war, malingering was a perennial occurrence. The Medical Officer doling out the number nine (laxative) pills to those unfortunates deemed more than capable of continuing in the trenches became a ritual in the Rifles (see Figure 7.1). Surprisingly, there were few convictions by the Battalion Commander for malingering. The casualty books record only four occasions between the August and September attacks on the Somme when punitive sanctions were invoked, and then the punishment was merely two to three days' deduction of pay. It was taken for granted that men would report sick without a cause

---

[42] 1/6th Battalion King's (Liverpool) Regiment Casualty Books 2–3, KRC, MLL, 58.83.537a–b; Ledger books of Field General Courts-Martial, 1915–19, PRO, WO 213/1–24.
[43] G. Dallas and D. Gill, *The unknown army: mutinies in the British Army in World War One* (London, 1985), 101–21.
[44] 1/6th Battalion King's (Liverpool) Regiment Casualty Books 2–3, KRC, MLL, 58.83.537a–b; Ledger books of Field General Courts-Martial, 1915–19, PRO, WO 213/1–24.

PHASES OF THE WAR:—4. Our Doc. at Work.

Figure 7.1 'Our Doc at work': Captain A. Barrett Cardew, MC, RAMC, Medical Officer of the Liverpool Rifles.

in order to gain a few days' respite from the line.[45] This kind of short-term malingering appears to have been condoned by the Battalion hierarchy, as long as the men were not permanently lost to the unit.

What could not be tolerated was the more dramatic form of malingering, that of self-inflicted wounding. Self-mutilation was a desperate act perpetrated by individuals who had lost their ability to cope with the war. However, the Battalion Commander could not afford to be compassionate when the offence struck at both the manpower resources and the morale of his battalion. A soldier who shot himself in the hand or foot, unlike the malingerer, was rejecting his role as an infantryman and attempting to remove himself permanently from the war. In all but two cases in the Rifles, this warranted a court-martial.

For the Rifles, self-inflicted wounding was the most frequently occurring court-martial offence during wartime. A total of nine men were court-martialled for shooting themselves in the hand, foot or neck to escape front-line duties, constituting 26 per cent of all trials.[46] By contrast, only 1 per cent of all courts-martial in the British army abroad were for

---

[45] J. W. Lorimer, Diary, LSM, Acc. No. 794.
[46] 1/6th Battalion King's (Liverpool) Regiment Casualty Books 1–3, KRC, MLL, 58.83.537a–b; Ledger books of Field General Courts-Martial, 1915–19, PRO, WO 213/1–24.

Table 7.1 *Court-martial offences committed by a representative sample of infantry battalions that served on the Western Front, 1915–18*

	Battalions				
	Regular	Service	Territorial		
Types of offence	1st Glosters	6th Cameronians	1/6th Gordons	1/14th London	1/6th Liverpool
Drunkenness	27	14	8	0	1
Escaping	4	0	0	0	1
Quitting post	1	0	0	0	3
Absence	14	12	2	9	3
Desertion	15	1	2	0	3
Sleeping	3	1	1	0	6
Cowardice	1	0	0	0	0
Insubordination	9	4	2	2	1
Disobedience	9	2	1	0	1
Section 40	14	17	9	7	4
Self-inflicted wound (S40)	0	0	0	0	9
Striking a senior officer	6	1	1	0	0
Theft	2	0	0	0	0
Fraud	1	0	0	0	0
Offence against an inhabitant	1	3	0	0	0
Unknown	0	0	0	0	2
Injuring property	0	0	0	0	1

Source: 1/6th Battalion King's (Liverpool) Regiment Casualty Books 1–3, KRC, MLL, 58.83.537 a–b; Ledger Books of Field General Courts-Martial, 1915–1919, PRO, WO 213/1–24; T. Bowman, 'The discipline and morale of the British Expeditionary Force in France and Flanders 1915–18, with particular reference to Irish units', unpublished PhD dissertation, University of Luton (1999), pp. 730–48

self-mutilation,[47] and amongst the representative sample of battalions in Table 7.1, only the Rifles had entries for self-inflicted wounds. Why should the Rifles have so many men with self-inflicted wounds and other battalions none at all?

---

[47] Percentage calculated from table (xi) Summary of analyses of proceedings of General, District and Field General Courts-Martial Abroad for the trials of Officers, Soldiers and Civilians, 4 August 1914 to 31 March 1920, War Office, *Statistics of the military effort of the British Empire* (London, 1922), 667.

This significant discrepancy highlights an interesting historical issue that has not yet been adequately accounted for. David Englander and James Osborne believed that self-mutilation was negligible,[48] and so it was, if the official court-martial statistics are to be taken at face value. Joanna Bourke too noted the apparent dearth of courts-martial for self-inflicted wounds, but suggested that official figures were underestimated.[49] Neither produced an explanation for their observations.

Part of the answer lies in the way in which court-martial details were compiled by the Judge Advocate General's Office during the war. Heading the pages of each court-martial ledger were seventeen categories to describe an offence, including the catch-all category 'miscellaneous'.[50] This category accommodated, among others, offences tried under Section 40 of the Army Act – conduct to the prejudice of good order and military discipline – that broad church that could encompass almost any misdemeanour.[51] As most cases of self-inflicted wounding were tried under Section 40, their numbers were subsumed in the miscellaneous group.[52] The high numbers of Section 40 offences across Table 7.1 gives credence to this theory. It is probable therefore that, contrary to the official indices, self-inflicted wounding posed a significant threat to the operations of the British army during the Great War.

Prosecutions for self-inflicted wounds in the Rifles began in December 1916. They were evenly distributed throughout 1917 and 1918 and do not correlate strongly with set-piece attacks. Indeed, only one man was court-martialled for shooting himself during battle. This was probably because self-inflicted wounds were more difficult to identify amongst the multitude of battle-injured men; but also because the monotonous 'quiet' periods in the trenches, with their attendant tension and anticipation, gave the men time to dwell upon what had happened to them and what was to come.[53]

---

[48] Englander and Osborne, 'Jack, Tommy and Henry Dubb', 598. See also N. Ferguson, *The pity of war* (London, 1998), 367.
[49] Coincidentally, Bourke uses statistics relating to injuries due to causes other than enemy action between February and July 1916 in the 55th Division to support her argument. Bourke, *Dismembering the male*, 86.
[50] Ledger books of Field General Courts-Martial, 1915–19, PRO, WO 213/1–24.
[51] This was despite the fact that Section 18 of the Army Act specifically mentions wilful self-mutilation. War Office, *Manual of military law* (London, 1914), 392.
[52] Admittedly, in some ledgers a hand-written column, entitled S.I.W. was added, almost as an afterthought, and it is from here that the official self-mutilation statistics were derived. However, offences were not entered consistently and on cross-referencing those court-martials recorded in the 6th Rifles casualty books with the Ledgers, it was found that a number of the cases had been entered under miscellaneous, despite the addition of the S.I.W. column.
[53] 1/6th Battalion King's (Liverpool) Regiment Casualty Books 1–3, KRC, MLL, 58.83.537a–b.

In general, self-mutilation followed two patterns that mirrored Charles Moran's analysis of endurance in the trenches. According to Moran, who was the Medical Officer for the 1st Battalion, The Royal Fusiliers, the first debilitating fear felt by a new soldier was that of the unknown. A minority were unable to conquer that dread, which may explain the actions of the five riflemen who wounded themselves within a month of joining the Battalion. If, on the other hand, a soldier survived his initial experience of warfare, his fear subsided and the drain on his endurance became slow and cumulative.[54] The remaining six men prosecuted correspond again to Moran's paradigm, taking on average eighteen months to resort to self-mutilation.[55]

Volunteers and conscripts alike were responsible for self-inflicted wounding,[56] but their offending pattern diverged dramatically. Volunteers spent an average of 23.8 months in the trenches before injuring themselves, compared with 2.4 months for conscripts.[57] This difference can be explained by the circumstances in which conscripts found themselves on joining the Battalion. Most of those conscripts court-martialled had been transferred from other battalions on small drafts.[58] Assimilation into the Battalion was harder for these men, who often joined the unit as individuals and thus lacked the support network of those with whom they had trained. In addition, although all conscripts came from the King's (Liverpool) Regiment, customs could differ from battalion to battalion, confusing and alienating new drafts.[59] The shock of the transition from training to the trenches was also more severe for some conscripts. Unlike raw drafts in the early years, there was often no opportunity for an acclimatization period,[60] and their formative experiences in the trenches proved overwhelming for a minority of conscripts.

---

[54] Lord Moran, *The anatomy of courage* (London, 1945), 69.
[55] 1/6th Battalion King's (Liverpool) Regiment Casualty Books 1–3, KRC, MLL, 58.83.537a–b.
[56] Four volunteers and seven conscripts.
[57] 1/6th Battalion King's (Liverpool) Regiment Casualty Books 1–3, KRC, MLL, 58.83.537a–b.
[58] The men were transferred from 1/8th, 12th and 19th Battalions of the King's (Liverpool) Regiment.
[59] For example, Private Campbell, when posted to the 9th King's, found his first guard on active service difficult. As he explained, 'the ceremony was different, we felt somewhat humiliated at being rebuffed at faults we are not to blame for'. W. H. Campbell, Diary, 11 October 1916, LSM, Acc. No. 484.
[60] On arrival in Belgium in February 1915, the men of the Liverpool Rifles were introduced to the trenches in stages. At first they trained behind the lines and then they performed carrying duties to the trenches, before graduating to manning the front line. Most drafts of 1915 and early 1916 would have joined the Battalion during relatively quiet periods and so would have had time to acclimatize.

The distribution of Section 40 offences suggests that self-inflicted wounds may have been an offence favoured by volunteer units, rather than the regulars. Section 40 offences dominated the court-martial profile of the Cameronians, the Gordons and the London Scottish, but were of less significance in the Glosters (see Table 7.1).[61] Certainly, it appears that self-mutilation was preferred to desertion as a method of escape in the Rifles. A wound provided an immediate and legitimate release from the trenches, and thus a self-inflicted wound, if undetected, allowed the soldier to return home with his reputation intact. An honourable reputation was of vital importance to the first Territorials, who set the trend of self-inflicted wounding. Conscripts followed the same tradition within the Battalion, maintaining a high rate of offending throughout 1918.

It is clear that self-mutilation was considered to be a problem for the Rifles. The sentences varied according to the period of the war, and the whims of the presiding officers, although they got noticeably stiffer in the aftermath of the Third Battle of Ypres. This trend continued into 1918, with self-mutilation incurring Field Punishment Number One, when previously Number Two had sufficed. Although the men were often transferred to Britain for medical treatment, they were sentenced on recovery to long periods of field punishment, which was completed either with their battalion or, if they had been medically downgraded as a result of their injury, with the Labour Corps.[62] It was important that the men should be seen to be punished for their crime, as a means of deterrence. Of the nine men convicted by courts-martial, only one soldier avoided field punishment, because he was declared insane. Four of the remainder served out their punishments with the Labour Corps and four with the Rifles (see Table 7.4).

Disobedience and insolence

Those who failed to comply with an order, displayed insolent behaviour or committed a combination of the two were usually charged with misconduct to the prejudice of good order. Offences included clear-cut cases of soldiers failing to observe routine orders, such as not extinguishing lights after 'lights out', or specific orders, for instance failing to deliver a message. There were also the more subjective military crimes, such as making an improper reply to an NCO and commenting on the fairness of an order.

---

[61] Section 40 offences accounted for over 35 per cent of all courts-martial in the representative Service and Territorial units and only 13 per cent in the regulars.
[62] 1/6th Battalion King's (Liverpool) Regiment Casualty Books 1–3, KRC, MLL, 58.83.537a–b.

Table 7.2 *Minor offences committed in the 6th Liverpool Rifles, 1915–19*

Offences	Year				Post-war	Total
	1915	1916	1917	1918	1918–19	
Over leave	0	1	4	12	4	21
Absence	1	2	1	13	6	23
Over a pass	0	2	2	1	0	5
Absent from parade	2	3	0	2	0	7
Not complying with order	1	14	0	0	0	15
Insolence	2	1	0	0	1	4
Insolence and disobedience	4	3	0	0	0	7
Connected with sentry duty	2	1	3	1	0	7
Negligently discharging arms	3	0	0	0	1	4
Reporting sick without cause	0	4	0	0	0	4
Drunkenness	0	1	1	3	0	5
Self-inflicted wounds (negligent)	0	0	0	2	0	2
Miscellaneous	2	5	2	2	1	12
Unknown	1	4	17	27	11	60
Total	18	41	30	63	24	176

Source: 1/6th Battalion King's (Liverpool) Regiment Casualty Books 1–3, KRC, MLL, 58.83.537 a–b.

The incidence of soldiers not complying with an order and insulting officers or NCOs traced a different trajectory from that of most military crimes committed in the Rifles. Their numbers peaked in 1916, accounting for 44 per cent of all minor offences for that year and then declined sharply thereafter (see Table 7.2).

To some extent, the apparent decline in disobedience and insolence during the latter years of the war may be misleading. In 1917 and 1918 there were numerous minor sanctions recorded in the casualty books without a corresponding offence, and it is probable that disobedience and insolence were responsible for some of these punishments. Nevertheless, the sheer strength of the trend towards declining trials for disobedience among the known offences is convincing and requires explanation.

As most recorded instances of insolence and disobedience were concentrated in the early years of the war, it was overwhelmingly volunteers, including a high percentage of the original Battalion of 1915, who were convicted.[63] This pattern can be explained by the nature of the social

---

[63] Eleven out of twenty-six offences of disobedience and insolence were committed by original members of the Battalion.

hierarchy in the unit during the early years of the conflict and its reconfiguration after 1916. As we saw in chapter 3, the ranks of the Rifles were filled initially with men of high social status. Such men regarded most serious military crime as dishonourable, but, frustrated by the lack of promotion opportunities, some became vociferous and powerful critics within a unit. Whilst the 6th Rifles undoubtedly cultivated an informal atmosphere which encouraged open discussion, there was still a need to establish boundaries. Thus, during 1915–16, when the leadership was under the greatest pressure from below, field punishment was employed as a method of imposing those limits. After 1916 the opportunities for promotion were there for the taking, discontent subsided, and the need to use field punishment as a means of control receded.

It is likely that disobedience remained a regular feature of Battalion life throughout 1917 and 1918, but it no longer posed the same threat to the cohesion of the unit. A plethora of other, more serious offences demanded the attention of the Battalion Commander, and the management of disobedience could be delegated to company commanders who were now more secure, having more opportunity to utilize their civilian social standing to bolster their authority.

Disobedience came in many forms. It was not always a negative action, nor was it necessarily a product of discontent. Taking the initiative sometimes involved contravening regulations, and this was recognized within the Battalion. Indeed, J. B. McKaig, who became Commanding Officer of the Rifles in September 1916, was not averse to disregarding restrictive rules himself. As a company commander, he ignored direct orders preventing him from patrolling No Man's Land, because he believed it was in his company's interests that he should be familiar with its section of the front.[64] Similarly, Sergeant Macfie braved the wrath of the Quartermaster to smuggle stores up to the front line, in order to ration the Battalion more effectively.[65] If initiative was to be encouraged, a balance had to be struck between enforcing rules and allowing some freedom of action.

Whilst the officers and NCOs might be the ultimate arbiters of what merited formal punishment, their decisions were not made in a vacuum. To avoid alienating their men, and thus failing in the fundamental objective of maintaining the efficiency of the unit, punishment had to be applied sensitively. The way in which a fraternization incident was handled in the Liverpool Scottish illustrates this point well. During November 1915 the Battalion was facing a unit of friendly Saxons. A general agreement to live and let live was operating, and Private Herd and his comrades on a

[64] *Greenjacket*, July 1927, 12.
[65] R. A. S. Macfie to Charlie Macfie, 24 October 1918, Macfie Papers, IWM, Con. Shelf.

listening post in No Man's Land spent a pleasant five days meeting with the Saxons and exchanging gifts in a nearby mine crater. Rumours of the fraternization circulated within the Battalion and eventually passed into its folklore.[66] According to Herd, the meetings were a result of boredom with trench warfare, and certainly not induced by a latent pacifism. They did not trust their enemy and took the precaution of slipping Mills bombs and bayonets into their pockets, in case of foul play during the encounters. The fraternization represented the kind of adventure many of the young men believed they were going to experience on joining up, and did not herald a rejection of the war. It ceased as soon as the Battalion was relieved.

It would have been counter-productive to court-martial these men. Their actions, although entirely contrary to army regulations, did not pose a threat to the operation of the unit and were an extension of the live and let live situation in which the whole Battalion was colluding at the time. Captain Davidson, recognizing this fact, merely reproved Rifleman Herd and his comrades 'with a twinkle in his eye' and the matter was not taken any further.[67]

The Territorials continued to eschew formal punishment wherever possible during the war and, as in pre-war days, attempted to fit the punishment to the crime. H. S. Taylor remembered one attempt to wean an amiable alcoholic in his platoon away from his military misdemeanours. Taylor suggested to the Platoon Commander that he might give the offender a stripe as he had 'read somewhere that such a method developed a sense of responsibility in an otherwise black sheep'.[68] It was a strategy rooted in middle-class notions of self-improvement, but unfortunately, in this case, was unsuccessful. Taylor explained that the man soon had to be demoted: 'our ex-lance corporal had managed to possess himself of the precious rum jar ... When found he was blissfully engaged, lying on his back, with the remains of the rum trickling through the sandbag into his mouth ... This could only lead to serious trouble and he disappeared from sight permanently.'[69] Although this attempt at creative discipline was ultimately unsuccessful and stronger measures had to be subsequently imposed, it shows that the Territorial tradition of seeking alternative punishments was alive and well in 1917.

---

[66] McGilchrist, *The Liverpool Scottish*, 57; E. Herd, Diary, 25–29 November 1915, KRC, MLL, 1981.850, 41–3; W. Bromley, Memoir, LSM, Acc. No. 544, 65.
[67] E. Herd, Note to diary in 1939, KRC, MLL, Herd Papers, 1981.850, 41.
[68] H. S. Taylor, Reminiscences, LSM, Miscellaneous File T, 6.
[69] H. S. Taylor, Reminiscences, LSM, Miscellaneous File T, 6.

Drunkenness

Drunkenness, the vice of the regular army, appeared only rarely in the punishment statistics.[70] Only one sergeant was convicted by court-martial for drunkenness alone, and alcohol played a part in three other convictions: absence, escaping and quitting a post. Similarly, only five punishments for drunkenness appear in the minor offence lists (see Table 7.2). That is not to say that the Battalion was teetotal. There was a general acceptance within the Scottish and the Rifles that alcohol could relieve some of the privations of the trenches and release nervous tension. The rum ration was gratefully received, and a blind eye was turned to heavy drinking before battle. Indeed, many of the Liverpool Scottish marched to the trenches at Hooge nursing hangovers.[71] Drunkenness threatened the efficiency of the Battalion only when a soldier was drunk on duty and it was only then that punitive sanctions were enforced.

Looting, theft and dishonesty

Theft within the Rifles was a rarity between 1915 and 1919. Only two soldiers received minor punishments and one was court-martialled. In August 1915 Rifleman Clarke received seven days' Field Punishment Number Two for tampering with company rations, a punishment equal to that given to an absentee from defaulters parade, apprehended by the military police during the same month. The next offence in March 1917 was committed by a lance corporal who removed government property from a billet and as a consequence lost his stripe. Finally, March 1918 saw the court-martial of Rifleman W. Pilling for making away with property from a hospital, and he was awarded fifty-six days' Field Punishment Number One.[72]

Unlike most offences discussed, theft was a crime familiar in civilian life, and it was viewed with contempt. In the trenches, the significance of the crime was magnified as it helped to destroy the essential trust between comrades in arms, and its seriousness was reflected in the relatively harsh punishments awarded.

---

[70] Spiers, 'The regular army', 46.
[71] A. Bryans, 'Hooge, the charge and after', 28 June 1915, Bryans Scrapbook, LSM, Acc. No. 545.
[72] 1/6th Battalion King's (Liverpool) Regiment Casualty Books 1–3, KRC, MLL, 58.83.537a–b.

If theft within the Battalion was taboo, attitudes towards stealing from the local populations in France and Belgium, otherwise known as looting, were more ambivalent. Throughout the war, despite orders to the contrary,[73] officers and men of both the Rifles and the Scottish plundered the countryside and the partially destroyed villages for food and furniture.[74] Looting was deemed acceptable if it provided for the immediate, basic needs of the men and alleviated the discomfort of living in the field. To legitimize this practice and reconcile their actions with their civilian values, looting was labelled as 'winning'.[75] In some cases, it seems that the war modified middle-class morality, but certain rules still operated. Looting for individual financial gain induced revulsion in many men, particularly when it involved the dead. Sergeant Macfie's reaction to looting on the battlefield was a typical one.

> We asked the men what they were looking for and I laughed incredulously when they said watches and money. But I had not gone eight paces before a man called 'Here's one'. He had rooted up a lump of black oily clay-like stuff from which protruded two black sticks, the bones of a soldier's wrist. And in the decaying mass around the bones was a strap, from which, working carefully with a knife and a stick he gradually extracted a watch. It was rather ghoulish.[76]

General trends

Between 1915 and 1918 there was a dramatic increase in the number of men tried by the Commanding Officer and by court-martial. Whilst orderly room trials fluctuated, the courts-martial followed a more consistent curve (see Figures 7.2 and 7.3). How can these patterns of offending be explained and what implications do they have for the nature of the disciplinary regime in the Rifles?

The offending profile of the Rifles was influenced by four main determinants: the social and ethnic composition of the Battalion, the experience of individuals, the amalgamation of battalions in 1918, and the Territorial disciplinary framework. The initial low rates of offending in 1915 can be attributed, in part, to middle-class attitudes towards crime. The rank and file were anxious to avoid any slur on their character, and in

---

[73] 166th Brigade Order, 13 January 1916, Y Company Army Book 152, Liverpool, Macfie Papers, LSM, Acc. No. 306.
[74] McKinnell, *The diary of Bryden McKinnell*, 24 November 1915; E. Herd, Diary, 28 September 1915, Herd Papers, KRC, MLL, 1981.850, 34.
[75] 'Every illegitimate method of obtaining possession of an article is called "winning".' R. A. S. Macfie to Jack Macfie, 19 February 1915, Macfie Papers, IWM, Con. Shelf.
[76] R. A. S. Macfie to Father, 23 August 1916, Macfie Papers, IWM, Con. Shelf. For a similar opinion see W. G. Bromley, Memoir, January 1916, LSM, Acc. No. 544, 75.

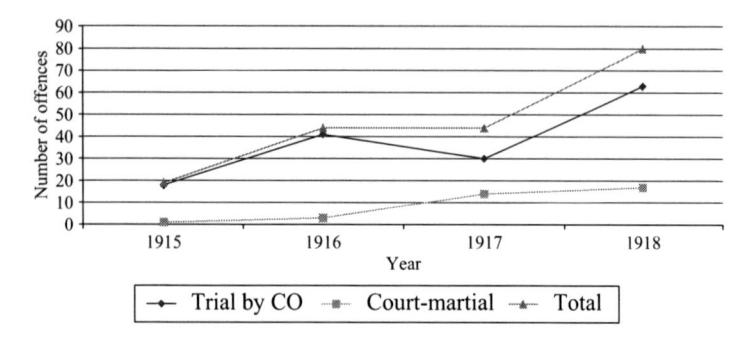

182   Command, discipline and the citizen soldier

Figure 7.2 Military offences tried during wartime in the 6th Liverpool Rifles, 1915–18.

many cases the threat of punishment was enough to dissuade them from committing a serious offence.[77]

The increase in offences tried by the Commanding Officer in 1916 was largely a product of the frustration of middle-class rankers challenging their superiors, and the corresponding reduction in 1917 a consequence of the promotion of some middle-class men and the beginning of a gradual shift towards a different social hierarchy within the Battalion. From 1917, men from lower social classes entered the Battalion and the types of offences punished by the Commanding Officer began to change. It appears that some of the new conscripts preferred to express their protest through more unambiguous and threatening means. The addition of absence, drunkenness and desertion to the litany of offences explains the increased need for courts-martial.

Englander and Osborne have suggested that war neurosis may have played a part in boosting military crime in the latter years of the war.[78] The evidence from the Rifles, however, shows that only nine offenders had hospital or field ambulance admissions for neurosis,[79] and the offences they committed spanned the whole war and covered a variety of crimes.[80] Wartime experience, on the other hand, took its toll,

[77] J. S. Handley, Memoir, Handley Papers, IWM, 92/36/1, 7.
[78] Englander and Osborne, 'Jack, Tommy and Henry Dubb', 599.
[79] Diagnoses included debility, neurasthenia, myalgia, shellshock and insanity. All these labels described forms of war neurosis during the Great War. Of course, the incidence of mental illness is likely to have been underreported. However, the fact that even one day's illness was recorded in the casualty book suggests that the low number of war neurosis cases amongst offenders is broadly accurate.
[80] Offences ranged from: failure to report for parade, in 1915; reporting sick without a cause, slackness on road guard and using insulting language to a superior officer, in 1916; to overstaying leave, proceeding to the transport lines without permission, absence and self-inflicted wounding, between 1917 and 1918.

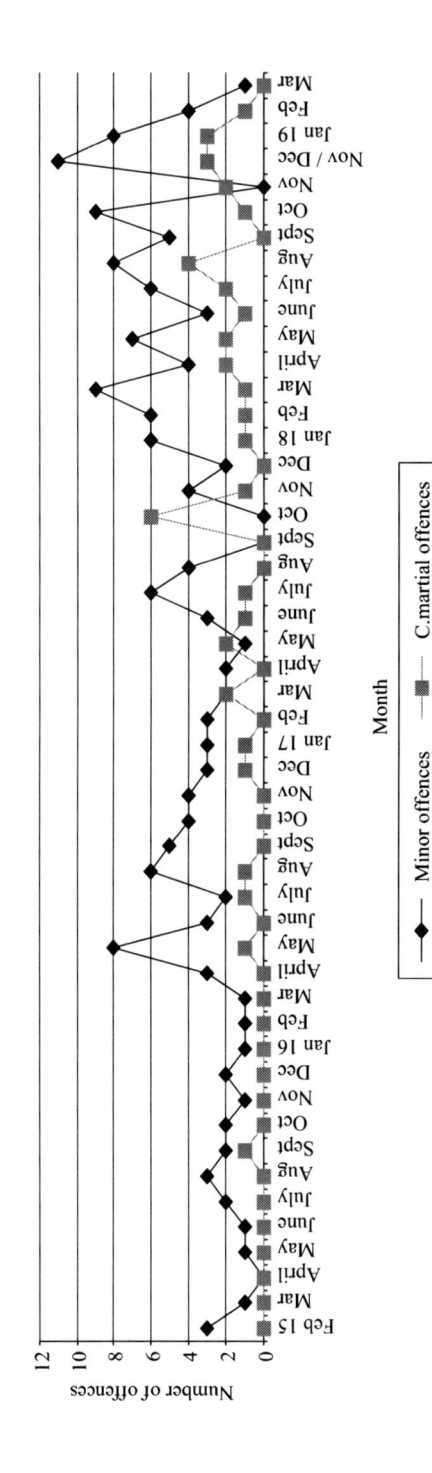

Figure 7.3 Offences committed in the 6th Liverpool Rifles, 1915–19, by month.

affecting the attitude of individual soldiers. An increasing number of war-worn men from all backgrounds began to overstay their leave, injure themselves deliberately or fall asleep at their posts in 1917, but this did not necessarily indicate that they were suffering from mental illness, and the numbers remained small. Indeed, although serious crime increased within the Rifles during 1917, the overall offending rate remained static (see Figure 7.2). It was not until 1918, with a more significant shift in the social and ethnic composition of the unit and the absorption of discontented drafts, that the trends of 1917 were accentuated.

The year 1918 began with the reorganization of the British army. In the 55th Division the 1/8th and 1/9th Battalions were reduced to cadre and transferred to their sister battalions in the 57th Division. The remainder of their men were distributed amongst the Territorial battalions in the 165th Brigade.[81] The 6th Rifles received 248 drafts from the 8th Irish and thirty-four from the 9th Liverpools.[82] Soldiers understood that if they returned to the front after a period of sickness, they might get redirected to a different battalion, and brand new drafts could be transferred *en masse* if battle casualties dictated. However, the disbandment of a battalion was a different matter, and the fact that these were first-line Territorial battalions that had to suffer the indignity of transfer to their junior unit, or worse, a different Territorial or Service unit, certainly rankled. An Officer of 1/9th Liverpools described the feelings of his men on the day the Battalion was disbanded:

> To a soldier his regiment is his home and to be called upon to leave it, to lose friendships and lose his comrades of many a tragic day, is for him, very bitter. It is not untrue to say that as the drafts were leaving and comrades were saying goodbye, some of the soldiers who had braved nearly every conceivable terror were almost in tears.[83]

The influx of men from the 8th Irish also added a new ethnic dimension to the Rifles. Irishmen had a reputation for being unruly, both in civilian life[84] and within the army,[85] and the 1/8th Liverpool Irish were noted for their poor disciplinary record. Writing to Lieutenant General Sir George Macdonogh after the war, Lord Derby described the Liverpool Irish Battalion as 'an unsatisfactory battalion throughout. Very insubordinate

---

[81] E. Wyrall, *The history of the King's Regiment (Liverpool)* (London, 1928), Part III, 606.
[82] 1/6th Battalion King's (Liverpool) Regiment Casualty Book 3, KRC, MLL, 58.83.537a–b.
[83] Wyrall, *The history of the King's Regiment (Liverpool)*, 607.
[84] In 1911, Irish natives accounted for one-tenth of all inmates in Lancashire prisons. D. Fitzpatrick, 'A curious middle place: the Irish in Britain, 1871–1921', in R. Swift and S. Gilley (eds.), *The Irish in Britain 1815–1939* (London, 1989), 165.
[85] Bowman, *Irish Regiments*, 20–1.

and slack in peace time and not too satisfactory during the War. We were never able to get a good CO for it and I do not believe ever shall as long as it is known as the Irish Battalion. The Irish in Liverpool are synonymous with all the lowest class.'[86] Coming from this type of insubordinate tradition, it is unsurprising that former 8th Irish soldiers, whatever their original background, should boost the offending statistics by bringing with them different regimental traits.

The surviving letters and diaries for 1918 do not dwell on discipline or the impact of the arrival of new drafts, but using the 1918 roll of Number 1 Platoon, A Company of the Rifles, it is possible to verify the above assumptions by ascertaining the personal background and experience of offenders. Eight men of the platoon committed a military crime during the course of the year. Of these men, a disproportionate number either were drawn from social class IV, were known to be Roman Catholic, had Irish connections, or had been posted from first-line Territorial units that had been amalgamated.[87] Each offender was defined by at least one of these characteristics which could label a man an outsider in a platoon composed of skilled working- or middle-class, Protestant, Englishmen. Excluded from the group, lacking allegiance to the Battalion and the men around them and deprived of a support network, such men were vulnerable to committing offences.

It is also possible that the Battalion hierarchy reacted to these new, suspicious drafts by tightening up the disciplinary regime. However, there is more evidence in favour of the proposition that the disciplinary system continued to retain its tolerant Territorial character, in spite of the changes in personnel. Whilst the number of summary punishments awarded soared in 1918, there was only a small increase in the numbers of courts-martial (see Figures 7.2 and 7.3). It was the Territorial system that protected the men of the Rifles from courts-martial and punished offenders within the confines of the unit.

Serious crime that threatened the physical and moral well-being of the Battalion had always been non-negotiable and attracted a court-martial. Thus those sleeping on a post received the same treatment in

---

[86] Derby to Lieutenant General Sir George Macdonogh, 18 April 1919, Derby Papers, LRO, 920 DER/17/28/3. This is more than an impressionistic view expressed by Derby. The 8th Irish had the highest number of executions of any battalion in the King's (Liverpool) Regiment during the Great War.

[87] Fifty per cent of offenders were Roman Catholic, although only 11 per cent of the platoon were of Catholic persuasion, 50 per cent of offenders were drawn from social class IV, when the platoon contained only 18 per cent from this class, 50 per cent were drawn from former soldiers of the 8th Irish Battalion, who comprised 12 per cent of the platoon, and 75 per cent were drawn from first-line Territorial units that had been disbanded.

Table 7.3 *Courts-martial in the 6th Liverpool Rifles and a representative sample of battalions that served on the Western Front, 1915–18*

Battalion	Year				Totals
	1915	1916	1917	1918	1916–18
1st Glosters (regular)	16	35	26	30	91
1st Border (regular)	–	52	27	40	119
2nd South Wales Borders (regular)	–	13	12	21	46
6th Cameronians (Service)	–	27	8	11	46
26th Northumberland Fusiliers	–	14	8	4	26
14th Royal Welsh Fusiliers (Service)	–	17	6	11	34
1/6th Gordons (Territorial)	3	3	7	13	23
1/14th London Scottish (Territorial)	0	3	5	9	17
1/6th Liverpool Rifles (Territorial)	1	3	14	17	34

Source: 1/6th Battalion King's (Liverpool) Regiment Casualty Books 1–3, KRC, MLL, 58.83.537 a–b; Ledger Books of Field General Courts-Martial, 1915–1919, PRO, WO 213/1–24; T. Bowman, 'The discipline and morale of the British Expeditionary Force in France and Flanders 1914–18, with particular reference to Irish units', unpublished PhD dissertation, University of Luton (1999), pp. 730–48

1916 as in 1918. However, by 1918, crimes such as leaving a post or leaving the trenches, that might have attracted a court-martial in other battalions, were punished, albeit harshly, by the Battalion Commander only.[88] Throughout the war the act of referring an offender to a court-martial in the Rifles was used only in the gravest cases to delineate the outmost boundaries of admissible behaviour.

Comparisons with court-martial statistics for other formations further substantiate this theory. In the Liverpool Rifles 0.88 per cent of those who served abroad were court-martialled; by contrast, 3.5 per cent of the British army abroad were tried.[89] Furthermore, if the random sample of British battalions in Tables 7.1 and 7.3 are examined, two divergent disciplinary models, the regular and the Territorial, emerge. In the Territorial model, the first two years of the war saw few courts-martial, followed by a steady increase through 1917–18.[90] For the regulars, the rate of courts-martial remained consistently higher than that of the Territorials throughout the

---

[88] 1/6th Battalion King's (Liverpool) Regiment Casualty Books 2–3, KRC, MLL, 58.83.537a–b.
[89] Percentage calculated using enlistment figures for the British Empire and court-martial figures for soldiers and officers (home and abroad), War Office, *Statistics of the military effort*, 740 and 669.
[90] The Rifles' large increase in 1917 is slightly misleading as five men were court-martialled on the same day for the same offence of sleeping on a post.

war. As for the Service battalions, they combined elements of the regular and Territorial models.[91] Their courts-martial peaked in 1916, when the officers were either all regulars, or inexperienced citizen soldiers and thus keen to stick closely to the rules. Thereafter, their figures resembled those of the Territorials (see Table 7.3). The regular and Territorial models are also defined by the offences committed. The regulars prosecuted more soldiers for drunkenness, absence, desertion and striking a senior officer. These offences rarely appeared in the courts-martial indices for Territorials (see Table 7.1).

The fact that the regular and Territorial models persisted throughout the war, despite their drafts being drawn from the same conscript pool from 1916 onwards, suggests that the tradition of a battalion had the greatest influence on the operation of its discipline system and the resultant court-martial figures. The Liverpool Rifles began the war with a relaxed disciplinary regime and continued to operate a tolerant system to the end of the war. They were helped, in part, through sympathetic commanding officers. During the conflict, each commanding officer was a Territorial himself, and from September 1916 Colonel J. B. McKaig led the Battalion. However, as Table 7.3 shows, Territorial disciplinary traditions in general were durable, and persisted to the end of the war, despite changes in officers and the social and ethnic composition of the rank and file.

Conclusion

Why were the Territorials able to maintain a relatively relaxed discipline system when faced by the trauma and miserable living conditions of the trenches? The solution to this question may lie in the fact that few men conspired to offend together.[92] Perhaps because of their tradition of inter-rank communication, the Rifles did not suffer from mass absences, desertions or mutiny.[93] It was collective offending that posed the greatest danger to a Battalion. As this rarely occurred, it was possible to deal with offenders on an individual basis.

---

[91] These trends have been noted by G. D. Sheffield, 'Officer–man relations, discipline and morale in the British Army of the Great War', in Cecil and Liddle (eds.), *Facing Armageddon*, 414, and Bowman, *Irish Regiments*, 203–4.

[92] One rifleman from the Battalion was convicted of mutiny whilst he was serving a prison sentence after the end of hostilities.

[93] The British army as a whole was relatively free from mutiny, especially when compared with the other European powers. However, as Tim Bowman has shown, minor mutinies were consistently occurring and multiple desertions and absences did pose a significant problem for some units. Bowman, 'The discipline and morale of the British Expeditionary Force', appendixes 2 and 3.

Offences were committed by two main groups of soldiers. The first was composed of those men who found assimilation difficult on joining the Battalion, and this constituted the largest group of offenders. The second held a tiny minority of soldiers who offended after long service in the trenches. Neither of these groups was large enough to pose a significant threat to the integrity and performance of the Battalion. Indeed, between February 1915 and November 1918 over 5000 men served in the Liverpool Rifles, yet there were only 187 offences which were formally punished.[94]

There was an awareness that in the trenches each soldier relied on the other in ways that were not replicated in civilian society. There simply had to be sanctions for behaviour that could compromise the safety of the battalion and put all its members in danger, but men would not accept the harsh disciplinary regime of a regular battalion. As in all other areas of Battalion life, the disciplinary regime could also become the subject of an unspoken bargain. Those in charge of the Liverpool Rifles remembered that the men, whether early volunteers or conscripts, were citizens in uniform, and for a punitive system to work effectively, it had to be perceived as fair.

Punishments had to be applied sensitively. In general, a soldier was 'crimed' only when necessary, taking into account his previous history and the circumstances of his offence. Moreover, whilst serious military offences could never be tolerated and always attracted severe sanctions, even here, offenders were generally punished within the Battalion, where the Commanding Officer could choose the nature and length of the punishment. During wartime the Rifles referred only thirty-five cases to courts-martial, thus shielding many men from a potentially harsher fate.[95] The officers of the Liverpool Rifles were aware that the punitive discipline system was a necessary component in maintaining an efficient battalion in the face of horrendous fighting conditions, but they also understood that it took far more than the threat of a court-martial to motivate their men to continue fighting the war.

---

[94] 1/6th Battalion King's (Liverpool) Regiment Casualty Books 1–3, KRC, MLL, 58.83.537a–b.
[95] 1/6th Battalion King's (Liverpool) Regiment Casualty Books 1–3, KRC, MLL, 58.83.537a–b.

Table 7.4 Courts-martial in the 6th Liverpool Rifles, 1915–19

Year	Offence	Punishment	Rank	Arrival	Trans. from	Left	Reason for leaving	With Batt?	Number of other offences	History
5/9/15	Neglect to the prej. While acting as a sentinel so negligently performing his duties as to shoot at and mortally wound a comrade	3m fpno1 (14/9/15)	Rfm	1/8/15	3/6th	11/4/18	Wounded	Y	1 of 1	Injured 31/7/17 and posted to 1/9 until 1/4/18
18/7/16	When acting as a sentinel, asleep at his post	To suffer death by being shot, confirmed by GOC cmding 165 Bde. Comm 6m IHL, susp. GOC 4th army (26/7/16)	Rfm	18/3/16	3/6th	4/4/17	Boils	Y	1 of 2	
3/8/16	Using insulting language at his superior officer	56d fpno2. Confirmed by Brig. Duncan	Rfm	3/3/16	3/6th	11/8/17	Wounded	Y	3 of 3	4/16 Myalgia 2d FAm. 7/8/16–18/8/16 Shellshock. Remained at duty

Table 7.4 (cont.)

Year	Offence	Punishment	Rank	Arrival	Trans. from	Left	Reason for leaving	With Batt?	Number of other offences	History
19/12/16	Conduct to the prej. Carelessly wounding himself in left hand (S40)	28d fpno2 (1/1/17) Confirmed by GOC 2nd Army	Rfm	18/11/16	3/6th	10/8/17	LC (PB)	Y	1 of 1	Wounded 19/12/16 in hand and never returned to the Batt.
20/1/17	Conduct to the prej. Wounding himself in neck (S40)	42d fpno1, after C of I found him of unsound mind (5/2/17)	Rfm	12/10/15	3/6th	23/10/17	Insane	Y	2 of 4	
10/3/17	Quitting post and drunkenness	10y PS (14/3/17) adm. No. 5 mil. prison. Comm 2y IHL (5/17) rj Batt 16/6/17	Rfm	2/4/16	3/6th	22/6/17	DOW	Y	1 of 1	Wounded knee 9/16
21/3/17	Conduct to the prej, SIW knee (S40)	42d fpno2 (9/4/17) with PB Batt from 28/6/17	Rfm	1/4/16	3/6th	28/10/17	LC (PB)	Y	1 of 1	Wounded leg 10/16
9/5/17	Disobedience	30d fpno1 (10/5/17)	Rfm	9/5/16	3/6th	15/2/19	Dispersal	Y	1 of 1	Wounded leg 7/16, 3 wks; face 9/16; back 9/17–2 wks

21/5/17	Absence	90d fpno1 (34 days remitted) (25/5/17)	Rfm	12/10/15	3/6th	23/10/17	Insane	Base details. PB 4/17	3 of 4
23/6/17	Conduct to the prej; SIW foot (S40)	14d fpno2	Rfm	8/12/16	3/6th	20/9/17	Wounded	Y	1 of 1	SIW 23/6/17. Ret. 13/8/17. Rewounded 9/17
22/7/17	AWOL at base details 70 days	Sentence not confirmed on account of insanity	Rfm	12/10/15	3/6th	23/10/17	Insane	Base details PB 4/17	4 of 4
5/10/17	Conduct to the prej; SIW (S40)	56d fpno1	Rfm	9/6/17	19th	25/1/18	LC (PB)	Y	1 of 1
26/10/17	Sleeping on post	5 years PS suspended (3rd Army – 10/11/17)	Rfm	12/6/17	9th NS	30/11/17	POW	Y	1 of 1
26/10/17	Sleeping on post	5 years PS suspended (3rd Army – 10/11/17)	Rfm	12/6/17	9th NS	30/11/17	POW	Y	1 of 1
26/10/17	Sleeping on post	5 years PS suspended (3rd Army – 10/11/17). Sentence remitted 10/2/18 1st Army	Rfm	15/9/17	2/6th	–	–	Y	1 of 1
26/10/17	Sleeping on post	5 years PS suspended (3rd Army – 10/11/17)	Rfm	25/12/16	3/6th	30/11/17	POW	Y	1 of 1	Wounded face 6–8/17

Table 7.4 (cont.)

Year	Offence	Punishment	Rank	Arrival	Trans. from	Left	Reason for leaving	With Batt?	Number of other offences	History
26/10/17	Sleeping on post	5 years PS suspended (3rd Army – 10/11/17)	Rfm	13/9/17	2/6 SStaffs	30/11/17	POW	Y	1 of 1	
6/11/17	Wounding Sergeant Hannah (S40)	Tried and acquitted by FGCM in his absence	Rfm	15/9/17	2/9th	30/11/17	POW	Y	1 of 1	
17/1/18	Drunkenness	Reduced to ranks	Serg	18/3/16	2/6th	8/2/19	Dispersal	Y	1 of 1	
18/2/18	Desertion	2y IHL adm. mil. prison 10/3/18	Rfm	30/1/18	1/8th	1919	–	Y	1 of 2	
18/3/18	Injuring/making away with property	56d fpno1	Rfm	16/12/17	18th	16/7/18	LC (PB)	Hospital	2 of 3	Sick 26/1/18 – Sent to 3 IBD 23/5/18
11/4/18	Conduct to the prej. Injured self negligently (S40)	60d fpno1 (18/6/18)	Rfm	Original	Original	25/9/18	DOW	Y	1 of 1	GSW buttock 5/15, ret. 6/17, then SIW foot 4/18 ret. 8/18
23/4/18	Drunkenness and escaping	6m IHL susp (4/5/18) rj Batt, remitted 26/12/18	Rfm	15/9/17	2/7th	17/2/19	Dispersal	Y	1 of 1	Sick after offence 30/6/18–16/7/18

11/5/18	Desertion from 55th DRC. Declared a deserter	Rfm	5y PS comm to 90d fpno1 (4/9/18) by GOC 55th Div. Balance of sentence remitted from 1/10/18	30/1/18	1/8th	17/9/18	Wounded (thigh)	Hospital	1 of 2	18/4/18–11/5/18 Hospital
30/5/18	Conduct to the prej. (S40)	Rfm	90d fpno 2. 30d remitted (2/6/18) by GOC 165 Bde	18/4/18	3/6th	15/3/19	25th	Y	1 of 1	
18/6/18	Conduct to the prej. (S40)	Rfm	60d fpno2	18/4/18	3/6th	1919	–	Y	1 of 1	
1/7/18	Conduct to the prej. Injured wilfully – self-inflicted (hand) (S40)	Rfm	2y IHL comm to 90d fpno1 (12/7/18) rj unit 10/10/18	13/6/18	1/8th	4/2/19	Dispersal	Y	1 of 1	
24/7/18	Leaving post	Rfm	12m IHL comm to 56d fpno1	12/9/17	3/6th	1919	–	Y	1 of 1	4 days eye April 1918
3/8/18	Absconded and arrested in Abbeville after 36 days	Rfm	Sentenced to death for desertion. (26/9/18). Comm. 5y PS. Committed to mil. prison 13/10/18. Comm 2y IHL. susp. (8/2/19) rj Batt 20/2/19	6/7/17	1/9th	1919	–	H IBD	3 of 3	NYD 10/9/17–26/11/17

Table 7.4 (cont.)

Year	Offence	Punishment	Rank	Arrival	Trans. from	Left	Reason for leaving	With Batt?	Number of other offences	History
14/8/18	Absence – 17 days 14/8/18–31/8/18	90d fpno1 (11/9/18)	Rfm	13/6/18	1/7th	28/12/19	Dispersal (miner)	Y	1 of 1	
17/8/18	Conduct to the prej. Injured negligently SI (hand) (S40)	56d fpno1 (27/8/18)	Rfm	15/7/18	12th	30/11/18	LC	Y	1 of 1	
22/8/18	Quitting post	12m IHL (22/8/18). Comm to 90d fpno1 by GOC 55th Div. (28/8/18)	Rfm	11/7/18	1st	19/1/19	Dispersal	Y	1 of 1	
22/10/18	Conduct to the prej, SIW hand (S40)	35d fpno1 comm to 35d fpno2 (completed)	Rfm	10/2/16	3/6th	15/2/19	Dispersal	Y	1 of 1	Shellshock 2½ wks beg. 18/9/16. Debility 22/7/18–29/8/18. Ret. from SIW 15/11/18
6/11/18	Unknown	90d fpno1 remitted 26/11/18 by GOC 55th Div.	Rfm	17/4/18	52nd	1919	–	Y	1 of 1	

Date	Offence	Rank	Sentence	Date	Unit	Date	Location	?	
6/11/18	Unknown	Rfm	90d fpno1 remitted 16/11/18 by GOC 55th Div.	14/5/18	1/5th	26/2/19	Flu	Y	1 of 1
17/11/18	Desertion apprehended by civil police 1/12/18 (2 wks)	Rfm	1y IHL (28/12/18), admitted to 2 mil. prison 26/1/19	13/6/18	17th	26/1/19	Military prison	Y	1 of 1
9/12/18	Absence – arrested after 24 days; imprisoned in guard room and escaped next day	Rfm	28d fpno1 and ff 21d pay by RW	13/6/18	1/7th	12/3/19	Military prison	Y	1 of 2
9/12/18	Absence	Rfm	6m IHL. Conviction quashed by GOC 5th Army (21/1/19)	17/6/18	1/8th	24/3/19	Dispersal	Y	1 of 1
3/1/19	Declared a deserter by C of I on 3/1/19 after escaping from guard room after a period of absence	Rfm	5y PS (1/3/19), comm 2y IHL (22/2/19)	13/6/18	1/7th	12/3/19	Military prison	Y	2 of 2

Table 7.4 (cont.)

Year	Offence	Punishment	Rank	Arrival	Trans. from	Left	Reason for leaving	With Batt?	Number of other offences	History
19/1/19	Absence and escaping from guard room 19/1/19–21/1/19	2y IHL (22/2/19)	Rfm	14/6/17	25th	1919	–	Y	3 of 4	VDG and VDS 9/18
24/1/19	Absence	4m IHL comm to 28d fpno2 (31/1/19)	Rfm	30/1/18	1/8th	21/1/19	Dispersal	Y	4 of 4	11/6/18–29/6/18 gassed
4/2/19	Joining in a mutiny in forces belonging to HM military forces	56d fpno1 to run concurrently with previous sentence	Rfm	30/1/18	1/8th	1919	–	Prison	2 of 2	

adm, admitted; AWOL, absent without leave; Batt, Battalion; Bde, Brigade; Brig, Brigadier General; C of I, Court of Inquiry; comm, sentence commuted; DOW, died of wounds; DRC, Divisional Reinforcement Centre; FAm, Field ambulance; ff, forfeits; fpno1, Field Punishment Number 1; fpno2, Field Punishment Number 2; GSW, gunshot wound; IBD, Infantry Brigade Depot; IHL, imprisonment with hard labour; LC, Labour Corps; LCpl, Lance Corporal; NS, North Staffordshires; NYD, not yet diagnosed; PB, permanent base; PS, penal servitude; Rfm, Rifleman; rj, rejoined; RW, Royal Warrant; S40, conduct to the prejudice of good order and military discipline; Sgt, Sergeant; SIW, self-inflicted wound; SStaffs, South Staffordshires; susp, punishment suspended; VDG, venereal disease – gonorrhoea; VDS, venereal disease – syphilis.

Source: 1/6th Battalion King's (Liverpool) Regiment Casualty Books 1–3, Liverpool KRC, MLL, 58.83.537 a–b, and Ledger Books of Field General Courts-martial, PRO, WO 213/1–24.

Part III

Attitudes and experience: the war and its aftermath

8 The experience of active service on the Western Front

The Territorial soldiers of 1914 entered the army motivated by an array of different factors ranging from a sense of local patriotism to fulfilling a desire for adventure. Few were prepared for the nature of the war they encountered and few had any comprehension of how long they would be in uniform. Trench warfare was something outside the realm of all previous experience and as such could not fail to impact on the initial attitudes of the Territorials. Through charting the wartime behaviour of both Battalions between 1914 and 1918 we can begin to understand how far their ideals and attitudes were changed by the experience of war.

By October 1914, the regular army was dangerously short of manpower and a number of Territorial divisions, including the West Lancashire Division, were plundered for units to be deployed on the Western Front. The Liverpool Scottish crossed the Channel in November 1914 as part of the first wave of reinforcements and was incorporated into the 3rd Division. They were chosen because of their pre-war reputation as an efficient battalion, although there were many private doubts as to the readiness of the unit.[1] The Rifles followed a few months later in February 1915 and joined the 5th Division.

Although the Battalions arrived three months apart and the men of the Liverpool Scottish were forced to endure the winter of 1914–15 in the trenches, the initial period of acclimatization and the attitudes expressed by soldiers followed a similar pattern. Both Battalions received a graduated introduction to trench warfare in the Ypres salient, lasting, on average, three weeks. The Battalions first trained in rear areas and performed carrying duties up to the trenches, before being instructed in the art of trench warfare by regular units and entrusted with holding a section of the line.[2]

The Battalions arrived in the Ypres sector to find exhausted regular troops grimly holding on to their trenches against an enemy greatly

---

[1] Lord Derby to Lieutenant General Sir Henry Mackinnon, 31 October 1914, LRO, 920 DER 17/33, and R. A. S. Macfie to Charlie Macfie, 27 August 1914, IWM, Con. Shelf.
[2] W. D. McDonald, Diary, November 1914, LSM, Miscellaneous File M.

superior in number, with overwhelming artillery support. The trenches, barely dug, consisted merely of sandbagged breastworks, and perhaps the greatest hazard of all was the lack of communication trenches. Thus, the inexperienced Territorials had to cross open ground to reach their trenches, an ordeal about which they complained bitterly.[3] This was their first experience of active service. Shellfire, death, physical destruction, miserable living conditions, and the realization that the Battalions had much to learn, all came as something of a shock to the middle-class Territorials.

Shellfire was the primary preoccupation of the new soldier. A few months after his first experience, Private Bryans explained the fears of the initiate: 'How I had subconsciously dreaded what my feelings would be and whether I would show them.'[4] Most men feared that they would lose their self-control under shellfire and betray themselves as cowards, but as Bryans found: 'Plenty of emotion came along yet it somehow seemed to differ from "fear" as one knew it in one's civilian days ... I could speak normally although I was surprised at myself, I felt that my pulse was racing, yet I didn't want to bolt in the least.'[5] After passing the first test of coping under fire, the 'poignancy of self-distrust'[6] faded and new preoccupations took their place.

Death, understandably, loomed large in the descriptions of the first months of the war. Witnessing their first violent death made an impression on new soldiers, increasing their fear of mortality and temporarily shaking their resolve. Sergeant Handley remembered his reaction to the death of his Captain in April 1915: 'I was stunned, shocked. I saw myself lying there – this was to be my fate! In a daze of fear I made my way safely back to the wood.'[7] Private Ellison chronicled a similar reaction to the first deaths in his platoon: 'I wanted to be physically sick, so did Frank Evans, but we quickly realized that would never do, so we carried on. I cleaned myself up a little and managed somehow to swallow some breakfast.'[8]

After the first fatalities most soldiers were able to discuss their experiences with friends who were coping with similar reactions. They recovered their composure and subsequent deaths became part of the routine.[9] Indeed, after

---

[3] N. F. Ellison, Diary and Memoir, Ellison Papers, IWM, DS/MISC/49, 25.
[4] A. Bryans, First time under shell fire, 13 March 1915, Bryans scrapbook, LSM, Acc. No. 545.
[5] A. Bryans, First time under shell fire, 13 March 1915, Bryans scrapbook, LSM, Acc. No. 545.
[6] A. Bryans, First time under shell fire, 13 March 1915, Bryans scrapbook, LSM, Acc. No. 545.
[7] J. S. Handley, Memoir, Handley Papers, IWM, 92/36/1, 4.
[8] N. F. Ellison, Diary, 7 March 1915, Ellison Papers, IWM, DS/MISC/49, 29. For a similar reaction in the Liverpool Scottish see W. G. Bromley, Memoir, LSM, Acc. No. 544, 12.
[9] J. S. Handley, Memoir, Handley Papers, IWM, 92/36/1, 7.

Figure 8.1 Private Walter Mills and Lance Corporal Thomas A. Robinson of the Liverpool Scottish in Q2 trench, St Eloi, near Ypres, April 1915.

the initial experience, death was mentioned in diaries, letters and memoirs only when a close friend was the victim, or in the aftermath of a large action.

The invidious living conditions, lack of adequate food and the poor equipment were also factors that influenced the attitudes of the men, as they learned to fend for themselves in the field. The learning curve, out of necessity, proved steep. The Territorials developed new ways to harass the enemy through improvised jam tin bombs, in the absence of an adequate supply of Mills bombs,[10] and after five months of trench warfare, Sergeant Macfie was able to write to his aunt that, 'men have learned by experience how to protect themselves and now don't fall ill so often'.[11]

Despite stinking trenches, the absence of glamour, the bereavement and the intermittent terror, a number of beliefs and attitudes sustained the early volunteers for the first eight months in the trenches. The Territorials were fighting to defend their homes and country. Whatever the original

---

[10] 'All that was needed was a Tickler's plum and apple tin, a primer of gun cotton, a detonator, some fuse, and as many small pieces of stone, iron and old nails as we could find.' *Greenjacket*, July 1924, 16.
[11] R. A. S. Macfie to aunt, 11 February 1915, Macfie Papers, IWM, Con. Shelf.

motivation for joining up, their actions now had moral purpose, and the war came to be viewed as 'a nation's last resort against enslavement'.[12]

The initial actions of their enemy did much to reinforce the moral dimension of the conflict. The physical destruction of buildings was a theme that dominated the writings of the Scottish and the Rifles throughout the war, but the progressive annihilation of Ypres provoked the greatest disgust, and galvanized the resolve of the soldiers. Aware of its history and once beautiful architecture, Bryans wrote for the majority of men when he lamented the ruined city: 'On all sides evidence of destruction, battered walls, broken edifices, discarded clothing, burning rafters and then the famous St Martin's Cathedral, now scorched walls and the floors a heap of broken images, stonework, chairs ... and to think a nation's manhood was guilty of this felonious act of sacrilege.'[13] The plight of the Belgian refugees also touched many of the Territorials, who became convinced of the inhumanity of their enemy and determined that their own families should not suffer in a similar way.[14]

Witnessing the after-effects of chlorine gas was another defining moment for the men of the Liverpool Rifles. In May 1915 a number of the Battalion volunteered to help men of the 1st Dorsets who had been subjected to a gas attack. Lieutenant Gordon described the scene: 'The railway cutting was full of the dead, the dying, the wounded and some almost mad with torture from the gas. The doctors could render but little help to those who were gassed.'[15] Gordon, who rarely expressed his feelings in his memoirs, felt moved to write, 'Their cruel and dastardly crime will never be forgotten by the troops who took part in this battle. Germany had pledged her word not to use poison gases.'[16]

Finally, for a minority of Territorials, the war was seen as a vehicle for the regeneration of British society. A variety of visions, some self-serving, others more altruistic, existed within the Battalions. Lieutenant Chavasse remembered that there was a general consensus among the officers that the war would eradicate complacency and be beneficial for England.[17] Most officers

---

[12] *Greenjacket*, July 1924, 13; H. L. Leaton, Diary extract, 16 February 1915 in *Progress*, July 1915.
[13] A. Bryans, Hooge the charge and after, June 1915, Bryans scrapbook, LSM, Acc. No. 545. Similar opinions on the destruction of Ypres can be found in: Undated cutting from *Liverpool Echo*, December 1914, Private W. Norris of Wavertree to a friend in J. Bedford, With the Liverpool Scottish, Scrapbook 1, LSM, Acc. No. 476.
[14] Undated cutting from *Liverpool Echo*, December 1914, Private Francis of the Liverpool Scottish to family in J. Bedford, With the Liverpool Scottish, Scrapbook 1, LSM, Acc. No. 476.
[15] S. E. Gordon, Memoir, Gordon Papers, IWM, 77/5/1, 109.
[16] S. E. Gordon, Memoir, Gordon Papers, IWM, 77/5/1, 104.
[17] N. Chavasse to father, 5 September 1914, quoted in Clayton, *Chavasse*, 61.

owned or worked within firms that traded throughout the Empire and were acutely aware of the growing economic threat posed by Germany. They saw the war as an opportunity to diminish the threat and perhaps to enhance and harness British military resources to safeguard the Empire in the future.[18]

Hopes for social and religious renewal were also cherished. On 4 June 1915, Lance Corporal Bryans was sustained by the belief that 'Out of this great struggle will emerge a new humanity with large outlook and a higher purpose ... mistakes must be made and on a mighty scale for the forces are elemental, but the men and the nations who in the end must win, will be those who put righteous dealing above brute strength and force.'[19]

The next challenge for the Territorials was that of battle. The Liverpool Rifles had the first experience shortly after their arrival in Belgium during the Second Battle of Ypres. At first, the main role of the Rifles was to support the front-line troops at Hill 60 by ensuring a supply of ammunition and food.[20] Their role changed on 5 May when the enemy succeeded in dislodging the Duke of Wellington's Regiment with yet another gas attack and the Rifles were required to counter-attack from Zillebeke Village. 'It is worth noting that this was practically the only occasion in the war when any part of the Battalion was called on to carry out the orthodox open order attack at five paces extension over open ground, with no covering fire except that provided by their own rifles.'[21] The Battalion suffered heavily in this action, but, 'without artillery or other support, and in the face of accurate machine gun and rifle fire, they had carried out their orders and advanced over open uphill country, with no cover save death traps of long grass and mustard, for almost a thousand yards'.[22] The Battalion history notes that this action made a great impression upon those who took part. They had proved that they could now attack and advance, as well as hold trenches, and began to feel they were now an asset to any regular brigade.[23]

The first attack of the Liverpool Scottish took place on 16 June 1915, against an enemy entrenched on Bellewaarde Ridge, between the village of Hooge and the Ypres–Roulers railway. The position afforded the enemy panoramic views of the British trenches and so had some tactical

---

[18] Bourne, *Britain and the Great War 1914–1918*, 230.
[19] A. Bryans, 'Are the Britons Phlegmatic?' 4 June 1915, Bryans Scrapbook, LSM, Acc. No. 545. These beliefs persisted into 1916, see E. Peppiette, Diary, 26 July 1916, LSM, Acc. No. 887.
[20] *Greenjacket*, July 1924, 20. Ironically, those withstanding the enemy onslaught in the trenches felt they were fortunate when compared to the rest of the Battalion who ran equal risks on carrying parties and suffered more onerous duties.
[21] *Greenjacket*, July 1924, 22.   [22] *Greenjacket*, July 1924, 25.
[23] *Greenjacket*, July 1924, 25.

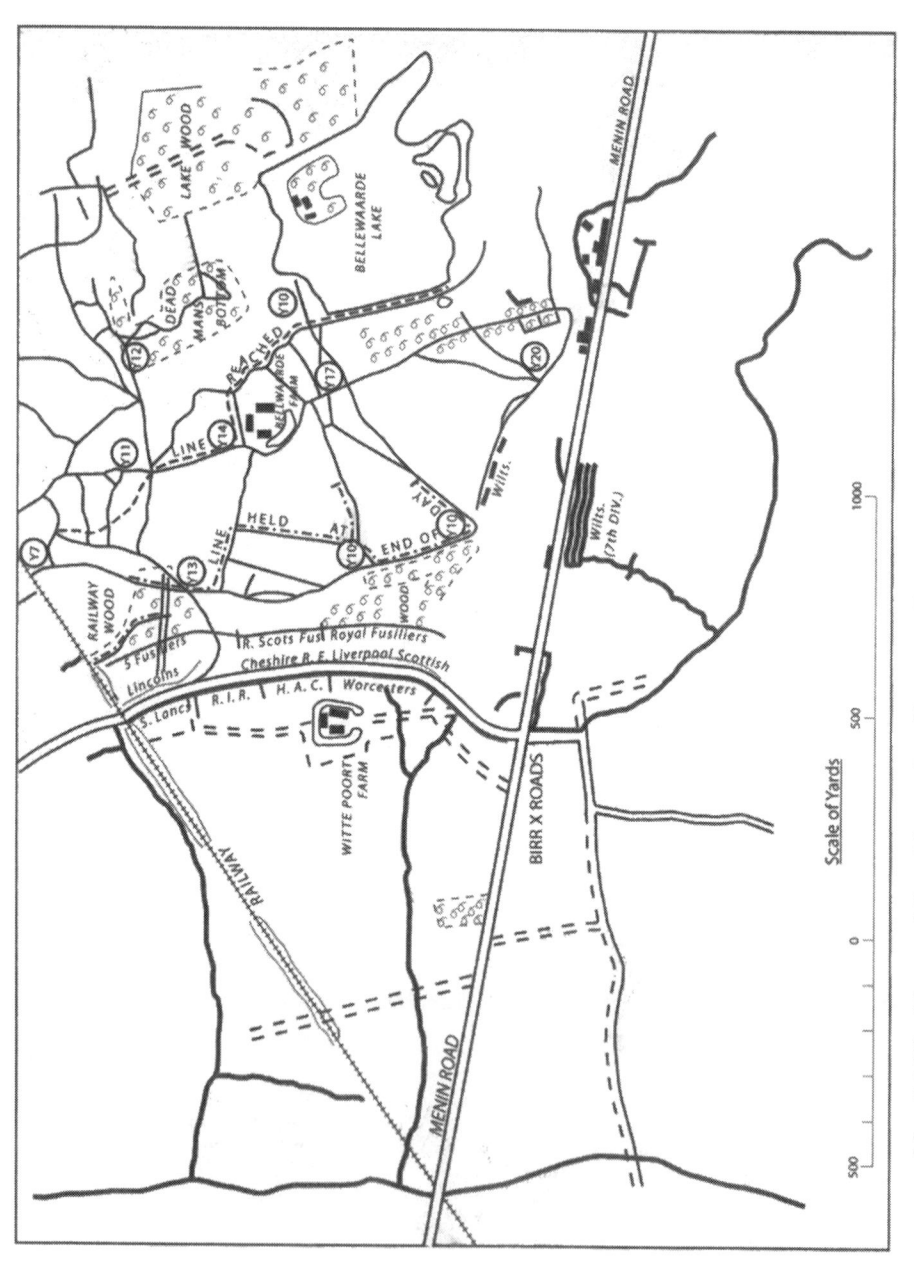

Map 8.1 The Liverpool Scottish attack at Hooge, 16 June 1915.

Figure 8.2 Men of Z Company, Liverpool Scottish, behind the lines on 15 June 1915, the day before the Battle of Hooge.

significance, but the action was designed to be a relatively minor operation to aid the British at Givenchy and French attacks at Vimy by pinning down German reserves.

Whereas the Rifles' attack at Zillebeke had been a hurried response, the Scottish spent many days practising their attack behind the lines, and had time to collect their thoughts before the assault. The Battalion appear to have been in belligerent mood as they prepared for battle. They had suffered greatly at the hands of enemy artillery since November 1914, but more importantly, they were anxious to create a reputation for their unit. 'We are about to make a name for ourselves. If we can only get amongst them with the cold steel, we'll give them fits', wrote a private to his friend in Liverpool.[24] An officer of the Scottish, Bryden McKinnell betrayed similar sentiments in his final diary entry when he wrote, 'we are going to justify our existence as Terriers and men – we middle-class business men'.[25]

At first glance, it appears that the Territorials were simply assimilating regular values of martial pride and unit rivalry. The Scottish were

---

[24] *Liverpool Courier*, 22 June 1915.
[25] McKinnell, *The diary of Bryden McKinnell*, 15 June 1915.

certainly keen to gain the battle honours they lacked from the Boer War,[26] and were anxious to prove themselves the equal of the regulars with whom they had served for eight months. As Bryden McKinnell showed, the Territorials, though well treated by the regular units in their Brigade, were aware that they were the inexperienced junior partners within the formations. Military glory in battle could dispel any negative images of Territorials that had circulated in pre-war popular culture and continued to persist amongst regular commanders.

McKinnell's quote also reminds us that the Territorials had wider preoccupations than those of the regulars and, whilst keen to demonstrate their martial prowess, were motivated by more than simply regimental rivalry. The Territorials already had a reputation based on the fact they were the 'middle-class business men' and civic leaders of Liverpool. To maintain that standing at home they needed to set a good example, and this required exemplary performances in all aspects of their conduct, from behaviour in billets to achievements on the battlefield.[27] Ability and bravery in battle had become linked with civilian integrity, and thus an impeccable military reputation was seen as essential by the Territorials, not just to assert their standing within the army structure, but to maintain their standing at home.[28]

Finally, we must not overlook the fact that they were eager to prove themselves as individuals. They saw battle as a personal challenge, and as before their first experience of shelling, the men discounted death but expressed similar misgivings about their ability to cope with the test of battle.[29] All were eager to take part, sick men attempted to get well, and there was much singing and joking on the way to the trenches.[30]

The operational orders for the Battle of Hooge were straightforward. Two regular battalions were to take the first line of enemy trenches.[31] The Liverpool Scottish, together with another battalion, were to pass through the first trench and assault the second line, capturing and consolidating

---

[26] *Liverpolitan*, May 1936. Formed in 1900, the Scottish had been able to send only one officer and 29 men to South Africa as reinforcements for other units.

[27] Similar sentiments were expressed by men of the Rifles. It was explained in the Battalion history that, 'we felt keenly that the great name of the Battalion in peace-time was our responsibility in war'. *Greenjacket*, July 1925.

[28] For more information on the Battle of Hooge and the importance of maintaining a reputation at home, see chapter 5.

[29] B. McKinnell, *The Liverpool Scottish* (Liverpool, 1919), 14 June 1915, and A. Bryans, Hooge the charge and after, June 1915, Bryans Scrapbook, LSM, Acc. No. 545.

[30] N. Chavasse, 'Ichabod' Account of the Battle of Hooge sent to his father, quoted in Clayton, *Chavasse*, 118. See also R. A. S. Macfie to father, Macfie Papers, 19 June 1915, IWM, Con. Shelf.

[31] These units were the 1st Battalion of the Royal Scots Fusiliers and 1st Battalion of the Northumberland Fusiliers.

these trenches. The battalions that had mounted the first attack were then to take the final objective, the third line of enemy trenches on the ridge.[32]

However, this neat battle plan did not correspond with the events that occurred on 16 June. The Scottish quickly learned that an attack never goes according to the original plan and that 'at drill an attack can be practised in an hour that in real warfare should take two days'.[33] For example, V and Z companies were forced to take the first line of trenches in their sector as the enemy had repulsed initial attacks around Railway Wood. The Battalion then continued to take their allotted objective, the second line.

At this point of the attack, the pre-battle enthusiasm had been transformed into aggression by the sight of the British dead, and German pleas for mercy were sometimes ignored.[34] The battle unleashed primitive feelings that, on reflection, shocked those who had taken part. Private Bryans, somewhat incredulously, likened the behaviour of his platoon to 'wolves after having a taste of blood'.[35] Sergeant Bromley also remembered that 'Some of our fellows ... had little mercy on them [the enemy] and used the bayonet freely.'[36] Whilst these actions could not be reconciled with the chivalric and honourable aspects of their Territorial identity, they were legitimized, to some extent, by the Scottish stereotype of the wild charge of the kilted warrior, derived from Highland tradition.[37]

On surveying the second line, it rapidly became clear that the trenches were little more than a ditch and offered no protection against shells or counter-attack. Major Thin thus ordered the remainder of the Battalion to assault the third line of trenches.[38] Unfortunately, this message did not reach all members of the Scottish, who, through the confusion of battle, had become mixed up with members of the other assaulting battalions.[39] Those who remained in the second line were severely shelled by enemy artillery and few escaped alive.

---

[32] McGilchrist, *The Liverpool Scottish*, 42–3.
[33] R. A. S. Macfie to father, 19 June 1915, Macfie Papers, IWM, Con. Shelf.
[34] For an overview of the killing of prisoners in the First World War see J. Bourke, *An intimate history of killing* (London, 1999), 182.
[35] A. Bryans, Hooge the charge and after, June 1915, Bryans Scrapbook, LSM, Acc. No. 545.
[36] W. G. Bromley, Memoir, LSM, Acc. No. 544, 49
[37] Bourke, *An intimate history of killing*, 58; J. Baynes, *Soldiers of Scotland* (London, 1988), 71, G. Urquhart, 'Negotiations for war', in B. Taithe and T. Thornton, *War: identities in conflict 1300–2000* (Stroud, 1998), 160.
[38] McGilchrist, *The Liverpool Scottish*, 42–3.
[39] P. Rayner, The Battle of Hooge – 16 June 1915 (1971), Rayner Papers, LSM, Miscellaneous File R, 2–5.

The soldiers who captured the third line of trenches fared better and repulsed German counter-attacks for eight hours, but the communication trenches were choked with the dead and wounded and the shelling remained intense. Lacking reinforcements, and with the enemy beginning to threaten both flanks, the survivors in the third line were eventually forced to retire to the old German first line, which was consolidated and held, allowing the High Command to claim a victory. For men such as Sergeant Bromley it was heartbreaking to be forced to evacuate trenches that had been won at so great a cost.[40]

The final gains from the battle were disappointing. Sergeant Macfie was not alone in suspecting that there had been 'a great deal of bungling' on all sides.[41] The impetuosity of both the Liverpool Scottish and the regular units led to the attack being pressed too quickly and too far in the early stages of the battle. The battalions became inter-mixed, making leadership and control difficult, and some men, carried away with the excitement, ignored orders, advanced beyond the final objective, and disappeared.[42] To some extent the rapid advance was inevitable, given the shallow second line, but it had the unfortunate result of the Scottish being shelled by their own artillery.[43] After an initial bombardment, the artillery had been instructed to support the attack by observation. This proved very difficult, as the telephone cables had been blown away by enemy bombardment, the runners were slow and vulnerable, and the brown canvas flags used to indicate the extent of the advance were obscured by smoke from shells exploding in No Man's Land. As a result, the artillerymen were not aware of the positions of their troops for most of the battle. Finally, the lack of dedicated reserves to support the attack and the absence of clear communication trenches ensured that reinforcements were not forthcoming and the hard-won third trench could not be held.[44]

The Liverpool Scottish paid a high price for a single line of trenches. They entered the Battle of Hooge 542 strong and suffered 400 casualties.[45] It is not surprising that the few men who trailed back to the Scottish camp in the aftermath of battle were exhausted and demoralized. Sergeant Macfie, who had not taken part in the attack, described the scene,

---

[40] W. G. Bromley, Memoir, LSM, Acc. No. 544, 51.
[41] R. A. S. Macfie to father, 19 June 1915, Macfie Papers, IWM, Con. Shelf.
[42] McGilchrist, *The Liverpool Scottish*, 45.
[43] J. Edmonds, *Official history: military operations, France and Belgium* (14 vols., London, vol. 2, 1922), 101.
[44] R. A. S. Macfie to father, 19 June 1915, Macfie Papers, IWM, Con. Shelf.
[45] McGilchrist, *The Liverpool Scottish*, 48. Many of these casualties, however, were lightly wounded and were quickly returned to the Battalion.

At last we heard the distant sound of pipes and after a while there passed through our gate a handful of men in tattered uniforms, their faces blackened and unshaved, their clothes stained red with blood, or yellow with the fumes of lyddite. I shouted for Y Company. One man came forward! It was heart breaking. Gradually others tottered in; some wounded, in various stages of exhaustion.[46]

In subsequent days the recovery of the remaining Liverpool Scots was nothing short of miraculous. Three days later Macfie was able to write of his men,

They are queer chaps: you will imagine that our camp is plunged in gloom. Not a bit of it. After a good sleep and a good meal the men at once recovered their spirits and are peacocking about in German helmets, taken with their own hands, and proudly showing their souvenirs and the rents in their clothing and recounting how they bayoneted Huns or how they had narrow escapes.[47]

The battle had been a success in terms of forging a military reputation for the Battalion. They gained recognition from their generals, the regular battalions in their Brigade and their home city, and for a few days their fame reverberated throughout Britain. They had accomplished their primary goal, to make a name for themselves, and this played an important part in helping the remaining soldiers to come to terms with the decimation of the Battalion.

The Scottish were withdrawn from front-line duties for three weeks following the battle and reinforced, often by soldiers who had been lightly wounded during the attack. The sense of elation that had supported the Battalion after the battle began to wane, and for at least two months following the attack, the Scottish felt that they had 'done their bit' and would have happily agreed to being withdrawn for a rest.[48]

August 1915 saw the welcome movement of the Liverpool Rifles to the Somme sector, where the conditions were a pleasant contrast to those in the Ypres salient. For two months the Rifles occupied the village of Vaux, facing the German held village of Curlu. Between the two villages ran the River Somme. Marshy areas fringed the banks and precluded the possibility of digging trenches. Consequently, both sides contented themselves with shelling their opponents' villages and dispatching patrols into the overgrown No Man's Land surrounding the river.

---

[46] R. A. S. Macfie to father, 19 June 1915, Macfie Papers, IWM, Con. Shelf. A similar description was offered by Sam Moulton in his diary: S. Moulton, Diary, 17 June 1915, LSM, Miscellaneous File M, Acc. No. 760/7.
[47] R. A. S. Macfie to father, 19 June 1915, Macfie Papers, IWM, Con. Shelf. Bromley also remembered how much he had enjoyed life following the Battle of Hooge. W. G. Bromley, Memoir, LSM, Acc. No. 544, 53.
[48] W. G. Bromley, Memoir, LSM, Acc. No. 544, 55. See also E. Herd, Diary, 26 June 1915, Herd Papers, KRC, MLL, 1981.850, 22.

Private Ellison certainly appreciated the change of scenery, informing his father in September 1915, 'This is more like the genuine article, fighting in open country. It is a welcome change from trench life.'[49] The Rifles were offered the opportunity of fighting the face-to-face chivalric war they had imagined before arriving in France. The situation was neatly captured in a newspaper article by Phillip Gibbs, appropriately entitled 'Gentlemanly ways of warfare'.

When a fight takes place, it is a chivalrous excursion such as Sir Walter Manny would have loved, between thirty and forty men on one side against somewhat the same number on the other ... It was a very sharp encounter the other night and our men brought back many German helmets and their trophies as proof of victory ... if all war was like this it would be a 'gentlemanly business' as the officer remarked, for one need not hide in holes in the earth nor crouch for three months below ground until there is an hour or two of massacre below a storm of high explosives. In the village on the marsh, men at least fight against other men and not against invisible powers which belch forth death.[50]

The Liverpool Scottish remained in the Ypres sector, but also encountered a quieter period in the trenches during autumn 1915. Indeed, in contrast to their belligerent attitude at Hooge, unofficial truces were observed on a number of trench tours in the St Eloi area. The members of one listening post went as far as fraternizing with the opposing Saxons. The proximity of the trenches meant that it was in their interests to maintain a quiet front, but the actions of the enemy also went some way to influencing their attitudes. Sergeant Bromley remembered refraining from shooting a German soldier who was wandering in No Man's Land. He felt that in view of the absolute trust of the enemy in the unofficial truce, it would have seemed like murder.[51] The Scottish made an attempt at night patrols, but the enemy reaction turned them into a farce. 'When they got near the German line they heard a voice say "Very good indeed, but if you keep to your left, you will find the going easier!" All the men in the post were standing up and watching the patrol's progress with the greatest interest. What could one do with an enemy like that?'[52]

In January 1916 the 55th (West Lancashire) Division re-formed and the Rifles and Scottish were, to the dismay of some, uprooted from their regular divisions. The Liverpool Rifles became a member of 165th Brigade and the Scottish part of 166th Brigade. As Territorial battalions

---

[49] N. F. Ellison, Letter to father, 11 September 1915, Ellison Papers, IWM, DS/MISC/49, 66.
[50] *Liverpool Daily Post*, 16 October 1915. Phillip Gibbs toured Vaux in October 1915 and spoke with Norman Ellison.
[51] W. G. Bromley, Memoir, LSM, Acc. No. 544, 64.
[52] McGilchrist, *The Liverpool Scottish*, 60.

The experience of active service 211

they had been distinctive amongst the regular units in their formations and now had to fight for recognition amongst their own kind. The compensation of serving with units composed of Lancashire men was not to make an impact until later in the war, after the battalions had haemorrhaged casualties, and in 1916 the men of both battalions 'felt in fact, all the emotions and fears of going to a new school'.[53]

The formation of the 55th Division had a positive effect on the provision of entertainment behind the lines, an important factor in maintaining morale.[54] Divisional sports were organized regularly and Lord Derby provided the capital to establish a divisional canteen, theatre and temporary cinema. There was also enough money to purchase laundry and bath appliances.[55] These facilities were a marked improvement on those available to the first members of the Liverpool Territorials in 1914 and 1915 and were noted appreciatively in letters and memoirs for the rest of the war.[56]

Between January and April 1916 the casualty rates for both Battalions were very low, the Rifles suffering only thirty casualties during these months, but the winter conditions proved trying.[57] Thus, when spring arrived in April, hiding the desecrated landscape, it had a marked impact on the spirits of the men. Private Ellison remembered, 'the fruit blossom opened and clothed poor battered Wailly with an appealing beauty. The night was filled with the song of nightingales. I cannot recollect any spring that thrilled me more.'[58]

It was not until August 1916 that the 55th Division played its first, direct role in the Battle of the Somme. Both the Rifles and the Scottish units were involved in the third attack on Guillemont village during 8 and 9 August. This was not an easy task. Guillemont, a key fortified village in the area of the second German position, had been delaying the British advance since 23 July and was not to fall into British hands until 6 September.[59] In the weeks leading up to their attack the men of the Liverpool Territorials were optimistic. They knew of July's heavy casualty

---

[53] *Ibid.*, 61.   [54] Fuller, *Troop morale and popular culture, passim.*
[55] Major General Jeudwine to Lord Derby, 3 February 1916, Records of the 55th (West Lancashire) Division 1914–19, LRO, 356 FIF 1/2/32.
[56] R. A. S. Macfie to Charlie Macfie, 13 March 1917, Macfie Papers, IWM, Con. Shelf.
[57] 1/6th Battalion King's (Liverpool) Regiment War Diary, January to April 1916, KRC, MLL, 58.83.501.
[58] N. F. Ellison, Diary and Memoir, Ellison Papers, IWM, DS/MISC/49. Wailly was a village defended by the Liverpool Rifles in the Arras sector from February to July 1916. See also R. A. S. Macfie to father, 26 April 1916, Macfie Papers, IWM, Con. Shelf. Noel Chavasse had a similar experience in March 1917, N. G. Chavasse to parents, 27 March 1917; N. G. Chavasse to parents, 30 May 1917, quoted in Clayton, *Chavasse*, 181.
[59] Gary Sheffield, *The Somme* (London, 2003), 20; Coop, *Story of the 55th Division*, 30; Wyrall, *History of the King's Regiment, Liverpool*, vol. 2, 321.

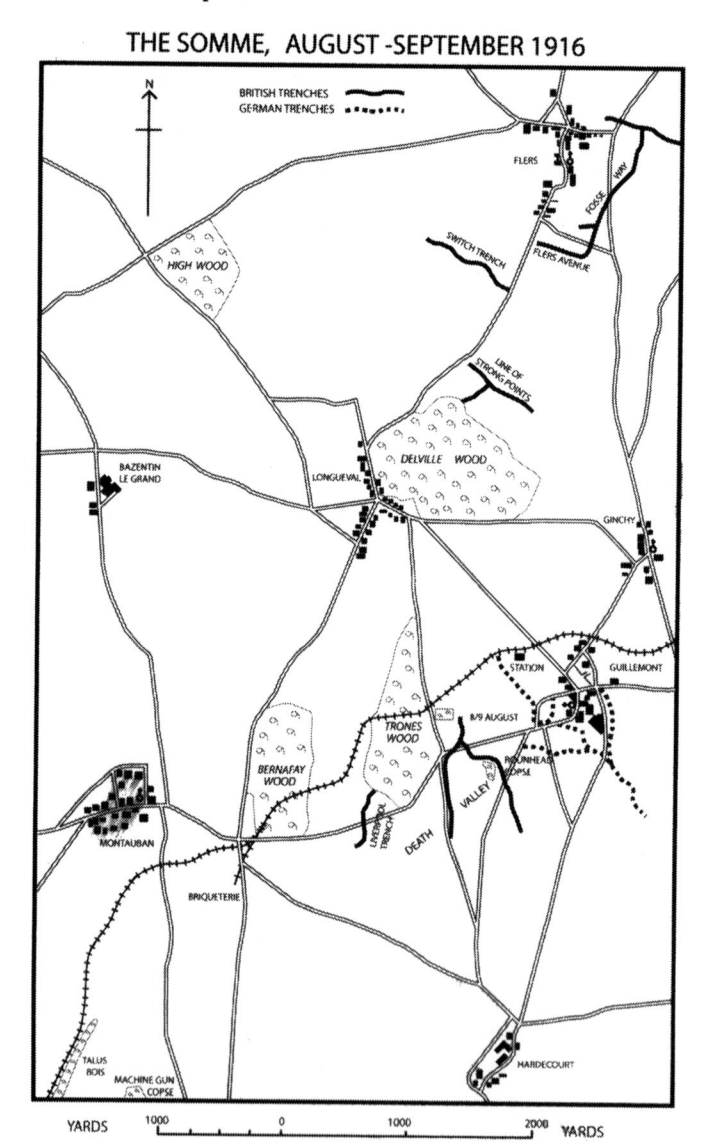

Map 8.2 Battle of the Somme.

toll and had experienced heavy shelling whilst digging communication trenches in the vicinity of Delville and Trones Woods, yet there was a sense that the Allies were making progress. Sergeant Macfie was able to convey a positive interpretation of the on-going battle to his father:

The experience of active service 213

Not far from my back is the old British front line. It is a curious sight and very inspiring. I suppose a month ago we would scarcely have dared to strike a match where we are. Now the valley is full of troops bivouacking like us, and at night the whole neighbourhood sparkles with their fires and candles, while in the afternoon, the divisional band comes and plays to us ... If war was always like this I do not think they would mind how long it lasted.[60]

Sixteen days later Macfie's tone had changed abruptly in response to the Guillemont attack. He wrote angrily to his father:

The want of preparation, the vague orders, the ignorance of the objective and geography, the absurd haste, and in general the horrid bungling were scandalous. After two years of war it seems that our higher commanders are still without common sense. In any well-regulated organisation a divisional commander would be shot for incompetence – here another regiment is ordered to attempt the same task in the same mind-closing way. It was worse than Hooge, much worse and it is still going on.[61]

Macfie's disgusted description was corroborated by many accounts of the action. The divisional attack had begun in the early hours of 8 August, but was not a complete success. The attack had succeeded on the right, but on the left it had largely been a failure, with the exception of a contingent of the Liverpool Irish which was cut off, but believed to be holding out in Guillemont village itself.[62] The Liverpool Scottish, then in reserve, were belatedly ordered to move to the front line to renew the attack.

Unfortunately, the initial failure had caused much confusion, and there was some doubt as to whether a second attempt should be made at all. Indeed, the Liverpool Scottish only received orders from the 166th Brigade to move to the trenches at 8 pm on the evening of 8 August. Before reaching the trenches, the Battalion was ordered to halt and await further instructions, delaying them for a further two hours, and when they reached Advanced Brigade Headquarters the expected guides needed to lead them to unfamiliar trenches could not be found. When the men finally reached their trenches at 3.45 on 9 August they had been on the move for over seven hours: 'heavily shelled for a great part of the time and with no chance whatever of getting any rest. They had had to force their way along roads and communication trenches full of men from the various units who had taken part in the attack earlier in the day and when they finally reached the front line they were tired out.'[63]

Yet fatigue was only one difficulty with which the Battalion had to contend. The trenches were new to the Scottish and there was no time for the men to familiarize themselves with the terrain over which they were

[60] R. A. S. Macfie to father, 29 July 1916, Macfie Papers, IWM, Con. Shelf.
[61] R. A. S. Macfie to father, 16 August 1916, Macfie Papers, IWM, Con. Shelf.
[62] McGilchrist, *Liverpool Scottish*, 77.   [63] *Ibid.*, 79.

214   Attitudes and experience

expected to attack. There was also no opportunity to explain the detail of their objectives, and consequently the instructions received at platoon level were inadequate. Sergeant Bromley remembered that his Captain, 'waving his hand vaguely in the direction of the German line said, "somewhere over there are the Germans and all you have to do, when our artillery barrage lifts, is to rush forward, capture the trenches, and go on through Guillemont, digging in and consolidating on the other side of the village."'[64] The result, according to the Battalion history, was that 'the attack was doomed before it began'.[65]

The assault was a disaster. The first line became so thinned that the men were forced to hide in shell-holes and wait for reinforcements from the next wave. The Battalion went forward three times, and each time the attack withered away under a hail of machine gun bullets. Lacking knowledge of the lie of the land, some soldiers ran parallel to their own trenches, rather than at the enemy, which contributed to the failure.[66] The surviving members of the Battalion retreated back to their jumping off trenches, only to find that they were choked with support troops, and were so poorly dug that they offered little protection.[67]

The Battalion lost 280 men out of 620 who took part in the action on 9 August 1916.[68] The casualties constituted only two-thirds of those at Hooge, but in this attack the first line was never taken and there was no compensatory eulogy of the Battalion in the aftermath. It was merely another unsuccessful action in the midst of a long-running battle and the demoralization of the men after the attack was marked. Private Campbell wrote in his diary that, 'An almost unconditional peace would be accepted by the boys here ... the tragedy of it, boys losing brothers and pals', but later in the entry added, 'I could not have stayed at home. I am glad I came out.' Campbell's sense of duty survived the experience, but it is clear that Guillemont had a profound impact on his view of war.[69]

The Rifles had a similar experience to that of the Scottish, although their fighting was more prolonged, and it was the intense shelling, accompanied by an epidemic of shellshock, that dominated the diaries and memoirs of the men.[70] Sergeant Handley recalled the experience

[64] W. G. Bromley, Memoir, LSM, Acc. No. 544, 85.
[65] McGilchrist, *The Liverpool Scottish*, 77.
[66] W. G. Bromley, Memoir, LSM, Acc. No. 544, 86.
[67] W. G. Bromley, Memoir, LSM, Acc. No. 544, 86.
[68] 1/10th Battalion King's (Liverpool) Regiment War Diary, August 1916, KRC, MLL, 58.83.509.
[69] W. H. Campbell, Diary, 27 August 1916, Liverpool, LSM, Acc. No. 484.
[70] H. C. Eccles, Diary, 10 August 1916, Liddle Archive, W/F 1915–18 (G.S.); 1/6th Battalion King's (Liverpool) Regiment Casualty Books 1 and 2, Liverpool, KRC, MLL, 58.83.537a–b; S. E. Gordon, Memoir, 13 August 1916, Gordon Papers, IWM, 77/5/1, 189.

in his memoir: 'The shells poured on us from all angles, except from immediately behind. High explosive tore up the earth and shrapnel burst in the air and showered bullets on us like rain ... we had to keep tightly up against the parapet wall to escape certain death from shrapnel, but only luck could save us from high explosive.'[71] Their ordeal began in the support trenches in front of Guillemont on 1 August, when the men were directed to join newly captured trenches to the old front line. Elements of the Battalion supported an attack on 8 August and took part in the same futile attack as the Liverpool Scottish on 9 August. Overall, the casualty list for August 1916 totalled 209, slightly fewer than that of the Scottish.[72]

The Scottish spent the rest of August and September digging fire and communication trenches and burying the dead, whilst the Rifles were in action again between 6 and 11 September, bombing enemy trenches and consolidating ground.[73] Between 12 and 24 September, the Rifles helped to strengthen defences around Flers and trained with a creeping barrage for their part in the forthcoming brigade attack. By 25 September 1916 the British were in a position to attack the strong German line of defence running in front of Morval, Les Bœufs and Guedecourt.[74] In their assault on Guedecourt the 165th Brigade was successful. The men closely followed the creeping barrage to secure their intended objectives, and captured a number of prisoners including five officers.[75] But success came at a price. The Rifles lost a host of experienced NCOs and officers who contributed to a total casualty list for September of 323 officers and men.[76]

The experience of the individual soldier on the Somme, as in all battles, differed in detail according to the battalion and even the company or platoon in which he was serving,[77] but 'to the average individual in the ranks, the Somme was merely a nightmare of endless hard work, miserable quarters and incessant shelling with a certain amount of fighting thrown in'.[78] The legacy of their tribulations on the Somme continued to affect the Battalions after their transfer to the comparatively quiet Ypres sector

---

[71] J. S. Handley, Memoir, Handley Papers, IWM, 92/36/1, 8.
[72] 1/6th Battalion King's (Liverpool) Regiment War Diary, August 1916, KRC, MLL, 58.83.501.
[73] Wyrall, *History of the King's Regiment, Liverpool*, vol. 2, 324–6.
[74] Ibid., 332.
[75] S. E. Gordon, Memoir, Gordon Papers, IWM, 77/5/1, 215; Wyrall, *History of the King's Regiment, Liverpool*, vol. 2, 335.
[76] 1/6th Battalion King's (Liverpool) Regiment War Diary, September 1916, KRC, MLL, 58.83.501.
[77] For example, before the Rifles' attack on 13 August 1916, B Company, which was intended to form the first wave, lost over 50 per cent of its manpower and had to be withdrawn to the support trenches, whilst C Company took over the attack.
[78] McGilchrist, *The Liverpool Scottish*, 88.

in October 1916, and it was to take them a number of weeks to recover from their exhaustion, and to regenerate their spirit.

In an attempt to come to terms with his experience, Private Campbell sought solace and meaning in renewed religious commitment. He confided to his diary, 'I assert that an experience of the front line such as the Somme would lead any man to throw up his hands to God in sheer desperation ... you must go on, bear all, suffer all, with the spirit of martyrdom, believing all is right with God.'[79] The Christian concepts of sacrifice and redemption were familiar to the men of both Battalions, most of whom in civilian life had attended church services regularly, and while few would have viewed themselves as Christian martyrs, there was a general belief that God was on their side[80] and that 'God helps those who trust in him.'[81]

Surprisingly, given the sectarian divisions in Liverpool, denominational differences were of little significance to the men in the trenches, and religious wrangling was confined to the higher echelons of the clergy in uniform. For example, although the Liverpool Scottish was nominally Presbyterian, Sergeant Macfie was keen to claim Father Pike, a Roman Catholic chaplain, for the Liverpool Scottish because of his personal bravery and commitment to the men in the front line.[82] By contrast, many of the padres in the Division were unwilling to spend time in the line and unable to put aside their religious and personal differences to provide an Easter service in 1917. Their lack of support provided to the 55th Division was regarded by many soldiers with a mixture of regret and contempt.[83]

In spite of the poor religious provision in the 55th Division, the men were able to draw upon their pre-war religious beliefs for sustenance, supported in many cases by their religious communities at home. Private Ralph Plunkett of the Liverpool Rifles told those at home, 'I do honestly think that the men out here have been brought nearer to God than they ever have been before.'[84] That there was no religious revival post-war[85]

---

[79] W. H. Campbell, Diary, 29 September 1916, Liverpool, LSM, Acc. No. 484. Similar views are also expressed by Private R. Plunkett, see *Young Crescent*, May 1916
[80] *Young Crescent*, August 1916.
[81] N. G. Chavasse to parents, 30 May 1917, quoted in Clayton, *Chavasse*, 182. See also E. Peppiette, Diary, 23 July 1916, LSM, Acc. No. 887.
[82] R. A. S. Macfie to Sheila Macfie, 7 June 1918, Macfie Papers, IWM, Con. Shelf.
[83] S. E. Gordon, Memoir, Gordon Papers, IWM 77/5/1, 264; R. A. S. Macfie to Sheila Macfie, 30 October 1917 and 7 June 1918, Macfie Papers, IWM, Con. Shelf; N. G. Chavasse to parents, 30 May 1917, quoted in Clayton, *Chavasse*, 182.
[84] Letter from Private Plunkett to his church magazine, *Young Crescent*, November 1917.
[85] Bourne, *Britain and the Great War 1914–1918*, 234.

does not detract from the importance of religious belief in helping soldiers through extreme circumstances in war.[86]

Between October 1916 and July 1917 the Battalions remained in the Ypres area and participated in mining warfare that had developed in the sector. Specialized tunnelling companies blew mines in No Man's Land and the infantry were required to capture and garrison the largest craters.[87] The raiding policy, imposed by High Command, was conducive to this type of warfare and the Battalions were required to dispatch regular patrols into No Man's Land and devise a number of large-scale raids on enemy positions. The first raids took place at the end of November 1916.[88] On 27 November the Rifles raided the German trenches opposite Railway Wood, whilst the Scottish attacked the Kaiser Bill Salient. The objectives of the raids were to kill and capture the enemy, damage enemy morale, identify the opposing enemy units, damage the enemy front line and his observation posts, and observe artillery damage to enemy trenches.[89] They proved very successful, with each Battalion rendering enemy front-line posts uninhabitable and capturing eleven prisoners apiece.[90]

Contrary to the belief of many historians, the November raids and those conducted in May and June 1917 do not appear to have been resented by the majority of soldiers.[91] There were probably a number of reasons for this. First, the raiders were almost exclusively volunteers, and neither Battalion was short of willing soldiers. For the November raid, the Rifles selected three officers and seventy-seven other ranks to take part and noted that 'many others were disappointed at not being chosen'.[92] The treatment the volunteers received in the build-up to the raid also provided powerful incentives to participate. At a time when the Battalions were engaged in back-breaking work, maintaining dilapidated trenches in harsh weather conditions, volunteers were withdrawn behind the lines for training and awarded extra privileges for their involvement.

---

[86] This conclusion is in opposition to that proposed by John Baynes, who was sceptical about the prevalence of religious adherence, particularly among the other ranks. J. Baynes, *Morale, a study of men and courage: the Second Scottish Rifles at the Battle of Neuve Chappelle 1915* (London, 1967), 202–5.
[87] S. E. Gordon, Memoir, Gordon Papers, IWM, 77/5/1, 232–70.
[88] S. E. Gordon, Memoir, Gordon Papers, IWM, 77/5/1, 232.
[89] Wyrall, *History of the King's Regiment, Liverpool*, vol. 2, 359.
[90] S. E. Gordon, Memoir, Gordon Papers, IWM 77/5/1, 232.
[91] For the negative effects of raiding see Fuller, *Troop morale and popular culture*, 64–5; Wilson, 'The morale and discipline of the British Expeditionary Force', 310–13. For an opposing view, arguing that the raids provided valuable practice for full-scale assaults, see Griffith, *Battle tactics on the Western Front*, 61–2.
[92] Wyrall, *History of the King's Regiment, Liverpool*, vol. 2, 360.

The opportunity to hone their tactical skill and inject some excitement into an otherwise monotonous existence proved an additional draw for raiders. The preparation was thorough. Volunteers familiarized themselves with the ground in front of their trenches through night patrols before training over full-sized replicas of enemy trenches to plan the most sensible way to assault their positions. By the time they were required to conduct the raid the soldiers were very familiar with the operation and most assaults went relatively smoothly.[93] Finally, the success of these raids between November 1916 and June 1917, together with a relatively low casualty rate, appears to have given the men a sense of achievement. Certainly, Private Rattray, who 'miraculously turned up in the German trenches', after being excluded from the Liverpool Scottish raid because he was underage, was said to have 'had the satisfaction of bringing back a fine large prisoner'.[94] In the Rifles, satisfaction was gained through the acquisition of undisclosed 'booty', and a successful raid inevitably attracted plaudits from senior commanders.[95]

Overall, raids proved a positive experience for both Battalions, but they occurred infrequently. A more common experience was that of patrolling. Those soldiers on patrols could also relish the opportunity to demonstrate their fighting skills by duelling with the enemy. 'We tried to ensnare a Bosch patrol round a moat in No Man's Land, but he was not daring enough',[96] wrote Major Gordon in April 1917. It seems that the notion of war as an adventure, so prevalent in 1915, remained a potent motivating force two years later. Indeed, the chivalric imagery chosen to illustrate a historical poem in the June 1917 issue of the Divisional Magazine served to underline the persistence of an ideal of heroic, individualized combat (see Figure 4.1).[97]

If some soldiers remained enthusiastic throughout the winter of 1916 and into 1917, a minority also began to feel the strain. Sergeant Macfie wrote to his sister that the winter of 1916–17 was the most severe he had ever experienced. A mug of tea left out in the open was frozen within minutes.[98] The pipe band of the Liverpool Scottish also suffered from the icy conditions, being unable to play because their breath immediately froze in their pipes.[99] The poor weather conditions sapped the strength of Private Ellison, who later remembered, 'we entered 1917 still half frozen and I was feeling the winter acutely and realised that my strength was

---

[93] *Ibid.*, 359–61.   [94] McGilchrist, *The Liverpool Scottish*, 88.
[95] Wyrall, *History of the King's Regiment, Liverpool*, vol. 2, 360.
[96] S. E. Gordon, Memoir, Gordon Papers, IWM, 77/5/1, 267.
[97] *Sub Rosa: Being the Magazine of the 55th West Lancashire Division*, June 1917.
[98] R. A. S. Macfie to sister, 21 December 1916, Macfie Papers, IWM, Con. Shelf.
[99] G. Warry, Diary, 30 January 1917, Warry Papers, IWM, 96/12/1, 7.

slowly ebbing'.[100] He returned home on leave in January, was medically regraded, and never returned to the front.

The gaps left by long-serving men such as Ellison and those who had been killed or gravely wounded on the Somme were slowly filled by uninitiated drafts from England.[101] They had to undergo a similar acclimatization process to the men of 1915, with the added benefit of practical advice from the veterans,[102] and they brought with them expectations and enthusiasms that were comparable to those of the original members in 1914 and 1915.[103]

In June 1917 each battalion embarked on extensive inter-arms training for the Third Battle of Ypres. Using aerial photographs, Royal Engineers mapped out the enemy's front-line trenches, strong points and machine gun emplacements with tapes and the infantry was responsible for digging out these replica defences. From 4 July training commenced for the Liverpool Territorials. 'Each platoon was taken slowly over the ground representing its position in the attack and all points were explained to the men by their platoon commanders.'[104] From 7 July three full dress rehearsals were carried out in which co-operation between artillery, contact planes and tanks was also practised.[105] There was an appreciation among the men that assault tactics had evolved in the year since the Somme actions, and the disillusionment felt after those attacks did not colour their attitude to the impending battle. Veterans and novices alike were anxious to be involved in the next big push[106] and anticipated a significant advance.[107]

On 31 July 1917 the 55th Division attacked in the opening phase of the Third Battle of Ypres around Wieltje, north of the Menin Road. The initial advance to their objectives on the 'blue line' was completed successfully, with minimal casualties along most of the front. Sergeant Bromley remembered passing the German front and

---

[100] N. F. Ellison, Diary, 7 March 1915, Ellison Papers, IWM, DS/MISC/49, 95.
[101] Ellison had served with the Liverpool Rifles in France and Flanders since February 1915, with two short periods of leave.
[102] G. Warry, Diary, November–December 1916, Warry Papers, IWM, 96/12/1, 4–6.
[103] This is consistent with Peter Simkins' argument that the resilience of the British army was sustained by a constant stream of new conscripts who had not experienced years of gruelling trench warfare. P. Simkins, 'Co-stars or supporting cast? British Divisions in the "hundred days", 1918', in P. Griffith (ed.), *Fighting methods of the Great War* (London, 1996), 60–1.
[104] McGilchrist, *The Liverpool Scottish*, 116.
[105] W. G. Bromley, Memoir, LSM, Acc. No. 544, 109. See also R. A. S. Macfie to Charlie Macfie, 8 July 1917, Macfie Papers, IWM, Con. Shelf; McGilchrist, *The Liverpool Scottish*, 116.
[106] H. S. Taylor, Reminiscences, LSM, Miscellaneous File T, 12.
[107] J. S. Handley, Memoir, Handley Papers, IWM, 92/36/1, 7.

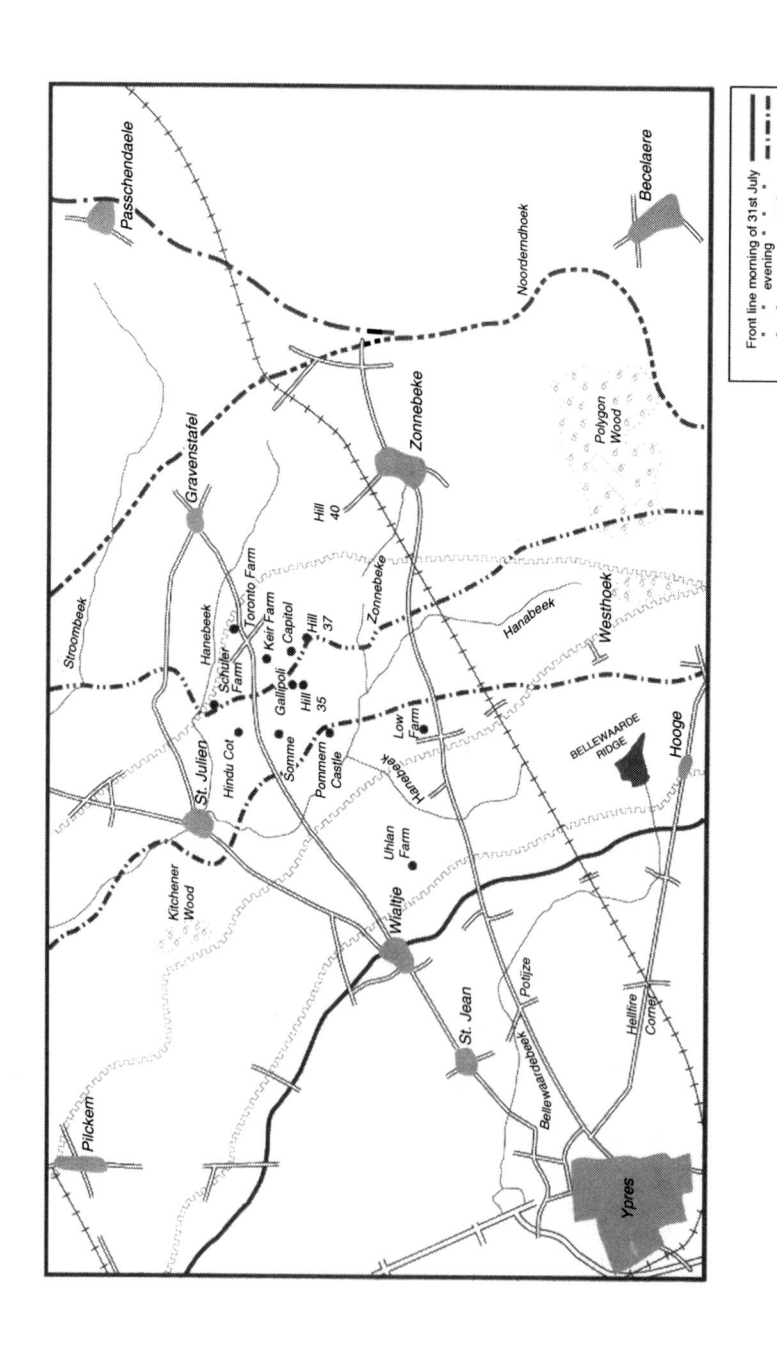

Map 8.3 The King's (Liverpool Regiment, Battle of Ypres, 1917.

support lines: 'it afforded us some satisfaction to see this, for we had not previously participated in an attack in which we had captured sufficient ground to include any guns'.[108]

The success of the initial attack was attributed to the preliminary training. The fact that 'Every man had in his head a mental picture of the ground over which he would advance and of the position of the objective of his own particular platoon and company'[109] meant that when the enemy concentrated on eliminating unit leaders the attack could still continue. According to A. M. McGilchrist of the Liverpool Scottish, 'If these men had not had an accurate idea of exactly what was required of them confusion and failure must have resulted.'[110]

Capturing their objectives may have proved relatively straightforward, but as the rain began in earnest, holding their gains pushed the Battalions to their limits. The weather conditions were so treacherous that the majority of D Company, Liverpool Rifles, sheltered in a captured pillbox, whilst small garrisons were posted in the captured German front line and rotated every two hours. On returning to the pillbox to rest,

men were exhausted, shivering and numbed in body and mind and one had to repeat an order several times to make them understand and then they would stare blankly and after hesitation obey... The new reliefs went forward each time without a murmur, although I could tell from the look on their faces that many of them would have walked to their deaths with a more pleasant expression... Throughout it all, however, their spirits did not waver, though after the flesh was weak. They knew it was 'for the great advance' and all took it willingly.[111]

The description is taken from a report to Divisional Headquarters by Sergeant Handley. Given the official nature of the report, Handley probably exaggerated the willingness with which the men fought. Indeed, in his memoir, he remembered being forced to threaten two stretcher bearers with a pistol to enlist their help in rescuing a wounded officer.[112] Yet despite the discrepancies between memoir and report, both Handley's accounts describe the heroic endurance of the troops in the face of appalling conditions and encapsulate the way in which many of the men viewed the attack in its aftermath.[113]

---

[108] W. G. Bromley, Memoir, LSM, Acc. No. 544, 114.
[109] McGilchrist, *The Liverpool Scottish*, 126.   [110] Ibid.
[111] Sergeant J. S. Handley, D Company, 6th Liverpool Rifles, 55th Divisional Narratives, 31 July–1 August 1917, Records of the 55th (West Lancashire) Division 1914–19, LRO, File 52A 356 FIF 4/1/176–82.
[112] J. S. Handley, Memoir, Handley Papers, IWM, 92/36/1, 10.
[113] 55th Divisional Narratives, 31 July–1 August 1917, Records of the 55th (West Lancashire) Division 1914–19, LRO, File 52A 356 FIF 4/1/131–220.

For a minority of soldiers the 'reports of a holocaust in a sea of mud' stripped away their sense of invincibility. After serving for thirty months on the Western Front CSM Jackie Shaw, a previously popular and jovial character, became deeply depressed, believing he was doomed in the next attack. It was a premonition that sadly came to fruition.[114] The Liverpool Scottish were also affected by the death of their Medical Officer, Captain Chavasse, who had done so much for the men, both in terms of medical aid and in organizing entertainment. A letter sent to the *Liverpool Daily Post* from a member of the Liverpool Scottish was typical of the response to his death. It read, 'no doubt you already know that the doctor has given his life. A life that I am convinced could not be spared. It is no boast to assert that the loss of him is as great as any the nation has ever suffered ... his memory is something that cannot die with me, as with thousands of others.'[115] His death came as a shock, in part, because in gaining his Military and Victoria crosses he had seemed invulnerable. His demise served to underline the precariousness of life in battle.

Despite the interminable casualty lists, most men recovered quickly from their exertions around Wieltje.[116] In addition to undergoing further training, particularly with regard to pillbox capture, they enjoyed the trips to the seaside and the sporting activities laid on to aid recovery. The Divisional Horse Show was particularly welcomed, not least because it attracted French and English nurses.[117]

The 55th Division did not attack again until 20 September 1917. This time the soldiers harboured fewer expectations of a breakthrough, but conversely, the next assault towards their objectives on the Menin Road Ridge, including Hills 35 and 37, proved very successful.[118] The problems of earlier attacks, caused by the inter-mixing of battalions and running into their own barrage, had not been eradicated, but the pillboxes that littered the front were successfully negotiated and Hill 37 was taken with relatively small losses when compared with the eighty to one hundred prisoners captured.[119]

As at Hooge, and on 31 July 1917, the prisoner count would have been even higher if all those surrendering had been afforded the necessary

---

[114] J. S. Handley, Memoir, Handley Papers, IWM, 92/36/1, 11.
[115] *Liverpool Daily Post*, 16 August 1917.
[116] The Liverpool Scottish lost 241 officers and men and the Rifles suffered 251 casualties. Battalion War Diaries of the 1/10th King's (Liverpool) Regiment and 1/6th King's (Liverpool) Regiment, August 1917, KRC, MLL, 58.83.501/509.
[117] W. G. Bromley, Memoir, LSM, Acc. No. 544, 118–20.
[118] J. J. Burke-Gaffney, *The story of the King's Regiment 1914–1948* (Liverpool, 1954), 55.
[119] 6th Liverpool Rifles, 55th Divisional Narratives, 20 September 1917, Records of the 55th (West Lancashire) Division 1914–19, LRO, File 52A, 356 FIF 4/1/955, 957, 962, 999, 1017.

protection. Corporal Hyam, an experienced NCO, rationalized his actions, on the grounds of military expediency, claiming that he was forced to put two surrendering Germans 'out of action', as he was 'unable to stop and tackle them and take them prisoners'.[120] Other soldiers took pride in detailing 'legitimate' kills. Lance Corporal Macnichol explained how he threw a bomb at an escaping prisoner 'which caught him in the back, but did not explode immediately, but dropped to the ground and then burst'. He concluded that 'it must have wounded him very badly, for he was found by the 5th King's when they went down the communication trench'.[121]

The experiences of 31 July had not dampened the determination to fight. Indeed, one lance corporal claimed that he detected a determination in the men that he had never seen before.[122] The success of the operation bred a new optimism and a renewed confidence in their tactical ability. Writing his memoir in hospital in late 1917, Major Gordon described the impact of the German surrender at Hill 37: 'This was an object lesson as there was no apparent reason why these Germans should not have held out for days and given us an infinite amount of trouble – it only went to prove that the Major General was right about "a few stout men with a machine-gun and rifles".'[123] His sentiments were also reiterated by men lower down the ranks,[124] and by those in command. In September 1917 the 55th Division was described as 'a good fighting division, possessing the right spirit' and a 'first rate division' by its army and corps commanders in their reports to GHQ.[125]

This was a significant achievement for a Territorial division. Although the German army had rated British Territorial formations highly, on a par with regular divisions in 1916,[126] in general, British commanders did not

---

[120] Corporal H. Hyam, 6th Liverpool Rifles, 55th Divisional Narratives, 31 July–4 August 1917, Records of the 55th (West Lancashire) Division 1914–19, LRO, File 52A, 356 FIF 4/1/201.

[121] Lance Corporal H. L. Macnichol, 6th Liverpool Rifles, 55th Divisional Narratives, 20 Sepetember 1917, Records of the 55th (West Lancashire) Division 1914–19, LRO, File 52A, 356 FIF 4/1/221. See also Lance Corporal H. E. Price, 6th Liverpool Rifles, 55th Divisional Narratives, 31 July–4 August 1917, Records of the 55th (West Lancashire) Division 1914–19, LRO, File 52A, 356 FIF 4/1/224.

[122] 6th Liverpool Rifles, 55th Divisional Narratives, 20 September 1917, Records of the 55th (West Lancashire) Division 1914–1919, LRO, File 52A FIF356/4/1/999.

[123] S. E. Gordon, Memoir, Gordon Papers, IWM, 77/5/1, 315.

[124] 'The last affair of 20th has proved that with determination, our infantry can overcome any obstacles put in their way by the enemy.' Lance Corporal A. Lee, 6th Liverpool Rifles, 55th Divisional Narratives, 20 September 1917, Records of the 55th (West Lancashire) Division 1914–19, LRO, File 52A, 356 FIF 4/1/221.

[125] Major General H. S. Jeudwine, To all ranks of the 55th (West Lancashire) Division, October 1917, Records of the 55th (West Lancashire) Division 1914–19, LRO, 356 FIF 5/2.

[126] Robert T. Foley, *German strategy and the path to Verdun: Erich von Falkenhayn and the development of attrition 1871–1916* (Cambridge, 2004), 185–6.

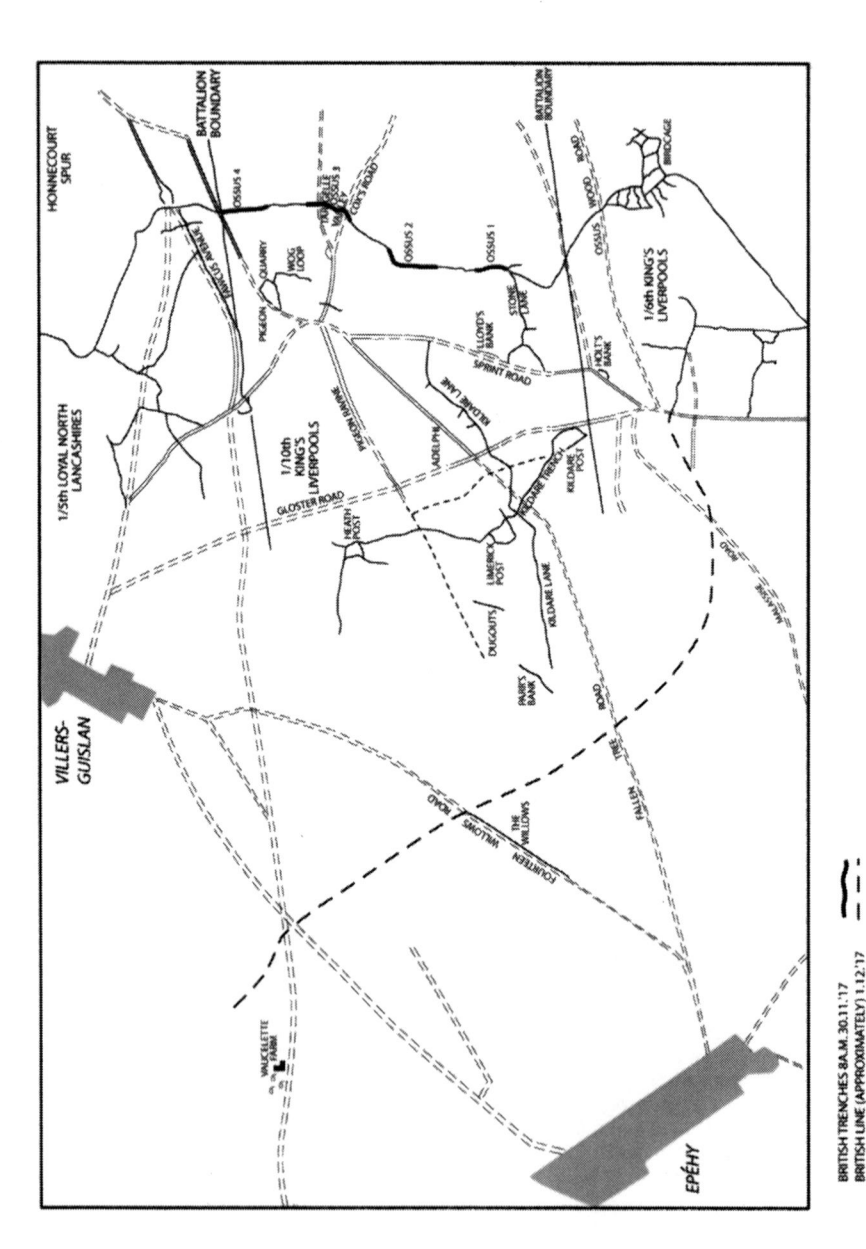

Map 8.4 German attack at Epéhy, 30 November 1917.

The experience of active service 225

view them so positively. Only half of first-line Territorial divisions were deemed reliable enough to be used as attack troops, and few Territorial formations were considered to be at the top of High Command's informal hierarchy of trustworthy units.[127] Undoubtedly prejudice played a part in the poor reputation of Territorials on the Western Front. They had been viewed with suspicion by regulars before the war and, often unfairly, this attitude persisted among higher commanders. Old attitudes were reinforced for some by the lax disciplinary regimes of Territorial units. Senior commanders who subscribed to the view that 'the best fighting battalions are those which salute best'[128] were unlikely to be won over by the informality of the Territorial unit.

The 55th Division was fortunate in escaping this negative image, at least until November 1917. Perhaps because of the quality of its divisional commander, Major General Hugh Sandham Jeudwine, who established a reputation as a tactician, the Division was regularly grouped with elite formations for attacks on the Somme and at the Third Battle of Ypres.[129] It has been argued that the practice of grouping assault formations together led to fruitful cross-fertilization of tactical ideas, and this may help to explain the tactical development and good fighting performance of the 55th Division in July and September 1917.[130] By contrast, their next encounter with the enemy was to be far from successful and was to cost the Division the trust of High Command.

In October 1917 the 55th Division was moved south. The Division was allotted over 7 miles of front line near Epéhy, north of Bourlon Wood, on the Cambrai front. In this area, the line was a series of fortified posts, strung together by ungarrisoned travel trenches used only for communication. When in the front line, the Liverpool Scottish concentrated their forward platoons in four main strong points named Ossus One, Two, Three and Four, as well as situating a company headquarters and two platoons in Pigeon Quarry, located behind Ossus One. Similarly, the Liverpool Rifles concentrated troops in the Birdcage, a small fortified salient fashioned from a quarry in the front line.[131]

There was no shortage of work for the Battalions. Strong points and trenches were in urgent need of repair and the Division was holding in excess of four times the frontage that it had held in the Ypres sector. On the positive side, the Epéhy front was assessed as a relatively quiet

---

[127] Griffith, *Battle tactics of the Western Front*, 82.   [128] Peel, 'The Territorial Force', 40.
[129] Griffith, *Battle tactics of the Western Front*, 80–2; Coop, *The story of the 55th Division*, 47 and 56.
[130] Griffith, *Battle tactics of the Western Front*, 82.
[131] McGilchrist, *The Liverpool Scottish*, 139.

backwater. It was deemed a safe place for the Division to recuperate and absorb new drafts, and, for the first few weeks in the trenches, peace prevailed. The Battalions worked hard to improve the line and the Liverpool Scottish were seduced by the luxuries of Pigeon Quarry with its range of dugouts complete with bunk beds, bath house and facilities to provide a hot meal for the men at the front. They improved the post still further by establishing a canteen and throughout November stockpiled whisky, rum and haggis in preparation for a smoking concert to be held on St Andrew's Day.[132]

On 20 November the divisional front was enlivened by the British tank assault on Cambrai to the north. The 164th Brigade of the Division was required to make a diversionary attack on their front in support of the main effort. The main attack on Cambrai was initially successful. The enemy retreated to a depth of almost 3 miles, but a lack of British reserves put a brake on further advance and the British were unable to take Cambrai itself.[133] On 30 November 1917 a German counter-attack of twenty divisions was launched. The 55th and its two neighbours, the 12th and 20th Divisions, were caught up in this counter-attack and overwhelmed by the enemy.

The German barrage began at dawn on 30 November 1917, and immediately cut all telephone communications. The smoke from the barrage and the early morning mist aided the enemy in penetrating the Division on the left of the 55th, which, in turn, enabled them to attack 165th and 166th Brigades in the flank and rear.[134] The experience of Lance Corporal Herd, who was running a canteen in Pigeon Quarry, was typical of those captured.

> Everybody took cover for a time, but in spite of strong dugouts dozens were killed and wounded ... The shelling ceased as suddenly as it had begun, but almost at once and as it seemed, from nowhere, the Germans were on us from the back of the quarry. In a moment we were completely surrounded ... we were like rats in a trap, but everybody fired like demons with machine-guns or rifles ... Rifle ammunition was getting exhausted and unless help could get to us soon we were done. It did not come, but the Germans did, hundreds of them, they must have been at least twenty to one and they marched us quickly, very quickly, and encouraged us with their boots into their lines.[135]

In writing his account, Herd, along with all other authors, was anxious to stress that his capture had been unavoidable, and thus may have

---

[132] Ibid., 140.
[133] H. Giblin, *Bravest of hearts: the Liverpool Scottish in the Great War* (Liverpool, 2000), 70.
[134] Ibid., 145–6.
[135] E. Herd, Diary, 30 November 1917, KRC, MLL, 1981.850.

exaggerated the strength of the defence.[136] Corporal Evans of the Liverpool Rifles certainly remembered the efforts of his unit in a less favourable light, although he personally emerged from the narrative with his reputation intact. Evans described how his comrades in a bombing post fled to the dugouts at the rear of the trenches at the onset of the barrage, and how a trench mortar officer and the sergeant of D Company had surrendered at the beginning of the attack.[137]

Mental and physical exhaustion may have played a part in their decision to surrender. Indeed, neither the Liverpool Rifles nor the Liverpool Scots had recovered from their exertions at Ypres two months earlier. The Rifles, for example, were severely under strength having received only 100 drafts during October 1917,[138] and such was the shortage of manpower within the Division as a whole, the Liverpool Scottish had taken over their trenches on 23 October and had not been relieved for thirty-nine days. According to the Battalion historian, this prolonged sojourn in the trenches had 'imposed a severe strain on the spirits of the men'.[139]

Yet despite their exhaustion, the narratives of prisoners of war and survivors of the battle reveal that the men of the 55th Divison were not cowed and defeated troops on 30 November 1917. Those who surrendered had not abandoned hope of their side winning the war. Corporal Evans remembered, 'We were not particularly despondent, indeed, we found cause for amusement in the shifts Jerry had to adopt for his transport.'[140] The men simply felt that they had been surrounded and, on this occasion, outfought. All narratives of capture complain about the absence of friendly artillery and counter-attack troops, which made it unlikely that the forward posts would have been relieved, even if they had fought to the last man.[141]

The survivors of the attack displayed a similar spirit. Few had secured their freedom through rapid retreat in the face of the enemy onslaught, and many held on to their positions with a strong-willed tenacity. The story of Limerick Post is one singled out by regimental and battalion histories as that of 'a very gallant fight by men who knew they were surrounded, who were called upon to surrender and refused, preparing to fight to the last'.[142] A composite group numbering eight officers and

---

[136] Although with its inadequate exits, Pigeon Quarry had been identified as a weak link in the line by the Battalion prior to 30 November 1917, McGilchrist, *The Liverpool Scottish*, 140.
[137] W. Evans, Account of capture, Evans Papers, IWM, Con. Shelf, 2–4.
[138] 1/6th Battalion King's (Liverpool) Regiment War Diary, October 1917, KRC, MLL, 58.83.501.
[139] McGilchrist, *The Liverpool Scottish*, 141.
[140] W. Evans, Account of capture, Evans Papers, IWM, Con. Shelf, 7.
[141] W. Evans, Account of capture, Evans Papers, IWM, Con. Shelf, 7; E. Herd, Diary, 30 November 1917, KRC, MLL, 1981.850.
[142] Wyrall, *History of the King's Regiment, Liverpool*, vol. 3, 559.

138 other ranks of Liverpool Scottish, Royal Lancasters and Loyal North Lancashires managed to hold Limerick Post, a strong point over 1000 yards to the rear of Ossus One, for twenty-two hours, despite being almost surrounded by the enemy. They held off three German attacks, one of which was mounted, using the communication trenches on their flanks, and eventually evacuated the position at 5 am on the morning of 1 December to join the remnants of their Division deployed in a defensive line in front of Epéhy.[143] The line guarding Epéhy did not break on 1 December, but the 55th Division had been pushed back over 2000 yards in less than twenty-four hours and had lost many men to German prison camps. In the Rifles, nine officers and 223 other ranks were posted as missing, whilst the Scottish had eight officers and 345 other ranks taken prisoner.[144]

This scale of loss could not be ignored, and a Court of Enquiry was convened to investigate the causes of the collapse of a previously 'first rate fighting division'. It listed the catalogue of misfortunes that befell the 55th, 20th and 12th Divisions on 30 November 1917. The Enquiry found that soldiers had been surprised in the outpost lines because the thick mist on the morning of the 30th had not permitted aerial observation of German lines. Hostile, low-flying aircraft had helped to intimidate troops, and the Enquiry admitted that 'the paucity of guns available for SOS action on the southern portion of the front facilitated the assembly of the enemy and his assault on our front lines'.[145] The lack of artillery on the frontage held by the 55th Division, caused by the removal of their guns to bolster another division, meant that the men at the front did not receive the necessary artillery support. These were just some of the minor challenges, identified by the Enquiry, which made the position of the 55th Division untenable when faced with a determined German attack. Their more serious criticisms centred around the lack of defence in depth, a corresponding absence of a doctrine for the defensive battle and poor training at junior command levels.[146]

---

[143] *Ibid.*, 560.
[144] 1/6th Battalion King's (Liverpool) Regiment War Diary, November 1917, KRC, MLL, 58.83.501; McGilchrist, *The Liverpool Scottish*, 156.
[145] Causes of the German successes, Court of Enquiry on the action fought south of Cambrai on November 30th 1917, 29 January 1918, Records of the 55th (West Lancashire) Division, 1914–19, 356 FIF 50/6/138.
[146] Causes of the German successes, Court of Enquiry on the action fought south of Cambrai on November 30th 1917, 29 January 1918, Records of the 55th (West Lancashire) Division, 1914–19, LRO, 356 FIF 50/6/142. Tim Travers suggests that by concentrating on tactical failure at a junior level, the Enquiry avoided asking awkward questions about command failures at Corps level and above. See Travers, *How the war was won*, 30–1.

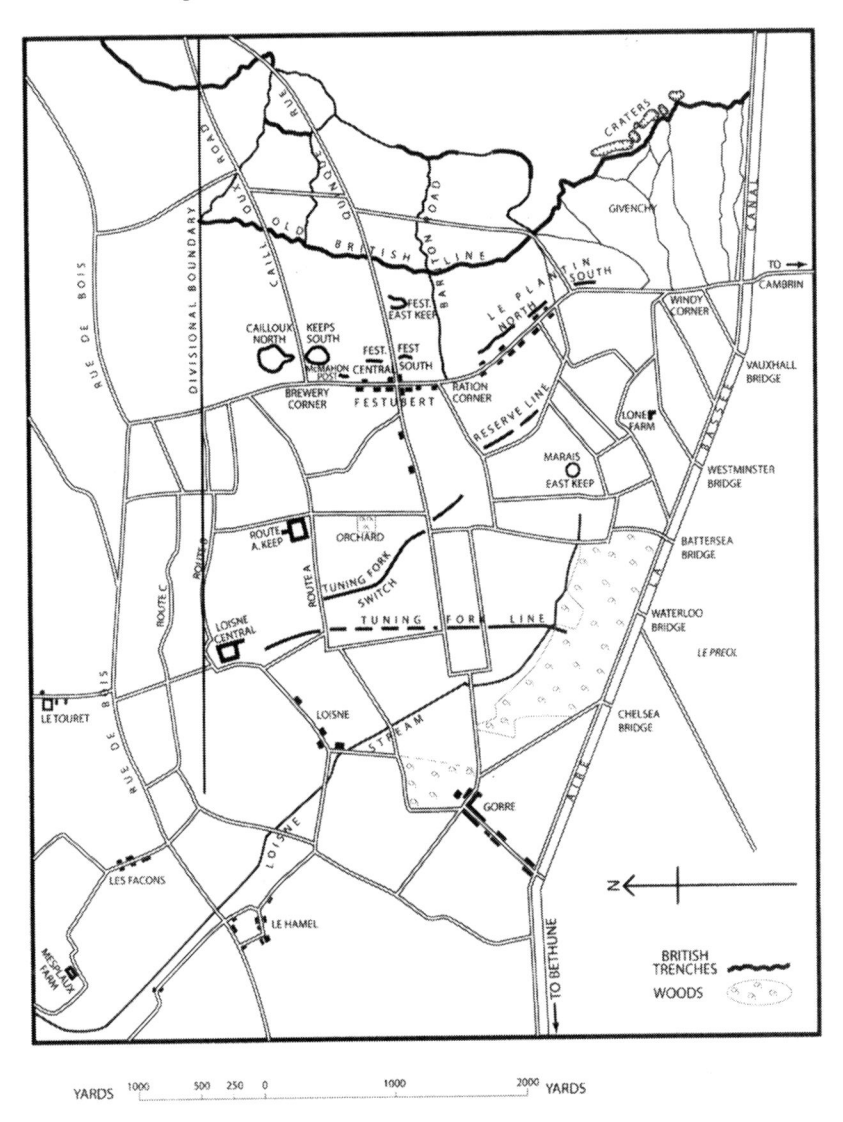

Map 8.5 Festubert–Givenchy Sector, 8 April 1918.

230   Attitudes and experience

There was by no means a consensus around the findings of the Report. Major General Jeudwine certainly felt that the 55th Division had been dealt with unjustly, and had annotated his copy with corrections, qualifications and comments. He described the accusations of poor defensive strategy as a 'personal advertisement' for Lieutenant General Ivor Maxse, a leading tactician and member of the Board who used the Enquiry to evangelize about the merits of systematic training.[147] Yet they cannot be dismissed out of hand. The counter-attack reserves were inadequate and deployed too late because of confusion over divisional boundaries to the rear, and the men, though not lacking in initiative, certainly lacked the direction that a clear, defensive plan would have given them. The British had spent most of the war on the offensive and had been trained in the art of attack. As the Enquiry highlighted, 'It is, in fact, easier to teach infantry to follow a barrage than to teach it to defend an area of ground which the enemy suddenly penetrates.'[148] An exaggeration, certainly, but platoon and section tactics did require some modification in order to fight a defensive action.

The Division laboured under a cloud of suspicion after the events of 30 November, especially as it was not completely exonerated by the Court of Enquiry.[149] It embarked on four months of retraining and developing divisional defensive tactics. In this period, Jeudwine spent a month preparing a training pamphlet on 'blob defence' at GHQ. The pamphlet, a simplified form of the German defence in depth scheme, was never published army-wide because GHQ attempted to implement the German system undiluted, but the 55th Division was trained and organized according to the principles Jeudwine and the committee laid out.[150] They were vindicated in April 1918 when the 55th Division stood its ground against another German onslaught while others fled. The defence of

---

[147] Causes of the German successes, Court of Enquiry on the action fought south of Cambrai on November 30th 1917, 29 January 1918, Records of the 55th (West Lancashire) Division, 1914–19, LRO, 356 FIF 50/6/154.

[148] Causes of the German successes, Court of Enquiry on the action fought south of Cambrai on November 30th 1917, 29 January 1918, Records of the 55th (West Lancashire) Division, 1914–19, LRO, 356 FIF 50/6/142.

[149] Causes of the German successes, Court of Enquiry on the action fought south of Cambrai on November 30th 1917, 29 January 1918, Records of the 55th (West Lancashire) Division, 1914–19, LRO, 356 FIF 50/6.

[150] 'Blob defence' described fighting in informal section groups or blobs, rather than in lines. The committee on which Jeudwine served advocated an outpost line, followed by a short zone of resistance containing machine gun nests and strong points, before a main line of resistance, instead of the three-zone system operated by the Germans. The final line of resistance was to be strongly held and if lost, was to be immediately recovered by counter-attacks. See Griffith, *Battle tactics of the Western Front*, 96; M. Samuels, *Command or control? Command, training and tactics in the British and German armies, 1888–1918* (London, 1995), 202–7.

Givenchy village helped to undo some of the damage wrought by the Cambrai débâcle and went some way to restoring the reputation of the Division in the eyes of the army.

Givenchy was a key sector of tactical and strategic importance to the British. Its elevation ensured that whoever held the village had excellent observation over the British rear, and Givenchy itself was a pivotal point in the defence of the coal mines between Cambrin and Loos.[151] Between December 1917 and February 1918 the Division reinforced and trained, before taking over the line between Givenchy and Festubert. There was much to do, as many experienced men had been lost in the previous November, but enough veterans remained to educate the raw recruits. In January 1918 sixty-four men who had fought with the Liverpool Scottish since 1914 were still serving with the Battalion, and these men still led by example. Five original Liverpool Scots were awarded medals for gallantry in the subsequent fighting around Givenchy.[152]

A complex defensive scheme was established within the 55th Division which ensured that, in the event of an attack, reserve units would be able to move into pre-arranged positions and launch local counter-attacks. The Givenchy sector had seen little fighting since the summer of 1915 and, in contrast to Epéhy, well-constructed defences existed. Behind the advanced posts there was the support trench, the Old British Front Line. To the rear of this was the Village Line, the main line of resistance. It was composed of a string of strong points from La Plantin South to Cailloux North Keep.[153] All posts in the line of resistance were garrisoned by complete platoons and had a field of fire that extended in every direction. In the event of enemy penetration, the garrisons were instructed to hold their posts at all costs, whilst the remaining platoons were to counter-attack immediately.[154] Jeudwine did not believe in 'elastic' defence in depth, as to lose the high ground in this important sector could have disastrous consequences.[155] He instructed his units that the Village Line was not to be yielded to the enemy. Finally, behind the Village Line were reserve lines, including Tuning Fork Switch and Tuning Fork Line, all of which were in good repair, and even protected by thick wire.[156]

---

[151] Lecture on operations at Givenchy–Festubert, 9 April 1918, RMC Sandhurst, 1928, Records of the 55th (West Lancashire) Division, 356 FIF 54/5, 4–5.
[152] W. G. Bromley, Memoir, LSM, Acc. No. 544, 133; Giblin, *Bravest of hearts*, 84–90.
[153] McGilchrist, *The Liverpool Scottish*, 162.
[154] Lecture on operations at Givenchy–Festubert, 9 April 1918, RMC Sandhurst, 1928, Records of the 55th (West Lancashire) Division, LRO, 356 FIF 54/5, 10.
[155] J. M. Bourne, *Who's who in World War One* (London, 2001), 145–6.
[156] McGilchrist, *The Liverpool Scottish*, 162.

The anticipated enemy attack, which began the Battle of the Lys, was launched on 9 April 1918 at 4.15 in the morning. The Scottish, with 166th Brigade, were in the rear, and the Rifles, with 165th Brigade, were in the right sector of the front. At the onset of the attack the Portuguese on the left flank fled, allowing the enemy to take 165th Brigade in the rear. According to the Divisional historian, it was 'in many ways a replica of the battle for Epéhy', but the failure of Epéhy was not to be replicated at Givenchy.[157]

The Brigade retreated to its line of resistance, whilst a defensive flank of some 2000 yards, at right angles to the main line of resistance, was formed by a number of units from 166th Brigade.[158] On the extreme right of 165th Brigade, the enemy succeeded in taking Le Plantin South, but the post was quickly recovered by counter-attack. On the left the situation was more serious. By 11 am Route A Keep, an important defensive post, had been lost to the enemy, and around midday the enemy were seen moving in front of Loisne Central, threatening the Brigade Headquarters situated just behind in Loisne Château.[159] The training sustained by 165th Brigade in the months leading up to this battle helped to ensure that the men did not collapse under the pressure, and, bolstered by the divisional reserve in the shape of the Liverpool Scottish, began three days of continuous counter-attacks to halt the enemy in their tracks.

Strong points changed hands numerous times before the end of the battle, and the fighting over Route A Keep is illustrative of these counter-attacks. At midnight on 12 April two companies, one from the Liverpool Scottish and one from the 13th Liverpools, advanced under an artillery and trench mortar barrage to recapture the Keep. The men of the Liverpool Scottish were detailed to capture the ruins immediately to the south of the Keep. The barrage advanced to within 50 yards of the objective, and when it lifted the men rushed in and took the enemy by surprise, acquiring nine prisoners and one machine gun. They then turned their energies to assisting the 13th Liverpools with the recapturing of Route A Keep itself. By 3.30 the strong point was again in the hands of the British.[160] It was held against enemy counter-attack until the Battalion was relieved on 16 April 1918. This was not the only time the Liverpool Scottish was ordered to recapture Route A Keep. Much to the Battalion's annoyance, the division who relieved them managed to lose the Keep in the days that followed, and the same company of the Liverpool Scottish was required to make another assault on the strong point on 24 April 1918.[161]

---

[157] Coop, *Story of the 55th Division*, 98. [158] *Ibid.*, 98. [159] *Ibid.*, 94–5.
[160] McGilchrist, *The Liverpool Scottish*, 177–8. [161] *Ibid.*

The citations for gallantry awards help to illuminate the experience of the attackers. Take, for example, the experience of Sergeant Samuel McKay. McKay was a knowledgeable veteran who had been a member of the Liverpool Scottish since 1914 and displayed courage and tenacity in support of the attack. On 23 April he was in charge of a party carrying Stokes Mortar ammunition to the vicinity of the Keep. A heavy enemy barrage wounded a number of the party, including the sergeant himself. McKay refused to be diverted by this setback and, after securing stretcher bearers for the injured, reorganized his party to ensure that all the ammunition was delivered to the post intact. His actions were deemed worthy of a Military Medal and the French Croix de Guerre.

The experience of Sergeant Duncan McRae is also instructive. McRae received one of a number of medals awarded to sergeants and corporals for assuming command in the absence of their officers. After his platoon commander was injured, McRae led his men to enter an enemy defensive post, attacking a German machine gun team holding up the frontal attacking party. This enabled the Liverpool Scots to advance in the sector without further casualties. He then garrisoned the post with his platoon and held it against counter-attacks for the next sixteen hours. Sergeant McRae was awarded the Distinguished Conduct Medal for his actions.[162]

Whilst there were many exceptional soldiers within the Liverpool Scottish, not everyone in the assaulting company had the same experience or courage. Some had to be guided to fulfil their appointed roles. For example, during the attack, Second Lieutenant Thomas Joseph Price volunteered to 'encourage' the company Lewis gunners forward from the ruins of a house where they were sheltering from the heavy counter-barrage laid down by the enemy. He succeeded in propelling them to suitable positions from which they successfully repelled German counter-attacks. It is unlikely that the gunners would have moved forward without the help of Lieutenant Price, but his actions were to cost him dear. Price was mortally wounded in front of Route A Keep and died of his injuries on the following day.[163]

The Rifles and the Scottish were undoubtedly engaged in a bitter fight to defend their front. Casualties were high, the Rifles losing 197 men during the month and the Scottish 273.[164] Hand to hand fighting was a prominent feature of the battle. There are numerous accounts of soldiers bayoneting the enemy to capture trenches and machine gun posts. The Territorials also suffered badly from the enemy's high explosive and gas

---

[162] Giblin, *Bravest of hearts*, 89.   [163] *Ibid.*, 88–9.
[164] *Ibid.*, 84–91; Battalion war diaries of the 1/10th King's Liverpool Regiment and 1/6th Battalion King's (Liverpool) Regiment, April 1918, KRC, MLL, 58.83.501/509.

barrage. Many men were buried alive, and although the efficiency of gas masks had improved since 1915, they were very unpleasant to wear and some soldiers still suffered from the effects of gas shells.[165]

Yet the enemy's use of gas no longer enraged the Liverpool Territorials, perhaps because they had experience of employing it themselves, and during the battles many Liverpool Scots displayed great humanity towards enemy prisoners of war. For example, Sergeant Albert Baybut, another soldier who had fought with the Liverpool Scottish since 1914, risked his life by rescuing a wounded German soldier under heavy sniper fire.[166] The compassion of the Liverpool Scottish was born of respect for the German soldier. That they admired his fighting abilities and his devotion to duty was highlighted by a story in the Battalion history. A Liverpool Scottish patrol, finding a wounded German warrant officer on the night of 11 April, acquiesced to his wishes to be 'left where he was on the chance that his own side might find him. He was given food and allowed to remain.'[167] When they returned the next night he was very weak and the patrol carefully carried him to their Battalion Headquarters to be sent for treatment. While the enemy sergeant was waiting to be evacuated, another German prisoner was brought in. This prisoner had given himself up during a lull in the fighting and, as McGilchrist recounts, 'It did one good to see the undisguised contempt of the [German] warrant officer, exhausted and suffering though he was, for the little skrimshanker.'[168] It was a contempt shared by British and German alike.

Beyond the medal citations and the Battalion history there are few eyewitness narratives of these actions. Most soldiers writing diaries and letters at this point were senior NCOs who remained at the transport lines throughout the battle. The accounts that did survive contained two common themes. First, the behaviour of the Portuguese troops was universally condemned. The Portuguese were deemed selfish and unreliable allies because their actions on 9 April had enabled the enemy to attack the 55th Division from the rear. Second, pity for civilian refugees, a theme familiar in the early years of the war, again appeared.[169] The plight of the refugees, as in 1915, strengthened still further the determination of the Territorials to ensure that such scenes would never be repeated in Britain.[170]

---

[165] Giblin, *Bravest of hearts*, 85–9. [166] *Ibid.*, 89.
[167] McGilchrist, *The Liverpool Scottish*, 178. [168] *Ibid.*, 179.
[169] In the Givenchy area many French civilians continued to live close to the lines. They were temporarily driven out of their homes in April 1918 by severe German shelling during their failed attack. W. G. Bromley, Memoir, LSM, Acc. No. 544, 143–5; R. A. S. Macfie to Sheila Macfie, 11 April 1918, Macfie Papers, IWM, Con. Shelf.
[170] W. G. Bromley, Memoir, LSM, Acc. No. 544, 145.

The experience of active service   235

The losses in the action, though high, were significantly lower than at Epéhy,[171] and, in being one of the few divisions during the German offensive to hold their portion of the front, capturing nearly 1000 prisoners and seventy machine guns, the men were aware of the significance of their achievements.[172] The defence of Givenchy, described by *The Times* as 'one of the brilliant incidents of this war',[173] merited a special supplementary dispatch from Haig himself,[174] and attracted much media attention. In April 1918 the 55th Division became a household name throughout Britain.[175] In this respect, the defence of Givenchy performed a similar function to the 1915 Battle of Hooge, raising the prestige of the Division within the army and at home. It was particularly important in the wake of the negative rumours that had circulated after the November fiasco.

May 1918 saw low casualty rates in the Battalions and the Liverpool Scottish numbers were boosted by the amalgamation with their second line. For old friends who were reunited, this had positive effects on morale, although some readjustment was necessary for the NCOs, as some posts were duplicated and the position was decided by seniority.[176]

Although the enemy abandoned his attack in April, the threat of a renewed assault persisted, ensuring that there was no relaxation for the Battalions. Sergeant Macfie complained as late as June 1918 that 'at night they [the Liverpool Scottish] have to sleep in their clothes and be ready to move off at half an hours notice'.[177]

At the end of June the threat of attack had receded, and although trench life was punctuated by patrols into No Man's Land, the trenches were quiet as a result of an influenza epidemic on both sides of the line. Such was the severity of the epidemic that the Liverpool Scottish was forced to send 200 of its soldiers to hospital in the space of two days.[178]

---

[171] Battalion War Diaries of the 1/10th King's (Liverpool) Regiment and 1/6th King's (Liverpool) Regiment, April 1918, KRC, MLL, 58.83.501/509.
[172] W. G. Bromley, Memoir, LSM, Acc. No. 544, 142; Coop, *Story of the 55th Division*, 106.
[173] *The Times*, 11 April 1918.
[174] See The 55th Division at Givenchy, 9–16 April 1918, Pegge Papers, MLHL, M198/6/6, 1–2.
[175] Accounts of the defence of Givenchy and the exploits of the 55th Division were printed in the *Daily Mirror*, 13 April 1918; *Daily Mail*, 15 April 1918; *Daily Telegraph*, 16 April 1918; *Liverpool Daily Post*, 12–22 April 1918; *Daily Chronicle*, 19 April 1918; *Manchester Guardian* 16 and 20 April 1918. A booklet containing a selection of newspaper cuttings and copies of congratulatory telegrams from army commanders and civic leaders in Liverpool was produced in June 1918 and distributed throughout the Division, to maintain their determination to fight. See The 55th Division at Givenchy, 9–16 April 1918, Pegge Papers, MLHL, M198/6/6.
[176] R. A. S. Macfie to Charlie Macfie, 19 April 1918, Macfie Papers, IWM, Con. Shelf.
[177] R. A. S. Macfie to Sheila Macfie, 7 June 1918, Macfie Papers, IWM, Con. Shelf.
[178] R. A. S. Macfie to Jenny Paton, 26 June 1918, Macfie Papers, IWM, Con. Shelf.

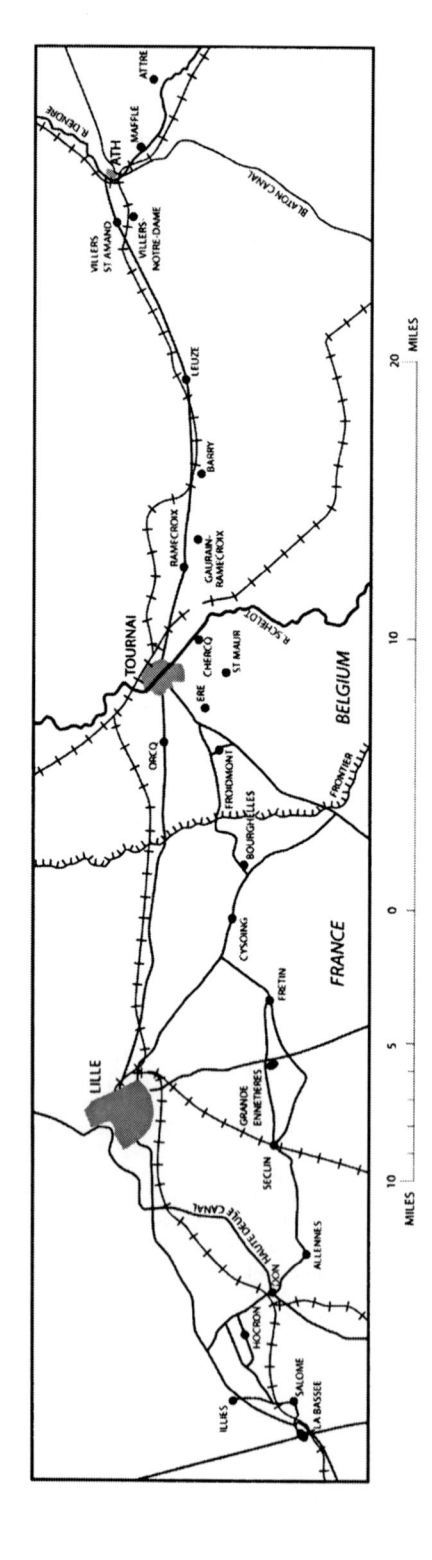

Map 8.6 The final advance, October–November 1918.

The experience of active service 237

Figure 8.3 Guard of the Liverpool Scottish, 7 September 1918.

By the beginning of July, resumption of open warfare was eagerly expected and Sergeant Macfie optimistically wrote home for his field glasses, followed by a request for new boots in August, 'in case we have to tramp to Berlin'.[179] Reports were received that the enemy was withdrawing in other parts of the line and on 2 September there were 'definite indications of a withdrawal' on the Liverpool Scottish front. By 3 September, the Liverpool Rifles were able to occupy the German positions, held by the enemy on 9 April 1918, without any resistance.[180]

Throughout September the 55th Division steadily moved in the direction of La Bassée, encountering some resistance, but gaining many prisoners. In the Liverpool Scottish, most of their casualties for the month were a result of booby-traps in enemy dugouts.[181] By the end of September the line had been advanced 4000 yards in the Left Brigade Sector and 2500 yards on the Right.[182] The mood of the men remained

[179] R. A. S. Macfie to Charlie Macfie, 3 July 1918, 29 August 1918, Macfie Papers, IWM, Con. Shelf.
[180] McGilchrist, *The Liverpool Scottish*, 226–7.
[181] R. A. S. Macfie to Sheila Macfie, 13 September 1918, Macfie Papers, IWM, Con. Shelf.
[182] Coop, *Story of the 55th Division*, 135–6.

238   Attitudes and experience

Figure 8.4 Soldier of the Liverpool Rifles, September 1918.

buoyant as they moved forward, although at this stage few expected the war to finish before Christmas.[183] Writing to his sister on the subject of a projected General Election, Sergeant Macfie expressed the view of his men: 'There will never be a chance for so simple a choice – fight it out or cave in – with no side issues that anybody will care a rap for. If you have any doubt about the verdict, you must be surrounded by a set of voters very different from those that I see.'[184]

In October the 55th Division moved into a truly mobile phase for the first time, advancing 5 miles on 3 and 4 October and halting at the Haute Deule Canal in front of Don. The Division was held here for a week, with the Liverpool Scottish taking heavy casualties in an attempt to secure the embankment, bristling with enemy machine guns. The advance resumed on 15 October, when elements of the 165th Brigade succeeded in crossing the canal and clearing the enemy out of his positions on the opposite bank.

---

[183] Macfie wrote to his sister that he did not expect leave before March 1919, and he suspected that it could be suspended if an important offensive was in progress. R. A. S. Macfie to Jenny Paton, 27 September 1918, Macfie Papers, IWM, Con. Shelf.
[184] R. A. S. Macfie to Sheila Macfie, 29 September 1918, Macfie Papers, IWM, Con. Shelf.

The experience of active service 239

The Battalions marched through a succession of villages: Seclin, Fretin, Çysoing, Bourghelles and Esplechin on the Franco-Belgian border. The Scottish and the Rifles were now treated as liberators. According to Macfie, 'This is quite the best part of the war so far. One village (French) where we stayed the night decorated the whole place and erected triumphal arches over the streets. Nearly every house produces French flags which they have concealed for years.'[185]

If the grateful response of those liberated motivated the soldiers in the final days of the war, the scorched earth policy and desperate stalling tactics of the retreating Germans incited contempt for their enemy. In some areas the French explained how their oppressors had stripped their villages of possessions, including horses and cattle, and the Liverpool Scottish found at least one village prepared for burning.[186] Sergeant Macfie also described an enemy gas attack on one village as 'particularly mean', in view of the fact that civilians lacked gas masks.[187] Gas, it seems, had acquired a semi-legitimate status as a weapon when used against combatants, but its use against civilians still caused outrage.

The 55th Division met no serious resistance until they reached the River Scheldt on 21 October, where again the Division came to a halt and prepared to attack the enemy defences. Fortunately, by 8 November, the enemy began to withdraw from his defences, and by 10 November the 55th Division reached the outskirts of Ath and took up positions to attack the town on the following day. The Division had advanced over 50 miles in the eighty days since leaving Givenchy.[188]

At 9.00 on the morning of 11 November, Lieutenant Colonel Munro, commanding the Liverpool Scottish, attended a conference of commanders to discuss the scheme of operations for the attack on Ath. It was during this conference that a message was received from Divisional Headquarters stating that hostilities were to cease at 11 am. There is no record of the Liverpool Rifles' reaction to news of the Armistice, but A. M. McGilchrist of the Liverpool Scottish describes the response of his Battalion: 'Troops and civilians at once went mad. All the church bells in the district were set ringing, the Pipe Band marched and countermarched up and down the village street through crowds of cheering Jocks and excited natives and the riotous scene would have made Donnybrook Fair seem like a prayer meeting.'[189]

[185] R. A. S. Macfie to Charlie Macfie, 24 October 1918, Macfie Papers, IWM, Con. Shelf.
[186] R. A. S. Macfie to Sheila Macfie, 26 October 1918, Macfie Papers, IWM, Con. Shelf.
[187] R. A. S. Macfie to Sheila Macfie, 26 October 1918, Macfie Papers, IWM, Con. Shelf. The village was probably Froidmont which was shelled with Yellow Cross Gas. See Coop, *Story of the 55th Division*, 149.
[188] Coop, *Story of the 55th Division*, 159. [189] McGilchrist, *The Liverpool Scottish*, 243.

After the Armistice the Territorials felt that they had completed their task. They had safeguarded their homes and families and wished to return to them as quickly as possible. There was now no incentive to endure the discomforts of army life, as Sergeant Macfie explained: 'I am very tired now and shall be glad to be demobilized. There's no fun in quartermastering when there are no shells and every day is exactly like every other day.'[190] Discontent with the slow demobilization began to permeate the battalions.

In an effort to occupy and distract the men, education and retraining programmes were instituted within the Battalions, and generous recreation periods were permitted whilst the units slowly demobilized. The Rifles returned home in May 1919, but the men of the Scottish were less fortunate, having been chosen to form part of the base staff to demobilize other cadres of the BEF. Individuals departed for England throughout the year, but the Battalion was not fully demobilized until November 1919.[191]

Conclusion

The mood of individuals and their units fluctuated according to their experiences. Physical factors – the weather, seasons, terrain, illness, the development of weaponry and tactics, and the provision of food and entertainment – all affected the general temper of both units, as did the psychological influences of bereavement, horror, boredom and comradeship. Success bred optimism, whilst demoralizing experiences, such as the action at Guillemont in 1916, invoked a lingering depression. However, as Audoin-Rouzeau has argued in relation to the French army, the connection between low morale and support for the war was tenuous. Even soldiers with low morale could continue to display a determination to resist the enemy and carry on the fight.[192] For the Liverpool Territorials, this will to resist was rooted in a set of attitudes that remained remarkably consistent throughout the war. Despite the paucity of conscript diaries and letters for 1918, it is possible to identify those beliefs that survived the experience of trench warfare.

Attitudes towards the enemy altered according to military expediency and to his behaviour, but the desire to end the war out of a sense of community solidarity was not countenanced. Whilst the men rarely

---

[190] R. A. S. Macfie to Sheila Macfie, 26 October 1918, Macfie Papers, IWM, Con. Shelf.
[191] 1/10th Battalion King's (Liverpool) Regiment War Diary, January 1919, Liverpool, KRC, MLL, 58.83.509.
[192] Audoin-Rouzeau, *Men at war 1914–1918*, 56.

expressed genuine empathy with their opponents, hatred, when it reared its head, was transitory and most commonly directed at the enemy unit which had transgressed their code of fair play. It could not be induced by army lectures, or bayoneting demonstrations.[193]

On the other hand, killing, albeit not primarily motivated by hatred, was celebrated by other ranks and their leaders alike.[194] Individual bloodthirsty deeds were bragged about and rewarded, and collective recognition was sought from the home front and the army for the military achievements of the Battalion and the Division throughout the war.

Similarly, the idea of war as an adventure did not die with the experience of industrialized warfare. Whilst there was a general acceptance that long service in the trenches induced war-weariness, and the opportunities for face to face combat were reduced when compared with previous wars, the desire to engage and outwit the enemy remained a motivating factor for a minority of veterans, as well as newly arrived conscripts, anxious to prove themselves in the field.[195]

The belief in the redemptive power of war, particularly the regeneration of society, was most frequently expressed at the beginning of the conflict, but could still be discerned at its close in a religious or personal guise. A number of soldiers, believing that their survival had a purpose, or some kind of duty attached, resolved to live a moral, uncomplaining life, or take an active role in building the peace after the war.[196]

The desire to protect their home and family was, however, the most important and enduring idea. It was the motivating force for many Territorials in joining up prior to and on the outbreak of war. The subsequent scenes of destruction and death they encountered on the Western Front strengthened their determination to prevent such scenes being replicated in their homeland, and militated against the effects of war-weariness. Once the Armistice had been signed, the reason for fighting had been removed. The Territorial had fulfilled his own objective and was no longer prepared to suffer the difficulties of army life, or the separation from home. Most soldiers gladly accepted their discharge with relief.

---

[193] See W. H. Campbell, Diary, 27 August 1916, LSM, Acc. No. 484.
[194] For an analysis of the pleasures of war see Bourke, *An intimate history of killing*, 13–43.
[195] See Ferguson, *The pity of war*, 360–2, for a discussion on the analogies drawn between warfare, hunting and sport.
[196] See W. H. Campbell, Diary, 29 September 1916, LSM, Acc. No. 484, and V. L. Morris, Diary, no date, LSM, Miscellaneous File M, Acc. No. 844/2, 1.

9   The aftermath of war

'In a few days time I shall be demobilized', wrote Frank MacDonald of the Liverpool Scottish; 'I wonder how I shall take to civilian life again.'[1] The Territorial soldiers had fought for and longed for their homes and families throughout the miserable years of war, but there were few who viewed their demobilization without some trepidation. And these were the lucky ones. For other, less fortunate Territorials, returned prematurely to their families with the physical and mental scars of war, the task of picking up the threads of their pre-war lives proved a still more daunting prospect.

And yet, assimilating back into civilian life proved easier than many had imagined. The post-war story of how some of the Liverpool Territorials coped with civilian life and the legacy of the Great War serves to reinforce the main themes that have emerged throughout this book. The majority of soldiers had remained stubbornly civilian in outlook for the duration of their service. Civilian culture had been exported to France and used by the soldiers to shape their environment and bolster morale. They had maintained their links with family and community tenaciously, and their hopes and aspirations had always been firmly located in the civilian sphere. Survivors undoubtedly had to make some adjustments on their return, but their values, prejudices and modes of thinking had not been radically altered by the experience of the army, facilitating a relatively smooth reintegration into civilian society.[2]

For Liverpool as a whole, the early 1920s were difficult economically. The Lord Mayor deemed the unemployment situation so acute in November 1920 that he postponed an appeal for a city war memorial, and Lord Derby received many requests for help from destitute ex-servicemen during the

---

[1] F. MacDonald, Diary, 31 August 1919, LSM, Miscellaneous File M, Acc. No. 514.
[2] The proliferation of diaries and memoirs related to wartime testified to the significance which men attached to their experience. Fewer men, however, felt the need to chart the aftermath of war and most accounts terminated on their discharge from the forces. The few voices that do emerge from the surviving documents are again those of the middle classes.

early years of peace.³ The men still retained an ill-defined sense of fair-play. Derby had been very influential in the army recruitment campaigns of 1914–15, and those who had answered his appeal expected recompense in peace. For the middle-class men whose family businesses had survived or whose firms had reserved their pre-war jobs, finding employment was more straightforward. The middle-class business and social networks were still in operation, which meant that if individual firms had not survived the war, the ex-soldiers were generally able to find suitable employment.

W. E. Cole, for example, who had served with the Scottish since 1908, returned to his post in the Staff Accounts Department at the Cunard Shipping Line. Cunard was particularly careful in re-employing ex-servicemen, and G. F. Hughes, who lost an eye during the war, was also reabsorbed into the company on discharge.⁴ RQMS Macfie returned to his directorship at Macfie and Sons.⁵ Major Arthur Gemmell reverted to his pre-war career as an obstetrician and gynaecologist,⁶ and whilst Private Ellison's apprenticeship to an African merchant was no longer available, he quickly found work in his uncle's firm of wholesale paper merchants.⁷ Lance Corporal Warry was discharged from hospital in 1919 minus his right leg, which had been amputated at the thigh. This did not prevent him from entering his father's firm in the raw and waste rubber trade for a year, until the business had to be closed as a result of the trade leaving Liverpool. He then had the opportunity to take a twelve-month course in book-keeping, after which he worked in the trade for three years and then became a travelling salesman, using a motor cycle and sidecar, an occupation he pursued until his retirement in 1983.⁸

Most men returned to careers that were commensurate with their prewar status. Wherever physically possible, they also rejoined their old clubs and societies, which as a result of the links maintained in wartime they had never really left. The Territorials may have temporarily abandoned their civilian employment in favour of fighting, but they had not lost the hopes,

---

[3] D. Boorman, *British First World War memorials* (York, 1988), 153; Letters from ex-servicemen to Lord Derby, February and March 1922, cases 1–83, Derby Papers, LRO, DER (17) 21/3. P. J. Waller notes that in August 1922 Liverpool has 30,800 unemployed, the majority being from the shipping and distribution industries. Waller, *Democracy and sectarianism*, 290.

[4] Biographies of Cunard employees compiled by the Liverpool Scottish Regimental Museum, LSM, Miscellaneous File C.

[5] R. A. S. Macfie, Summary of career, written on the sad occasion of the Lunds school controversy in justifying an unwonted excursion into local politics, undated (post-war), Macfie Papers, IWM, Con. Shelf.

[6] Arthur Gemmell was appointed to the Council of the Royal College of Obstetricians and received a knighthood in 1955. He was also Commanding Officer of the Liverpool Scottish, 1923–27. See index card, A. A. Gemmell, Officers' Index, LSM.

[7] N. F. Ellison, Diary and Memoir, Ellison Papers, IWM, DS/MISC/49, 106.

[8] G. Warry, Post-war reminiscence at end of diary, Warry Papers, IWM, 96/12/1, 14.

interests and ambitions of their civilian life. Many ex-soldiers went on to achieve prominence in public life, becoming lord mayors, deputy lieutenants and councillors.[9] Others colonized the emerging entertainment industry. Lieutenant Basil Rathbone made over ninety films in his long and varied Hollywood career, whilst his arch-rival within the Liverpool Scottish, Lieutenant James Dale, played Dr Jim Dale in the long-running radio programme 'Mrs Dale's Diary'.[10] Private Norman Ellison, who had spent his war filling his letters and diaries with descriptions of the flora and fauna of Flanders, ended his career fronting the natural history radio programme 'Nomad', and writing sixteen books on the subject.[11]

Not all ex-soldiers had successful, seamless post-war careers. In 1931 ex-Sergeant John McArdle was forced to ask the Liverpool Scottish Regimental Association for a loan to purchase a set of false teeth, in order to make himself presentable at job interviews,[12] and a minority of members applied to the Association for help in finding work during that year.[13] Much of this middle-class unemployment, however, was caused by the economic depression, which began to affect Liverpool in 1930, and was not always a direct consequence of wartime dislocation.

On the other hand, the war had seen dire economic consequences for those middle-class families who had lost their breadwinner, particularly if he had died post-war from the effects of war service.[14] The widow and

---

[9] Colonel J. B. McKaig became Deputy Lieutenant of Lancashire in 1924 and Chairman of the West Lancashire Territorial Association during the Second World War, and received a knighthood. F. M. Tweedle was appointed Lord Mayor of Birkenhead in 1931. Major W. W. Higgin held the posts of High Sheriff of Cheshire and Deputy Lieutenant of Cheshire. Lieutenant Pegge MC was a Conservative councillor in Manchester from 1937 to 1966 and an alderman from 1960. Correspondence relating to membership, Liverpool Rifles' Association Papers, MRO, 356 RIF 3/1, 3/3; Undated newspaper cuttings in J. G. C. Moffat's Scrapbook, LSM, Miscellaneous File M, Acc. No. 199; Preface to papers of W. J. Pegge, MLHL, Pegge Papers, M198.

[10] Basil Rathbone is primarily remembered for his characterization of Sherlock Holmes in the 1940s. Giblin, *Bravest of hearts*, 286 and 331.

[11] Ellison presented over 300 'Nomad' programmes between 1945 and 1963 and contributed articles on natural history to the *Liverpool Echo* and *Cheshire Life* for twenty-five years. Newspaper cuttings re reunion dinners, Liverpool Rifles' Association Papers, MRO, 356 RIF 3/8.

[12] Liverpool Scottish Regimental Association minute book, 8 October 1931, LSM.

[13] Liverpool Scottish Regimental Association minute book, 17 September 1931, 22 October 1931, 3 December 1931, LSM.

[14] A number of ex-soldiers were believed to have died prematurely from injuries or illnesses attributed to the war. D. E. Sproat was medically discharged in 1915 and died of his wounds in 1920; J. D. Boulton died 12 July 1921, aged 31; A. B. Selkirk MM died in 1932 from shrapnel in his lungs; Charles Jackson was severely wounded in 1917 and died aged 32 in May 1931. See undated newspaper cuttings in J. G. C. Moffat's Scrapbook, LSM, Miscellaneous File M, Acc. No. 199. Often, dependants did not receive state help if the Ministry of Pensions disputed the fact that the death was related to the war.

children of Lance Corporal John McKie Graham were struggling to survive in 1931, being virtually penniless and faced with eviction, whilst Mrs Parry was forced to apply to many different charitable organizations to afford the school fees and books for her daughter's education.[15] For these families, the war had catastrophic and permanent financial and social effects, but it was the absence of the father, husband, son or brother that was hardest to bear.

Mourning began the moment families were notified of a death, but the reality of the situation was often suspended until the end of the war. On 5 February 1916 Private John Evans wrote to his church magazine from France, 'I know from home that you are acquainted with the death of my brother Sam. I cannot yet, owing to the circumstances, fully realize my loss, but I do know I have lost a brother that cannot be replaced and one that I shall miss exceedingly when I come home.'[16] As families were reunited in the wake of the Armistice, absences became more apparent and loss accentuated. A similar experience occurred on a wider scale within local institutions and the nation as a whole. Commemoration of the dead became a psychological necessity for individuals and communities coming to terms with the experience of four years of war.[17]

By 1918, the war had made Britain a more centralized state.[18] However, the mindset of returning soldiers and their communities was still focused at the local level. They had fought to protect their families and locality, and it was here, more than anywhere else, they wanted their sacrifices to be recorded and remembered. The following discussion investigates the character and function of commemoration in Liverpool at personal, local community and civic levels.

Personal commemoration

The process of memorialization had become an integral part of coping with bereavement, and the most affluent middle-class families possessed the means and opportunity to create individual memorials to those they had lost. Throughout the war such families had been able to command personal memorial services for their dead[19] and had brass plaques and

---

[15] Liverpool Scottish Regimental Association minute book, 3 December 1931, 7 January 1932, LSM.
[16] *Young Crescent*, March 1916.   [17] Winter, *Sites of memory, sites of mourning*, 29–116.
[18] Winter, 'Popular culture in wartime Britain', 330.
[19] A. Twentyman, St Nicholas Church, Liverpool, 10 December 1914; F. H. Turner, St Andrew's Church, Rodney Street, 19 January 1915; W. S. Turner and C. D. H. Dunlop,

246   Attitudes and experience

stained glass windows placed in their local churches.[20] The Dickinson family erected memorial cottages on their estate to commemorate the sons they had lost,[21] and Robert Buchanan, a founding member of the Liverpool Scottish, whose son had been killed in 1915, gave several hundred acres of his Bosbury estate for the agricultural training of disabled officers.[22]

Individual commemoration did not have to be on a grand scale. The Turner family collated the obituaries of their sons to form In Memoriam booklets, which were distributed among friends and relatives,[23] and the parents of Tommy Fardo sent a mounted photograph of their son in response to all letters of condolence.[24] What was significant about all these forms of individual memorialization was the need to mark the individual sacrifice. Each family sought to ensure that their son's contribution, and their loss, did not become obscured by the experience of mass bereavement within the local community.[25]

Local commemoration

The firms, schools, universities, churches, sports clubs and societies through which the middle classes had defined their identities and conducted their pre-war lives also sought to mark the individual sacrifice of their missing members. From the start of the war, many of these organizations formed rolls of service, listing those members who had relinquished comfortable

---

Sefton Park Church, 6 July 1915. These two officers had been killed at Hooge, 16 June 1915, alongside many of their comrades in the Liverpool Scottish. A memorial service for all those who had died in the battle was held, but it is significant that individual commemoration remained important and possible for middle-class families. See J. G. C. Moffat's Scrapbook, LSM, Miscellaneous File M, Acc. No. 199, and In Memoriam booklets of F. H. Turner and W. S. Turner, MAL, DX 184/3–4.

[20] Brass plaques: St Nicholas Church, Liverpool, Lieutenant G. B. Burton, 6th Rifles; St Matthew and St James Church, Mossley Hill, Captain E. C. G. Buckley, 6th Rifles and Second Lieutenant V. B. Leitch, 10th Scottish; St James Church, New Brighton, Second Lieutenant J. C. Barber and Lieutenant C. B. Astley, 10th Scottish. Marble memorial in Sefton Park Unitarian Church, G. F. Rimmer, 10th Scottish. Stained-glass window in St Nicholas Church, Sergeant H. H. Massey, 10th Scottish. See database 'Merseyside war memorials' compiled by G. Donnison and D. Evans, LSM. I am grateful to David Evans for providing a print-out of this information.

[21] J. G. C. Moffat's Scrapbook, LSM, Miscellaneous File M, Acc. No. 199.

[22] See Liverpool Scottish Officers' Index, A. Buchanan, LSM.

[23] In Memoriam booklets of F. H. Turner and W. S. Turner, MAL, DX 184/3–4.

[24] Mr and Mrs Fardo to R. A. S. Macfie, 1918, Macfie Papers, IWM, Con. Shelf.

[25] Bob Bushaway has made a similar point with regard to the 'obsession with lists and rolls'. He claims that this reflected the need of the bereaved to see recognition of their individual loss. B. Bushaway, 'Name upon name: the Great War and remembrance', in R. Porter (ed.), *Myths of the English* (Cambridge, 1992), 139.

The aftermath of war   247

lives to fight in the trenches. As men were killed, rolls of honour were also formed.[26]

In part, these rolls were motivated by the need to support soldiers through providing public recognition and appreciation of their endeavours. They were also the first efforts at commemoration. Commemoration in this context can be seen as an act of citizenship.[27] Clubs, societies and institutions used the rolls of service to affirm their moral integrity and sense of duty, which helped to justify their position and reputation within the wider society.

After the Armistice a substantial number of organizations continued to display their rolls of service.[28] Rolls of honour were also given greater permanence through engraving the names on memorials[29] or printing lists of the dead in elaborate books, often accompanied by biographical details.[30] In peacetime the public display of rolls served similar purposes to those in war. The rolls of service ensured that those who returned, who had fought to protect their families and way of life, felt that their efforts had been recognized. They also confirmed that the soldiers had always been part of their community throughout the long years of war, at least in spirit.

The rolls of honour themselves expressed a sense of pride in the contribution of their individual community to the war effort. At the same time, they articulated a sense of loss and grief, marking the absence of many individuals who had been important members of that community before the war. By listing the dead and highlighting their sacrifice, these memorials were also a reminder of the debt owed by the surviving community to those who did not return.[31]

---

[26] The description 'roll of honour' did not always refer to lists of the dead. For the purposes of this discussion, however, all rolls commemorating those who died will be referred to as rolls of honour and the rolls referring to men serving in the armed forces will be classed as rolls of service.

[27] Winter, *Sites of memory, sites of mourning*, 80.

[28] See, for example, the rolls of service for Trinity Presbyterian Church Mission, Bootle (Men's Bible Class); Booth Line Company; St Helen's Church, Sefton; St John the Evangelist, Rice Lane, Walton and Cunard Steamship Company Roll of Honour, which also listed those men who served. Merseyside war memorials database, LSM.

[29] For example: Liverpool Exchange Newsroom, Liverpool Masonic Hall, Liverpool Postal Workers Memorial, Merchant Taylors School. Merseyside war memorials database, LSM.

[30] For example: Birkenhead Park Rugby Football Club illuminated memorial scroll; memorial booklet of Cunard Line clerical staff; Sewell, *Rugby football internationals*. Merseyside war memorials database, LSM.

[31] Jay Winter has suggested that one of the central themes of rituals and ceremonies surrounding war memorials was that of the duty of those that remained to 'remember the dead by dedicating themselves to good works among their fellow men'. Winter, *Sites of memory, sites of mourning*, 97.

This was certainly part of the intended function of the memorial in Trinity Presbyterian Church, Claughton.[32] The church lost thirty-one men from its congregation as a result of the war (at least five of whom were Liverpool Scots). They were commemorated by a Celtic cross of white Mansfield stone outside the church and two alabaster and marble rolls within. At the unveiling on 9 May 1920, the minister, the Reverend William McNeill, concluded his speech to the children of the parish with the following words: 'Many of you, boys and girls, will pass this cross on your way to and from school. I hope you will often stop and look at it for a moment. And, as you look, you will perhaps hear it say: you are not your own, you boys and girls, you are bought with a price.'[33] Thus memorials were to be a constant visual reminder of the sacrifice of a community and of the duty of all those that remained to discharge the debt owed.

The belief in the redemptive power of war had survived in the trenches. Indeed, McNeill supported his message with a letter sent to him by a member of the congregation who was subsequently killed in the war: 'If God asks me for life, I shall not shrink. Only do you who remain see to it that our sacrifice is not in vain. Do not let the world of men slip back into the slough of indifference from which they have been partly raised.'[34] Most survivors had not been radicalized by the experience of the trenches. Soldiers returned from the front with the same social and political prejudices with which they had left, but the scale of death and injury they had witnessed could not be ignored. When counting the cost of war in the wake of the Armistice, there was a great need to derive meaning from loss.

The idea of discharging a debt of honour was attractive to many individuals and communities and was not just the preserve of the religious. It implied that suffering and death had been worthwhile and involved positive actions, which could prove cathartic for those who grieved and for those ex-servicemen who were suffering the guilt of the survivor.

The nature of the 'debt' itself proved difficult to describe. It was discussed in the vaguest of terms at both religious and secular memorial ceremonies, but can be broadly defined as follows. The men of Liverpool had saved their families from the 'very worst horrors'[35] of invasion, and in doing so had preserved their way of life and the idealized values of British

---

[32] Claughton was a middle-class district on the outskirts of Birkenhead.
[33] *Our Church News: Trinity Presbyterian Church, Claughton*, 30 May 1920, Provincial and church records, MRO, 285 TRI 13/3, 15.
[34] *Our Church News: Trinity Presbyterian Church, Claughton*, 30 May 1920, Provincial and church records, MRO, 285 TRI 13/3, 7.
[35] J. B. McKaig, Commanding Officer of the Liverpool Rifles, in *Liverpool Daily Post*, 22 December 1925.

society. Those that remained thus had a duty to live up to the values for which men died. Communities were required to behave in a more moral, equitable and self-sacrificing way, were obliged to care for those affected by war, and had a duty to work for lasting peace.[36]

By the end of the 1920s, the equitable society remained an unattainable dream, whereas the preservation of peace still appeared as an achievable ideal. It was, understandably, the latter element of the 'debt' that was stressed during the 1930s.[37] By contrast, immediately after the war, the conception of this 'debt' was much more fluid. The practicalities of how it was to be discharged could be interpreted in different ways, according to existing traditions within institutions or the preoccupations of the individual.

For some institutions, the initial memorial had a utilitarian component which contributed, in some small way, to the provision for the sick or disadvantaged. For instance, the Liverpool Scottish Battalion funded a cot at the Liverpool Children's Hospital alongside its elaborate symbolic memorials.[38] Others redirected and extended charity efforts. The Trinity Presbyterian Church founded a Manor Hill Hospital fund that paid for day trips for permanently disabled soldiers throughout the 1920s. Those church members who ran the fund explained that: 'It has been a great privilege to provide these pleasures for we owe these men a great debt. Many have lain in hospital for seven years or more, and many have only weary years of helplessness before them. By our continued "acts of remembrance" we may give them some repayment.'[39]

J. G. Colthart Moffat, who had directed his pre-war energies to volunteering and the Liverpool Scottish, served as an ex-soldier representative on a committee that ran a home 'for children of those whose deaths were not officially recognized as having been caused through army service, or for children of ex-servicemen whose parents are unable or unfitted to provide for their upbringing.'[40] He also spent his military pension

---

[36] Adrian Gregory has argued that the war gave the idealized values of British society – decency, peace, fairness and social harmony – a certain degree of real meaning in the aftermath of the war. A. Gregory, *The silence of memory: Armistice Day 1919–1946* (Oxford, 1994), 5.

[37] Ibid., 118–42; D. W. Lloyd, *Battlefield tourism: pilgrimage and the commemoration of the Great War in Britain, Australia and Canada, 1919–1939* (Oxford, 1998), 178–9.

[38] *Liverpool Scottish Regimental Gazette*, July 1922, 12. The Scottish also erected a bronze memorial with a casket which contained an illuminated roll of honour and was displayed in the Battalion Headquarters. A carved oak memorial was commissioned for the Battalion Church (St Andrew's, Rodney Street), and a donation was made to the Scottish National War Memorial. Merseyside war memorials database, LSM.

[39] *Our Church News: Trinity Presbyterian Church, Claughton*, October 1925, Provincial and church records, MRO, 285 TRI 13/3, 5.

[40] Cutting from *Liverpool Echo*, 9 December 1920, in J. G. C. Moffat's Scrapbook, LSM, Miscellaneous File M, Acc. No. 199.

ensuring that the 'aged and broken residents' of Guillemont, the village where he was wounded in 1916, never lacked food and fuel. In 1927 he wrote an article in the *Daily Telegraph* in which he exhorted other old soldiers who had 'made good' to adopt a French village and help the poor, as an 'act of thankfulness that we are alive'.[41]

The promotion of peace was also taken seriously by Trinity Presbyterian Church, whose members formed an active congregational branch of the League of Nations in 1922.[42] Their objectives were echoed by Norman Ellison, whose pilgrimage to the cemeteries of his dead comrades around Ypres in 1923 prompted him to write: 'It was up to us who remained to carry on and see that no such terrible wastage of life ever occurred again ... such was the bounden duty those rough crosses conveyed to me.'[43] However, it was not until 1927 that Ellison began to consider writing a 'truthful' account of the war for the benefit of his family and warn the younger generation of the waste and horror of modern warfare.[44]

Colonel McKaig, who continued as the Commanding Officer of the Liverpool Rifles after the war, felt that the Territorials had become 'unfashionable' by 1923.[45] After the signing of the Locarno Treaty in 1925, he delivered a speech in which he warned, 'we must not turn all our swords into ploughshares', and stressed that 'the Territorial Army should be supported because it is part of the machinery for bringing about final peace'.[46]

In Liverpool, few saw their duty to the dead involving joining the Territorials, a trend also identified in the Lancastrian town of Bury during the 1920s and 1930s. In his exploration of the links between the Lancashire Fusiliers and their recruitment area, Geoffrey Moorhouse suggests that although the people of Bury remained proud of their regiment, the human wreckage left by the war ensured that most men avoided direct involvement in the Territorial Army.[47] Yet poor levels of recruitment in Lancashire cannot be solely attributed to the experience of the

---

[41] Cutting from the *Daily Telegraph*, 24 February 1927, J. G. C. Moffat's Scrapbook, LSM, Miscellaneous File M, Acc. No. 199.
[42] *Our Church News: Trinity Presbyterian Church, Claughton*, October 1922, Provincial and church records, MRO, 285 TRI 13/3, 8.
[43] N. F. Ellison, 'Three musketeers and a gunner', Account of pilgrimage, 1923, LRO, Unlisted catalogue, item 534.
[44] D. Lewis (ed.), *Remembrances of Hell: the Great War diary of writer, broadcaster and naturalist Norman Ellison* (Shrewsbury, 1997), 107.
[45] Recruiting and Discharge Committee minute book, 2 February 1923, West Lancashire Territorial and Auxiliary Forces Association, LRO, 356 WES 19/2, 136.
[46] *Liverpool Daily Courier*, 22 December 1925.
[47] Moorhouse, *Hell's foundations*, 190–2, 200.

Great War. Undoubtedly some men were dissuaded from joining up by personal or familial knowledge of warfare, but the Territorials had never been 'fashionable' in peacetime and the difficulties faced by the recruiting committees in the 1920s were the same as those faced a decade earlier.[48]

The Territorials had returned to their pre-war position in civic life. Their reputation was certainly enhanced, for they had proved themselves in war, but there were too many other distractions with which the young men of Liverpool chose to fill their leisure time. The individual Battalions themselves reverted to selective pre-war recruiting criteria, which reduced the pool of potential recruits.[49] The influx of conscripts had failed to alter substantially the traditions of the Battalions in wartime, and they were restored to their old composition in peace. Those ex-soldiers who re-enlisted in the Rifles and the Scottish were mainly those of middle-class status who had been members pre-war or had been early wartime recruits.[50] Social selection had been reimposed and the Battalions again became exclusive clubs, catering for the elite of Liverpool, with social functions high on their agenda. Indeed, in 1920 the Liverpool Scottish was awarded a grant for entertainment from the West Lancashire Territorial Association with the aim of stimulating recruitment.[51]

The majority of the wartime rank and file, irrespective of their social class, did not re-enlist, but an affinity with each Battalion was maintained. Annual dinners and reunions, often in conjunction with the serving Battalion, were well attended throughout the 1920s.[52] When the old comrades Associations were formed in the 1930s, the Liverpool Scottish were able to attract 1000 members and the Rifles 700.[53] These Associations met in the sergeants' mess of their respective Battalion

---

[48] Employers still proved troublesome in refusing to allow Territorials time off for camp, or allowing them extra holiday. Recruiting and Discharge Committee minute book, 4 December 1925, West Lancashire Territorial and Auxiliary Forces Association, LRO, 356 WES 19/3, 80. Lord Derby also complained that the financial cutbacks within the Territorial Army were having an adverse effect on recruitment. *Liverpool Courier*, 25 March 1926.

[49] General Purposes Committee minute book, 7 June 1921, West Lancashire Territorial and Auxiliary Forces Association, LRO, 356 WES 10/5, 2.

[50] The number of re-enlistments is not known, but of the few identified, all are pre-war or early wartime Territorials. For example, Sergeant D. Carr joined up on 1 September 1914 and rejoined as a private after discharge on 22 July 1920. A large percentage of the post-war officers had served during the war.

[51] Recruiting and Discharge Committee minute book, 11 August 1920, West Lancashire Territorial and Auxiliary Forces Association, LRO, 356 WES 19/2, 3.

[52] Eight hundred past and present members attended a Liverpool Scottish Ball in 1926. *Liverpool Courier*, 20 January 1926.

[53] *Liverpool Scottish Regimental Association Gazette*, September 1932, 46, and Liverpool Rifles' Association minute book, 2 September 1935, Liverpool Rifles' Association Papers, MRO, 356 RIF/1/1.

252   Attitudes and experience

headquarters and maintained close connections with the activities of the present units. The primary objects of both Associations were to perpetuate comradeship between old members and serving Territorials, which had the added advantage of helping to maintain Battalion traditions. The Scottish also had a charitable element, aiding those ex-soldiers who had fallen on hard times.[54]

The Associations were essentially social clubs with a military theme. The annual trips organized were often pilgrimages to the continental battlefields and the Scottish National War Memorial or to military tattoos, but they were never exclusively Great War societies. All ex-Territorials, both pre- and post-war, were entitled to join, and 'wives and sweethearts' were encouraged to accompany their partners on both pilgrimages and outings.[55] Comradeship in the trenches had never reduced the horizons of the soldier to an exclusive, immediate group, and consequently the Territorial Associations in peacetime were never the exclusive veterans groups, hostile to civilian society, that have been described by Eric Leed.[56]

These groups of ex-Territorials included men who had thoroughly enjoyed their experience of war,[57] alongside those at the opposite end of the spectrum, who meditated on the horror and waste of the conflict.[58] All, it seems, retained a pride in their old units. The ex-Territorials had not been alienated from either their communities or the army by their war experience and were participating in a well-integrated social organization that grew naturally from the existing Territorial structure.

Throughout the 1920s it was the act of commemoration that kept the veterans in touch with their units and with each other. For the Liverpool Rifles, the annual commemoration centred on a memorial dinner, which was held in February, the month the Battalion first crossed to France in 1915.

The Scottish had a more spectacular ritual, which occurred annually on 16 June, the anniversary of the Battle of Hooge. This date had been marked by the Battalion throughout the war, with a sports day where possible, and

[54] Liverpool Scottish Regimental Association minute book, 24 August 1930, LSM, and Liverpool Rifles' Association minute book, 8 December 1934, Liverpool Rifles' Association Papers, MRO, 356 RIF/1/1.
[55] For example, eighty members' wives and sweethearts visited the National War Memorial in Edinburgh to lay a wreath and read the Liverpool Scottish Roll of Honour that was placed there. *Liverpool Scottish Regimental Association Gazette*, June 1932, 26. Charles Kimball also notes that women were actively involved in ex-servicemen's groups. See C. C. Kimball, 'The ex-service movement in England and Wales, 1916–1930', unpublished PhD thesis, Stanford University (1990), 236.
[56] Charles Kimball also disputes Leed's argument that ex-servicemen's groups were hostile to civil society and intent on exclusively perpetuating the comradeship of the trenches. Kimball, 'The ex-service movement in England and Wales, 1916–1930', 150.
[57] F. MacDonald, Diary, 31 August 1919, LSM, Miscellaneous File M, Acc. No. 514.
[58] Lewis (ed.), *Remembrances of Hell*, 107.

The aftermath of war 253

had always incorporated a speech by the Battalion Commander.[59] In peacetime, the Scottish held a memorial service at Battalion Headquarters, including an address by the Commanding Officer, a blessing by the padre, and wreath laying at the Battalion memorial. It was followed by a march of serving Territorials and ex-soldiers through the principal streets of Liverpool, headed by the pipe band.[60] The ceremony served many of the same functions as Armistice Day. It recognized the sacrifice of the dead, and there was an emphasis on the need to dedicate oneself to good works, although this often took the form of a recruitment plea.[61] Yet the tone of the day differed from the sombre mood of 11 November. Hooge Day was a livelier event, in keeping with the sports days held during the war, because it was also an opportunity to celebrate the achievements and valour of the Battalion.[62] And the Battalion did not celebrate alone. As late as 1932, thousands of people lined the main streets of Liverpool to watch the spectacle of the Liverpool Scottish marching past.[63]

Civic commemoration

The military achievement and sacrifice of Liverpool as a whole was commemorated at civic level. Ironically, given the present obsession with the Pals Battalions, it was the 55th (West Lancashire) Division that came to represent the city in the aftermath of the war. On receiving the freedom of the city in July 1919, Field Marshal Sir Douglas Haig wrote to the Lord Mayor: 'in the gallantry of their action in the field, Liverpool yields to none of the cities of our Empire. I need only instance the performance of the Liverpool Battalions of the 55th Division last April at Givenchy, where Liverpool men displayed the finest qualities of courage and devotion.'[64] It was the fame generated by its stand at Givenchy that elevated the 55th above other Lancashire Divisions. This, together with the strong established links between city and county, ensured that the Division would become a symbol of Liverpool's war effort.

---

[59] 'June 16th – Anniversary of attack at Hooge ... Divisional band played and we had sports in the evening.' E. Herd, Diary, 16 June 1917, Herd Papers, KRC, MLL, 1981.850.
[60] In June 1932 150 ex-soldiers and 300 serving Territorials took part in the parade. *Liverpool Scottish Regimental Association Gazette*, June 1932, 19.
[61] At the unveiling of the Liverpool Scottish memorial in 1923, Lord Horne took the opportunity to remind those present of the continuing responsibility that rested on the shoulders of the Territorial Army, especially as the regular army was being reduced in size. *Liverpool Scottish Regimental Association Gazette*, July 1923, 12.
[62] The same situation occurred in Bury, where Armistice Day remained sombre, whereas Gallipoli Sunday was a celebration. Moorhouse, *Hell's foundations*, 155.
[63] *Liverpool Scottish Regimental Association Gazette*, June 1932, 19.
[64] Letter distributed to ex-servicemen on the occasion of the visit of Field Marshal Sir Douglas Haig to Liverpool, 5 July 1919, Macfie Papers, IWM, Con. Shelf.

254   Attitudes and experience

Figure 9.1 55th Divisional Memorial at Givenchy, France.

The first memorial to the Division was erected amidst the ruins of Givenchy in 1920. The stone cross bearing the Divisional symbol, motto and history had been commissioned by the 55th Division Comrades Association to commemorate those who had died and the achievements of West Lancashire men. It was followed in 1925 by two further memorials. One took the form of a statue of a soldier and an angel in Liverpool Cathedral; the other was the new West Lancashire Territorial Association Headquarters, also located in Liverpool.[65] The £20,000 to pay for these memorials was raised by public subscription, which gives some indication of the esteem in which the Division was held in the aftermath of the war.[66]

---

[65] *Liverpool Courier*, 19 January 1925.
[66] Open letter from the 55th Division Comrades Association Committee canvassing subscriptions to the 55th (West Lancs.) Division Memorial Fund, 22 November 1919, Derby Papers, LRO, 920 DER (17) 28/3, unsorted box file R.

The aftermath of war 255

Figure 9.1 (cont.)

The Division was not just commemorated through its own efforts. The civic authorities, anxious to celebrate achievement and promote city pride, as well as commemorating the dead, followed the example of the Comrades Association. Givenchy was 'adopted' by the city of Liverpool and another memorial was erected, again paid for by all sectors of Liverpool society.[67] The resulting memorial hall, fully furnished with cinematograph, piano, games and a library, was intended to be 'a centre of education and recreation'.[68] Its opening was attended by a welter of civic dignitaries from Givenchy and Liverpool, as well as the requisite military and ex-service representatives, and the ceremony included a play performed by Liverpool schoolchildren.[69]

In his opening speech, the Lord Mayor of Liverpool expressed Liverpool's pride in the men who had protected Givenchy. Those who had fought were receiving the recognition they sought throughout the war. As one observer put it, the memorial was an acknowledgement that 'Fighting Lancashire saved British arms from something we dare not even now contemplate.'[70]

The fact that so many Liverpool citizens now reposed in the cemeteries around Givenchy also made the area a symbol of Liverpool's loss, and the

---

[67] For example, the schoolchildren of Liverpool raised money to buy a piano for the hall. *Liverpool Daily Post*, 27 September 1924.
[68] *Liverpool Daily Post*, 27 September 1924.   [69] *Liverpool Daily Post*, 22 August 1924.
[70] *Liverpool Daily Post*, 27 September 1924.

Figure 9.2 Memorial Hall at Givenchy. Memorial plaque on building reads: 'In Memoriam: The City of Liverpool to the Commune of Givenchy'.

links established with the village ensured the city retained symbolic links with her dead. This was the second theme of the Mayoral speech: 'Watch over our dead', he concluded, 'and we will watch over your living.'[71]

More than the 55th Divisional Memorial, this village hall expressed the pride and grief of a whole city, of all civilians and ex-soldiers touched by the war, and was particularly important for a city which, as yet, had no central cenotaph. Indeed, it is significant that the memorial plaque did not mention the 55th Division, reading simply 'The City of Liverpool to the Commune of Givenchy.'

In 1925 the planning for the main civic cenotaph in Liverpool began. Until this time, Armistice Day ceremonies were held at a wooden cenotaph, conveyed to and from St George's Plateau in the heart of the city by a handcart.[72] It was funded by the Corporation to ensure that it was not associated with any one group and represented a monument to which the 'lowest and highest in the city have contributed',[73] but from the

[71] *Liverpool Daily Post*, 29 September 1924.
[72] Newspaper cutting, *Liverpool Daily Post*, 16 August 1930 in Liverpool cenotaph memorial volume, LRO, Hf 942.7213CEN, 45.
[73] *Liverpool Echo*, 11 November 1930.

The aftermath of war 257

beginning, the project courted controversy. There was debate over the size and site of the cenotaph,[74] and a religious dispute over the nature of the opening ceremony on Armistice Day 1930, an uncanny echo of the religious disagreements of the clergy of the 55th Division in 1917.[75]

The war had not healed the rifts in Liverpolitan society, and there was no new civic community forged by the conflict. Although religious tensions had decreased over time, Liverpool was still divided by class and religion. Memorials abounded at the level of the association and institution, commemorating the dead according to their pre-war affiliations. Yet the men had also fought for the wider community, their city and their county. Although they often had different conceptions of their city, a sense of civic pride had motivated many soldiers in the trenches, and it was only fitting that a central cenotaph should commemorate their effort, and mark their loss.[76]

Most Territorials from the Liverpool Scottish and Liverpool Rifles had successfully merged back into civilian life, their pre-war ambitions and interests substantially intact, but all had been indelibly marked by the experience of the Great War. There could have been few families in Liverpool who had not been touched by loss. The huge crowds that flocked to the unveiling of Liverpool's cenotaph illustrated the continuing depth of feeling associated with the war and its commemoration, which affected young and old alike.[77] A young schoolboy, born after the end of the conflict, summed up the mood of the city on 11 November 1930 when he remarked to a friend: 'It's raining. It's always raining on Armistice Day. We couldn't make enough tears.'[78]

[74] There was much debate over the correct place for the cenotaph and as late as 1933, three years after the unveiling, there was still discussion over whether it should be removed from its site in front of St George's Hall. See newspaper cuttings, 1927–33, in Liverpool cenotaph memorial volume, LRO, Hf 942.7213CEN, 93.
[75] For an analysis of the dispute concerning the inclusion of a short civic service in the unveiling ceremony, which was finally resolved by allowing each denomination to lead a prayer, see Gregory, *The silence of memory*, 200–1. See also newspaper cuttings, 1930, in Liverpool cenotaph memorial volume, LRO, Hf 942.7213CEN, 49–50.
[76] In October 1929, frustrated by the lack of a permanent cenotaph, and the lack of respect it implied, ex-servicemen's organizations made a formal appeal to Liverpool Corporation to ensure that the promised memorial was unveiled before the next Armistice Day. Newspaper cutting, *Liverpool Courier*, 1 October 1929, in Liverpool cenotaph memorial volume, LRO, Hf 942.7213CEN, 39.
[77] The *Sphere* estimated the crowds on and around St George's Plateau, where the cenotaph was unveiled, as being in excess of 50,000. Liverpool cenotaph memorial volume, LRO, Hf 942.7213CEN, 80.
[78] *Liverpool Echo*, 11 November 1930.

Bibliography

ARCHIVAL SOURCES

IMPERIAL WAR MUSEUM, LONDON (IWM)

Clegg Papers, 88/18/1
Coop Papers, 87/56/1
Douglas Papers, 66/274/1
Ellison Papers, DS/MISC/49
W. Evans Papers, Con. Shelf
Gordon Papers, 77/5/1
Handley Papers, 92/36/1
Macfie Papers, Con. Shelf
Warry Papers, 96/12/1

KING'S REGIMENT COLLECTION, MUSEUM OF LIVERPOOL LIFE (KRC, MLL)

Herd Papers, 1981.850.
1/6th Battalion King's (Liverpool) Regiment Casualty Books 1–3, 58.83.537a–b
1/6th Battalion King's (Liverpool) Regiment War Diary, 58.83.501
1/10th Battalion King's (Liverpool) Regiment War Diary, 58.83.509.
R. A. S. Macfie Papers, 4.315
Traynor Papers, 1976.5901
Turner Papers, Letters of W. S. Turner, 1987.155.17g
Turner Papers, Letters and newspaper cuttings, 1973.163.5

LIDDLE COLLECTION, UNIVERSITY OF LEEDS

Brownell Papers (G.S.)
H. C. Eccles Papers (G.S.)
T. D. Fisher Papers
H. S. Taylor Papers
T. W. Wood Papers (G.S.)

LIVERPOOL RECORD OFFICE (LRO)

Derby Papers, 920 DER (17) 10/2, 17/3, 21/3, 26/1, 26/4, 28/3
Ellison Papers, unlisted catalogue, item 534, 611

Bibliography

Liverpool cenotaph memorial volume, Hf 942.7213CEN
Liverpool Rifles Association Papers, MD 162
Records of the 55th (West Lancashire) Division, 1914–19:
  356 FIF 1/2/32
  356 FIF 2/1/232
  356 FIF 3/Part I
  356 FIF 4/1/131–978, 983, 985–7, 999, 1017
  356 FIF 5/2
  356 FIF 11/1/602
  356 FIF 13/2/642, 649–51, 671
  356 FIF 14/2/796, 805–6
  356 FIF 44/6/15
  356 FIF 45
  356 FIF 48/2/72
  356 FIF 50/6
  356 FIF 50/6/138, 142, 154
  356 FIF 54/5
  356 FIF 9/2/211
Records of the *Liverpool Daily Post and Echo*, 331 GRA 4/1
West Lancashire Territorial and Auxiliary Forces Association: 356 WES 10/5, 19/1, 19/2, 19/3

LIVERPOOL SCOTTISH REGIMENTAL MUSEUM TRUST (LSM)

J. Atherton, Miscellaneous File A
J. Bedford, Scrapbook 1, Acc. No. 476
W. G. Bromley Papers, Acc. Nos. 544, 687
A. Bryans, Scrapbook, Acc. No. 545
J. A. Burden, Letters, Acc. No. 1122
W. H. Campbell Papers, Acc. No. 484
Chavasse Papers, Officers Miscellaneous File
Colonel J. R Davidson to Colonel Blair, in uncatalogued scrapbook
G. Donnison and D. Evans, Merseyside War Memorials Database
Draft Book, 10th Liverpool Scottish, King's (Liverpool) Regiment, 1914–16, Acc. No. 19
Lieutenant Colonel D. D. Farmer VC, MSM, Autobiography, Miscellaneous File D
Liverpool Scottish Attestment Book, Acc. No. 32
Liverpool Scottish Officers' Index
Liverpool Scottish Other Ranks' Index
Liverpool Scottish Regimental Association minute book, Shelf 2
Liverpool Scottish Regimental Museum, Biographies of Cunard employees, Miscellaneous File C
J. W. Lorimer Papers, Acc. No. 794
McClymont Papers, Miscellaneous File M
F. MacDonald Papers, Miscellaneous File M, Acc. No. 514
W. D. McDonald, Diary, Miscellaneous File M
R. A. S. Macfie Papers, Acc. Nos. 306, 315

J. G. C. Moffat, Scrapbook, Miscellaneous File M, Acc. No. 199
V. L. Morris, Diary, Miscellaneous File M, Acc. No. 844/2
S. Moulton, Diary, Miscellaneous File M, Acc. No. 760/7
Newspaper Cuttings Scrapbook, Acc. No. 14
E. Peppiette Papers, Acc. No. 887
Pinnington Papers, Miscellaneous File P
Rae Papers, Miscellaneous File R
Rayner Papers, Miscellaneous File R
H. S. Taylor, Letter to Liverpool Scottish Museum, Folio 2
H. S. Taylor, Reminiscences, Miscellaneous File T
Matron Whitson, Diary 1915–1919, Acc. No. 1104

MARITIME ARCHIVES AND LIBRARY, MERSEYSIDE MARITIME MUSEUM

In Memoriam booklet of F. H. Turner, DX 184/3
In Memoriam booklet of W. S. Turner, DX 184/4

MERSEYSIDE RECORD OFFICE, LIVERPOOL (MRO)

League of Welldoers, 1856–1986, 364 LWD 23/1/84
Liverpool Rifles' Association Papers, 356 RIF/1/1, 3/1, 3/3, 3/8, 4/3
Provincial and church records, 285 TRI 13/3

NATIONAL ARCHIVES, PUBLIC RECORD OFFICE, LONDON

Army Council Instructions, WO 293/5
Ledger Books of Field General Courts-Martial, WO 213/1–24
Ministry of National Service Papers, NATS/1/400–1, NATS/1/868
Directorate of Organisation, PRO, WO 162/6

MANCHESTER LOCAL HISTORY LIBRARY (MLHL)

W. J. Pegge Papers, M198/1/2/1; M198/6/5–6

INTERVIEWS

A. Rimmer, with the author, 20 December 1998

PUBLISHED SOURCES

CONTEMPORARY JOURNALS, NEWSPAPERS AND REVIEWS

Caldian
Daily Chronicle
Daily Dispatch
Daily Mail
Daily Mirror
Daily Telegraph
Greenjacket

Hornsley Journal
Liverpolitan
Liverpool Courier
Liverpool Daily Express
Liverpool Daily Post
Liverpool Echo
Liverpool Scottish Regimental Association Gazette
Liverpool Scottish Regimental Gazette
Manchester Guardian
Peronne Gazette
Sub Rosa, Being the Magazine of the 55th West Lancashire Division
Sunday Graphic
The Times
Young Crescent

OFFICIAL REPORTS AND COMMAND PAPERS

Census of England and Wales, 1911
PP 1921, Cmd 1193 *General Annual Reports of the British Army (including the Territorial Force) for the Period from 1st October 1913 to 30th September 1919*
Hansard, 5th Series, LXXII, 1474; LXXIII, 994–5; XCIV, 626; XCVII, 1548; XCVII, 1558; XCVII, 1565
Registrar General's Decennial Supplement to Census of England and Wales, Part II, *Occupational mortality, fertility and infant mortality*, 1921, ciii–cxiv
War Office, *Field Service Regulations, part II organisation and administration (Reprinted with amendments to October 1914)* (London, 1914)
War Office, *Manual of military law* (London, 1914)
War Office, *Rights and duties of Territorial soldiers* (London, 1912)
War Office, *Service in the Territorial Force: terms and conditions* (London, 1912)
War Office, *Soldiers died in the Great War 1914–1919* (vol. 13, London, 1920)
War Office, *Statistics of the military effort of the British Empire* (London, 1922)

BOOKS AND ARTICLES

Ackerley, G. L., 'Memoir of R. A. Scott Macfie', *Journal of Gypsy Lore* 3rd series, 14 (1935), 20–50
Adams, R. J. Q. and Poirier, P. P., *The conscription controversy in Great Britain, 1900–1918* (London, 1987)
Anderson, G., 'The service occupations of nineteenth century Liverpool', in B. L. Anderson and P. J. M. Stoney (eds.), *Commerce, industry and transport: studies in economic change on Merseyside* (Liverpool, 1983), 79–92
Armstrong, W. A., 'The use of information about occupation', in E. A. Wrigley (ed.), *Nineteenth century society* (Cambridge, 1972), 191–253
Ashworth, T., *Trench warfare, 1914–1918: the live and let live system* (London, 1980)
Audoin-Rouzeau, S., *Men at war 1914–1918: national sentiment and trench journalism in France during the First World War* (Oxford, 1992)
Babington, A., *For the sake of example* (London, 1983)

Banning, S. T., *Military law made easy* (Gale and Polden's military series London, 1917, 11th edn)
Barnes, B. S., *This righteous war* (Huddersfield, 1990)
Baynes, J., *Morale, a study of men and courage: the Second Scottish Rifles at the Battle of Neuve Chappelle 1915* (London, 1967)
  Soldiers of Scotland (London, 1988)
Beckett, I., 'The nation in arms, 1914–18', in I. F. W. Beckett and K. Simpson (eds.), *A nation in arms: a social study of the British army in the First World War* (Manchester, 1985), 1–35
  'The Territorial Force', in I. F. W. Beckett and K. Simpson (eds.), *A nation in arms: a social study of the British Army in the First World War* (Manchester, 1985), 127–63
  'The Territorial Force in the Great War', in P. H. Liddle (ed.) *Home fires and foreign fields: British social and military experience in the First World War* (London, 1985), 21–37
  'The British Army, 1914–1918: the illusion of change', in J. Turner (ed.), *Britain and the First World War* (London, 1988), 99–116
  'The real unknown army: British conscripts 1916–1919', in J. J. Becker and A. Audoin-Rouzeau (eds.), *Les sociétés européennes et la Guerre de 1914–1918* (Paris, 1990), 339–56
  The amateur military tradition 1558–1945 (Manchester, 1991)
  '"Revisiting the old front line": the historiography of the Great War since 1984', *Stand To: The Journal of the Western Front Association*, 43 (April 1995), 10–14
Beetham, M., '"Healthy reading": the periodical press in late Victorian Manchester', in A. Kidd (ed.), *Manchester in the late nineteenth century* (Manchester, 1990), 167–92
Belchem, J., 'The peculiarities of Liverpool', in J. Belchem (ed.), *Popular politics, riot and labour* (Liverpool Historical Studies 8, Liverpool, 1992), 1–20
  '"An accent exceedingly rare": scouse and the inflexion of class', in J. Belchem, and N. Kirk (eds.), *Languages of labour* (Aldershot, 1997), 99–130
Bet-El, I. R., *Conscripts: lost legions of the Great War* (Stroud, 1999)
Blunden, E., *Undertones of war* (London, 1928)
Bohstedt, J., 'More than one working class: Protestant–Catholic riots in Edwardian Liverpool', in J. Belchem (ed.), *Popular politics, riot and labour* (Liverpool Historical Studies 8, Liverpool, 1992), 173–216
Bond, B., 'The Territorial Army in peace and war', *History Today*, 16 (March 1966), 157–66
Boorman, D., *British First World War memorials* (York, 1988)
Bourke, J., *Dismembering the male: men's bodies, Britain and the Great War* (London, 1996)
  An intimate history of killing (London, 1999)
Bourne, J. M., *Britain and the Great War 1914–1918* (London, 1989)
  'Midland Territorials at war: the 46th (North Midland) Division, 1914–1918', paper given at the Midlands at War conference, 9 November 1996
  'The British working man in arms', in H. Cecil and P. Liddle (eds.), *Facing Armageddon: the First World War experienced* (London, 1996), 336–52

'British generals in the First World War', in G. D. Sheffield (ed.), *Leadership and command: the Anglo-American experience since 1861* (London, 1997), 93–116

Who's who in World War One (London, 2001)

Bowman, T., 'The discipline and morale of the British Expeditionary Force in France and Flanders 1914–18, with particular reference to Irish units', unpublished PhD thesis, University of Luton (1999)

Irish regiments in the Great War: discipline and morale (Manchester, 2003)

Brophy, J., *The bitter end* (London, 1928)

Brown, Malcolm and Seaton, Shirley, *Christmas truce: the Western Front, December 1914* (London, 1984)

Bryson, R., 'The once and future army', in B. Bond (ed.) *'Look to your front': Studies in the First World War* (Staplehurst, 1999), 25–62

Buck, M. L., 'Feature review: between mutiny and obedience. The case of the French Fifth Infantry Division during World War I', *War in History*, 3 (1996), 116–17

Buitenhuis, P., *The Great War of words* (London, 1989)

Burke-Gaffney, J. J., *The story of the King's Regiment 1914–1948* (Liverpool, 1954)

Bushaway, B., 'Name upon name: the Great War and remembrance', in R. Porter (ed.), *Myths of the English* (Cambridge, 1992), 136–67

Carmichael, J., *First World War photographers* (London, 1989)

Carter, T., *The Birmingham Pals: 14th, 15th and 16th (Service) Battalions of the Royal Warwickshire Regiment* (London, 1997)

Churchill, R. S., *Lord Derby, King of Lancashire* (London, 1959)

Churchill, W., *The world crisis* (London, 1965 edn)

Clayton, A., *Chavasse: double V.C.* (Barnsley, 1992)

Colls, R., *Identity of England* (Oxford, 2002)

Cooksey, J., *Pals: the 13th and 14th Battalions, York and Lancaster Regiment* (Barnsley, 1986)

Cunningham, H., *The Volunteer Force* (London, 1975)

D'Aeth, F., 'Present tendencies of class differentiation,' *Sociological Review*, 2, 4 (October 1910), 267–76

Dallas, G. and Gill, D., *The unknown army: mutinies in the British Army in World War One* (London, 1985)

Davies, F. and Maddocks, G., *Bloody Red Tabs: General Officer casualties of the Great War 1914–1918* (London, 1995)

Davies, S., *Liverpool labour* (Keele, 1996)

Dennis, P., 'The County Associations and the Territorial Army', *Army Quarterly and Defence Journal*, 109, 2 (1979), 210–19

The Territorial Army, 1906–1940 (Woodbridge, 1987)

Dewey, P. E, 'Military recruiting and the British labour force during the First World War', *Historical Journal*, 27, 1 (March 1984), 199–223

Dunn, J. C., *The war the infantry knew* (2nd edn, London, 1987)

Edmonds, J. (ed.), *Official history: military operations, France and Belgium*, 14 vols. (London, 1922–48)

Eksteins, M., *Rites of spring: the Great War and the birth of the modern age* (New York, 1989)

Elton, O., *C. E. Montague: a memoir* (London, 1929), 193–4
Englander, D., 'Soldiering and identity: reflections on the Great War', *War in History*, 1, 3 (1994), 300–18
  'Discipline and morale in the British Army, 1917–1918', in J. Horne (ed.), *State, society and mobilisation in Europe during the First World War* (Cambridge, 1998), 125–43
  'Mutinies and military morale', in H. Strachan (ed.), *The Oxford illustrated history of the First World War* (Oxford, 1998), 191–203
Englander, D. and Osborne, J., 'Jack, Tommy and Henry Dubb: the armed forces and the working class', *Historical Journal*, 21, 3 (1978), 593–621
Ferguson, N., *The pity of war* (London, 1998)
Fitzpatrick, D., 'A curious middle place: the Irish in Britian, 1871–1921', in R. Swift and S. Gilley (eds.), *The Irish in Britain 1815–1939* (London, 1989), 18–31
Foley, Robert T., *German strategy and the path to Verdun: Erich von Falkenhayn and the development of attrition, 1871–1916* (Cambridge, 2004)
French, J., *1914* (London, 1919)
Fuller, J. G., *Troop morale and popular culture in the British and Dominion Armies, 1914–1918* (Oxford, 1990)
Fussell, P., *The Great War and modern memory* (London, 1975)
Garwood, J. M., *Chorley Pals: 'Y' Company, 11th (Service) Battalion, East Lancs. Regiment* (Manchester, 1989)
Gibbs, P., *Battles of the Somme* (London, 1917)
  Realities of war (London, 1920)
Graves, R., *Goodbye to all that* (4th edn, London, 1966)
Gregory, A., *The silence of memory: Armistice Day 1919–1946* (Oxford, 1994)
  'Lost generations: the impact of military casualties on Paris, London and Berlin', in J. Winter and J. L. Robert (eds.), *Capital cities at war* (Cambridge, 1997), 57–103
Grieves, K., 'War correspondents and conducting officers on the Western Front', in H. Cecil and P. Liddle (eds.), *Facing Armageddon: the First World War experienced* (London, 1996), 719–35
  'Lord Derby in Liverpool; military recruitment and dock labour', paper given at Liverpool and the First World War Conference, Merseyside Maritime Museum, Liverpool, 21 November 1998
Griffith, P., *Battle tactics of the Western Front: the British Army's art of attack 1916–18* (London, 1994)
Haig-Brown, A., *The OTC and the Great War* (London, 1915)
Harry, E., *From crime to court martial: a simplified rendering and index of those parts of the 'Manual of military law' and 'King's Regulations' which deal with a soldier's offences and punishments* (London, 1918)
Haste, C., *Keep the home fires burning* (London, 1977)
Hiley, N., 'Making war: the British news media and government control, 1914–1916', unpublished PhD thesis, Open University (1985)
  'You can't believe a word you read', in *Newspaper History* (1994), 89–102
Hoggart, R., '"Them" and "Us"', in P. Joyce (ed.), *Class* (Oxford, 1995), 239–49
Hudson, R. N., *The Bradford Pals* (Bradford, 1993)

Hughes, C., 'The New Armies', in I. F. W. Beckett and K. Simpson (eds.), *A nation in arms: a social study of the British army in the First World War* (Manchester, 1985), 99–125

Hynes, S., *A war imagined: the First World War and English culture* (New York, 1991)

James, E. A., *British regiments in the First World War* (2nd edn, London, 1976)

Janowitz, M. and Shils, E., 'Cohesion and disintegration in the Wehrmacht in World War II', *Public Opinion Quarterly*, 12 (Summer 1948), 280–315

Keir, J. L., 'Some aspects of a Territorial division from within', *Army Review* (July 1914), 129–41

Kimball, C. C., 'The ex-service movement in England and Wales, 1916–1930', unpublished PhD dissertation, Stanford University (1990)

Knightley, P., *The first casualty* (London, 1978)

Lawton, R. and Pooley, C. G., 'The social geography of Merseyside in the nineteenth century', Final report to the Social Science Research Council (Department of Geography, University of Liverpool, 1976)

Lee, J., 'The SHLM project: assessing the battle performance of British divisions', in P. Griffith (ed.), *British fighting methods in the Great War* (London, 1996), 175–81

Leed, E. J., *No Man's Land: combat and identity in World War One* (Cambridge, 1979)

Lewis, D. (ed.), *Remembrances of hell: the Great War diary of writer, broadcaster and naturalist Norman Ellison* (Shrewsbury, 1997)

The Liverpool Organisation, *Book of Liverpool civic week* (Liverpool, 1928)

Lloyd, D. W., *Battlefield tourism: pilgrimage and the commemoration of the Great War in Britain, Australia and Canada, 1919–1939* (Oxford, 1998)

Lovelace, C., 'British press censorship during the First World War', in G. Boyce (ed.), *Newspaper history: from the 17th century to the present day* (London, 1978), 307–19

McClymont, E. I. M., *Soldier poets: more songs by the fighting men* (2nd Series, London, 1918)

McEwen, J. M. (ed.), *The Riddell diaries* (London, 1986)

McGilchrist, A. M., *The Liverpool Scottish 1900–1919* (Liverpool, 1930)

McInnes, I. and Mitchinson, K. W., *Cotton town comrades: the story of the Oldham Pals Battalion, 1914–1919* (London, 1993)

Mackenzie, S. P., 'Morale and the cause: the campaign to shape the outlook of soldiers in the British Expeditionary Force, 1914–1918', *Canadian Journal of History*, 25 (August 1990), 215–31

Politics and military morale: current affairs and citizenship education in the British Army, 1914–50 (Oxford, 1992)

McKibbin, R., *Classes and cultures: England 1918–1951* (Oxford, 1998)

McKinnell, B., *The diary of Bryden McKinnell, Liverpool Scottish* (Liverpool, 1919)

Maddocks, G., *Liverpool Pals: a history of the 17th, 18th, 19th and 20th (Service) Battalions of the King's (Liverpool) Regiment, 1914–1919* (London, 1991)

Marquis, A. G., 'Words as weapons', *Journal of Contemporary History*, 13 (1978), 467–98

Marquis, F. J., *Handbook of employments in Liverpool* (Liverpool, 1916)

Marshall, S. L. A., *Men against fire: the problem of battle command in future war* (New York, 1947)

Messinger, G., *British propaganda and the state in the First World War* (Manchester, 1992)

Milner, L., *Leeds Pals: a history of the 15th (Service) Battalion (1st Leeds), the Prince of Wales's Own (West Yorkshire Regiment) 1914–1918* (London, 1991)

'Writing about the Gulf and the First World War', paper given at Unit histories: problems, limitations, value, conference, Chester College, 12 July 1997

Mitchinson, K. W., *Gentlemen and officers: the impact and experience of war on a Territorial Regiment, 1914–1918* (London, 1995)

Montague, C. E., *Disenchantment* (London, 1922)

Moorhouse, Geoffrey, *Hell's foundations: a town, its myths and Gallipoli* (London, 1992)

Moran, Lord, *The anatomy of courage* (London, 1945)

Morris, P., 'Leeds and the amateur military tradition: the Leeds Rifles and their antecedents, 1859–1918', unpublished PhD thesis, University of Leeds (1983)

Muir, R., *History of Liverpool* (2nd edn, London, 1970)

Naylor, J., *Lancashire biographies* (London, 1917)

Old Comrades Committee, *The 21st Battalion of the Manchester Regiment: a history* (Manchester, 1934)

Oram, G., *Death sentences passed by military courts of the British Army 1914–1924* (London, 1998)

Worthless men: race eugenics and the death penalty in the British Army during the First World War (London, 1998)

Military execution during World War One (Basingstoke, 2003)

Orchard, B., *Liverpool's legion of honour* (Birkenhead, 1893)

Osborne, J. M., *The voluntary recruiting movement in Britain 1914–16* (London, 1982)

Owen, W., *Poems* (London, 1920)

Peaty, J., 'Capital courts-martial during the Great War', in B. Bond (ed.), *Look to your front: studies in the First World War* (Staplehurst, 1999), 89–104

Peel, Lieutenant Colonel the Hon. S., 'The Territorial Force', *Army Quarterly*, 1, 1 (1920–21), 36–54

Perry, F. W., *The commonwealth armies: manpower and organisation in two world wars* (Manchester, 1988)

Price, R. N., 'Society, status and jingoism: the social roots of lower middle class patriotism 1870–1900', in G. Crossick (ed.), *The lower middle class in Britain 1870–1914* (London, 1977), 89–111

Pugsley, C., *On the fringe of Hell: New Zealanders and military discipline in the First World War* (London, 1991)

Putkowski, J. and Sykes, J., *Shot at dawn* (Barnsley, 1989)

Rathbone, B., *In and out of character* (New York, 1962)

Reeves, N., *Official British film propaganda in the First World War* (London, 1986)

'Through the eye of the camera: contemporary cinema audiences and their experience of war in the film, Battle of the Somme', in H. Cecil and P. Liddle (eds.), *Facing Armageddon: the First World War experienced* (London, 1996), 780–98

Reid, A. J., *Social classes and social relations in Britain 1850–1914* (Cambridge, 1992)
Robb, G., *British culture and the First World War* (Basingstoke, 2002)
Robert, J. L., 'The image of the profiteer', in J. Winter and J. L. Robert (eds.), *Capital cities at war: Paris, London, Berlin, 1914–1919* (Cambridge, 1997), 104–32
Roberts, Robert, 'The class structure of the "classic slum"', in P. Joyce (ed.), *Class* (Oxford, 1995), 236–9
Rose, T., *Aspects of political censorship, 1914–18* (Hull, 1995)
Rothstein, A., *The soldiers' strikes of 1919* (London, 1980)
Royle, E., 'Regions and identities', in E. Royle (ed.), *Issues of regional identity in honour of John Marshall* (Manchester, 1998), 1–13
Samuels, M., *Command or control? Command, training and tactics in the British and German Armies, 1888–1918* (London, 1995)
Sanders, M. L. and Taylor, P., *British propaganda during the First World War* (London, 1982)
Sassoon, S., *Memoirs of an infantry officer* (London, 1930)
 'Base details,' and 'The General', in R. Hart-Davis (ed.), *Siegfried Sassoon: the war poems* (London, 1983), 60, 67
Schneider, E. F., 'What Britons were told about the war in the trenches, 1914–1918', unpublished DPhil thesis, University of Oxford (1997)
Sellers, L., *For God's sake, shoot straight* (London, 1995)
Sell's Ltd, *Sell's world press* (London, 1919)
Sewell, E., *Rugby football internationals* (London, 1919)
Sheffield, G. D., 'The effect of war service on the 22nd Battalion Royal Fusiliers (Kensington) 1914–18, with special reference to morale, discipline and the officer–man relationship', unpublished MA thesis, University of Leeds (1984)
 'Officer–man relations, morale and discipline in the British Army 1902–1922', unpublished PhD thesis, University of London (1994)
 The Redcaps: a history of the Royal Military Police and its antecedents from the Middle Ages to the Gulf War (London, 1994)
 'Officer–man relations, discipline and morale in the British Army of the Great War', in H. Cecil and P. H. Liddle (eds.), *Facing Armageddon: the First World War experienced* (London, 1996), 413–24
 'A very good type of Londoner and a very good type of colonial: officer–man relations and discipline in the 22nd Royal Fusiliers, 1914–18', in B. Bond et al., *'Look to your front': studies in the First World War by the British Commission for Military History* (Staplehurst, 1999), 137–46
 Leadership in the trenches: officer–man relations, morale and discipline in the British Army in the era of the First World War (London, 2000)
 The Somme (London, 2003)
Simkins, P., *Kitchener's Army: the raising of the New Armies, 1914–16* (Manchester, 1988)
 'Everyman at war', in B. Bond (ed.) *The First World War and British military history* (Oxford, 1991), 289–313
 'Co-stars or supporting cast? British divisions in the "hundred days", 1918', in P. Griffith (ed.), *British fighting methods of the Great War* (London, 1996), 50–69

'The four armies 1914–1918', in D. Chandler and I. Beckett (eds.), *The Oxford illustrated history of the British Army* (Oxford, 1996), 241–62

Simpson, K., 'The Officers', in I. F. W. Beckett and K. Simpson (eds.), *A nation in arms: a social study of the British army in the First World War* (Manchester, 1985), 63–97

Smith, L. V., *Between mutiny and obedience: the case of the French Fifth Infantry Division during World War One* (Princeton, 1994)

Spiers, E. M., *Haldane: an army reformer* (Edinburgh, 1980)

The Army and society 1815–1914 (London, 1980)

'The Regular Army in 1914', in I. F. W. Beckett and K. Simpson (eds.), *A nation in arms: a social study of the British army in the First World War* (Manchester, 1985), 37–61

'The Scottish soldier at war', in H. Cecil and P. Liddle (eds.), *Facing Armageddon: the First World War experienced* (London, 1996), 314–35

Springall, J. O., *Youth, empire and society* (London, 1977)

Stanley, F. C., *History of the 89th Brigade* (Liverpool, 1919)

Stedman, M., *Manchester Pals: 16th, 17th, 18th, 19th, 20th, 21st, 22nd and 23rd Battalions of the Manchester Regiment* (London, 1984)

Salford Pals: a history of the 15th, 16th, 19th and 20th Battalions, Lancashire Fusiliers 1914–1919: a history of the Salford Brigade (London, 1993)

Stirling, J., *The Territorial divisions 1914–1918* (London, 1922)

Stouffer, S. A., et al., *The American soldier: combat and its aftermath* (New York, 1965)

Strachan, H., 'The morale of the German Army 1917–18', in H. Cecil and P. Liddle (eds.), *Facing Armageddon: the First World War experienced* (London, 1996), 383–98

'The soldier's experience in two world wars: some historiographical comparisons', in P. Addison and A. Calder (eds.), *Time to kill: the soldier's experience of war in the west, 1939–1945* (London, 1997), 369–78

Taylor, A. J. P., *An illustrated history of the First World War* (Harmondsworth, 1965)

Terraine, J., *The Great War* (Ware, 1997)

Thompson, G., *Liverpool scroll of fame*, Part I, *Commissioned officers* (Liverpool, 1920)

Threlfall, T. R., *The history of the King's Liverpool Regiment* (Liverpool, 1915)

Travers, T., *The killing ground: the British army, the Western Front and the emergence of modern warfare, 1900–1918* (London, 1987)

How the war was won: command and technology in the British Army on the Western Front 1917–1918 (London, 1992)

Turner, W., *Pals: the 11th (Service) Battalion (Accrington) East Lancashire Regiment* (Barnsley, 1987)

The Accrington Pals trail (London, 1998)

Van Creveld, M., *Command in war* (Cambridge, 1985)

Wadsworth A. P., 'Newspaper circulations, 1800–1954', *Transactions of the Manchester Statistical Society* (1954–55), 1–40

Waller, P. J., *Democracy and sectarianism: a political and social history of Liverpool 1868–1939* (Liverpool, 1981)

Walton, J. K., *Lancashire: a social history 1558–1939* (Manchester, 1987)
Walton, J. K. and Castells, L., 'Contrasting identities: north-west England and the Basque Country, 1840–1936', in E. Royle (ed.) *Issues of regional identity in honour of John Marshall* (Manchester, 1998), 45–77
Ward Lock and Co., *Guide to Liverpool, Birkenhead and New Brighton* (London, 1912)
Watson, Janet S. K., *Fighting different wars: experience, memory and the First World War in Britain* (Cambridge, 2004)
Wheelan, P., *The Accrington Pals: the 11th (Service) Battalion (Accrington), East Lancashire* (Preston, 1986)
Whitmarsh, A., 'The development of infantry tactics in the British 12th (Eastern) Division, 1915–1918', *Stand To. The Journal of the Western Front Association*, 48 (January 1997), 28–32
Williams, B., *Raising and training the New Armies* (London, 1918)
Williams, P. H., *Liverpolitana* (Liverpool, 1971)
Wilson, J. Brent, 'The morale and discipline of the British Expeditionary Force', unpublished MA thesis, University of New Brunswick (1978)
Winter, D., *Death's men: soldiers of the Great War* (London, 1978)
Winter, J. M., 'The decline of mortality in Britain, 1870–1950', in T. Barker and M. Drake (eds), *Population and society in Britain 1850–1980* (London, 1982), 100–20
  The Great War and the British people (London, 1986)
  World War One, 1914–1918 (Oxford, 1988)
  'Catastrophe and culture: recent trends in the historiography of the First World War', *Journal of Modern History*, 64 (1992), 525–32
  Sites of memory, sites of mourning: The Great War in European cultural history (Cambridge, 1995)
  'Popular culture in wartime Britain', in A. Roshwald and R. Stites (eds.), *European culture in the Great War: the arts, entertainment and propaganda* (Cambridge, 1999), 330–48
Winter, J. and Robert, J. L. (eds.), *Capital cities at war: Paris, London, Berlin, 1914–1919* (Cambridge, 1997)
Wurtzburg, C. E., *History of the 2/6th Battalion, The King's Liverpool Regiment 1914–1919* (London, 1920)
Wyrall, E., *The history of the King's Regiment (Liverpool)*, vols. 1–3 (London, 1928–35)
Young, P. and Bellen, J. (eds.) *Whitbread book of Scouseology, 1900–1987* (Liverpool, 1987)

Index

absent without leave 168, 169–70, 171, 180, 182, 187
Aigburth 31
amalgamations 60, 72–4, 184, 185, 235
Anderson, A. S. 25, 26
Army Council 65
Ath 239
Audoin-Rouzeau, S. 54, 240
Australia 59, 76

Barber, J. C. 26
Barnish, L. 43
battalion traditions 7, 9, 19, 20, 48, 63, 130, 132, 139, 145, 146, 163, 165, 175, 176, 187, 251
  local identity 9, 57–8, 59, 77–9, 80
  local uniformity 57, 58–74, 77, 88, 117
  regional identity 65, 76, 80–7, 88, 141, 147
  regional uniformity 58, 60, 61, 62, 63, 64–6, 67–74, 77, 88, 117, 125, 159
  Scottish identity 30, 31, 207, 226
  social uniformity 25, 29–30, 31–6, 41, 44–7, 48, 49, 51, 55, 56, 141, 150, 160, 165
Baybut, A. 234
Beaverbook, Lord 104
Bebington 59
Beckett, I. F. W. 4, 19, 72
Bedfordshire 59
bereavement 58, 240, 245, 246
Berkshire 64, 65
Birkdale 59
Birkenhead 9, 25, 26, 59
Blackpool 80
Blair, G. A. 47, 145, 159
Blundellsands 59
Bohstedt, J. 16

Bottomley, H. 116
Boulton, W. J. 92
Bourke, J. 174
Bourne, J. M. 53, 154
Bowman, T. 163, 165
Bristol 10, 64, 65
British Army Formations
  armies
    3rd Army 92
  divisions
    2nd Division 67
    3rd Division 67, 199
    5th Division 199
    12th Division 226, 228
    20th Division 226, 228
    30th Division 67
    55th West Lancashire Division 67, 71, 78, 81, 82, 84, 87, 102, 111, 112, 152, 159, 184, 210, 211, 216, 219, 222, 223, 225, 226, 227, 228, 230, 231, 234, 235, 237, 238, 239, 253, 256
    57th West Lancashire Division 184
  brigades
    6th Brigade 67
    164th Brigade 226
    165th Brigade 154, 184, 210, 215, 226, 232, 238
    166th Brigade 81, 141, 155, 210, 213, 226, 232
  regiments
    King's (Liverpool) 67, 69, 70, 72, 103, 175
    Lancashire Fusiliers 250
  battalions
    1st Dorsetshire 202
    1st Gloucestershire 176
    1/6th Gordon Highlanders 176
    11th East Lancashire 69
    1st King's (Liverpool) 67
    1/5th King's (Liverpool) 17, 27, 70, 223

270

Index

1/6th King's (Liverpool) (Liverpool Rifles) 3, 5, 16, 17, 19, 25, 26, 27, 29, 30, 31, 32, 35, 41, 42, 43, 44, 45, 48, 49, 50, 51, 52, 54, 58, 60, 61, 67, 69, 72, 78, 92, 113, 125, 126, 129, 134, 136, 140, 142, 144, 146, 159, 160, 163, 165, 166, 167, 169, 170, 171, 172, 173, 174, 176, 177, 178, 180, 181, 182, 184, 185, 186, 187, 188, 199, 202, 203, 209, 210, 211, 214, 215, 216, 217, 221, 225, 227, 228, 232, 233, 237, 239, 240, 250, 251, 252, 257
2/6th King's (Liverpool) 17, 31, 32, 60, 62
3/6th King's (Liverpool) 32
1/7th King's (Liverpool) 17
1/8th King's (Liverpool) (Liverpool Irish) 17, 184
2/8th King's (Liverpool) 17
1/9th King's (Liverpool) 17, 70, 184
1/10th King's (Liverpool) (Liverpool Scottish) 3, 5, 6, 16, 17, 19, 20, 25, 26, 27, 30, 31, 32, 34, 35, 37, 42, 43, 44, 45, 48, 49, 50, 51, 52, 54, 58, 60, 61, 70, 72, 74, 75, 77, 78, 79, 91, 92, 93, 95, 97, 103, 105, 106, 107, 108, 110, 113, 114, 115, 126, 127, 130, 132, 134, 136, 137, 139, 140, 141, 142, 144, 145, 146, 150, 152, 156, 157, 159, 160, 178, 180, 181, 199, 202, 203, 205, 206, 207, 208, 209, 210, 211, 213, 214, 215, 216, 218, 221, 222, 225, 226, 227, 228, 231, 232, 233, 234, 235, 237, 238, 239, 240, 242, 243, 244, 246, 248, 249, 251, 252, 253, 257
2/10th King's (Liverpool) 60, 62, 72
3/10th King's (Liverpool) 47, 136
13th King's (Liverpool) 67, 70, 232
16th King's (Liverpool) 46, 159
17th King's (Liverpool) 67
19th King's (Liverpool) 67
1/4th Leicestershire 69
1st Lincolnshire 78
10th Lincolnshire 69
1/14th London 176
12th Manchester 78
21st Manchester 70
2/6th North Staffordshire 69
8th North Staffordshire 69
52nd Nottinghamshire and Derbyshire 69
1st Royal Fusiliers 175
6th Scottish Rifles 176
2/6th South Staffordshire 69
51st Welsh 69
Brocklehurst, Captain 159
Bromborough 59
Bromley, W. G. 7, 127, 132, 140, 141, 146, 156, 207, 208, 210, 214, 219
Brophy, J. 15
Bryans, A. 200, 202, 203, 207
Buchanan, R. 246
Buckinghamshire 64, 65, 66
Burden, J. A. 53, 94
Bury 250

Cain, B. 160
Cambrai (1917) 102, 112, 147, 159, 225, 226
Court of Enquiry 102, 228, 230
Cambridgeshire 65
Cammell Laird 34
Campbell, W. H. 6, 80, 150, 214, 216
Canada 59, 76
Carruthers, H. 160
censorship 6, 87, 89, 90, 91, 94, 95, 102, 104, 105, 106, 107, 110, 113
Chavasse, F. J. 160
Chavasse, N. G. 49, 137, 150, 202, 222
Cheshire 10, 43, 44, 64, 65, 117
churches
    Crescent Congregational 97
    St Andrew's Presbyterian 52
    Trinity and Palm Grove Methodist 25
    Trinity Presbyterian, Claughton 115, 248, 249, 250
Clarke, Rifleman 180
Claughton 59, 248
Clegg, H. 16
Cole, W. E. 243
command relationship 7, 56, 134–61, 163–88
commemoration 103, 105, 109, 245, 246, 247, 248, 252, 255, 257
comradeship 52–4, 55–6, 100, 113, 240, 252
conscription 18, 34, 35, 59, 62, 63, 123, 131
conscripts 52, 80, 130, 131, 132, 133, 157, 175, 176, 187, 241, 251
Coop, J. O. 95
Costin, Rifleman 168
Cottesloe, Lord 72
courts-martial 162, 163, 165, 166, 167, 168, 169, 170, 171, 172, 174, 175, 176, 179, 180, 181, 185, 186, 187, 188

272 Index

Cumberland 64, 65
Cunard Shipping Line 11, 79, 243
Cunningham, H. 27
Cunningham, R. D. 26

Daily Chronicle 111
Daily Mail 115
Daily Mirror 114
Daily Telegraph 250
Dale, J. 244
Davidson, J. R. 46, 47, 159
Delville Wood 212
demobilization 125, 145, 240, 242
Derby, earl of 34, 47, 71, 72, 80, 100, 124, 125, 129, 159, 160, 184, 211, 242, 243
Derby Scheme 54, 131, 211
desertion 168, 170–1, 176, 182, 187
disciplinary system 2, 7, 56, 121, 135, 136, 141, 146, 162–88
disobedience 176–9
Don 238
Douglas, P. 91
drafting of troops 58, 62, 66–72, 87, 88, 127, 175
Drew, F. W. M. 146
drunkenness 170, 180, 182, 187
Duncan, F. J. 142, 146, 147, 152, 168

Eastham 59
Eccles, H. C. 42, 50
Edmonds, J. E. 152
Ellison, N. F. 11, 29, 50, 92, 116, 129, 144, 169, 200, 210, 211, 218, 219, 243, 244, 250
Englander, D. 91, 174, 182
Epéhy 225, 228, 231
Essex 65
Etaples 169, 170, 171
Evans, J. 245
Evans, W. 133, 227

Fairrie, A. 47
Fardo, T. 246
Farmer, D. D. 45
Festubert 70, 171, 231
field punishment 164, 168, 169, 170, 171, 176, 178, 180
Fifty-Fifth Division Comrades' Association 254, 255
Flers 215
Formby 59
Fyfe, F. A. 107, 108, 110, 115

Gallipoli 71
Gemmell, A. 243

Gibbs, P. 111, 210
Givenchy, defence of 38, 69, 111, 152, 230, 231, 232, 235, 253, 254, 255
Goering, H. 7
Gordon, S. E. 7, 28, 30, 48, 49, 50, 133, 142, 153, 202, 218, 223
Graham, J. M. 245
Gregory, A. 33
Guedecourt 215
Guillemont 211, 213, 214, 215, 240, 250

Haig, Sir Douglas 253
Haldane, A. 157
Haldane, R. B. 18, 74
Hamilton, Sir Ian. 71
Handley, J. S. 19, 27, 28, 35, 38, 125, 142, 169, 200, 214, 221
Henderson, G. F. R. 135, 136, 143
Herd, E. 93, 110, 178, 179, 226
Herefordshire 64
Hertfordshire 65
Heswall 59
Holmes, S. 7
Holt, R. 13
Hooge, Battle of (1915) 103, 105, 106, 107, 109, 110, 112, 114, 115, 127, 129, 134, 180, 203, 206, 208, 214, 235, 252
Hoylake 59
Hughes, G. F. 144, 243
Huntingdonshire 65
Hyam, H. 223

Imperial Service Obligation 74, 125
Ireland 15
Irish 15, 16, 17
Izzett, D. 107

Jaeger, Captain 146
Jeudwine, H. S. 71, 142, 147, 148, 149, 150, 151, 152, 153, 154, 157, 158, 159, 168, 225, 230, 231
and regional motivation 81, 82, 87, 147

Kendall, P. D. 43
Kentish, R. 141, 142
Kitchener, Lord 50, 71

La Bassée 237
Lancashire 10, 17, 43, 44, 58, 59, 61, 64, 65, 71, 76, 82, 83, 84, 86, 87, 117, 124, 211, 250
Lancaster 84
rose of 81, 82, 83, 84, 87
Laybourne, J. 160
League of Nations 250

Index

Leaton, H. L. 97
Lee, A. 152
Leed, E. 2, 252
Levey, J. 151
Lindsay, R. C. 26
Liscard 59
literature, disillusionment 1
live and let live system 113, 133, 178, 179, 210
Liverpool 9, 10, 11, 12, 13, 15, 16, 17, 21, 22, 25, 26, 27, 32, 42, 43, 44, 47, 51, 59, 60, 66, 71, 75, 76, 78, 79, 80, 92, 93, 97, 99, 100, 102, 103, 110, 113, 114, 115, 116, 117, 125, 134, 159, 242, 243, 244, 245, 248, 250, 251, 253, 254, 255, 256, 257
Liverpool Clerks' Association 11
Liverpool Courier 105, 106, 115
Liverpool Daily Post 21, 31, 100, 105, 107, 109, 111, 222
Liverpool Echo 77, 105, 112, 115
Liverpool Express 105
Liverpool Rifles' Regimental Association 251
Liverpool Scottish Regimental Association 244, 251
Liverpool Scottish Regimental Gazette 74
Liverpool Scroll of Fame 44
Locarno, treaty of 250
London 10, 34, 36
London County Council 34
looting 181
Lorimer, J. W. 131, 157
Lovelace, C. 104
Lusitania, sinking of 113, 114
Lyon, W. M. 101

McArdle, J 244
Macartney, H. M. 106
McClymont, E. I. M. 103, 154
Macdonald, F. 242
Macdonald, J. L. A. 156
Macdonogh, G. 184
Macfie, R. A. S. 6, 48, 52, 55, 79, 81, 82, 91, 92, 95, 96, 103, 113, 115, 116, 124, 126, 127, 129, 130, 131, 136, 144, 145, 155, 156, 157, 178, 181, 201, 208, 209, 212, 213, 216, 218, 235, 237, 238, 239, 240, 243
McGilchrist, A. M. 78, 221, 234, 239
McKaig, J. B. 169, 170, 178, 187, 250
McKay, S. 233
McKibbin, R. 27
McKinnell, B. 6, 49, 205, 206
McKnight, A. 41
McMullen, C. N. 152

McNeill, W. 115, 248
Macnichol, H. L. 223
Macpherson, I. 70, 73, 74
McRae, D. 233
Macready, Sir Nevil 67, 69
malingering 137, 139, 157, 171, 172
Malleson, H. 95
Manchester 9, 10
Manchester Guardian 104
Marquis, A. G. 104
Mather, A. 160
Mather, N. 42
Maxse, I. 230
Mersey, River 9, 13, 59, 76
middle-class attitudes 5, 10, 12, 15, 20, 25–6, 28, 29–30, 51–2, 54, 56, 129, 136, 139, 150, 160–1, 165, 178, 179, 181, 182, 200, 205, 206
middle-class clubs 25–6, 27, 243, 246–7, 251
middle-class employment 11–12, 49, 243–4
middle-class residential areas 13
Military Service Acts 73, 75, 124, 125, 131
Militia 17
Moffat, J. G. C. 52, 126, 144, 145, 249
Molyneux family 10
Montague, C. E. 112
Moorhouse, G. 250
Moran, C. 175
Moulton, S. P. 93
Muir, R. 15
Munro, D. C. D. 146, 239

National Service, Ministry of 65
National Service League 18, 21
New Armies 4, 5, 50, 57, 62, 71, 78, 102, 129, 130, 135, 253
New Brighton 59
New Ferry 59
Norfolk 65
Norfolk Commission 18
North Western Recruiting Area 65
Northcliffe, Lord 104
Northern Daily Dispatch 105, 115
Northern Recruiting Area 65

Osborne, J. 174, 182
Oxfordshire 64, 65
Oxton 25

penal servitude 168, 171
Peppiette, E. A. 6, 31, 54, 131
Peronne Gazette 152

Phillips, J. 159
Pilling, W. 180
Pinnington, W. E. 150
Plunkett, R. 216
Preston 137
Price, T. J. 233
propaganda 86, 89, 113

Rae, G. B. L. 136, 137, 148
Rathbone, B. 7, 244
Rattray, J. S. 218
recruitment 21–2, 25, 29–34, 41, 57, 58, 59, 62–6, 74, 87, 88, 124, 243, 250, 251, 253
Red Baron 7
regular army 2, 4, 5, 7, 12, 17, 18, 34, 62, 74, 78, 84, 121, 122, 123, 124, 126, 134, 135, 136, 139, 141, 142, 143, 145, 146, 165, 176, 180, 186, 187, 188, 199, 206, 208, 211, 223, 225
religion 15, 257
 Protestantism 16, 185
 Roman Catholicism 16, 185
Remarque, E. M. 116
Renison, W. J. H. 26
Roberts, Lord 35
Russell, E. 100
Russell, Lord 159

St Eloi 210
St Helens 10
Salvidge, A. 16
Sassoon, S. 116, 154
Scotland 15
Scottish 15, 19, 21
sectarianism 16, 17
Sefton Park 31, 79
self-inflicted wound 171, 172, 173, 174, 175, 176
Shaw, J. 222
Sheffield, G. D. 163
shellshock 182, 214
Shropshire 64
Simkins, P. 77
Smith, L. V. 122, 133, 134
social change 2–3, 11, 25
soldiers
 attitudes towards the enemy 110, 113–14, 202, 207, 210, 222–3, 234, 239, 240–1
 attitudes towards the home front 89–117, 144–5, 158–60
 attitudes to religion 98, 99, 203, 241
 attitudes to war 7, 92–3, 107, 110, 132, 151, 179, 184, 199–202, 202–41

civilian outlook of 1, 2–3, 5, 7, 8, 9, 25, 42, 48–9, 52, 56, 75–6, 78–9, 122, 124, 125–34, 135–9, 136, 143–5, 145–6, 160–1, 165, 180, 188, 206, 241, 242, 243–4, 247
civilian skills of 147, 148, 157–8
morale of 7, 25, 51, 51–5, 77–88, 91, 93, 129–30, 133, 136, 141, 172, 175, 184, 199–241, 242
Somme, Battle of the (1916) 53, 54, 57, 70, 129, 131, 141, 142, 147, 169, 171, 211, 215, 216–17, 225
South African War (1899–1902) 18, 45, 206
Southern Command 64, 65
Southport 9, 59
Special Reserve 18
Stanleys 10
Stockwell, Brigadier General 147
strikes 12–13
Sub Rosa: Being the Magazine of the 55th West Lancashire Division 82, 86, 87, 113, 116, 152, 218
Suffolk 65

Taplin, E. 16
Taylor, H. S. 79, 179
Territorial Army 4, 250, 251
Territorial Force 4, 5, 17, 18, 19, 21, 22, 26, 27, 43, 50, 57, 61, 62, 69, 74, 78, 81, 91, 102, 123, 124, 125, 126, 129, 130, 135, 136, 141, 143, 145, 146, 162, 165, 186, 187, 223, 225
 County Associations 18, 21, 47, 124
 West Lancashire Territorial Association 19, 21, 47, 71, 80, 159
The Times 43, 106, 235
Thin, E. G. 207
Training Reserve 62, 63, 64, 65
Trones Wood 212
Turner, F. H. 43, 91, 140
Turner, W. S. 90

Vaux 78, 134, 209
Volunteer Force 17, 19, 27
volunteering 17, 75, 122–30, 132, 145, 159

Wailly 211
Wales 15, 64, 65
Wall, Lieutenant 81
Wallace, G. 171
Wallasey 59
Waller, P. J. 27
war memorials 245, 247, 248, 249, 252, 254, 257

Index

at Givenchy 254, 255, 256
Liverpool cenotaph 242, 256, 257
Scottish National 252
War Office 18, 20, 63, 67, 73, 88, 125, 160
Warry, G. 54, 131, 137, 243
Warwickshire 64, 65
Welsh 15
West Derby 31
West Kirby 59
Westby, Captain 50
Western Command 64
Westmorland 64, 65
Whitson, Matron 100
Widnes 10
Wieltje 219, 222
Wilkinson Green, Brigadier 155
Williams, B. 63
Williams, J. 167, 170, 171

Winter, J. M. 32
Wirral 9
Worcestershire 64
working-class attitudes 16, 27, 34
working-class employment 12
working-class residential areas 13
Wurtzburg, C. E. 31
Wylie, B. 54

Yeomanry 17
Young Crescent, 97, 98, 99, 114
Ypres 43, 93, 106, 199, 202, 209, 210, 217, 227, 250
Ypres, Second Battle of (1915) 38, 49, 113, 203
Ypres, Third Battle of (1917) 41, 69, 95, 111, 115, 150, 152, 167, 176, 219, 225

Zillebeke 203, 205

Studies in the Social and Cultural History of Modern Warfare

Titles in the series

1 *Sites of Memory, Sites of Mourning: The Great War in European Cultural History*
   JAY WINTER
2 *Capital Cities at War: Paris, London, Berlin 1914–1919*
   JAY WINTER AND JEAN-LOUIS ROBERT
3 *State, Society and Mobilization in Europe during the First World War*
   EDITED BY JOHN HORNE
4 *A Time of Silence: Civil War and the Culture of Repression in Franco's Spain, 1936–1945*
   MICHAEL RICHARDS
5 *War and Remembrance in the Twentieth Century*
   EDITED BY JAY WINTER AND EMMANUEL SIVAN
6 *European Culture in the Great War: The Arts, Entertainment and Propaganda, 1914–1918*
   EDITED BY AVIEL ROSHWALD AND RICHARD STITES
7 *The Labour of Loss: Mourning, Memory and Wartime Bereavement in Australia*
   JOY DAMOUSI
8 *The Legacy of Nazi Occupation: Patriotic Memory and National Recovery in Western Europe, 1945–1965*
   PIETER LAGROU
9 *War Land on the Eastern Front: Culture, National Identity and German Occupation in World War I*
   VEJAS GABRIEL LIULEVICIUS
10 *The Spirit of 1914: Militarism, Myth and Mobilization in Germany*
   JEFFREY VERHEY
11 *German Anglophobia and the Great War, 1914–1918*
   MATTHEW STIBBE
12 *Life between Memory and Hope: The Survivors of the Holocaust in Occupied Germany*
   ZEEV W. MANKOWITZ
13 *Commemorating the Irish Civil War: History and Memory, 1923–2000*
   ANNE DOLAN
14 *Jews and Gender in Liberation France*
   KAREN H. ADLER
15 *America and the Armenian Genocide of 1915*
   JAY WINTER (ED.)
16 *Fighting Different Wars: Experience, Memory and the First World War in Britain*
   JANET S. K. WATSON
17 *Vienna and the Fall of the Habsburg Empire: Total War and Everyday Life in World War I*
   MAUREEN HEALY

18 *The Moral Disarmament of France: Education, Pacifism, and Patriotism, 1914–1940*
   MONA L. SIEGEL
19 *National Cleansing: Retribution against Nazi Collaborators in Post-War Czechoslovakia*
   BENJAMIN FROMMER
20 *China and the Great War: China's Pursuit of a New National Identity and Internationalization*
   XU GUOQI
21 *The Great War: Historical Debates, 1914 to the Present*
   ANTOINE PROST AND JAY WINTER
22 *Citizen Soldiers: The Liverpool Territorials in the First World War*
   HELEN B. MCCARTNEY

Lightning Source UK Ltd.
Milton Keynes UK
174247UK00001B/113/P